# Sorcerers of the Silver City

*Happy Birthday*
*Sr Javery*
*lots of love*
*xxx*

Russell Knowles

*Russell Knowles*

93 93/93

Copyright © 2016 Russell Knowles

ISBN: 978-1-63491-589-2

All rights reserved. No part of this publication may be reproduced, stored in a retrieval system, or transmitted in any form or by any means, electronic, mechanical, recording or otherwise, without the prior written permission of the author.

The characters and events in this book are fictitious. Any similarity to real persons, living or dead, is coincidental and not intended by the author.

Published by BookLocker.com, Inc., St. Petersburg, Florida.

Printed on acid-free paper.

BookLocker.com, Inc.

2017

First Edition

**Dedicated to:**

Angelos, Brigid, Carole, Crow, Daniela, Demi, Don, Duncan, Edie, Mags, Micheil and Sophie.

**Thanks to**:

Alayna, Angie, Gillian and Rogé

for all their encouragement and feedback.

**Special thanks to:**

Carole for all the invaluable editing and feedback.

&

Rob Bignell (inventingreality.4t.com) for editing the initial manuscript and for all his hard work, patience and feedback.

Author website: https://russellknowles.wordpress.com/

# Contents

I: The Fool ..................................................................................... 1

*Chapter 1*:   Altered States in Council Estates ............................... 5

*Chapter 2*:   You know, when you grope for Luna? ..................... 37

*Chapter 3*:   Here we come to call thee forth .............................. 63

*Chapter 4*:   The Hippie, the Dippy and the Downright Lippy ..... 74

*Chapter 5*:   The Green and the Grey ....................................... 125

*Chapter 6*:   The Doors of Reception ........................................ 162

*Chapter 7*:   Never Mind the Bollox .......................................... 181

A: The Ordeals ............................................................................ 233

*Chapter 8*:   Get a fix on Getafix ............................................... 235

*Chapter 9*:   Out of the woods and into the frying pan ............ 261

*Chapter 10*:   Karma Police, Arrest This Man ............................. 292

*Chapter 11*:   Under the streets beneath the waking world ....... 325

*Chapter 12*:   The Prince and the Queen of Night ...................... 343

*Chapter 13*:   We are all Stars .................................................... 367

O: The Force ............................................................................... 401

*Chapter 14*:   The Empire Strikes Back ...................................... 403

*Epilogue*:   When will we three meet again? ........................... 439

# I: The Fool

*Prologue.*

This is a story of hope; there may be another way! You know!? A third path between religion and science, logic and fantasy; between actual life and death. I came to see a glimpse of a twilight that exists where actual magick can be used by all to reach their true potential. Well, I was convinced for a while there, but I suppose I'm less sure now. The account that follows is a true story of events which took place in Aberdeen, Scotland, throughout the 1990s. I thought it was worth retelling the story, if only to help figure these things out for myself you understand? You can read it and make your mind up for yourself.

Ok, so I will first mention some very early memories, as they always felt relevant. I remember it was in the summer of 1972, on some Saturday evening on a planet far, far from here. Well, actually it was Aberdeen on the north east of Scotland; it's just that, for all intents and purposes, the seventies were another planet compared to now. My parents were preparing to go out for the evening. My uncle and his girlfriend were babysitting my little sister and I and so we were packed off to bed. I have a very vivid memory of my little sister asleep in the bed across from mine; I have a good clear memory of instances from my infancy like this. We lived at the top of a three story block of council flats on Hilton Drive, in the Woodside area of town. Hilton Drive and the surrounding streets were relatively peaceful, as it was heavily populated by old people who religiously scrubbed and polished stairs, washed cars, windows and pottered in the garden. They were forever bent over in gardens as we walked past, greeting the family with their leathery, smiley-weathered faces while little yappy dogs sneered through rows of provocative gleaming teeth between gaps at the bottom of hedges. I would be quite confused as a child at the apparent dichotomy of 'kind, friendly old buffer/ugly vicious little dog.'

This was one of those few occasions where my parents could afford or find the time to go out for the evening. My young sister and I were already in bed as they said their goodbyes to the babysitters. The next memory that follows is of watching them go downstairs, going out the door and starting down the long driveway towards the street and bus stop. I slipped behind a wall and watched them; I felt a sense of curiosity and abandonment. 'Why are they going without me?' Even though I was sure I'd never ventured out this far on my own as yet, the wall, the environments were familiar to me, but I was not 'me' completely; I was 'my shadow.' I remember that this state of being for me was as natural and as real as my waking self. I obviously never really questioned it and I had come to accept this as just 'becoming my shadow-self;' just something that was a part of my regular experience. Indeed, my body was a shadow, a black outlined facsimile of my real body. I was also quite sure that I could go and see other members of my family whenever I wanted or faraway places with people I knew, but never really questioned how I knew them. The people that I met while out and about like this were as familiar to me as the other adults in my life.

The memory continues as I followed my parents through the streets of Woodside; I felt the spirit of the place and watchful eyes, which I knew were not there on normal school days, peering at me acceptingly from old buildings and overgrown paths. Some parts of Woodside were left for the succession of nature. Where kids would run feral over amalgamated back gardens behind tenement flats of imposing grey granite; a warren of closes led out to warped and buckled metal fencing while long grasses sprouted unhindered out of old mattresses and rusting garden tools. Nature seemed to have re-taken some of the place; knarled trees towered over quaint old buildings and houses; long abandoned bomb shelters stood quietly on overgrown, bumble bee-visited waste-ground behind shops and worn advertising boards, crisscrossed with small tracks known only to cats and children.

I remember Woodside, as a child walking along the street with my granddad, the streets were a hive of activity as people bustled around attractive looking shop fronts with their wares displayed on the street, the chatter of people tinged with the friendly tone of village community familiarity.

As I explored this environment as my shadow, often emerging out of all the buzzing, crawling insects and rubble, an image of a kind woman just seemed to form at will from tree stumps or old chairs and bees. I knew her as a kind of mother, though I knew she wasn't my actual mother. I had come to know that, like a watchful parent, this female form was never far away from me. I didn't know who she was but I instinctively felt that she had lived among the bushes and walkways far longer than I had been there. She was just a part of it, as if her body was made out of all the vegetation and stones. I felt perfectly at home whilst out on walkabout with this woman's presence watching over me.

My shadow-self walked along behind my parents remaining unseen, popping my head around corners and feeling very naughty but triumphant that they couldn't see me. I know that I'm hard to be seen as my shadow. I watched them walk further away but then sometimes found myself inexplicably far ahead of them waiting for them to walk past where I was waiting. This was a game of daring, though I'd never been caught like this. The gardens buzzed and hummed with life as if everything was that bit more 'consciously alive.' The stillness of nature coexisting at ease with our civil remains, I found, were very comforting. I took it all for granted; the memory fades.

As well as this, though, I had memories of clearly seeing little fluttering black shapes that would buzz close to my face and zing around the room. When it began to quiet, the air would become filled with movement, filled with different presences. However, as I grew a little older, I developed a profound fear of these occasional black shapes, as well as a fear of the dark that every child has—sleeping with my head under the blankets, creating little air holes which ventilated my little nylon-cotton den, ably protected by the never sleeping Action Man on night watch.

Of course, infancy eventually fades into nostalgia and as I grew older I reasoned that they were just memories of vivid dreams that had survived from young childhood, before I could make sense of the world. As a kind of introspective loner, there were also times in my childhood when I felt irrevocably drawn to nature. I would sit alone in woodland beside the river Don, trying to experience the "oneness" of everything, thinking that if I stayed quiet enough I would be absorbed by it, a sense of really trying to experience the "spirit" of the place. This was, I suppose, an extension of my curiosity about the big questions in life that every curious person philosophises about at some point. I was trying to recapture the childhood memories of nature.

Later, science became the only logical tool for understanding nature for me. I studied Biology and Psychology, holding the belief that these two disciplines alone could combine to produce an 'all you need to know guide about life and human behaviour past, present and future,' much like perhaps, Douglas Adams' 'Hitchhiker's Guide to the Galaxy.' Move aside religion, stop your efforts philosophy, shut up and listen political studies – all these fields in my view would be redundant without science. We should look to the light of the sciences and be illuminated by its power to provide forensic self-awareness. After all, the rationality of science is the pure distillation of common sense!

## *Chapter 1*:
## Altered States in Council Estates

At the age of ten, my family left that house in Hilton Drive and Woodside to move up the hill to the industrial estate of Northfield on a little street called "Briar Brae." This wasn't some picturesque little lane populated by bushes and small thatched cottages with smoke drifting from the chimneys as the image of the name might suggest! No, this was more a little brae of identical harling-coated council terraced flats which blended in with the uniformity of the rest of the network of very similar housing throughout that part of the estate.

Where Woodside Primary School had been an old victorian brick building with solid old wooden doors, Cummings Park Primary on the other hand was prefabricated- fake and falling apart. Kids had kicked holes in the walls along the corridors out of frustration, where they remained festering in the corridor landscape. It was a million miles away from the nice leafy Woodside Primary where I had been familiar with every bush, tree and battered signpost, where I had known nearly every person since infant school. Now I felt like an alien locked in a parallel universe devoid of spirit or feeling, where even the birdsong seemed suppressed and out of place.

So here I was, the new kid in the classroom; I'd never understood before why the new kids always seemed so shocked, so shy. Now I was experiencing that first hand as the teacher did the introduction routine. If you've never been the new kid in class, then you'll not understand what I mean. Joining the class a good third of the way through the final primary year made me feel like I was crashing someone else's party. I was naturally very quiet on the first day, but then just seemed to remain so for the duration of my time there. I never found a way of fitting in, I always felt like an outsider. In the playground, I resorted to sitting on a small mound of grass with my back to the fence, absorbed in comics, my way of achieving perfect escapism while I was forced to go there.

Inevitably, like some rite of passage, I got into a fight; the reasons were totally contrived, but I realised I had no choice as I was swept along by the throng of people. An appointed person had been named as having been calling me names behind my back. He had been singled out by the collective will of the group as someone with approximately similar fighting stats as myself – both bantam weights with an unclear resumé of past bouts. Having no choice, I walked up to him and threw a punch. There was no real aggression in me at all and I just sort of jutted my fist forward robotically in the general direction of his face, which felt a little bit rude, I know, but I was in unchartered territory. In my mind, I had psyched myself to do as much Bruce Lee-like moves as I could remember, but it all seemed to come out as one kind of awkward laying of fist-on-face type scenario. His jaw clicked a wet *schtuk* sound as it moved a little bit and then we both just then looked at each other in a perplexed manner, not knowing what to do next. I really didn't want to hit him again; my part of the deal was done and it was his turn. He didn't know what to do either; but what he did do was make me feel terrible for years and years later, as he just said, "Oh come on now, Sean, mate, you know I didn't call you names, I thought we were pals?" Well that was hardly fair at all; I never saw that coming, for fuck's sake! A ten-year-old boy being all 'grown up and Hugh Grant-like' on school politics. Of all the luck! Most people just exchanged a few slaps and then forgot about it, but oh no, he had to go and say that.

I bit my bottom lip and said sorry, he teared up a little and then so did I; I had never felt so bad in all my life. The others in the group surrounding us both, expecting blood and gristle to be flying by now were also quite confused, like the lumberjacks from the Monty Python sketch they looked at each other with uncertainty and then disapproving scowls. No wonder this guy hadn't been in many scraps; now he was just upsetting everybody! The crowd gradually dispersed; their sense of boredom and anti-climax almost made me feel guilty for not being battered. I thought that I had won the fight by default, as in I had thrown the one and only punch and, unfortunately for my opponent, his use of psychological warfare had not yet been recognised by his peers at that time. Of course, in actuality, I think he won the fight; that is if months, nay years even, of subsequent lost sleep and abject self-loathing on my part were to have been factored into the final scoring. (I mean, fuck me, he said he thought we were pals..!).

My time at Cummings Park eventually came to an end. It had been a complete exercise in endurance and survival. My self-esteem and sense of identity had taken a severe bashing, as I just wasn't like my peers; though as a glasses-wearing, comic-reading science and sci-fi enthusiast, it was lucky that they hadn't beaten me to death with a shovel before Christmas. Luckily, they just seemed to leave me alone, which meant I just sort of dissolved into the background. However, I was given a little reprieve as I progressed to Northfield Academy Secondary School, where I was introduced to Science and Science teachers for the first time. There I found solace with other people who read Arthur. C. Clark and actually looked forward to going to Science classes. Soon I had some friends, similarly shy sorts and I had found a niche for myself, where other slightly nerdy kids could stay out of the way together, lucky not to be collectively beaten to death with shovels before Christmas!

Though my self-esteem was still extremely low and I had seemed to remain younger and not quite as sussed and mature as my peers. I felt like I had somehow missed a few meetings. To me, my peers seemed to change almost overnight, talking about jobs they were going to go into, having regular girlfriends, experimenting with new styles, clothes, cologne and careers, whereas I still had the stupid nerdy bowl cut, uncool clothes, social awkwardness and an overzealous wanking habit. I never even considered further education, as I imagined that was exclusively for clever or gifted people. I just felt kind of inept and downtrodden all the time.

Although very much grounded and interested in Science, there were some aspects that I kept to myself. Perhaps being quite introverted made me aware of the *para-social* environment we all may contribute to and live within. Para-social, to coin a phrase, is a bit like paranormal in its meaning. It is a name I've chosen to sum up how coincidences, luck and social ripples affect us all in a large group (or sea) of people. I'm talking about things such as *déjà vu* or people turning up on cue when they are needed. People may just shrug off such occurrences or at best say "that was weird," or "well, that was meant to be!" However, for me in my teens the frequency and predictability of some of these types of effects were just undeniable and unprecedented. Therefore my perception of these types of things forced me to take them more seriously and actually think about them. I normalised these events to myself to the point that I could predict with complete accuracy when, for example, if I dreamt about someone I hadn't met for a while, I would bump into them randomly very soon afterwards in town. I had no choice but to shrug and compartmentalise this intuitive knowledge of how aspects of our para-society worked. I understood that these were more than coincidences, as often I would dream of meeting people in places I had never visited before, which I'd seen in the dream with exceptional detail. I came to accept this persistent pre-cognition as just part of ordinary life. I felt that certain people who I had some kind of sub-conscious connection to, were connecting to me. Somehow I could see this connection happening where, I suppose, most could not. I came to think therefore that there is a kind of fate, a shared connection but only if the people involved are fated to subconsciously process the notion of each other, if you like; a fate that we knit together subconsciously. I could sort of tell that often they had been thinking about me too! Since *information* underpins reality at a quantum level and information can be shared instantly, this may be an unspoken or unconsidered aspect of human society.

I think it's true to say that some people, who are less socially able, in some ways tend to compensate in another mental faculty, such as science or mathematics. Call it the nerdy factor. Society, social interaction and social navigation are orders of magnitude more sophisticated in humans than any other animal. It requires significant computing power to see into another's mind, to second guess another's motivations, to use humour, wit and metaphor to say something but mean another. It requires Machiavellian intelligence and meta-cognition in excess to live in our societies. This is the so called "theory of mind" that our closest relatives, the next smartest of the great apes, chimpanzees can only match an ability of that of a four year old child. (Indeed, it is a widely accepted theory that our emerging social skills were a major driving force for the fairly rapid evolution of our large brains).

So it seems to me that the mental energy required for such feats of mental gymnastics are re-distributed for other processing in people who lack social skills. These may be redistributed towards 'para-social interactions,' perhaps. Autistic people have incredible brains that sense and process the world very differently from the average person. They tend to perceive details and patterns that, presumably socially processing, brains cannot afford to attend to.

The fact is that people with a deficit in one sensory attribute generally compensate by becoming more developed in another. So perhaps socially withdrawn people who are also very sensitive and empathic in general, like me at this time, may be better able to perceive para-social patterns. Being more of an introverted person may also mean that the radar for internal mysteries of the mind can more easily pick these effects out.

I also (admittedly) came to realise that not only could I test this, but I could in fact consciously influence this effect; like whenever I concentrated on a particular person with any degree of emotional energy. That is, I could apparently affect their behaviour towards me or even affect them in a way that benefited me. I should have been bullied a little; everyone else even slightly geeky was, without a doubt at times. However, I could sense when anyone would be thinking of targeting me in any way and I could take evasive action, such as fantasising that there was a thick brick wall between us. Sometimes I could feel 'persistence' in the air. The only way to describe it is, like an atmosphere that I could feel and sense. Consequently, if I began to get anxious, concerned or annoyed with any key person, they would go on holiday and return as if they had forgotten me. A sense of protection was also there, like the lady of my dreams when I was my shadow, looking after me.

And this was part of the schism I had. On the one hand, I'm a dedicated scientist, versed in the ways of logic and rationality. I read Conan Doyle's Sherlock Holmes religiously, impressed by his super-human powers to shine insight and logic onto a situation and solves puzzles using data, exactly like any good scientist. Sherlock Holmes is without doubt my favourite superhero! I'm even appalled and disappointed that Conan Doyle himself was duped by Victorian mediums and charlatans into believing in ghosts and fairies. Sherlock Holmes wouldn't be that easily fooled! He wouldn't entertain ideas of the paranormal at all! However, simultaneously, I seemed to have an intuitive awareness that waking reality, which we all seemed to have some consensus on, was just the tip of an iceberg. A sort of stage version, where behind the wings or behind the scenes, were kept from sight, away from ordinary perception.

Looking back now, I can surmise that if these processes work for the good of individuals within our complex societies, then it would be "positively selected for" (in terms of natural selection) through evolutionary time! I'm willing to bet, in fact, that if a correlation study were done, there would be a positive correlation between this type of coincidental arrangement between people, déjà vu and even premonitions within closed groups or small villages, rather than an impersonal sprawling social landscape such as big cities, in comparison!

I was happy to leave school but had no real aspirations or concept of what I might do next. I had passed enough exams, especially in sciences. Despite that, I still felt really stupid – especially socially – compared to my peers. I dressed in black and avidly listened to 'indie' music of the eighties like Joy Division, New Order, The Smiths, The Cure, the Sisters of Mercy, The Fall, The Jesus and Mary Chain, Sonic Youth, The Pixies, Dinosaur Jr. and so on to name but a few, all the alternative bands really. I would avidly listen to the John Peel show and nip out the next day and buy vinyl of the bands he played. I would spend hours flicking through vinyl after vinyl buried in Aberdeen's only alternative record shop (a godsend to people like me) the One-Up on Diamond Street. Many of these alternative bands just appealed to some core sense of belonging that I was searching for. These bands weren't main-stream at all; in the eighties an indie kid would be almost despised by mainstream pop culture society for being a bit weird or an outsider. This made us weird outsiders identify all the more with the concept.

Whilst rooting around in the One-Up, I discovered a punk group called CRASS, who were the quintessential anarcho-punk band, rebelling against all the crass and hypocrisy in the world. These guys actually did it for real and lived their lives in a hippie/punk commune outside and apart from 'the system.' They became my absolute heroes, representing something worth aspiring too. For the first time in my life, through music and punk, I was beginning to find my niche. I wasn't a mere husk floating through life; I had convictions, passion and definite views on how the rights of the individual should have more precedence. In other words, I was a fan of human beings, believing in an innate goodness in people. CRASS' war chant of "There's only one way of life" woke me up, breathing life into my personality and soul. I listened to CRASS' "Christ the Album" all the time, the little cuts from adverts and politician interviews followed by their white noise guitars and angry lyrics and sloganeering really struck a chord with me. I felt aligned to this thinking, emancipated from damaging outmoded conventions; I felt that the human spirit could overcome the human instinct for intolerance and dominance culture. Despite my rather pessimistic views of human nature (especially since reading insightful authors like Desmond Morris), I felt that CRASS were correct in their view that cultural and social change could be improved; not by a large movement or revolution but by small individual changes, by people living their lives their way, "there's only one way of life," as the Levellers were to echo later. I felt that John Lennon was not just a dreamer and sure, he wasn't the only one; counter-culture, I felt, stood for evolution in a good direction, towards a fairer world. I began collecting more records by bands with a social conscience, from Bob Dylan to Public Enemy.

By the end of the eighties I had landed a job in a laboratory connected with Aberdeen's oil industry in Dyce on the outskirts of Aberdeen. This was a large chemical services company testing and quality controlling many aspects of offshore industry. The daily work could be anything from testing a lube oil sample checking for an erosion signature or checking water samples for quality. Much of the work was actually routine, involving calibrating and using spectrographic instruments, making solutions and preparing many, many samples. The large lab was delineated into many smaller sections, each consisting of long white benches holding up occasional hooded instruments and eye-level shelving resplendent with glassware. The latter ranged from beakers that never seemed to be used and volumetric flasks containing stock solutions. Working opposite me was a character called Sandy Rourke; he was a couple of years younger than I was but, like me somehow, didn't seem to quite belong there among the smart quietly confident people who swished around in lab coats like they had been trained to wear them on some science cat-walk. It seemed to me that the many pens in their top pockets were no mere affectations; I would bet they used them often, in ways I may never aspire to understand. Sandy seemed more down to earth to me, speaking in a more familiar style, as he started almost every sentence with a long drawn out "fauck-kin..." in the same manner that most people used the "umm" or "erm" expression. For example:*"Fauck-kin, watched 'at film ye' were spikin' aboot the ither night, fauck-kin'-like fuckin' shite it was an 'aw!"* I actually found this endearing and so I related to him far better than the majority of those identifiable 'middle-class graduate types.' Sandy was working his Youth Training Scheme placement and so, only being a few months out of school, he should have been as perplexed and as anxious as I was. So I was both comforted and intrigued that he didn't seem in the slightest bit intimidated by these alien surroundings of pipettes, plugs and pens in labcoats; often walking around his side of the lab like he owned the place. On the first day of meeting him, I clocked his chino-baggy jeans and spikey blonde hair and almost dismissed him as a fairly conventional type who was probably not quite on the same wavelength as me. He had a very round, pockmarked face with a wry sardonic look that made me think he was ever so slightly untrustworthy. He also walked like a thug, which I noticed was more on purpose than some physiological accident of birth. So, together with his strong 'doric' accent, I was also close to dismissing him as a bit of a wide boy perhaps!? My shameless stereotyping instincts turned out to be quite wrong of course, as he turned out to be that bit shrewder than I had given him credit for and altogether much more fucking untrustworthy. Though once I noticed his Smiths T-shirt under his labcoat, that was that; we were friends! Sandy even liked a lot of goth and indie bands that I did; and, as we were both from Northfield, as I soon found out, we had a fair bit more in common than anyone else in the building. He lived ten minutes away from me up the road, a stone's throw from Northfield Academy, so we commuted in together on the same bus as well. I felt kind of safe knowing he was working a few feet away. I hid with my back to the fence away from the other 'graduate type' kids, though instead of comics, I could speak about Smiths songs and living in Northfield with fauck-kin' Sandy!

This was the year of Baggy; The Stone Roses, the Happy Mondays and James were hitting the charts. Drug culture had taken off in Britain in a big way, due to the whole Hacienda rave scene spreading out from Manchester. Recreational drug use hadn't been huge while I was at school; I had just missed it or hadn't really noticed it. However, Sandy Rourke's year had embraced acid house and 'Madchester' wholeheartedly and he was a confirmed weed smoker. I was becoming bored of playing computer games in my room with only Morrissey and Robert Smith for company. I can simply say the scientist in me wanted to experiment; I mean, even the great Sherlock Holmes blissed out on the odd opiate.

Consequently, Sandy introduced me to cannabis resin. Though, as I mentioned, he was a bit of an untrustworthy character and enjoyed getting other people overly stoned. I had never tried the so-called 'magic mushies' before, but he had been going on about them for so long that I gave in. I also decided that I should try them at least once. I had heard tales of their hallucinogenic properties and was a little apprehensive, as one would be, about their mind-altering power. I therefore requested that Sandy start me on a fairly weak brew; Sandy nodded enthusiastically replying, "Aye, aye nae bother min...fauck-kin', dah worry you'll jist get a slight stoned feelin' and it'll be a bit o' a laugh that's aw'."

We had picked them that afternoon; I had felt really conspicuous wandering around the local playing field in full view of the housing estates occasionally going down on bended knee, plucking little brown liberty caps out of the grass. Being a little older, all the people I had been at school with were starting to get married and be proper adults, but I didn't really feel in step with them. Sandy wasn't fazed however; he'd dart off and then shout with glee as he landed on a large cluster of them. He was virtually eating them off the field, half council estate boy half rabbit, as he scooped handfuls into the muddy little Tesco carrier bag tightly gripped by his left side pocket (like a little illegal doggie bag of shit) and others still, straight into his hungry mouth. I'd never seen him so focussed, certainly not at work...as he was quite laid back, to say the least, when it came to that!

We took them back to his house and boiled them up in a pan. I had no idea what the correct dosage was.

"That looks like an afa lot, Sandy! Must be over a hundred in there?" I said, a little nervous of the quantity he kept heaping into the water like some weird demonic version of Jamie Oliver.

"Fauck-kin...na min; you need a lot of 'em to get enough of the psychoactive compound into solution...it's for the baith o' us mind!?"

I relented, he was the expert. "Aye fair enuff, you look like ye kaen fit yer dein' onywy." Well I had to have faith that he knew what he was doing, as I didn't really have a clue!

As I looked at those little dirty stalks simmering in Sandy's parents' kitchen, I felt that it was very strange that they had been embedded underfoot amidst the dirt of the playing field not two hours before. I was used to getting all my food from clean, sanitized supermarket plastic trays. Plus, this was actually against the law, which did lend a bit more of an edge to the proceedings. As I watched their illegal little bodies float about the pan in an inch of water, they seemed to threaten of all the untold dangers yet to come and yet look so small and pathetic all at the same time.

We decided to sit and watch MTV whilst drinking the 'mushie tea' on Sandy's advice (it was 1989, everybody found MTV trippy and exciting back then!). The brew was disgusting, brown and oily and tasted like acrid mud. Like the playing field should taste, as you might expect, with years of Northfield feet having trod upon it over time.

"Nuthin's happenin'," I said, after a cup of it, 'so far, so good,' I thought. However, Sandy, as if by magic (like Mr. Ben's tailor) was standing at my shoulder with the pan and strainer in hand,

"Have some maaaair, have some mair go'oan. We've nae hid enough 'at's why!"

I tentatively took another half cup. Sandy went and boiled up the mushrooms for a second time and then squeezed them in his hand to wring every ounce of "trippy juice" outa them. We drank the dregs; Sandy even started picking them out of the strainer one by one, chewing on them. I watched their glistening bodies wriggle on his fat bottom lip before being sucked in his mouth like some slug spaghetti. I found this way too disgusting and decided to pass on that. Watching him sip up the little slithery stalks made me wonder whether a person could get addicted to mushies. Though as I watched their glistening bodies slither into the side of his mouth, like some fucking depraved toad eating slugs, I became quite assured that, I at least, definitely never could, gadz or fit, right? (Doric for yuk or what).

I had downed a cup and a half and was now committed. I sat and waited, wondering what the hallucinations would be like. The only reference I had was the film "Yellow Submarine," and I supposed I would see colours and have visions like 'Lucy in the Sky with Diamonds' complete with a great soundtrack. That wouldn't be bad; it certainly worked for the Beatles anyway and I liked that film. Although, you do tend to forget how weird, scary and repressive that film can be, don't you!?

Soon the fast graphic adverts on MTV started to get a bit wild and a weird 'elasticized feeling' crept up on me, from the back of my head onwards over my head to my face. I began to have that feeling of bouts of complete lack of control. I started sweating, then momentarily felt detached from my body and very strange, I composed myself as best as I could and turned to speak to Sandy on the next chair, clearing my throat a little to try to conceal my panic.

"Erm aye, right enough, I'm eh...startin' to feel a luttle bitty weird," I said, but as I turned my face towards him, I found Sandy glaring at me with a huge grin on his now red and puffy, pockmarked face, like a Cheshire cat. A mixture of supreme glee and fascination was etched on his face, looking like perhaps a twisted person who had been watching a cow walk towards a land mine. Then suddenly, this vision of the Cheshire cat face seemed to hurtle away from me until it was far away at the end of a long corridor, then just as quickly it elastically snapped back into place.

"Wowh! Shit, oh fuck, oh fuck, oh fuck," I said as I shook my head and hung onto my knees, in case the former was going to fall off into my lap or something.

Sandy was ecstatic however, obviously on seeing the desired reaction from me. "By the way," he said looking at me with a peculiar glint in his eye, "we've just had one fauck-kin' <u>massive</u> dose o' mushies!"

He was nodding his head in approval and eyeing me with the sort of look that should be accompanied with a thumbs up! He was acting like he was doing me a favour (the puffy-faced cunt). This film definitely wasn't going to feature a nice cartoon John Lennon in a groovy submarine but was more like being trapped in a lift with a fucking annoying and slightly deranged blue meanie! I just looked at him incredulously, hoping it was a bad joke, but my hopes faded as I realised that no such admission was forthcoming. I was in for a long evening.

Sometime later, I don't know how long, there was a knock on the door. In walked four of Sandy's mates from the local area. They noisily piled into his house, "Fit's happenin' fat boy? A'right Roorkie ye fat basterd, fit ye dein'? *etc.*" I became alarmed and nervous; I'd never met any of them before. As typical in Aberdeen, all their names ended in an 'ie;' Johnie, Stuartie, Frunkie and Boabie! I immediately thought Frunkie was quite a 'freaky Frunkie,' as he had a very apparent receeding hairline, despite just being a year out of school (poor bastard). I mean, if this had been the 1930s, he would be smoking a pipe and be a dad by now or something. But here he was grinning in his Megadeath t-shirt with a forty-something hairdo. I don't know, it just didn't seem right to me, it made him seem daft, retarded even and desperate for attention; mushies didn't cure my prejudices, clearly! They all took one look at us and immediately realised we were very, very stoned.

"Mushies? Wayyyyy!"
"Aye!"
"Wow, gie'us some?"

"Neen left, we've just had them all, the "hale lot of 'em itween iz!" Sandy said knowingly and proudly.

Johnie slapped Sandy on the shoulder playfully; "Fuckin' fat cunts ate 'em a'!"

I smirked out of politeness but I was really on guard. I didn't quite get this kind of blokey piss-take camaraderie. I felt a little embarrassed that they'd insulted Sandy in his own home about a half a dozen times before they reached the living room. Sandy, though, seemed in his element; I would have felt crushed. I didn't understand these guys at all, the way they looked, the way they dressed. I was only three years older, perhaps, but felt like I came from a different time. They were all rock dudes, sporting a very American style thrash metal look; which to me seemed desperately fake in a Doric fishing town in Scotland (says the goth-indie kid, punk). They all wore converse trainers that looked smelly and falling apart. They all had the same black jeans as well, with dangling chains or straps (for some reason). An array of denim and baseball style jackets and caps filled my view. (Stuartie reminded me strongly of Judd Nelson's character from the Breakfast Club). I also couldn't understand how Sandy could function in such a cool sober kind of manner. Sandy and I obviously were in different places really. Though I began to "feel" the world through his eyes, almost accidentally or unwilling by osmosis, while watching him speak and make gestures eagerly into the void of the room. I mean, I could see that, despite sharing a physical reality, his version was completely different to mine. It was a very strange and almost an out of body realisation, as I began to feel every tick and fibre of his now transparent insecurities in full Technicolor brilliance. In that state, I could see through him and inside his mind as if I had X-ray vision, my natural empathic abilities having been now magnified to the point of psychic awareness. I watched him desperately trying to impress his mates. It was painful to feel.

However, my more immediate issue was the strain of grappling with conversation with new people, which was a huge venture that needed all my concentration and defences at the best of times. Although my initial prejudices of the poor, 'follicley fucked' Frunkie actually proved somewhat correct, as in an effort to impress the crowd, he promptly grabbed an aerosol off a shelf in Sandy's room and proceeded to spray it right up his nose and shout,

"Well then, fuckin' right boys, let's get hiiiiiiiigh!"

I was shocked; I'd never witnessed such a flagrant and insensible disregard for personal health. Everyone knew that solvent abuse was really dangerous and stupid, surely? I wondered for a second whether this past behaviour had been responsible for making his hair fall out like that!?

Sandy just looked at him perplexed. "Fauck-kin', wise up Frunkie, 'that's ma fuckin' feet spray!"

Sandy had some problem with his feet; I don't know what it was, except to say it must have been a fairly severe fungal infection because when he took his shoes off, people in Norway must have screwed their faces up if the wind was in the right direction. His room was actually impregnated with a slight "feety" odour, especially on the blankets and furnishings. It was quite unpleasant.

In response, someone then spoke for the crowd: "Waahh, the boy's sniffin' fuckin' feet spray, Harhar, 'Feil Frunkie, - Feil Frunkie Feetspray' - what a fuckin' dickhead!" (Feil is Doric for stupid). Everybody laughed at him, as he shrugged and started to regard the label with a look of disdain. Feil Frunkie was clearly used to this treatment as Boabie's main stock phrase to any interaction seemed to be, "Fuckoff-Frunkie ya-fuckin' freak min!" They obviously went back quite a long way! With my now acquired, somewhat enhanced, state of empathy, I observed Frunkie's entire ego implode and whimper down like a failed soufflé. I, myself, was a bit perturbed by this time and was starting to wonder just what the hell I was getting myself into, though I was relieved that there was someone in the room that might draw any antipathy away from me. 'Thank fuck for Feil Frunkie and his Feetspray,' I thought! As I started to long for the sanctity of my lonely existence in my bedroom in Briar Brae playing boring computer football games interspersed with bouts of uninspiring masturbation.

I didn't think the evening could get any worse, but it proceeded to tax my sensibilities in new ways. As the smallest of social interactions usually demanded my full attention, as anyone who has been overly stoned will know, even the two times table is tricky in that state of mind. Stuartie had a small orange ball with him that they all started tossing around between them, in front of my eyes saying, "See ony tracers, min? See ony fuckin' tracers, min?" They were excited that we may be able to see tracers following the ball or anything else that was wafted past our faces, including their wiggling fingers accompanied by a "Whuhoooooo" sound and "Trip-paaaaay" in alarmingly strange spooky voices. Tracers were clearly a big deal and a known benchmark for the official "trippy" experience. I mean, they even carried a 'special ball' around, apparently just for these occasions...fuck me!

Although I did see tracers, they made me feel a bit sick, so I put my hand over my eyes, "Woaah, steady there, guys, 'at's a bit too much tracers in one go, they're too trippy." This evidently made them feel highly delighted, "Yayy, the boy's seein' tracers a'right! He's all right ini-he?" With a slap on the shoulder, I was part of the gang, as easy as that, tracertastic!

However, as happy as they apparently were with their new friend, they had no idea whatsoever of my advancing state of paranoia and vulnerability. Someone eventually had the bright idea of going outside for a walk about. I objected strongly but when questioned on why not, I was completely unable to think up a sensible retort as to why we shouldn't. So of course we ended up walking along the street, but my legs were walking three feet in front of me on their own. I was sure that any passer-by would be aware of this and see that I was stoned and so I tried to look as inconspicuous as I could, trying to command my legs back under my body as I walked. I was afraid that I would bump into someone I had gone to school with. Then I would appear as the retard, surely! Getting stoned with the kids; I mean, as we walked down the road the boys were pushing each other into hedges and whooping and hollering. Frunkie's trainers rolled into view as he went too far, showing off, rolling right into a garden. I hid my face; a girl I fancied in year two lived around here. It might be her house; she may have kids of her own by now! What an affront! Frunkie caught us up to the sounds of window banging and Boabie's; "...freak-min!"

I don't know how I managed to disguise my total and utter dread and panic. Well, I suppose as a neurotic kind of introvert I had become quite a master at disguising my insecurities in sober society.

This, though, was a whole fresh kind of Hellish experience to me; I seemed to manage carrying out bits of conversations with Sandy's mates. Oddly, as they'd been so stoned together so often before, they had become accustomed to talking within that 'stoned kind of trippy reality,' as half-finished sentences and confusion just brought laughter and amusement. It actually made you more liked by the group as everyone else was doing it. I felt terrible, as it occurred to me, *'so this is how really dumb people at school operated!'* Having to be re-told everything and seemingly not being capable of holding any information for more than ten seconds at a time. Then it struck me, '*gawd, many of the people in my classes had been stoned!*' That's why they giggled and found it hard to remember stuff, or care. It didn't matter that you did not take anything in; all that was important was the continuity of this shared platform of social stoner-cohesion with your mates. In fact, the dumber you were, the more acceptable you became.

I wasn't suited to it, I hated it; life is for inquiry and wonder, not giving up and revelling in some cloud of stupidity because you really can't be bothered doing anything else. Sure, it's ok for an hour or so, but this was a way of life for these guys and like consistently playing Atari Pong, I would very quickly get bored of it.

We walked to the chip shop. The strange thing about young people just going for a walk is that it's never quite random. It always tends to gravitate towards a corner shop or chip shop despite no one actually declaring that this is the real destination. Why is that? And why do people always then buy soft drinks when they have bottles in the fridge at home? And why does at least one person open a drinks can right outside the shop and spill it down their front, so it looks like they've pissed themselves? Then for the next minute or so their mates go, "Whaay, stupit fuckin' dickheed, check oot the boyyy, irin bru a-oer his fauck-kin coupon and a-thin'." Anyway, I was too out of it to answer these insights! We got chips, which I hoped would sober me up a little, but I wasn't really able to taste them. The worst part though, was that I just couldn't remember how to swallow and large clumps of soggy chips splattered on the ground all around me, falling from the corners of my mouth as I chewed them perplexed by what to do after this action. It seemed that mushie trips were impervious to attempts at sobriety.

We also got beers and upon hearing that alcohol brings you out of a trip, I began gulping them down like a man possessed, praying that I would get back to normal, as I was quite uncomfortable by this time, very paranoid and completely unable to process information in any sensible manner. I would swap familiar drunk inebriation for a mushie trip any day (aside from the fact that it was much more socially acceptable to be publicly drunk in Northfield and I was still worried I'd bump into someone I'd been to school with). I had also become acutely worried that I may never actually be normal again and be forever one of Sandy's mob obediently following him around for chips and beer, with a whole new bunch of zombie mates, changing my name to Seanie.

Forever vying for acceptance by spraying feet spray up my nose and being ridiculed by former classmates and their children and becoming "that guy" who spills food and drink on himself outside the chipper and all his mates go, "Fauck-kin' whaahaayyy."

Back in Sandy's room was one of the longest evenings of my life; I had never been so stoned and totally couldn't handle it. The feeling of just not wanting to be there was intensified a hundred-fold in my addled brain, but I just couldn't get up and leave, as I just couldn't reason enough to do this. I had become a nauseous, paranoid space on the bedroom floor, trapped there unable to assert my free will on any part of it. Worse still, his mates liked metal music such as Slayer and Anthrax, which they played loud as fuck, obliterating any chance of a peaceful nice relaxing trip. It became the demonic soundtrack to the personal hell I was trapped in.

Eventually, I started to come down a little. Feeling a little relieved that the beer had worked its magic and more convinced that my brain wasn't permanently broken, I made my way down the road to my house. I quietly crept through the front door, as my parents were asleep. I opened my bedroom door and flicked on the light switch. A fluttering sound broke the silence and the biggest moth I think I've ever seen attacked the light shade in the middle of the ceiling. I wondered for a few seconds whether this was a hallucination, as the room and windows had been closed for the day and surely I would have noticed this thing the night before. I opened the window and gently guided the beast outside. I left the window open a little for fresh air and carefully made my way over to the computer chair before slumping into it, summoning up energy for my next move, taking off my DM boots, as I knew it was going to take some concerted effort.

Shortly after, a fluttering broke the silence again and I became aware of feeling a 'mothy sort of presence' again. I looked around; another identical moth was on the curtain. "Aah for fucksake! It's like bloody Borneo in here tonight," I muttered to myself, as I had to repeat the process aaalll over again. Some minutes later, I sank onto my bed and decided to rest there for a while, assimilating the evening's proceedings. I had finally tried (or succumbed) to the seasonal mushroom eating pastime of the average Northfielder! I smiled at how bad, bold and experienced I now was; a mini rite of passage had been tentatively made, even with Sandy's strong brews and I had lived to tell the tale. Although, after vomiting somewhat and half believing that my brain had been rendered permanently disordered, I did wonder however, 'what was the attraction exactly?'

As I smirked, I became aware of a very small whisper that seemed to start way back in my mind and enter the reality of the stillness of the room. My body went cold as again the voice whispered my name. I opened my eyes still stoned, thus not considering the unlikely weirdness of the situation and answered out loud, "What? Who's there?" And as I sat up on my elbows, another moth flitted across the room. I curiously watched its zigzag flight mock me and then alight on the far wall.

I immediately felt very perturbed as hair stood up on the back of my head. The whole room seemed to shrink with a threatening silence as my head swam a little. 'Fuck me, that moth just spoke to me!' I shook my head and grabbed my temples; this was a little freaky to say the least! I spoke out loud to reassure myself, "Demonic moths!? For Christ-sakes? I must be going mad." I then thought how much of a fool I had been to trust Sandy. 'The bastard! He's broken my fucking brain.' But the sudden rationale that this was all drug-induced seemed to ease my fears a little. "You're a mouldy tattie-crisp!" I said out loud to break the tension, mimicking Ebenezer Scrooge. It worked; the sweat on my forehead gave way to the relief of a giggle as my own little analogy amused me as my face contorted with a smirk. I swung my legs off the bed and made my way over towards the brown cloth-like night visitor. I held my hand up for a second, contemplating splatting the scary bat–sized insect, but as quickly as I had thought this, I immediately sensed that that would be a bad idea and that I would regret it immensely. I lowered my hand feeling slightly ashamed to have considered it at all. Anyway, I tried never to kill insects; they were complicated animals after all and often beautiful close up. Also, I often did feel the need to bond with their kind; believe it or not, they were the only other living things which regularly intersected my life in this room!

"I'm here!" In a flash, the voice sounded louder, definitely female and strangely familiar, almost stunning me! I reeled a little. I knew I was out of it, but this felt more real – more significantly real – than anything before. "Fuck amm fuckin' trippin' min," I said to myself in an effort to assert some street normality back onto the scene. I faced the curious object on the wall; it now seemed to hum with electricity and instantly I felt a pang of childhood memories, *put the ink on the paper, it's a mess, fold it...and it creates anew, a butterfly! Out of chaos, out of nothing, perception is altered.*

"Perception is altered...perception is altered," I muttered aloud." Why not a moth? I asked myself, why doesn't anybody say they've made a moth?" Butterflies get all the press!

"Why not a moth?" I now said to myself again, the words streaking across the wall, caressing the brown patchwork on its symmetrical wings. I regarded it. "What were you saying? What are you saying?" I mouthed, standing still staring expectantly towards the winged shape, almost expecting an answer. Strangely enough, I wasn't scared, only intrigued, as the moth looked earthy, like the mushrooms, caked, crisp and singed, made out of cloth as if delivered to the palpable reality of the world in a rush. I walked up to it; I could see clearly now that this moth was connected to the mushrooms somehow. "An agent of them, even," I said to myself as I stared at it contrasted against the dirty-cream woodchip of my wall. It looked serenely beautiful, almost awesome, revealing never ending detail and beauty against the monotony of the man-made uniformity of paint and paper. I felt stupid to have thrown the other one out so quickly (or indeed, this was probably the same one). "I had no idea!" I said again, apologetically, as I took the time to try to fully take in its beauty. I suddenly felt incredibly lucky to behold the intricacies of this small unique animal before me. Now a wondrous sight, allowing me to drink in its presence for free as my eyes followed the design of the wings, the detail in each flake looking perfectly placed. I mused that I could almost see each colony group of cells and the colours and textures were almost too overwhelming to behold. Mottled bands of earthy brown contrasted with subtle darker rings on the top. Occasionally, a quick flexing movement of wing revealed a mesmerising bright flash of a secret burnt orange band underneath, which stole my complete attention, as it hypnotically communicated this celebration of "just being orange" directly into my nervous system. I gasped under my breath at the shock of it, an orange-ness sinking through my mind then body and resonating in my core. I could almost taste it.

I pondered this as I stared awestruck at the wall. 'Seems like nature had invented orange long before any human had decided to label it *orange*,' I thought and included it on cave paintings, cravats, wallpaper catalogues, or plastic toy cars; strange when you think about it. We don't actually *own* anything! The biblical mind-set kind of lets on that we do, that nature was all invented for us, yet there was something far older and far less concerned with human affairs involved here. A secret, just sitting in plain view on my wall; all you had to do was be a bit less sober to notice it, perhaps!? We should feel lucky to behold all that exists, not just assume we're entitled to it all.

I became aware that my mind was whizzing and flinging up too many separate attempts to describe and analyse the insect in front of me. 'When's it going to end, where is the moth now?' I thought. Immediately and in a flash I knew it all, knew the moth didn't end, it was on the wall, in my mind, my childhood, in every pattern my eye ever followed, in chaos and in order, across time and in my room now and in my head. 'Some of reality is made of imagination,' I thought, 'and so the universe *is* partly imaginary!' It was all relative! 'Relativity...YES! Relativity! Reality is relative, imagination is relative!' I thought that I was onto something, I grappled to articulate it. "Relative is real-i-tivity...realitiv...Awh No! Fuck! Ah lost it, fuck it!" I couldn't string a single thought together; my mind had lost the grasp of it, maybe forever! Fuck, how many stoned people have seen the secrets of the universe, only to have lost it," I chuckled out loud, "bugger it, I'm hungry!" I gently cupped the moth and again let it out into the cool dark air rushing past my window, out into a quiet world where the mystery of moth flight silently awaited its arrival. I ate something; I wish I could remember what unlikely combination of things it was as it was the best thing I have ever tasted, ever! I eventually feel asleep and thankfully in the morning my brain seemed quite back to its normal self. I didn't really feel like killing Sandy anymore, for the time being anyway.

I felt like such an idiot afterwards, that life was not fair, as life had a way of making me feel kind of stupid and gormless. Therefore to everybody else, it was written on my face and thus it gave them license to regard me as a gormless stupid no hoper, but it wasn't fair as I never actually wanted to get that stoned with Sandy. I should've been at home doing my own thing. Life, it seemed, was just full of frustrating obstacles put in my way because of the will of other people!

My stoner education had been inevitable though, at the lab; on the bench behind mine on the other side was our mutual friend, Wally Fraser. He was bit of a scary guy from the Broch- further up the north east coast, as he had an uncompromising biker vibe about him, though this was contrasted with an obvious intellectual mind which was revealed whenever he spoke. He was about two years younger than me, again of Sandy's 'more stoner' generation. He was quite strange, a typical intellectual, nerdy type who wore khakis and big boots all the time, hated authority and life in general and had a fixation with drug taking. It seemed to me that he definitely had the kind of look of a person most likely to be carrying a range of concealed weapons on his person. Our boss, occasionally, used to wind him up and be mean to him for some reason. Let's just say that if I was his boss, I wouldn't! (As on the day he finally might 'go postal' on us, he'd be the first to get it!). Wally's face was partly obscured by large 'owly' glasses which sat authoritatively on a pug nose. You could see that he'd spent his entire life being much more intelligent than his peers, as this had now crystallized into a permanent state of sarcasm, while his eyes conveyed almost constant amusement at other people's ignorance. I knew this as no mere speculation, as often his historical or pop culture references clearly went over my head to which, his twinkle in eye stare and tightlipped smile-come-grimace response conveyed that he was mentally chalking up yet another group of facts that I didn't know!

Sandy had been finding out about him just before I arrived and had recognised a potential hash soul mate. I was working right between the two biggest hash heads I would ever come to know, so what chance did I have? There were a couple of other guys who worked there as well, such as rock dude Freddie and a few others that came and went. We all went out together to the Mudd club, every Monday night, Aberdeen's best indie club as well as the rock night on some Thursdays. I loved it, as I loved throwing myself around the dance floor to the music I was really into; tracks by the Wonderstuff and Jesus Jones sounded transcendent to me; Janes Addiction and Smashing Pumpkins were simply ethereal. I felt a kinship to all the black-dressed student types in there. At first I was mesmerised by the way they moved on the dance floor and quickly found a similar type of style of dancing, as if the music was moving my body and limbs. Either it would be the slow hypnotic goth beat and disjointed sweeping guitars which seemed somehow to resonate at the same pace and sense of mood as my very soul, or to the sub-pop grunge, like Mudhoney or Nirvana, making me hurl my head and body in a sort of tribal trance.

This was more than just a place to mingle for me; I was plugged in physically and spiritually. I belonged there and the DJ kept putting on song after song that belonged to me! Like the "Passenger" (the Iggy Pop song & Jim Morrison poem). A good night would see me up there for hours. The lift I received from the music was addictive; from the tribal connection to the grunge sound and almost spiritual ecstasy from goth rock like the Mission or Fields of The Nephilim. T-shirts were everywhere, "Pop Will Eat Itself," the Inspirals' "Cool as Fuck," "Death to the Pixies." It was indie heaven; people dressed and looked alternative, which inspired me to keep doing the same.

We also spent hours in Wally's flat. It was a total fucking state of affairs with doors hanging off their hinges, sticky carpets covered in horrible things; a scene straight out of the Freak Brothers. We would all get stoned and lie on the floor listening to Led Zep or Pink Floyd. I found this a bit boring most of the time, but I didn't mind Hendrix; I've got to admit that that sounded unearthly under the influence, as did the Mission. I was the only sort of indie dude, as they were all more rock orientated. I once played The Jesus and Mary Chain, which I considered perfect for listening to after a smoke or two, but Wally lunged over claiming, "Jeezuz-man what the fuck wiz that? All I could see were big brown stripes flying at ma head, keep it mellow man, mellow!" as he looked for his Masters of Reality CD. But I didn't want mellow; you can keep that for when you're in your seventies. I wanted emotional music or something that mirrored my inner angst and drive.

During this time I still lived with my parents and inevitably the two worlds would collide. On one occasion after scoffing a hash cake at the flat (as being assured by Sandy Rourke that it was fine and much nicer than smoking) and then getting dropped off at home, I went to get my tea and sat in the living room where my family and sister's new boyfriend were watching T.V. whilst eating their dinners from their laps, sort of like the Royle family watching 'Only Fools and Horses' or something. I didn't think the hash cake had any effect, but began to feel a bit out of it in the kitchen all of a sudden, even trying to make tea with cold water, for instance. I hadn't bargained on the delayed effect! By the time I sat down, I was dedicating the full power of my brain (that I could muster) just to coordinate eating and swallowing.

"Hey Sean, this is Geanie's boyfriend Wattie...y'kaen, fae the lut-til shoapie!?" (*i.e.* The smaller of the two nearby shops) someone said a tad overly incongruously politely to introduce the poor nervous and brill-creamed lut-til shoapie mannie sitting with my sister in the corner.

Mashed potatoes toppled from my mouth and splatted around me on the table, as again I was forgetting how to swallow and eat, lacking the required concentration for simple multitasking. I was indeed familiar with 'Wattie fae the lut-til shoapie.' The lut-til shoapie was just around the corner and down some steps fae the big shoapie. A sparse dusty little room comprising open 'cash n carry' boxes, selling mainly fags and confectionery, barely qualified as a shop in my book anyway. A red-eyed monster now looked up at the lut-til shoapie Watt.

"Oh yeah, right yeah, hello erm..." I reached into my back pocket and slapped £1.50 on the table, "I'll have a cream egg an'a bounty Wattie, cheers mate!" Luckily everybody just thought I was being funny and giggled.

My mum flashed me a look of daggers though and stuck up for the nervous Wattie grinning in the corner, sandwiched behind my sister, as if to prevent him making a run for it.

"Ignore him Watt, he's jist being a bit of an arsehole as usual," she said politely.

I looked a bit confused; sure that this was the usual sort of script when talking and dealing with Wattie and I began recounting in my head what the difference in this case might be, but for the life of me just couldn't figure it out. In fact, I didn't even know what I was figuring out, just that my mind was whizzing around in circles trying to figure out something!

I hit a filling with my fork; a metallic throbbing intensified and spread across one half of my face and wouldn't go away, making it now totally impossible to eat. "Mawwwwuurahhh," I groaned as I spat food back onto the plate, open mouthed and face now screwed into a fine involuntary Quasimodo impersonation. I held the one side of my face with both hands, dropping the fork loudly onto the table. "Mawwwwurrahhhh."

My mum looked very embarrassed as she quickly tried to stem the shenanigans from me. "He's nae ay-wiz like this, Watt!" She then rounded on me. "Fit the hell's a-wrang wi' you the-day? Pull yourself tigither will ye, stop acting the fuckin' goat!" Then amusingly turning towards Wattie, she said in her best posh voice, "I do apologise on his behalf this evening, he should have a bit more manners;" as my sister's new boyfriend regarded me fearfully, no doubt worried that "Mungo" might leap across the table at any moment and bite his ear off or something. I guess he was wondering just what the hell he was getting himself into! He'd always distrusted me, failing to understand my goth/indie kid look. He was a fool who thought comics were for fools. Our conversations were always out of sync; but now he had to tolerate me in my own house. Clearly at this moment though, I was further giving all indie kids a really bad name with the 'conventional' lut-til shoapie mannie social set.

I sank back into the sofa, the metallic pain further spreading across my cheek, my hands clamped over my face, tongue lolling as I uttered, "Fillin', fillin'," in an effort to explain my apparent antisocial behaviour.

"Fillin'? But you've hardly touched it!" my confused and now irascible mother continued, "Hiv you been eating shite fae 'at bloody lut-til shoapie again? Oh…Sorry, sorry Watt, I didnae mean it like 'at!" My now blushing parent was sending me a look that could kill. Clearly, scaring off a possible sister-suitor in such a way was not on at all.

However my mum's annoyance was currently furthest from my mind as a new predicament was now unfolding; as I sat back in the sofa I began to realise that I was sinking into it, part of my legs disappeared and the back of my head became enveloped in the cushions behind me. 'Oh my god, I'm melting into the sofa,' I thought, 'they're gonna notice this and figure out that I'm stoned!'

Unbeknownst to me, in reality, I was merely sliding off the couch towards the floor in slow motion. I, however, was convinced that I was falling further into a quicksand brown corduroy cushioned nightmare with large flat fabric buttons, terrifying I can assure you!

"Bloody cheap shite sofa!" I yelled in an attempt to share my frustration and give some explanation for my uncivil sinking behaviour. "Nay my fuckin' fault, see what happens!?' I shrieked in protest. "See what happens fin ye buy cheap shite!"

My mother stood up, arms at her hips, which was like a shaolin ready position for her, I was seconds away from getting a mighty slap but she was restraining herself. Close to tears with rage and confusion she retorted,

"Fa' d'ye think yer spikin' till? Nithing rang wi' this hoose! Yoo should think yersel lucky tae bide in a hoose wi' sofas 'n tee-veeess and a'thing like 'at! Some folk's got nithing, ye kaen 'at?" She shook her head looking to everyone else tutting with one of her stock phrases, "Ye bring 'em up's best as ye can and 'ats the bloody thanks ye get!"

My dad who had been watching me with interest decided to intervene before my Ma attacked me.

"Fit's a-dae wi ye min," he said sternly, with brow wrinkled, as he now watched me trying to do the back stroke, hands flailing a mere one and a half feet to his left. I sank, twisting around and desperately clawing at the armchair as I went, moaning and preparing to have to hold my breath.

"Is he a' right like?" said Wattie, regarding his own plate of potatoes with some suspicion and obviously rethinking the offer to come for tea one evening.

My sister just frowned nonchalantly, "He's niver been a'right 'at boy!"

I reached over manically and sank my fingers onto my dad's knees, he winced "Ooh-ya bastard yeh!"

My mum immediately rounded on him and without the least bit of irony, "Language Sean!?" She quickly composed herself. "It's nae ayewiz like this, Watt!"

Meanwhile, I felt corduroy touch my mouth and I started a loud series of gasping reflexes. "I canna breathe, a' canna fuckin' breathe! Heeelllllp!"

My mum darted towards me. "Is he choking, is he chokin'?" she said with grave concern. Choking, like loose and dangerously unused coat hangers and plastic bags seemed to trigger the most desperate life threatening panic building within her. "Sean, Sean!" she frantically beckoned to my dad to act and this he did by pounding my back with the flat of his hand.

I felt my face sink into the cushion with each slap, "Fuckin' murrrrderers," I gasped out with my last breaths.

My mum was wringing her hands "Do ye need a bit o' loaf? Get the loaf, somebody get the loaf!" Whenever we choked on food as kids she'd feed us mounds of bread to dislodge it; I don't know where she'd heard this from but it had become an instinct for her to reach for loaf in these crisis situations.

However, what I needed was a French stick to cling to, to haul me out of this furniture come quicksand nightmare. Eventually my dad grabbed my arm and effortlessly hoisted me up, "Oh thank you!" I said as I hugged him for saving my life, "Oh God, thank you!"

With that, my dad escorted me through to my room, "He's been drinking 'at's a'!" As he poured me onto the top of my bed he gave me a knowing look. "I'm gan tae be ha'in' a word with you and yon Sandy Rourke when he next comes around here!" he said sternly and walked out as I heard the faint voice of my Ma, still perturbed in the background, "A'm black affronted!!" before the door shut on me.

I was just glad to be alive. I crawled off the bed and slid onto the floor; I didn't fancy going through that again. He did, though, have a rather stern word with and he threatened to have us both locked up if I ever came home in that state again. We were a bit more careful after that.

However nothing lasts forever, as any good Taoist worth his salt will tell you. Sandy & Wally inevitably took their drug habits to another level. One Friday evening, as I was working overtime, I was surprised to see Sandy and Wally huddled over a fume cupboard, which was odd because they hardly ever worked overtime, if at all and especially never on a Friday evening. In fact, I was usually the only person labouring there like the underpaid and overworked idiot that indeed I was. I hadn't sussed that one could tell their boss where to go and live to tell the tale. I still assumed that I had to keep doing what the boss asked and be grateful that I had a job to keep me away from doing things which I actually would prefer to do with my time, such as reading, improving myself and not breathing in carcinogenic solvents, y'know? Things like that!

We were the only three left in the building. "Hey what are you two up to?" I asked.

"Ah," said Wally authoritatively, with his finger raised in the air, pointedly, in an exaggerated nutty professor kind of way (except for the fact that he did actually speak and act like that all the time). "We're making amphetamine here and if the organic synthesis is progressing accordingly, then we're only a few steps away from producing pure amphetamine!" He grinned like a triumphant schoolboy. Sandy looked on excitedly then chipped in,

"Fauck-kin,' course then we can cut it wi' sucrose from the stores and sell it on, make a fuckin' fortune and have enough to use ourselves for free," he said assuredly. They had it all worked out and they had talked themselves into thinking it was fool-proof, especially Sandy, who was clearly thinking, like Del boy, that 'This time next year, we'll all be millionaires!'

Wally had planned this for some time. He hadn't had a great deal of Organic Chemistry knowledge at the time, having only just sat his

OND Chemistry on day release at college, which was like the senior school Higher Chemistry level, a sort of introductory level course. It may enable you to remember all the homologous hydrocarbons and balance equations, but string together complex organic synthesis? Nuh! However he had gone around asking the Chemistry lecturers how to synthesize 'A' from 'B' carefully trying to conceal 'C' as much as he could. By asking different individuals about different parts of the process and pretending he was asking out of innocent curiosity, he had obtained a full list of all the stages and ingredients of chemical synthesis of amphetamine, together with catalysts and quantities required, starting from base products. This was before the age of home PCs and internet access. His next move was to stealthily obtain the ingredients bit by bit, by occasionally adding these to the monthly roster of chemical orders. The store-man and general caretaker had no real knowledge of advanced Organic Chemistry and so ordered them, none the wiser. Wally then went into the storeroom when the orders arrived, intercepted his 'additions' and hid them away in a little locked cupboard he had set aside and now this Friday evening was the night. You had to admire his resourcefulness and patience.

I was a bit scared and started to get paranoid, which is probably why they hadn't let me in on it earlier. Anyone could come in at any time, how were they going to explain this massive round flask and distillation apparatus, with frothy bubbling liquids inside it?

"Right now," said Wally in his enthusiastic sort of school teacher way of talking, "Let's add some of this...and a powdered zinc catalyst...and it should turn yellow...right; there it goes...good!"

I watched for a bit, slightly impressed I admit and then went to carry on with my work, slightly nervous, expecting someone to come walking in any minute. I went to the toilet and as I walked past the front door I looked out into the car park. Parked there all on its own was the lab boss' Volvo! I panicked and concluded that he had come back and was in his office a mere few feet from the laboratory and dark deeds. I ran like the actor 'Jim Dale' from one of the *Carry On* films, back into the lab, trying to both shout and whisper at the same time (while using panic-stricken body language to great effect) that the boss was here and his presence in the lab was surely imminent. Together, efficiently and in silence and with a heightened state of alert, Wally and Sandy set to work robotically pouring liquids down drains, switching off heaters and dismantling what they could. It was like watching a tape on fast forward; it was incredible and very well coordinated.

However, it soon transpired that the boss had merely left his car there to catch a train into town so he could go out on the piss. After some debate as to whether suitable violence should be advocated against me, I was subsequently banished from the project while they returned to work continuing their fiendish ambitions for drug self-sufficiency. Huddled together like a pair of alchemists from antiquity, they set to work, hoping to create their "gold" out of ill-gotten chemicals, acids and powdered metals.

I almost wish it had happened for them, but whatever dried product they ended up with later that evening, it sure wasn't amphetamine and rather like when Percy in *Blackadder II* when trying to turn base metals to "gold," instead invented "green," they it seemed, had invented "shitey fucking yellow!" We all three gazed at the mound of sickly coloured powder resting on the ominously discoloured and charred filter paper.

"Bloody hell", I said, "wasn't there a Blue Peter warning about not trying this at home?"

Sandy, sensing my negativity, retaliated; "Fauckk-kin'; well we're not at fuckin' home ya cunt, we're in the lab urn't wi!?"

I turned to look at him realising that it was pointless to start an argument; all babies look good to their parents and this was definitely their baby and I was slagging it off. I smiled and with wide eyed resignation agreed, "Aye, aye, fitiver min!"

We looked again, the other two more adoringly than I. I suddenly became glad that I hadn't been included in the original venture and took an almost involuntary step back from the worrying pyramid of greyish yellow devil dust.

"Well all that's left now is to test it," said Wally, the chemical engineer in charge.

"Don't fuckin' look at me!" I said as I gestured towards it as one would a pile of radioactive waste. "As far as I'm concerned, I never even saw you guys!"

Sandy looked all serious for a moment and glancing at Wally, turned towards me, his very shadow seemed to grow larger, looming over me, "Aye damn right, you neva saw nuttin'!" he said in an ominous tone with a New York twang.

I regarded him coolly. "Oh fuck off Sandy. You've been watchin' far too many gangster films; you twat head!" I sneered at him a little, looking at Wally and nodding my head towards Sandy; the threat evaporated and Wally's head swivelled in his owl-like fashion from Sandy to me and back again which was his way. I had long since learned that Sandy was all mouth and that as soon as you stood up to him he immediately acted like it was all a joke, that he was just pretending!

"Ah right, ah right, Fauckk-kin', A wiz only fuckin' jokin' min." He looked at Wally incredulously and shrugged.

Wally was clearly quite amused himself. "All right Sandy, I've got an offer for you that you can't refuse! You said you were willing to test it; fuckin' fire in!"

Sandy didn't need to be asked twice. I watched in awe as Sandy took massive snorts of the stuff and then cop his head back, his eyes reeling in an expression which was for all the world like a kid being handed down a giant ice-cream cone from a gigantic heavenly confectionery, but with a simultaneous kick in the groin at exactly the same time. His big unshaven chin jutted into the air in both triumph and an expression of 'crime does pay.' Sandy blinked and instinctively held onto his nose, presumably to check it was still there. Before the verdict was even pronounced, however, Wally brushed past my shoulder and I did a double take of disbelief as I watched him eagerly bend down face first into the evil discoloured mound to do the same. Like a greedy hound from some pet food advert. He didn't even wait to see the reaction from Sandy, presumably him still being alive at that point was all the encouragement he needed.

Sandy was by this time dancing about, "Fauckk-kin' hell what a hit, what a hit!" I admit I was eventually foolish enough to try a very tiny snifter, perhaps out of curiosity, getting caught up in the excitement and Wally's absolute conviction that it couldn't be anything but "pure amphetamine" by now and by the fact that Sandy was acting like he had just ingested pure delight in a test tube. The powder immediately irritated the lining of my nose, it was clearly very acidic! It occurred to me, even with my limited knowledge of chemistry at the time that the substance should have been purified before use, perhaps by crystallisation or further distillation. I had seen him add powdered zinc to it and it should, therefore, still be there; God knows what else was in there!? I went to thoroughly rinse my nose, ignoring the discomfort of water flooding upwards through my nostrils, as I reasoned it was less bad for me than burning chemicals, solvents and toxic metals. Sandy and Wally, however, were convincing themselves that the party was on, Sandy was sniffing more accompanied by a Homer Simpsonesque "Whoo-hooo!" So this was the sound of a man sniffing random corrosive chemicals. I was amazed at their capacity for denial; there was nothing psychoactive about this powder. 'It was clear this guy could get high on fucking talcum powder,' I thought.

They had filled several large plastic screw top vials with it. Sandy was jubilant, saying "Fauckk-kin'...check all that oot; there must be a few hundred quid's worth there, eh? Not bad for one night's work."

Wally grinned with an expression of agreement. But as the night wore on they were forced to accept that perhaps their dream hadn't worked. Of course I knew that, but played along with them. Well, I couldn't be honest with them and tell them my point of view; I mean you can't be yourself with your mates, can you? Well I couldn't, as I actually didn't really know what being myself actually was. Life was clearly more about pleasing others and acting in a manner to fit into their needs, going with the flow so that people won't talk about you behind your back and so on!

Wally was the first to tentatively bring up the notion of plausible disappointment in the venture. "Eh...the hit disnae seem to last very long, though, dis it?"

"Nah nae lang enuff min, an' fauck-kin', de ye feel a slight burnin' sorta feelin' up yer snitch like?" Sandy asked inquiringly.

The fact his nose was bright red and had started to drip with blood, a mere few minutes earlier made this statement all the more absurd.

"Aye it is wee a bit...nippy right enough!" agreed Wally, wiping blood and snot on his lab coat sleeve. "The problem here, you see, is that we don't have enough of the active compound per gram!" This piqued Sandy's interest; here was an academic lifeline to his 'tomorrow we'll be millionaires' dream, which was fading by the second. The solution was obvious; just take higher doses!

So they resorted to taking the vials with them to the pub, mixing it into their beers and downing it. I half expected to see them sink below the pub table followed by, a few moments later, a hairy hand coming back up and them staggering upright with hair bursting out of their T-shirts, kind of like those two monsters out of *Carry on Screaming*. I don't know how many times they attempted this, but I have a feeling that Sandy, probably, consumed the entire batch.

This was an indication of how out of hand their appetites and consumption of drugs was starting to become. Sandy kept going on about ecstasy and speed. I didn't want to try it after the memory of the mushrooms, but they would never let up. However, I was resolute, but the constant badgering was getting fucking annoying. Wally, just seemed to live for the consumption of heroic doses of anything he could acquire, where he would then talk and philosophise deeply for hours. I could never figure out whether he was an eccentric genius or a lost cause. I felt sorry for him; he always seemed like an individual that carried a lot of sadness in his voice and eyes and it was becoming obvious to me that he just wanted to escape life. He eventually got sacked, partly for missing too many days, but mostly for experiencing recurring, sudden and horrendous flashbacks which made him frequently jump and drop pieces of glassware without warning. I watched him leave the office smiling (and apparently being followed out by a line of red lobsters that had been distracting him all week, *i.e.* the whole lot of them got the sack together). He waved over and said goodbye. I was really saddened and so was Sandy. I realised that I'd come to really like and admire the man, despite the fact that he clearly thought that I was a bit boring and straight. Well, it wasn't his fault that he felt like that! I clearly brought that on myself because of my lack of personality. We said we'd keep in contact, but I felt like it was the end of an era.

Of course, Sandy eventually got into raves and E in a big way and despite his best efforts to introduce me to the scene, I wasn't overly into it. Eventually, things got the better of him and he became quite ill. Though, eventually I did go to a few raves with him and liked it. I found that I could get high just listening to the beat; everyone assumed I was on E and I was definitely in the same place. I noticed, however, that they all burned out a lot quicker than I did and needed chemical stimulation to keep going. Also, they were going to have bad downers the next day, whereas I, on a natural high, just felt nicely relaxed and happy the day after. Of course this meant that the next morning I would get on everyone's tits as I would have lots of energy and be restless, whereas everyone else just wanted to mope about smoking dope, feeling ill, looking withdrawn and zombiefied, or just asleep! I was aware that it annoyed everyone that I wasn't in the same "drug place" as them, not quite part of the in-group.

Playing the slightly idiosyncratic obstinate character wasn't going to wash with the group much longer. I could sense that they weren't happy with me for not joining in wholeheartedly with their shared lifestyle choices. I wasn't bound by that; I felt compelled and driven to find something else. I kept quiet about this and avoided the confrontation. I suppose I went along with a lot of things just to fit in, as I was eager to please people. Well, it makes for an easier life, doesn't it? Although, despite not being able to assert any will on the group, I did have an obstinate manner of thinking that made me feel like it was imperative to do my own thing which 'welled up' from somewhere.

I didn't want to mope about all day, instead revelled in getting up early, filling a flask with coffee and with a bunch of compilation tapes and enough food and spliffs to last the day, disappearing into the countryside on my bicycle, quite content to be on my own, going in no particular direction on some mini adventure. I appreciated a nice bit of blow on these occasions, instead of sharing a large repulsive soggy doob around a bunch of zombies fixating on Mario endlessly scampering along the screen. Instead I would find a nice tree with a view or a standing stone and just sit watching the clouds serenely flow over the countryside. I felt being stoned should be a route to melting into nature, not to dissolve in front of some shite T.V.

On the last rave I went to with them, Sandy got quite ill and kept being sick and was looking quite distressed, red, puffy and confused. I had seen him get paranoid before, but this was much more pronounced than I had ever seen him be. His eyes darted around in a highly alert state, as if he was awaiting the grim reaper himself to part the crowd and come straight for him. He couldn't last on the dance floor for any more than five minutes at a time. I was a bit worried and stayed with him, his other newfound rave mates not really giving a toss. He had taken a fuck load of E's, so all I could do was watch out for him. Most of the night I ended up sitting with him in the chill area or standing around the toilet, as he knelt in the cubicle being quite sick! As we walked back to the near deserted chill room, I asked him if he was feeling ok to go downstairs, as I wanted to burn up some energy and get my flood of endorphins, which for me had become quite addictive as well.

"Nah, fauk-kin,' jist bide here min, wi' kin chill for a while aye?" he responded. It didn't have to be said; it was just an unspoken and understood thing between us that he didn't want to be alone. When it came down to it, I was one of the few people he could rely on to get him out of bother if it came to it.

The next day I phoned him, ostensibly to get his reaction to the night before and see if was feeling ok; however his upbeat response completely took me surprise,

"Fauckk-kin' good fuckin' night last night? Fauck-kin'...fuckin' kickin' min!?" I was amazed; he had completely blanked the hellish events of last night from his mind! That night marked the last time I would spend an evening with Sandy, as we gradually grew apart. I had become tired of the constant pressure to take drugs, followed by the constant sniping that I was less cool or a "bit straight" because I wasn't one of them, mainly by Wally, but I knew he was right. I didn't fucking want to be one of them, didn't ask to be, I just didn't quite articulate that at the time. Later, Sandy became so paranoid that he went completely off the rails and wouldn't leave the house, the drugs having caused a chemical imbalance in his brain. Later his life went from bad to worse – very much worse!

For all the cool, the street cred and image associated with the "scene" and drug culture, this is it what it boiled down to – stoned folk mindlessly watching games consoles, dirty flats with doors off hinges, feeling sick and paranoid, pretending to be happy and free from conventions. Slowly having your will siphoned from your soul!

That stoner life, to me, was clearly an excuse for indulging in laziness, with a lack of any aspirations, but all the time conforming to the idea of an enlightenment that never comes, of a Nirvana that just is not there. What does inevitably come is burial in bills, addiction, disillusionment and slow (or not so slow) death, surrounded by messed up people who are only friendly because you make them feel as if it is acceptable to be a drop out, while you have to act or become as fucked up as them or worse, for some sense of acceptance.

## *Chapter 2:*
## You know, when you grope for Luna?

I had become friendlier with rock dude Freddie who worked in another part of the laboratory, due to our mutual appreciation for supping real ales in my favourite Aberdeen pub, the Prince of Wales, especially Orkney Dark Island, which came like a brown milk shake on tap. Freddie was also sort of one of the crowd, but was somehow a little more immune from the "uncool" label that others had given me. Freddie just liked beer! It was just accepted that Fred had a kind of coolness that people respected whether he had anything to say, or not or despite not doing drugs like the rest of them. I had found Freddie a constant source of fascination, as he seemed absolutely untouchable by the crowd. Nobody seemed to mind if he said he didn't want to take a hit of speed or a smoke. His response of "Nah, A can't really be arsed with that the now," was all it would take, whereas if anyone else tried to say that, they'd be ridiculed and bitched about behind their backs, or more likely directly to their face. Freddie just emanated a unique kind of personality that everyone responded to as if he was from a universe with different rules or something. It was quite amazing and anywhere we went people would know him. Random people we'd never seen before or never saw again would stop and shake his hand and he'd chat a little with them, always laid back and matey like; "Woah, Freee'ed, fit's happening min? This is my girlfriend, hey have you met Freddie?"

The odd thing to me was that Freddie didn't seem to do anything or even say anything that appeared deserving of such adoration and recognition. I found this quite frustrating at times and longed to crack the secret where I could enter a room and not feel like Mr. Buzzkill. People were just at ease with Freddie. See, I'd be sitting in the coffee room early with only the pretty young receptionist for company and inevitably, the atmosphere would be strained. Conversation would not flow and if it did, then I'd be the one who would derail it before long. However, if Freddie strode in (looking like almost exactly like Slash from Guns 'n' Roses, with big rock afro, tight black jeans and converse trainers; always dishevelled and bleary eyed), the atmosphere would immediately just chill out. He didn't seem to have to say anything, but the few words he did say here and there carried an easy friendliness that seemed to create conversation around him, like a catalyst. I agonised for months during situations like these, analysing and noting his personality and effect on people. I would make mental notes and go over these like a fixated mathematician working through many permutations of the enigma code, wondering whether I could discover some "Freddie formula" and then utilise this myself, to finally feel some social acceptance at last.

Perhaps it was the rock star look that Freddie projected. Even if he sat quietly, not bothering to say anything at all, burped and then left the coffee room, people would still comment, "Freddie, eh? Some guy?" and then others would concur, "Oh yeah, Freddie yeah, cool dude like;" as if the inquisition were about and any negative slander would be met with instant ostracization by the others. Like there had been a meeting and Freddie's coolness had been voted through as statutory law. I just couldn't understand it; they even had me doing it as well. Of course I knew, just knew, that when I sat and said nothing and then left they would be mocking me, saying I was too quiet and a socially inept pain in the arse! I knew this for sure because sometimes I was so overlooked in a crowd that people had actually slagged me off like that when I was still fucking sitting not ten feet away from them in a slightly crowded room, seemingly failing to notice that I was actually still there!

I guess at the time, I didn't realise that the reason why Freddie was so accepted was because he wasn't doing what I was doing, *i.e.* he wasn't analysing me or comparing himself to anyone else. He was just at peace with himself and doing what all good conversationalists do. Instead of fixating on himself constantly, he was thinking about other people's issues and having a genuine interest in them. Whereas he used his heightened sense of empathy to tune into others and make them feel at ease, I used my heightened sense of empathy to pick up and amplify any unease people had with me. Then I'd use it as a self-fulfilling prophecy to fuel my sense of estrangement. It was that simple, but my current self couldn't help me back then. Then I suppose, also, Freddie didn't care about potential bitching and backstabbing from us guys. He was getting laid regularly and was just that bit more mature than us. We were all uptight lab workers in our late teens and early twenties, all virgins and all geeky to some degree. We all looked up to Freddie for the simple reason that he was liked by women and they frequently agreed to shag him. Everybody else was probably agonising over his secret and going over permutations in their heads as to how he did it, just like I did.

As I didn't particularly smoke to any great extent anymore and had by this time been fairly obviously dropped by the other guys, I found that Freddie was more than happy to tolerate my company in the pub after work or during our day release days at college. With Fred, I discovered the joys of whiling away the time with a mate getting steadily happily drunk on all manner of real ales. I had found my drug of choice and was leaning on it as much as Sandy and Wally had leaned on theirs.

To me, the bar culture was less contrived; there was no need to be overly political or cool. I suppose I was a bit too straight - give me a good seat in a good pub a nice foamy pint, some company and a good jukebox any day. I gave him CRASS tapes, which he liked and understood. I sensed a bit more of a kinship with Freddie on these types of issues, which I mostly kept to myself and tried to generate some shared interest with him. I thought that most alternative people would have an intuitive understanding of counter culture and emancipation of the human spirit.

Fred introduced me to a lot of local gigs. There were a few bands that developed a bit of a profile at the time, especially Missing Jane who did a fantastic punk version of Fairport's Matty Groves and the Lorelei, which had a huge following in Aberdeen. These were folk/rock cross-overs in the style of New Model Army or the Levellers. I found I was frequenting all the alternative bars, which were also student haunts and I began to like that lifestyle. Freddie actually knew the Aberdeen bands (of course); it turned out that he'd been to school with many of them, as they were mostly art students and in with a cool crowd. I was kind of fascinated by this emerging following and they interestingly all seemed to hail from the same area – Dyce in the North of Aberdeen. They were creating a scene all of their own.

New Model Army was the punk band that I began to listen to more and more. They also had a folky/Celtic flavour, meaning they were rather more melodic, musically and easier on the ear than the likes of CRASS or a Flux of Pink Indians, which were, admittedly, a little bit corrosive. New Model Army and Justin Sullivan were skilled in making their songs more emotive, articulating a sensibility that the singer and the fans both understood. This is why New Model Army fans really love them; the songs are an articulation of a sense of justice and social awareness you just never got with pop music and in that sense, it is real rock and roll. A lot of their songs made intuitive sense to me. As well as the social observations, there was a mystical quality running through many of their lyrics which I felt an emotional connection to. For instance one song, *White Coats*, was quite meaningful to me. This is an insightful song of how scientists quite blindly interfere with ecology and nature, usually for the worst (white coats = lab coats).

The song also referred to a female type of deity, which represented the Earth. This message was very clear; you can pray all you want, but science, the march of civilisation, technology and progress have resulted in the ecosystems of the world being relentlessly plundered, manipulated and polluted in our drive to exert our will on nature. This is by no means a new idea, but the song also resonated with the "knowledge" that there was something "living" about the natural world, or at the very least, that we would definitely be better off 'thinking of it' that way as we depended on its (fragile) life support systems.

I experienced an emotive instinct when I heard that song, which I can describe as a feeling that welled up inside of me accompanied by a strong sense of presence. The early and strange memories of the knowledge I had of the nature of a place taking the form of a woman there to protect me, was edging back into my mind for more scrutiny. I had buried that memory as an infantile fantasy of course, though now something had rekindled the emotional memory I had of this 'voice of the environment.' Similarly I kept having flashbacks to the strange moth voice after Sandy's mushies and I felt that that moment had somehow allowed these memories a route back from the delete bin, as it were and "opened my head" up to them once again.

At the same time, I was listening to bands like Alien Sex Fiend, Killing Joke, Red Lorry Yellow Lorry, Jene Loves Jezebel, Dead Can Dance and This Mortal Coil and the Pagan sounding Sisters Of Mercy, All About Eve, Dream Disciples, The Mission and Fields Of The Nephilim, the superb and eccentric Julian Cope and the awesome and original Bauhaus. I was drawn to this music and though, in terms of the Sisters, Mission and the other Goth bands, that was how electric guitars would have sounded like if they were invented and played in Victorian times. Many of these bands, it seemed to me, shared a mystical quality both in their lyrics and in their sound. I didn't know at the time whether this influenced me at a deeper level, or whether I always had a predilection for it, but I began to feel the same deep emotional connection to the Goddess inspired by this music. The Sisters of Mercy – Marian, is another good example of a song which affected me like this. This was akin to the prickly feeling one gets when you hear a moving piece of music, or poetry for the first time. Why I should feel this, despite being a rationally minded scientific type person and atheist was quite a stunning feeling for me. Previously, I sorta felt that Karl Marx had had a point, that "religion was the opium of the masses." This emotional connection to a notion of the Goddess wasn't rational, it was deeply emotional and a part of my very being. I was curious as to whether other people had a strange and instinctive notion of a feminine spirit of a place like this. I was intrigued; could the members of New Model Army also have had dreams like mine as children? Was it real? Could other people secretly do what I did but keep quiet about it?

I thought of this as I cycled around Aberdeenshire; alone in nature, I wanted to get back to that childhood state of awareness, to see the environment without preconceptions. I had a sense that as adults, we tended to screen things out, or filter out important sensations. I wanted to have some "living" connections to the environment, but I couldn't. I felt like I was too rooted in rationalism, though I couldn't shake the feeling that our waking reality was just only a portion of a more complete, larger reality that was just sitting there, just "being," hidden from view to the uninitiated.

As much as I liked Freddie and the days we whiled away in the pub playing pool and supping pint after pint, I found I was still suffering from a bit of imposter syndrome. I just didn't belong anywhere; I felt it and I was sure everyone else did, too. I couldn't just relax and chew the fat and be at ease with people. I couldn't express myself; my personality did not flower at all. I was closed within a shell that locked me within its walls and in turn shielded the world outside from it. I could sense that Freddie thought my interests in alternative viewpoints were a little idiosyncratic. I tried to engage him a few times in conversation about New Model Army lyrics or the relationship between anarko-punk and the idea that there was something "else," something a little bit beyond the human. But he returned my questions often with a raised eyebrow and a blank face. Often he gazed into the pub's thick air; he had a very laid back brain which kept you waiting and slowed the pace of life and conversation. He always took just a little too much time to respond and thus it was oddly relaxing talking to him. Sometimes I'd think he wasn't going to respond at all, even though I was becoming used to this. I would wait and wait for him to reply and then I'd begin to repeat or carry on the conversation only to be cut short as I was spoken over by Freddie finishing his train of thought. He got me every time! It would invariably leave me in a Martin Freeman-like in *The Office* double-take of slight disbelief, as if he was perhaps taking the piss or something, but he never was. Ironically, Freddie liked quite fast speed metal, but I imagine if he ever did pick up a guitar it would sound more like Nick Drake played at 33.3 rmp (when it should have been 45 rmp...google it if you're not an Eighties kid).

Sometimes Freddie got a little bit bored with my probing and he responded a little uncharacteristically condescending to my question about the lyrics to *Whitecoats*.

"Soooo...aye...like how do you square this...religious type of a 'feeling' of an organic, living and kinda...conscious Earth with common sense and like...modern science in 'at?"

I felt a little bit embarrassed as I held my face teetering on the edge of my little pint sized little frothy brown pond of inspiration, the third one of the afternoon. However, as I hovered there, savouring the hoppy aroma, I found that I did have an answer of sorts, which I never particularly knew I had. You know, that feeling that you have when you're in an exam and despite having done virtually no obvious revision for a topic, a five page essay starts to take shape somewhere in your mind? No, well if you don't know that feeling then join the ranks of people I've been on courses with who hated me just as much. I didn't care; no one liked me anyway!

I hovered and I pondered and then I stepped off the diving board and dived into the thought forming in my head.

"Wellll, biologists (such as Steve Jones) right? Have been pondering and talking about the concept of *emergent properties* in nature for some time. Now if I have got it right, it's like swarm behaviour emerges from the almost robotic behaviour of individual ants in a colony and similarly consciousness emerges from the behaviour of individual neurons in a colony that we call a brain. Perhaps the biosphere is a little bit deserving of being labelled 'living' more than we give it credit for." Freddie frowned, a kind of I-wish-I-had-never-asked kind of frown, as he watched me from the other end of the wooden table in the Prince of Wales on that Thursday afternoon when we should have been at college on day release. I carried on,

"Well...of course, the rather esteemed scientist James Lovelock has postulated these types of feedback controls with his model of Daisy world and ultimately the Gaia hypothesis, hasn't he?" Freddie pursed his lips and nodded, I could sense he was becoming annoyed with me, as I could feel in that moment that he was thinking that I was full of shit, talking in an erudite manner on Biology and Science in a way just to sound well-educated and pretentious. I could feel a deep knot of 'ineptitude' forming in the pit of my stomach so shrugged and shifted in my seat to appear less pretentious and intelligent. However, I was compelled to keep going against my better judgment, as I felt I had a point to clarify both to Freddie and indeed myself.

"So, like, these are compelling arguments and observations that living processes are distinct from non-living processes in that they arise as a consequence of adaptation and further influences on their surroundings. A feedback emerges which creates a self-regulating ecosystem on a planetary scale." I knew Freddie would have knowledge of the Gaia hypothesis, as we were both chemists after all. Although, just because we worked in industry in school leaver jobs, it didn't give us the right to try to appear intellectual on the subject and although Freddie nodded in affirmation, his sudden grasp of his lower lip and downward glance to his rollie cigarette box betrayed, albeit subconsciously to me, his discomfort with my monologue. Again, regardless, I kept on, hoping to finally answer the question.

"James Lovelock of course, distances himself from any suggestion of awareness or deliberate design and quite rightly so, it's just maths in action! I mean, there is no need to invoke such supernatural notions to fill in gaps and as a disciple of Charles Darwin myself, I would also have to abhor any such suggestions." I paused to gesticulate intellectually for a moment and failing miserably to disguise any semblance of extreme nerdiness poking through, continued with a very apologetic "Ermmmm...without due reason of course anyway!"

Freddie set light to a small tube of shabby tobacco dancing from his lips. Little incandescent threads were consumed in a briefly defiant red glow before dying in a flash, their smoke hungrily consumed by Freddie's indifferent mouth. Perhaps he had a fleeting thought to just set his whole head on fire to escape my verbal onslaught. He cradled the Zippo in his hands and then studied it for a moment, as if the etching on it was much more interesting than my speech. I took a sip of my beer watching him closely for approval to continue. Whether

Freddie was going to reply or what he was about to eventually say, I'll never know. I quickly gulped to make way for the next point from the amber bitter and calm liquid that was satisfying me, as only good real ale can, at the back of my throat.

"So I suppose I can concede that the Earth may be as complex as a large single living cell in a manner of speaking, but I can in no way concede this imbues the place with a form of consciousness or awareness and thoughts and personalities. I mean, wise-zup right?"

Freddie was smiling politely, but answered in a quite begrudging fashion, "Aye...wise up!" I felt that this definitely had a double meaning aimed at me and immediately felt stupid and my feelings that I was just useless at communicating were compounded. I felt apologetic as I supped my beer, contemplating how to prove to Freddie that I did understand that I had been a bit boring there for a moment. Freddie slowly tapped ash into the pub ashtray in a comforting, languid motion and strangely the object obeyed the action as the ash itself seemed to fall in moonwalk-like slow motion from the tip of his rollie into the round dirty tin ashtray. I was taking the time to just consider how fucking strange that was when he, again surprised me momentarily by talking into the void he seemed to always manage to create. It was actually infectious and after a while I found myself aping this behaviour (as I usually did with all personalities that I evaluated as being effective) but I almost scared myself by how much I began to think and sound like him at times. Freddie punctuated the slow motion scene,

"Yeah...well..." (Enough time to read a Calvin and Hobbes cartoon in a nearby paper, for instance) "...If you don't believe that a Goddess is real...kinda...like you and me, what can you say about it in a religious way? I mean New Model Army..." Freddie's pupils slowly rotated to the upward position and stared there momentarily (pause, but just sit tight, don't interrupt, a qualifier will be along in just a moment, I repeat, this is not an opportunity to retort or reply). "......are intimating...you think anyway...that people believe in a Goddess of sorts...And you're starting to feel like there's a Goddess in your head...sorta uninvited like...But you're saying it's all imaginary and not actually real, like people say that God is real, kinda-thing?."

I sighed. That actually was a tough question, but I suppose I had to provide an answer. It was good chatting to Freddie about this, as it helped me clarify the beliefs that were starting to ferment in my head.

"Yeah, well first of all, I see a place for religion, obviously what all cultures have in common aside from language; appreciation of art and music, is a spiritual belief system, often also tied into both a creation myth and some helpful pointers of life after death. I suppose that's the beginning to end fairy-tale for bedtime piece of mind reading." I nodded and looked for appreciation at this phrase, but Freddie just supped his ale and looked into the distance. I felt that most of the time I was there to keep him from looking like an lone-drinking alcoholic, as he just seemed to look over at the bar thinking about his next beer. I continued, happy to be given uninterrupted full reign for my thoughts.

"Also, religion and spirituality are clearly linked to some sense of communal identity and morals; they provide a framework of guidance on how to act in times of stress and a reassurance that there is more to life than the mere struggle for existence. You could say that these are intelligent needs that are met by whatever religion or meme is created and sustained to meet that need and perpetuate it within a group. It was something that was necessary for our survival and part of our core humanity. It was 'selected for' by natural selection as it obviously must have provided our early small ancestral groups with a survival advantage." I was getting louder and starting to make pointed motions down into the table.

Freddie glanced around the largely empty bar at this time in the early afternoon and perhaps he was thinking whether his innate coolness would be compromised by a public show of scientific proclamations. However the three auld mannies, who collectively gave that side of the bar an almost reassuring whiff of urine and cologne, sat doing the crosswords at the bar with their pints of beer that seemed to be slowly evaporating rather than actually being drunk, were no threat to his street cred. I, however, was actually happy for once in my life and sat back casually wafting a newly lit rollie in my right hand like a professor's pipe.

"For me, you see, this notion of a "goddess' is similar to a humanistic view of the world," I said. "I feel as if it is our own subconscious mind that somehow contributes to some deep-rooted concept of a connected Gaia and *we* provide 'it' with a personality and all its associated abilities. I once had a bit of a magic mushroom-induced insight that perhaps to quantify all of reality as we know it we have to include actual elements of the human imagination!! I think the quantum physicists call it the observer collapsing the wave function, if you will! Imagination is *also* part of reality, or part of the universe, just as gravity and electromagnetic radiation are, though not perhaps in the same physical sense." Again I ventured into the plausible as I nodded manically and gestured like some manic T.V. boffin of the Eighties and continued apologetically again.

"Ahem, yes erm...during the initial pre-human reality, perhaps imagination was not part of reality. But now, factor in humans and you also eventually factor in imagination as part of our universe! Don't you agree with that?" I looked triumphantly at Freddie. It had been a long winded way to get to my point but I had made it out alive and Freddie still seemed awake and engaged.

Freddie nodded. "Aye...Aye! I think I know exactly what you mean."

I wasn't sure whether he was about to tell me what he understood by that or whether this was just an informative statement. I drew in a longer than usual drag of my rollie to waste time, a second or two later I raised the beer to my lips to drown and expunge the acrid DNA-mutating toxic taste from my tongue and mouth. Freddie just sat staring into the smoke filled air of the hauntingly quiet pub back room as his eyes seemed to look neither outward nor inward. I cleared my mouth sat forward and began to make my point,

"It's like–"

Freddie's voice then eclipsed mine.

"Kinda...like the same logic as the zen story: 'If a tree falls in a forest and no-one or no-thing is around to hear it...will it make a sound,' kind-da thinnng?"

I loved how he ended every nearly sentence with the slow deliberate *"kinda-thing?"* I had started doing it on a regular basis with people neither of us knew.

"Yeah, yeah exactly and the answer is simply 'no,' sound is mere vibrations, energy transducing and propagating through the air! But once you have a brain and imagination and 'experience' you have also, a 'sound' of a tree falling and the 'experiences' of a sound and forest, which becomes very much part of that reality, part of that universe! Reality is constructed by human beings isn't it?"

Freddie shrugged. "A suppose so."

I smiled as a teacher egging on a student to make the conclusion. "So by the same logic, does a Goddess exist or is there a 'spirit' to nature? No! But once you factor in a human brain and imagination, then an 'experience' of spirits, gods, goddesses, call it what you will, *can* exist. I mean, the Goddess Gaia exists just as much as any character in literature, with a personality and essence of her own and she will continue to exist long after we are dead and gone."

Freddie rolled another cigarette and then checked his watch. "Maybe we should head out!?"

That was an unusual thing to say, as we had by now came to the mutual consensus that afternoons for the next few weeks of lab work were for the pub. I mean, what the fuck did we need lab work practice for at college? We worked in labs! If we had to make up molar solutions or figure out how to get a substance into solution, we just did it, almost automatically, whereas the full-time students just stared helplessly at charts and data booklets with looks of dread and abject confusion on their faces and sometimes even crying.

I ignored Freddie's signals that the conversation was over and waved my rollie around in front of me animatedly and again a little Eighties T.V. boffin-like.

"It's like Fred, that I feel that there is something there, just out of reach, but my church isn't a construct of pews and stained glass pictures, my church is out there, the breath-taking reverence of the natural world!" More people who had entered the bar with shopping bags beneath them were turning a head towards us now and I became suddenly self-conscious and red in the face. Freddie was smirking at me,

"Olright ya da hiv tae campaign for Greenpeace the now...I wish I had never asked!" But my chuckle concealed a disappointment, as I knew that perhaps Freddie was a not a 'Crasstafarian' after all, he used music to express himself, not to find himself like I did.

So I couldn't fully talk to him about my feelings and insights. Or I couldn't, for example, discuss with Freddie strange recurring dreams that I'd always had. My dreams, perhaps, showed that my mind was becoming more receptive to what I was struggling to comes to terms with. I hadn't heard of Carl Jung's notion of a collective unconscious at that time; however the archetypal male and female deities were keen to reveal themselves to me regardless, despite me not having had the memo.

These recurring dreams in question actually started when I was around eleven years old; I was standing in Northfield playing fields, close to the secondary school that I had just started to attend. Right next to the playing fields was a large transmitter mast, owned by British Telecom; it was about three hundred feet high and covered with lightning conductors and discs. You could see it from miles away; it was a bit of a landmark and stood out when you first catch sight of Aberdeen from a distance. Northfield is one of the highest points in the profile of Aberdeen; the mast has bright red lights on it to make the structure more visible to aircraft landing at Dyce airport. In my dream, lots of people are on the field walking around with school bags. In the middle of the field, near the foot of the transmitter, is a large crate about ten-feet high. I, like other people, look into this crate. Bright red eyes stare back and a powerful threatening presence emanates from them. I walk away but as I do so the crate flies apart, unleashing the terrible presence inside. The beast is all powerful and raging; it destroys parts of the mast and even throws people near to it around like spent rags. People are fleeing everywhere; eventually it fixes its eyes on me and lumbers towards me. I can't make it out except it's big and hairy, just powerful and unstoppable. I run like the wind, along streets I know, desperately trying to find cover. Though no matter how much I try to outwit it, I can't shake it off; it's always behind me, at the same sort of distance, tracking me, waiting for me to slip up. Throughout my life, ever since I first had this dream, I had intermittent recurrences of the thing chasing me through completely unrelated dreams. For instance, I had dreams of being at my grannie's house and then suddenly, the thing is outside or trying to get up the stairs and I have to climb out of a window or try to find a hiding place. I have to keep running.

However, around this time I had a very curious and vivid alteration that happened in this recurring dream, where even now I can remember it very clearly. The dream started with me walking past my old house in Hilton Drive where I lived as a child and as usual, I realised 'the thing' was watching me. I pretended not to notice and kept casually walking; the idea being that once I rounded a corner, I would leg-it at full speed and hopefully escape. After this I was running through a forest in the snow and 'the thing' was still tracking me. I was aware I was leaving tracks, but there was nothing I could do about it. But now a curious transformation took place, 'the thing' was no longer the unidentified muscular hulk that chased me all those years but had transformed into the humanoid figure with antlers and the legs of a deer. The immense power and presence was still there. The figure then ran parallel to me through the trees; I often couldn't see him, but I knew he was there tracking my movements, he was more at home in the forest than I was. His powerful limbs kept moving through the snow, antlers swaying from side to side. I saw a chink of light though the trees and made my way towards it. I was very happy and relieved to make out streetlights, through the trees. Yes! Civilisation, I love civilisation, I may be safer there. I ran towards the street and emerged from the woods, within the triangular glow of a street light a few feet away. There stood three women. I hurried towards them, thinking that talking may help make me feel like everything was normal and take my mind away from the dark forest. As I began to speak to the women, one of them, an old woman, turned around and pointing behind me said, "Is he with you, son?"

I turned around to see that the antlered figure had turned into a young king wearing a golden crown and holding a sword. He was dressed in a long blue and glittering gold regal robe and was standing motionless, staring at me. He was no longer terrifying, but benevolent and regal, gaining my respect. Without saying a word, I walked over to him, now less afraid; I understood that he was connected to me somehow. I knelt and then I realised that I had the sword. I realised that I may have to prove myself to acquire the crown as well. I got into my car and drove away, as the young king sat quietly in the back. These very clear symbols emerged in my dreams before I had become consciously aware of their spiritual significance.

Idly sitting watching telly one evening, I chanced upon a bit of a television programme about different religions. This is one of the benefits of watching all kinds of random television, every now and again something actually informative pops up. I think it may have been the A-Z of belief, an informative programme made for young people, like snub T.V. at the time, probably instigated by Janet Street Porter. This took the form of an interrogation by young people of some representative of that religion. What caught my attention was an initial interview by Carl McCoy of the Fields of the Nephilim (one of my favourite goth bands); this is where I had switched on to it, so I continued to watch it with interest. It was about Paganism, which was something I knew very little about and hadn't realised this was even considered a religion in particular or that the Nephilim or McCoy were involved in any way. The interviewee representing the faith was getting a hard time from the interrogators, being asked about animal sacrifice and other such nonsense. He was answering sensibly but was floundering in places, due to the rapidity of the onslaught (From multiple questionnaires). I found myself shouting at the screen, "Just explain that; why don't you just clear up this point!" Somehow I had acquired a lot of knowledge and a great deal of intuitive understanding of a subject I hadn't been particularly consciously aware of. This articulation made me quite excited. So that was it, I was a Pagan and no doubt about it. Maybe there were other people who had had childhood experiences like me!? Wow, perhaps New Model Army were Pagan?! Christ, maybe I was part of a social group of some kind after all. By now I often lay awake feeling the actual presence of something that you could equate with the Goddess, as an inner emotional up-welling within me connecting to her (if that doesn't sound too strange?). It was as if my soul was calling to her and she was calling to it. Me, who rationally didn't actually believe in the existence of souls or of hidden spiritual dimensions or gods or deities, was experiencing this, undeniably. This notion was at the core of my schemata of the world.

    I was a rational person, but I had much more sympathy for a view of the world which had more in common with a hippie Pagan person than any biology textbook. I was a scientist at heart but disliked the way that technology had been used to ill-effect, tainting our environment, food-chain and perhaps damage our climate. And despite the fact that I couldn't explain it or even rationalise it, I was feeling a strong affinity and connection to a deity figure that I knew very little about and had no obvious rational reason to do so. I rejected patriarchal misogynistic society with its crass media, repressed conditioned culture and felt aligned instead to the 'fresh air in my face Paganism' with its love of freedom, life and an unrepressed human condition. To use an analogy, I didn't believe we were born tainted with sin separated from the wonder of nature; as a biologist, naturalist and Pagan I believe we are very much part of the natural world, we arose and evolved with it.

    So I realised that I was Pagan, but wasn't even aware what a Pagan did for a living or where they did it. I knew I was something more specific than a Pagan. I was aware, somehow, that a witch was a healer who worked with some esoteric forces of nature, wise like some old Taoist priest, having a say over life and death. I instinctively understood that there may be a wholly and singularly "human" kind of knowledge that wasn't marred by conventions. This was in accord with my anarchistic type of belief, that there is a "humanness," which is real, uncorrupted by social conventions, society or politics. This was it, I had to find out more, to see if there was such a thing in existence as a witch and perhaps find a wise old woman who would be willing to teach me the craft, but I thought that unlikely, since if any did exist, they were probably solitary and unwilling to publicise themselves.

I got myself down to the bookshop and had a look at the mind body and spirit section. There to my astonishment was a book on the subject, *Wicca – the old religion in the new age,* by Vivienne Crowley. I bought it with a heightened state of expectation, pouring over it on the back of the bus home like it contained the missing key to link all knowledge and wisdom. I digested it quickly; it was a good book for me, as it linked spirituality with psychology, more specifically Jungian psychology, as Vivienne herself was a psychologist. This was a language I could understand. The book was an explanation of Wiccan rituals and roots with an explanation of the deities. These God and Goddess and their various personifications are interrelated with cycle of life through the Celtic wheel of the year, the seasons of the Earth and the rhythms of night, day and the moon. Further, the God and Goddess didn't exist as external, sitting on *some cloud*, but were the anthropomorphic personifications of the energy or state related to a changing season - interacting with human psychology or consciousness. In a sense it is a product of the collective imagination, but driven by environmental, cosmic and external forces on/to the imagination. I much preferred the concept of psychological construction which exist down the ages, as the Jung's archetype of the collective unconscious represent, rather than the idea of a giant supernatural God that our western sensibility provides us with. I mean, that's just feels silly in this day and age.

I was compelled to write to Vivienne expressing my beliefs and thanking for her writing that book. Right on cue, The Mission released *Deliverance*; the lyrics were highly emotive to me starting "Believe in magic believe in lore..." followed by *"Give me Deliverance..."* Whereas, most people would have found this a load of hocus pocus and mere mystical image playmaking, I found it a cry for initiation. Thankfully, despite the best efforts of hundreds of years of persecution, there seemed to be some kind of community and tradition of Paganism that remained intact! Why didn't we get this at school?

Vivienne promptly replied to my letter. I was ecstatic; she was very cordial, explaining that Wicca was a fast growing religion as people of all walks of life were becoming disenchanted with the lack of spiritual guidance on offer which held the actual planet we live on and the myriad of life upon it, as central to its doctrine.

Well, it seemed like common sense to me, the Earth was real; we're standing on it, its solid, that doesn't require a great deal of faith. To love it and revere it was common sense, quite a healthy religious tenet. Similarly the Moon, the changing of the seasons, they are all quite real and tangible as well. We've evolved according to their rhythms. This rhythm of life is in our very DNA. To live your life in accord with them as opposed to the central heating timer, the alarm clock and streetlight timers, is surely more real and is probably more concurrent with a more harmonious state of being.

Vivienne also informed me that there was a Pagan Federation network and that there was a representative for the Scottish branch, Clarisse, of whom she included the name and address. I wrote to Clarisse explaining that I was more than interested and that I wanted to meet and join other Wiccans if possible. Clarisse wrote back explaining that there was a group affiliated to the Pagan Federation in a town outside Aberdeen, she had passed my details to the priestess and that also, since another new person had just written to her from Aberdeen, she had sent my address to her and vice versa; this was a young English literature student called Mara. So I wrote and very shortly got a reply from her. She was looking forward to meeting me, saying she was new as well and that the priestess was really sound. We were to meet in the Prince Of Wales (where else?). I had to look out for a woman with pink hair! Well that definitely wouldn't be too hard in Aberdeen in 1990.

The next day, I also received the letter from Mags, the high priestess also telling me she would meet me in the Prince Of Wales. Fantastic choice of venue, I thought, as I was already very familiar with that place on my drinking days/evenings with Freddie, but then where else would Pagans choose to meet in Aberdeen but the Prince of Wales? This is one of the city's oldest pubs, with its large fireplace, wooden floor throughout, which I think came from a church; certainly all the church pews along the walls did. It once boasted the longest bar in Scotland, as it went the whole length of the building. The pub was the first bar in Aberdeen to sell a good range of real ales long before it became fashionable. There was always a pleasant murmur playing around the bar, which was frequented by students, locals and shoppers alike, laden with bags from the town. There was no loud music, though occasionally the melodies of the buskers in the back room would fill the air. It was the perfect and a much loved city pub. The locals stopped it being torn down to make way for a Tesco mini market earlier that year.

I felt it was a magical place for me already, the closest thing I had to *Cheers.* So it was a pleasant surprise to me that they choose to meet there. I told Freddie and he seemed a bit miffed, "What? English student? What is this Pagan Federation, a fuck-in' dating agency?" I knew this would annoy him and it was fair to say that this had also crossed my mind.

I was quite nervous on the day; it was early afternoon and I felt like I was on my way to an interview. I had built up pictures of them in my head especially of Mara; I had visions of a long haired hippie/gothy/student type who was completely in tune with me. I arrived fairly early, ostensibly so I could get a couple of dark island milk shakes down me first. As the appointed time came closer, I took to scanning around the bar. A little distance down the bar sat a middle aged woman with a long flowing brown dress and wild wavy dark brown hair. The more that time wore on, the more I became convinced that this had to be Mags, as she fitted my mental image of a witch very well. So I attempted to get eye contact from time to time to make sure she noticed me.

The bar was becoming a little busier and it was now ten minutes or so past the appointed time for the meeting. I kept looking over, waiting to see if she would acknowledge me and make some sign. 'Shit,' I thought, 'why didn't we plan some sort of lapel rose or something!? The fucking Prince of Wales is full of people and they could all be Pagans for all I know, why wasn't I a bit more precise!? 'This woman surely must be Mags! She'll be waiting for me to introduce myself to her and if I don't, she'll leave, thinking I've stood her up!' There was no sign of Mara, so she had to be late; well she was a student of the arts, so she probably wasn't even out of bed yet! Plus she was taking the bus all the way from the bridge of Don, a fair bit away from the town Centre. I looked over again agitatedly and she caught my eye and gave a cursory smile back in response to my stare. I thought 'Gawd, this could be a test for all I know!' I couldn't take it any longer so I hopped off the bar stool and made my way to the probable witchy woman along the bar. She eyed me expectantly as I walked up to her looking as friendly as I could. I tried to make myself clear over the loud mumour of voices playing across the bar.

"Hi there, sorry, but are you Mags by any chance?" I asked tilting my head forward and smiling, half closing one eye in a gesture as if to present one cheek to her in case she felt the urge to slap it.

"Look" she said," I'm sorry darlin', but I'm actually waiting for someone ok!"

"What?" I was a bit thrown. What might she have mistook 'Are you Mags' for? I hope it wasn't a euphemism for anything rude, was it? I concluded that she hadn't heard me correctly due to the loud background noise and that I hadn't been clear and so I stammered on,

"I'm sorry I just though perhaps you were waiting for me!" She frowned as if I had said something corny, so I continued hopefully, "I'm supposed to be meeting Mags here, you see?"

But she wasn't listening to me by now anyway and was looking over my shoulder at someone who had just come through the door to whom she was raising her hand in greeting. Annoyingly I found that people often ignored me like that, even though I hadn't finished what I had to say! A large man walked past me and put his hand on her shoulder, as they exchanged greetings, he said "Sorry I'm late," before turning to me, "Who is this then?" he continued, perhaps a bit overly quizzically, looking down at me where I was standing awkwardly clutching my pint, looking from one to the other. He was huge and had that Tom-Selleck 'older guy that works out iron muscle' thing going on, which just made my muscles just give up on the spot and go limp in response.

"Sorry," I replied, nervously swallowing, trying to string some words together in an attempt to explain and make myself as absolutely clear as possible. "I was just here to meet an older woman and…and I just thought there was, y'know…a chance, maybe…y'know!?" I mumbled as I vaguely motioned with a few nervous nods of my head towards the woman by his side! I knew the words had not come out quite right, but I hoped by gesticulating towards her he would understand the explanation that was in my head, but just wasn't quite arriving at my mouth intact, as my lips continued to dry up under the stress.

The man jolted his head upright, making him seem even taller than he already was, his eyebrows contorting to make an exaggerated quizzical look, which I mused, for a moment in between abject alarm, was like a 1920s silent movie villain. To my added frustration, he evidently couldn't grasp that this was a simple case of mistaken identity either. What the fuck was wrong with these people?

"Who are you calling 'old' son?" he said. "Is it no' past your fuckin' bedtime? Go on home to your bed before I fucking send you home to yer Ma in a fucking shoebox!"

'Well how very rude,' I thought. His moustache, though, did have an air of authority that made me in comparison, with my very smooth twenty-something face, look very young and inferior. It didn't help that at that age; I looked about seventeen and although I thought I was bit indie, alternative and cool, my Batman symbol badge might have conveyed something otherwise to this chap. I was a bit scared by his sudden and completely unprovoked aggression. Clearly he was thinking I had made some kind of a move on his girlfriend. I immediately felt a mild sense of injustice at this thought. I mean, sure I had mulled it over but since I hadn't actually carried this out in any fashion as yet; in my mind, I thought, 'this could not be farther from the truth, how dare he!?'

I began in my best Sherlock Holmes style to convey calm and good sense.

"My good sir, the woman in question, while not bad looking I agree, is in fact old enough to be my mother!" I realised that I probably shouldn't have used the "old" word again, however, I had to convey that I wasn't trying to hit on her as she wasn't actually in my age range and that perhaps I was the one who was inferior to her. "Now that doesn't mean she's not good for you, of course, but I assure you, I certainly wouldn't do that!"

He must have misunderstood the intended version of "do that," clearly interpreting the words in some alternative syntactical way! All I heard was,

"Ya insolent fucking little bastard, I'm gonna fuckin' killyaa."

His girlfriend screamed and held onto his arm with both hands as it swung backwards to punch me. I actually didn't have any confidence that her body weight would impede the movement of this arm to any significant degree and that she would just flail in the wind, like a flag, behind it. His other hand shot forward to grab my lapel and a huge hand loomed towards my face like some machine from a car wrecker's yard. He had no regard at all for all my badges, as they scrunched and jingled in his closing fist. The only thing I did appreciate about his clenched fist on my jacket is that it couldn't, by the laws of physics, also now be employed to hit my face with it. My pint went flying all over my already quite humiliated and quite scared looking, smooth twenty-something face like water off a duck's back as people stepped aside. All I could do was grip my remaining beer and try grinning up at him through a moist face. It was half a grimace in rediment for a massive punch in the face and half a grin in an effort to appease him in some way (as if he found me cute, he might not kill me...unless he was like one of those baby seal clubber people, of course).

I almost expected the bar to start chanting "Fight, Fight, Fight," just as what had happened the last time at primary school. Fortunately adults don't quite do that (only think it) and the woman pulled her boyfriend back, "With he's just a lad; let him go, he didn't mean anything by it." Fortunately for me, amazingly she seemed angrier at him than at me. He started to release his grip a little and the barman and a few customers ran over and helped to calm him down.

I decided that saying anything else was pointless and liable to cause further unwanted confusion and as actions are louder than words, I made my apologies and promptly spun around, just as the women was pulling the man, still staring at me, like a 1920s silent movie villain, closer to the bar. 'Forfucksake,' I thought to myself, 'trust me! What perfect bloody timing.' Also, my Batman badge was never the same after that and kept falling off, another measure of how unfair life is sometimes.

I was drenched in beer, so I decided to go to the toilet and get cleaned up. As I made my way there, I was confronted by a very bubbly young woman with shaved scalp resplendent with a shock of purple hair. As we looked at each other I had a feeling of recognition, despite having a very different mental image in mind. I could see as well in that instant that she had the same impressions of me.

"Are you Sean?" she said.

"Yeah" I stammered, a little taken aback.

She was wearing a sort of vest that was torn at the neck, she looked just like Tank Girl in the flesh, complete with big boots and a couple of nose rings and the same tattoo as Tank Girl on her right shoulder (which I thought was very daring and cool).

"Oh fuckin' wow Tank Girl! Or is it Mara?" I said. "Though I thought you had pink hair?"

"Oh yeah, sorry" she sniggered, "I dyed it again! I thought you didn't have beer and snot all over your face! Are you all right, darlin'?"

We seemed to hit it off straight away, despite my lousy first impression, though annoyingly the initial "I feel so sorry for you vibe" never seemed to fade as fast as I would have liked it too. I mean, it took many years, in fact, to wear off! I liked Deadline comics, Tank Girl and comics in general and clearly, she did too. We agreed that these seem to be the most important things in life, music, films and comics. Mara added literature onto that group. She took my hand and led me through the crowd to Mag's table. I felt like I was being rescued from the aggressive normality of society to a psychedelic and magical doorway somewhere in the pub, home at last! I was introduced to Mags, who was very nice and personable, not to mention very knowledgeable, she was a little older than I expected with a long ponytail of grey hair. She was very chirpy and had a great laugh; she clearly enjoyed Mara's company. Mara was extremely ebullient, talking exuberantly on any subject; she had a great sense of humour and a very keen mind, her eyes twinkling with intelligence. She had a Lancashire accent, which I found amusing and engaging; she had both French and Irish grandparents, which seemed to imbue her with very talkative and philosophical genes. Of course, I found their company a bit intimidating as I still considered myself not a great conversationalist and my knowledge was limited in comparison to theirs. Plus I kept scanning around every five minutes looking for Magnum P.I. and I was beer stained and perturbed.

I was acutely aware that this was sort of like an interview and was a little anxious that I had to impress, to get through the door as it were. I spoke to Mags, explaining that I had read the Vivienne Crowley book, but in fact felt that I was drawn to it even before that. I told her that I was very drawn to a goddess figure in nature and also that I felt that it resided deep within me. She nodded occasionally and agreed, seeming to identify with the point. I felt quite relieved to be speaking to people who seemed to know exactly what I was talking about and seemed to share many of my experiences. Upon mentioning the fact that as a child I had vivid experiences where I seemed to become my shadow and met a woman who emerged from the very environment, Mags especially raised an eyebrow in recognition to this and nodded smiling. As I tried to explain that it was actually strange for me as a scientist to come to terms with spirituality and one that professes a reality of magick and the stuff of fairy tales, I could see that Mag's especially understood where I was coming from.

At the end of the evening, I then broached the subject of whether I could actually join the circle. I was expecting her to ask me a lot of questions, but she just regarded me for a moment and said, "Yes well traditionally one had to wait a full year and a day before being allowed into the magick circle." My heart sank a little, a year seemed an awful long time! "However" she said matter-of-factly, which was her way, "I think you have already had your year and a day period and so you're welcome to come along to the next Esbat and see if it is for you."

My father, although not overly religious, did have some kind of Christian belief in God, thanks to a Catholic background from my hard as nails Granddad from the east end of Glasgow. He was thus deeply suspicious of my interest in all things Wiccan and perhaps at the time did not understand that Paganism did not mean non-Christian. He would often sidle up to me when I was reading books on the subject! "Fuck ye readin' min?"

"Well, it's a book aboot magick and Wicca and stuff...it's interestin'!"

He would shake his head and tut. "I said to yer mother, I told her, dinna buy him *Lord of the Rings* last Christmas, but oh no, would she lus-in?!"

I soon developed an interest in herbs as well and was fascinated that I could harvest herbs, such as nettle and dandelion, from the garden from which I could dry and prepare tea or tinctures, all free and good for your health! I liked the idea of recognising and getting back to nature, even in a council estate, rather than yanking it out of the ground as a mere nuisance then throwing it on the compost heap. However, once my dad soon got wind of this he became quite derisory about it, as you might expect a father to be.

I came home one day to find him in my room, looking very scornful! "Right you! I'm nae fucking aboot here. I want the truth, now the truth mind! What have you been bringing into this hoose!?"

I thought for a minute he was going to hold up a book about Aleister Crowley that I had bought (although I had barely understood a word of it anyway). "What is the meaning of this!?" He could hardly verbalise properly, such was the emotion and pent-up confusion in his voice. He pointed into the open cupboard; I peered in slowly, looking towards what he was pointing at. "Yer mither's really distraught! I've just stopped her getting the police. Tell me! Fit...is that?"

He was pointing at a huge bunch of dandelion leaves which I'd hung upside down in my cupboard for drying. "Dandelions Da!" I said emphatically.

He scoffed as if that was the best I could do, "Dandelions!? Dandelions? You expect me to believe..." Then he stretched over and plucked off a leaf and looked at it closely, he was a builder and worked outdoors often. I could see the recognition dawn on his face, they were dandelion leaves, but perhaps just not in the context he was used to seeing them in! Then he looked at me suspiciously. "Why, fit you fucking smoking dandelions for? You're even mair depraved and I realised min aren't ye?"

Meanwhile my mother was hovering outside in the lobby wringing her hands, "Am getting the police, am getting the police and nae havin' drug smugglin' in this hoose!" Then muttered to herself about how she thought she'd brought us up much better than that and that's the bloody thanks ye get.

My dad was still looking a bit confused and was examining the leaves closely tentatively smelling them and eyeing me with a scary I'm still considering disowning you, kind of look.

"Tell us the truth now, as we're gan tae find oot one way or another, yer maws a' for getting the polis in aboot."

I shrugged. "I've been selling 'em to Sandy Rourke and his mates for months Da, they seem to fuckin' love 'em, figured it was healthier for them in the long run as well...dandelions like?!"

My dad's eyes widened in horror! "You've done fit?"

I continued on coolly and matter-of-factly, which I knew was making my dad even more concerned than the fact that I might by smoking items from his garden!

"Oh I never *technically* lied or anything, they asked me if I could get any weed and I said, 'Fuck yeah, I know where I can get my hands on heaps o' weed!" I eyed him triumphantly. "Am makin' a fuckin' fortune Da!'"

Of course, you can never lie to your dad convincingly, for although I didn't smile at all, he could tell that I was repressing one. He looked me in the eye and gave a knowing smile which made me reciprocate, the game was up. Of course this was made further obvious by him with the expression, "C'mon min, dinna come the cunt wi' me!"

I explained that it made a tea that was good for the liver, was a diuretic and basically wasn't a bad wee soothing drink as well! I held up a mortar and pestle I'd bought from Debenhams.

"There's flowers you can use, too, see? You grind them up and then put them in a strainer," which I now held aloft triumphantly in my right hand, "and Bob's yer uncle Da! Herbal tea...for nuthin!"

I thought producing something for nothing might impress an old Aberdonian like my dad, but from the look on his face, it didn't seem to impress him half as much as I might have expected it to. He called through to my mum,

"It's ok he's just making dandelion tea, thinks he's a hippie child now or some-fuckin'-thing, some sort of flower power shite!"

Now, this annoyed me somewhat; I mean, they were from the sixties and always ranting on about the Beatles, Stones or bloody Woodstock. But as soon as I get in on the act, it becomes 'flower-power shite.' I always felt disappointed that they refused to identify that punk and Paganism were an extension of what they had brought me up with, *i.e.* namely the Beatles and the Stones and pretty much all the 'thinking for myself,' values they had instilled me with. I found their reaction quite telling and disapointing that the counterculture of the sixties obviously hadn't quite blossomed like it had threatened too. They never got it off the ground back then; what a drag, in hindsight just too many...snags! My mother came through, actually, literally wringing her hands, worry etched into her eyes for a most dramatic effect. She tentatively looked at the plants in my dad's hands, "Are ye sure it's..."

He calmly nodded before she could finish, "Aye."

"And he's making them into some kind of tea?"

"Aye, 'at's right, an herb tea. I've heard of them right enough, ye kin drink 'em...it winna kill ye!"

I found it hard to believe that the one piece of health advice he might have heard about herbal tea was, "*it winna kill ye*," but I sensed this was not the time for that discussion.

My mum looked over at me, not quite sure what to make of it. "Fit's wrang wi' ye min?" she said. I explained all over again, somewhat exasperatedly, trying to be understood, but Ma was less than impressed.

"Dandelions!? But ye'll kill yerself! Eating things aff the grun' like that! Gadz-sake!"

"I washed 'em Ma!" I protested.

My Ma really didn't like the idea though; she was a very clean, clean freak. She eyed them incredulously.

"But they're aff the grun! All muddy...and beasties and dog's pee on them an iverything!!"

I sighed. "Well, all vegetables start off from the grun, Ma!"

But to her that was different, "Oh dinna be stupe-it! That's different; they've been through a supermarket and are a' cleaned up and everything by the time we get 'em!" She walked out muttering, "He's aye dee'in sum-ming' weird."

My dad just eyed me for a second! "Flooers as well? Whar' did ye get this idea fae?"

I went over to the bedside cabinet and brought out a book on herbs. My dad still eyeing me picked it up and leafed through it. He handed it back to me, clearly making his mind up in some regard.

"Jist dinna mention ony mair o' this tae yer Ma, she worries aboot ye enough as it is!" He walked out and turned to look towards the cupboard and then back towards me, as I stood in the middle of the room still clutching a book on herbs and holding a tea strainer. "Get yerself a fuckin' girlfriend min, for fuck's sake!"

As a result of this, I decided to sit them down and talk to them about my interest in all things spiritual and in particular Wicca. I thought it was about time to explain my notions of this spirituality that had become central to my core beliefs. I also, admittedly, may have been driven by some desire to garner their disapproval, for my own amusement, to shock the "old establishment," as an act of rebellion, to suit my punk credentials.

But alas no, my burley builder dad just found it amusing. It was very hard to shock people who had been teenagers in the Sixties. This just gave my dad ammunition to last him a lifetime. Such as holding his fingers in a cross and shouting "back witch" when we were vying for the toilet in the mornings or if he got as much as a headache he'd sit with a cross on his head. I suppose they represented a microcosm of how society at large still viewed Wicca.

My mum's response was fairly consistent as well,

"You're a fuckin' nutter you min, you can't just have a normal hobby can ye? No, no; you have got to go and...and...tinker with forces that you can't understand!"

Other teenagers in the neighbourhood were meanwhile experimenting with hard drugs, house burglary and premature parenthood! My parents, however, appeared to be more worried that I was turning into Dr. Frankenstein!

## *Chapter 3:*

# Here we come to call thee forth

The day came when I had the chance to go to my first circle and meet the others. [There are circles that occur every full moon known as Esbats and there are also Sabbats that take place at key times of the year. You already know all about the latter! Think about the festive season where you get nostalgic about the good old days, the passage of time and feel the need to be with family. This is a Sabbat we call Yule and part of the mystery of this Sabbat is the knowledge that life waits in midwinter to be reborn. How about Easter (after the Germanic Goddess Eostre) where animals come into 'oestrus' and begin breeding 'like rabbits;' (chocolate bunny anyone?) and the symbol of reproduction is the fertilised egg. The mystery of this time is of new starts, renewed vigour, promise and new beginnings. You already know this because we in the UK and Europe never stopped living our lives according to the rhythm of these festivals. Perhaps these key times are imprinted onto our genetic biological clocks. This would make sense, given that we've adapted and developed within that rhythm for tens of thousands of years.]

Wicca and Paganism just afford us an actual psychological route into these mysteries; what it means to be part of nature. Yeah we keep it real.

So a full moon circle came at last. I waited on the Great Northern Road as instructed by Mara to get my lift out there. I didn't know what to expect. I had in mind something like a V.W. campervan full of hippies smoking and playing Crosby, Stills and Nash full whack out of the window or a bunch of punks and goths screaming around the corner in a scene mindful of Hanna Barbera's wacky races. So I was somewhat bemused and perhaps a little bit disappointed when a small caravenette gradually rolled into view with a stream of angry drivers trailing behind them like an unwilling parade. In the driver's seat was an elderly and slightly overpolite gentleman called James. His wife Priscilla smiled from the passenger seat. "Hillo, hillo! Nice to meet you!" she said. They were very, kind of upper middle English. Aside from a small goddess-shaped pendant on Priscilla's necklace, you would have no clue whatsoever that these people were witches. They were much more like what I would imagine as the archetypal middle England Anglican Church go-er types. Exactly the type that comedian Eddie Izzard describes as having no arm muscles and wear knitted jumpers. They hailed from around Hertfordshire and were up in Aberdeenshire to live a peaceful life with access to the Highlands.

I stepped inside and said hello to Mara, who introduced me to everyone including a guy called Don who was about my age and sat grinning at me with a huge smile. He wore a leather biker jacket and a kilt with huge Doc Martin boots that jangled as he walked. In fact, it all seemed to make him move in slow motion. He was a singularly weird character but was instantly likeable. He wore black face make up and so I sensed a fellow goth right there. He was also part of the circle and had been going along for an only few months before I had arrived. His non-judgmental friendliness had a way of putting you at ease and people took to him right away. I found him instantly trustworthy and a good presence to have around. I quite admired the way Don could just chat to anyone about anything with relative ease, as I obviously still found the act of making conversation a bit of an effort and a little stressful. He wasn't camp at all; you wouldn't assume he was gay, but he had sex on the brain and made lewd comments about practically every guy in the vicinity. Once he got into his innuendo frame of mind, there was no off switch. At times, talking to him was like trying to have a normal conversation with a full on Frankie Howerd; which sounds terribly annoying, but I found this very endearing.

Driving from Aberdeen to Newmachar was the best part of twenty miles away. I was excited and filled with anticipation as the full moon glowed in the dark sky, beaming over fields and glinting through trees. The illuminated familiar globe seemed to me now charged with an ominous and meaningful presence. The journey should have taken maybe thirty minutes or so but took a heck of a lot longer due to James' reluctance to go more than thirty miles an hour.

We arrived at Mags' house in a quiet cul-de-sac of small semi-detached bungalows. We must have looked strange us all piling out of the van like that; a bunch of leather clad people in Doc Martins laden with casseroles and the obligatory potato salad. An unlikely band of misfits visiting an old woman in the middle of the quiet suburban haven on a Saturday night, as next door neighbours eyed us nervously in front of flickering family friendly television. Mags, however, was completely unconcerned, greeting us at the doorway barefoot, robed and wearing a crescent moon head decoration. As we wafted past along the path, I saw a woman turn her head and glance out of a living room window whilst an older, balding man, presumably her husband sat glued to Noel Edmunds house party. He looked bored, slumped in a chair with his face on his hand, while the woman eyed us suspiciously. I nudged Don, leaning in to not be overheard, "Think his name might be Aaaabinaaaaar..?" Brilliantly, I thought anyway, referencing Bewitched. Don, however, just looked back at me somewhat confused; "I dae kaen fit hees ca'd! Fuck should I kaen?" Then thinking for a moment while I gave an expression reminiscent of Wally Fraser in conversation with me, he continued! "mmm...looks mair like a Bert to me onwy!"

Waiting within was the high priest, an upper class university lecturer with big bushy eyebrows called Ernest, which was shortened to Ern, but James and Priscilla pronounced more lovingly as *Erneh* or *Erneh old chap*. Erneh, we didn't know at the time, had been a part of one of Gerald Gardner's original covens down in Bricketwood Hertfordshire in the 1950s. James and Priscilla both knew him from that earlier incarnation. He had a broad smiley dimpled face and quite small eyes set within narrow slightly slanted and intellectual bushy eyebrows, which made him look constantly curious. Straight away he reminded me of a quintessential vicar type. The fact that he spoke with a very educated English accent with a slight but endearing stutter added to his addled old professor look (He actually was an extremely on the ball, old professor). He really was like some stereotypical Ealing Studios magician from some old gothic horror film, or Terry Thomas in a robe, if you could imagine such a thing?

Gerald Gardner was the guy who spearheaded Wicca as a religion after the repeal of the law banning witchcraft in 1957. With Doreen Valiente, he started covens and wrote rituals and initiation rites based on High magick ceremonies such as those of the Golden Dawn and from material from his own initiation, by Dorothy Clutterbuck, into a traditional English folk-religion coven. *The New Forest Coven*, it was believed by some, contained within it elements of original British sorcery (one that had survived the burning times and in secret, passed down the generations). So this was by all accounts very much the real deal. I did not have a great deal of knowledge about Gardner at the time so I didn't think to ask Erneh too much about him. Years later all of us would remark that we bloomin' wish we had!

I was filled with a sense of wonder as the billowing incense filled the living room, drifting around the many books on bookshelves and cute little terracotta dragons and knick nacks. I was relieved that I had found this as Mags drew the circle; as the final quarter was secured we all stood silent, facing the altar, then suddenly the High priestess disrobed and everybody else followed suit. I didn't know what to do; I put my hand to the neck of my robe, but hesitated. *'Maybe I'm not supposed to,'* I thought. Maybe I wouldn't be expected to strip off on my first day? However, I felt a bit of the odd one out as I stood there in a room full of naked people. I made a concerted effort to avert my gaze from people's bodies. I was sweating; Don and Mara had actually mentioned a couple of times that they did their rituals skyclad, as was the way in Gardnerian Wicca and now it suddenly dawned on me that that didn't mean 'mostly outside.' Duh!

After the chanting and building up of "power," my head felt a little fuzzy but apart from that I didn't feel or experience much which was a bit disappointing. However I did very much feel like I belonged there and Mags remarked that I fitted in so well that she kept forgetting that it was my first circle. I knew what she meant, I felt like I very much belonged and despite my usual imposter syndrome, I actually felt comfortable, for once.

Attending circles was odd sometimes; I got the whole synchronicity of life with the seasons and even the idea of gods and goddesses, though I had come to the decision that the latter were mere mental constructs. I didn't see myself like the sort of new-agey deluded sort. However, there were occasions where episodes that qualify as paranormal did occur. For example, we sometimes did pathworkings, group visualisation based on the paths connecting to the tarot. Tarot could be seen as a series of episodes or ordeals within the patchwork of creation and its interrelatedness to human consciousness. It is the basis for much of western magick and esoterica. During one particular pathworking, which was always lead by Erneh, I decided to pick up a crown and place it on the head of a statue that guarded the doorway to the astral realm we were trying to gain access to. When that figure was described again by Erneh, as we left back through that doorway, he casually mentioned the crown, even though he hadn't the first time and I hadn't mentioned it, as we were all in a trance state visualising the scenes. This sort of thing wasn't unusual and I just sort of accepted it.

Although I did not then accept this as defining proof of telepathy of course, as such an event was not a 'test' of any theory.

Sabbats were slightly more exciting as they involved celebrating through ritual enactments an aspect or myth representing the change of the season and the relationship of that with the human psyche. This made absolute sense to me as I can't think of many other religious practices where human beings attempt to interface their minds with some notion of the entire planet, universe and everything. This is not the mere passive state of being in a universe of cause and effect only, but actually being in the universe with some semblance of intent and destiny. I mean, are we part of this world, or are we just passing microbes crawling over its skin? Sabbats were a way of connecting with what was going on. Everyone can feel it getting cold, or see flowers opening, so it's a natural step to try to connect with the fuse that lights the green flower, as it were. All Wiccans really want is freedom for the individual and the soul to live in accordance with nature.

The worst thing about the circles, however, was not the nakedness which you really don't notice after a short while – but trying to remain serious at key times. We were such a rowdy bunch of new kids and Erneh was a very serious academic person. Often during what was called "the Wiccan rune" (an initial circular chant of raising power, written by Doreen Valiente), whilst all holding hands, Erneh would get into the part, his voice booming louder and louder with each verse. He really was old school. He was very theatrical and a little bit too much for us to take. After having admitted our amusement of this to one another one evening among ourselves and having a good laugh about it, it became impossible to keep a straight face each time it happened. If I dared look in Mara's direction, all she needed to do was raise an eyebrow and smirk and I'd be off. It was the same with Don; his shoulders used to bob up and down as he silently laughed to himself. I'd usually be right behind him. Sometimes I would just explode from too much inner pressure and start gasping for breath really loudly. This would have a chain reaction effect on the other two and subsequently other student Wiccans who might pop in and out of the circle from time to time and we'd all start to laugh uncontrollably. This was all going on as we were flinging ourselves round and around in Mags' front room. Fortunately, Erneh was so loud that his voice drowned us out and he never seemed to notice, but Mags did of course. Eyeing us with a knowing look afterward, she'd just say, "Yes, well mirth is as relevant an energy, if not more so, in a magick circle!" Don especially could laugh forever and it was an infectious chortle that always had a feedback effect on me, which in turn would make him laugh again.

After the ritual, robes went back on and the eating, drinking and general relaxing began. We sat around the circle passing food around drinking and red wine from the chalice; it was fantastic. Often I'm ashamed to admit I could hardly concentrate on the circles, just wanting to skip ahead to the post circle food drink and socialising. We, the younger contingent, were quite restless and noisy, often giggling and being silly. This is when I realised the full extent of Mags' brain power and wealth of knowledge, as no matter which subject we talked about Mags knew virtually everything there was to know about it. She was very intelligent, had trained to be an M.D. but dropped out to raise her family and now worked as a research scientist for the university. She was a year off retirement age. She had a photographic memory and could recall rafts of poems, songs and anecdotes. If her memory was jolted by something someone said, she'd chuckle "That reminds me of this one…" and break in to a little song or poem.

She had a wealth of knowledge about the local area and history, which I doubt many other people had. Her house was surrounded wall to wall with bookshelves stacked with books. Mara, an English student and lover of books and literature, would slowly peruse them, periodically gasping to herself. She would leave with books crammed under her arm. With Erneh also being a scholar of the English language and Mara mid-way through her degree and being very bright anyway, with an impressively broad general knowledge, the conversation often became a little highbrow. I would often feel somewhat inferior, but then I had Don there, a Kincorth lad who also probably felt exactly the same way. It's not quite so bad feeling inferior when you have a friend to feel inferior with. Don and I would just look at each other and he would strike up a conversation about the Terry Pratchett book or comics that he was reading.

As time went on, I sensed the power being moved around the circle, being built up via chanting. I could feel the power, which was very uplifting. I also became more sensitive to how the changing of the seasons felt at each Sabbat. I did try to throw away the script and just feel the role I had to play. I was feeling the power of the God too and when the God was invoked into Erneh I began to fill with power, which

I always instinctively directed towards him to aid the complete invocation.

Don was initiated first. I wondered whether Mara and I were next, but Mags never said anything. We both felt ready, for the light that never goes out but for me that night a strange fear gripped me (and I just couldn't ask). Eventually I pushed Mara into the kitchen while Mags prepared tea after a circle, ushering her forward whispering, "Ask her, go on! Ask her, ask her, ask her." Mara then duly asked. Mags looked and said, "Oh yes you're both ready, sure!" We were a bit perplexed and asked her how come she hadn't spoken to us about it? "Well you only had to ask me," she said. This was Mags' way; she had an extremely Zen-like approach to things, nothing ever put her up nor down, what happens, happens! It was very frustrating at times.

When Mags intimated that I was ready to be initiated, I felt a slight feeling of bliss and for a split second I felt almost invincible, as if I was exactly where I should be, feeling exactly as I should. I hadn't noticed that I wasn't recounting past conversations in my head quite so much, although I still did. Neither was I comparing myself to Don as much or analysing his actions or searching for data as to why people would like him better than me. I was, for a second, at peace and for a moment I felt strangely whole. I wondered if this was how normal people felt all the time!? Was I still ill? If it was how normal people felt, it was a wonderful feeling.

This was the summer of 1991; I had passed the Higher National Certificate (HNC) in Chemistry with flying colours. The HNC was based on the first two years of a degree course for those people in employment as job training. The result was a little surprising as I had spent a great deal of time getting drunk with Freddie, who himself had to re-sit two of the modules. Suddenly it occurred to me that I could go to university to study Biology, something I would actually want to do with my life! I had options and I fathomed that university might be full of New Model Army-loving Pagan punks like myself and Don or really cool and clever alternative people like Mara. I had savings and figured it would be good fun to go; I mean, I never thought I would be good enough to sit an HNC, but then again I had passed it whilst spending most of the time in the pub. Clearly then, I had the necessary skills to be a proper student. My parents were a little apprehensive about me quitting a perfectly good job and probably suspected that I just wanted to avoid work by being a full-time student (they were basically right). I realised that I could avoid these discussions by just moving in with Mara full-time.

I joined Freddie at the pub for our weekly beers and to chat about work stuff, which was our norm. However, something had shifted and I no longer felt compelled to discuss things I actually didn't care too much about. I mentioned the idea of becoming a full-time student to Freddie expecting a bit of support, but he just grinned when I told him and he made out that I might be punching a little bit above my weight. Suddenly it flashed across my mind that Freddie had just been using me as a person to sit at the pub with and to waste the time away. He had no real interest in me or my life and in fact he didn't like the idea of me leaving the workplace, as that didn't fit in with his idea of who he thought I was; who the work crowd had decided that I was (in my absence, kinda thing). It was odd, I realised that despite some people being your friend they don't actually like it when you're smart or show any promise. It was a strange sense of empowerment that pushed me to my feet and made me head towards the door. "Well, I'll be seeing ya Fred, I think I'll just toddle down to the university and talk to them about courses and stuff."

I hadn't realised before that you could just go to a place like a university and talk to people about options, but that's exactly what I did. Ironically, as I waved goodbye to Freddie – despite the fact that we both frequented that pub an awful lot and both lived in a small town, saw the same bands and both worked at the same place – I never actually saw him again. He broke his leg doing something daft whilst a bit pissed later that day and he didn't show up to work for my final month there. That was really strange. After eventually gaining his HNC he soon went straight to working offshore. I always wanted to catch up with him for another beer at some time, but it's like our universes just drastically and suddenly diverged!

I was accepted into a Biology course at The University of Aberdeen. Almost the entire campus was set in an area known as Old Aberdeen, complete with cobbled streets and five hundred year old buildings. It was a lovely place, the next oldest University in Scotland after St. Andrews. In the past I had taken the wrong turn, looking for a careers interview just after leaving school one day and had ended up walking among the throngs of students. I was totally intimidated; how could people do degrees? They must be geniuses or something. And now I was going there and I had more than the necessary entry requirements. Again, at the same time, ambivalently, I retained the attitude that I probably wouldn't be good enough to stay on for the complete course, but it was worth a go!

The day of initiation into Wicca also arrived. The rite involved being lead around blindfolded. This proved to be a good way to engage in such a magical activity, as when Mags talked to the quarters I saw them as well as felt their presence. By the time the blindfold was removed, I was really surprised to find myself in her front room.

Relationships forged in a magical group like that are very binding and strong; I belonged there and we could speak about anything. Eventually Don and I talked about dreams and their significance. I hadn't spoken of the content of my recurring dream yet to anyone and was curious about the strange metamorphosis into a dream filled with apparent Wiccan symbolism (The three women were surely the three aspects of the Goddess – *i.e.* Maid, Mother and Crone; and the antlered deer-man was very clearly the Wiccan Horned God). This was powerful proof for me that something was welling up from a place in my subconscious which I had no direct conscious access to. I hadn't learned about the obvious symbolism until long after the dream. To set the ball rolling I asked Don whether he had any experience of recurring dreams, or knew anything about them. I was interested to know if he had had any similar experiences running up to initiation and whether he had any information about them. Instead he started to describe a recurring dream he'd had as a teenager, whilst at school in Kincorth, an area at the very South of Aberdeen. He told me that he had dreamt that the transmitter mast in Northfield had come to life; that the two red lights, which can be seen for miles in Aberdeen, had transformed into big glowing red eyes. The creature, as it now was, broke free from its holdings and started running amok, killing everything in its path and in Don's words, 'becoming like a Norse Berserker killing indiscriminately.' It then chased Don through his dreams and many a night Don dreamt of it chasing him down, always there, never managing to completely give it the slip. I finished the sentence for him. "And it seemed to follow you always at the same distance, tracking you, hunting you, keeping you in its sights?"

"Yes, yes that's it exactly!" he replied, "But years later the beast morphed into the Horned Lord of the forest!!"

Incredibly, the last dream he had of it quite recently was that he had found himself at the Northfield tower, but discovered that the

Horned Lord had given up chasing him and there in a mound of grass was a sword sticking out. He tried to pull it out, like King Arthur, but annoyingly awoke before he could complete this! I mean, fuck me!! Right?

A few days later, Mara passed me in the kitchen whilst somewhat absent mindedly musing aloud, "I had a dream about you the other night, Sean!"

I raised an eyebrow in expectation; conversations that start like this usually end up being either: i) quite hurtful and insulting, or ii) quite awkward, or iii) all three. "Oh aye?" I said tentatively.

She stopped momentarily and continued in a slightly bemused manner, "Yeah, you were in your car, you stopped and let me in. You had horns and when I got in there was a guy with a sword in the back seat with me!"

"Go on, go on." I urged, excitedly.

"Well that's all it was. He didn't say 'owt, bloody rude he wir, it wer really vivid though; bloody weird or what!?" She said in matter of fact Lancashire tones as she slurped her tea and walked off. I sat down by the table in awe; this was weird! I was really impressed and quite astounded that a guy on the other side of town was having an identical dream to me, probably around the same time, only to meet up and be involved in a magical relationship some ten years later. Not only that, the woman who I shared a flat with and who had arrived at the coven around the same time, in her dream had hopped a ride in my car – which was also was a feature of my dream. There was a definite inescapable connection going on, somehow. It all smacked of destiny, a shared pull or calling to the craft perhaps, an unconscious union. Why Northfield for Don in his dream? It was certainly not that unusual for me to dream of this location as I lived there, but Don? He lived far away on the other side of town, Kincorth, which was on the opposite hill that looked over to Northfield and the mast with red lights which he could see far away in the distance. After that dream, Don always had an aversion to those red lights. And Mara as well, I mean, WTF?

Rationally it made no sense at all, but to my personal private sense of coincidences and para-social synchronicities, the phenomena of meeting up and sharing dreams of events that were yet to occur, fitted in quite nicely. So even though I couldn't explain it I was, instinctively, somewhat at ease with the idea. Also, we were working with the Tarot, when you think about it; these symbols have the ability to liaise with information ahead of time. In our case, the same process had obviously been at work in reverse. We were all definitely going to meet and do tarot pathworkings when Don and I started having the dreams in our teens.

It was amazing. The circles were very much becoming places of power, to feel this shared sense of intent or for want of a better word 'energy,' was very empowering. There is nothing like it. Once you get a taste of working in a group like that you wouldn't want to operate as a solitary again. Group magick is very addictive. Sure, social dynamics usually always cause rifts and friction, especially if there are a lot of dominant personality types and 'egos' present, but the group mind operating on the magicks bypasses all that and makes it worthwhile.

## Chapter 4:
## The Hippie, the Dippy and the Downright Lippy

So, I had developed an attitude where I should at least try things despite thinking that I was probably going to fail. I was self-aware enough to realise that I needed to learn the hard way if need be; I needed to build up my social skills, which I understood were still spectacularly worse than average. Although, as I gradually passed exams, there was proof therein, that I had some intelligence in the sphere of the sciences at least. I eventually moved into digs near the university as the accommodation office technically didn't allow extra students living in the one bedsit (with Mara). Besides that, it had become a bit cramped with Mara and others. I went to all my lectures and actually revised for exams. I loved studying Biology, Astronomy and Psychology. I knew a few different people but not many on my course as they all lived in halls together. I spent a lot of time sitting in the central refectory, or "the Ref" as it was known, reading comics like Sandman, Swamp Thing, Hellblazer, Batman and the Sandman spin offs which I loved. By second term of first year, I had settled into university life and had realised what the minimum amount of work required was for acceptably passing courses and dividing the rest of the time up by going to the ref' and the student Union. I especially haunted the snooker hall and the bar in the basement known as the dungeon. This was the most perfect place for me, painted all black with walls adorned with luminescent comic book characters. My absolute favourite was an eight foot tall perfect rendition of the Joker on Alan Moore's 'the Killing Joke,' graphic novel on the far wall by the bar. The juke box pumped out indie tunes all night and the beer, considering it was a student hangout , wasn't half bad and very cheap!

Whilst in the dungeon one evening I was approached by a tall figure wearing a large hat and long coat. It was a guy called Paul Alder who was in there as much as I was. He was a Wiccan who had come to the coven one night after getting in touch with Mara to "come in from the cold," as he put it. He had a very soft upper class accent which was exactly like Hugh Grant in *Four Weddings and a Funeral*; he used the word "fuck" almost every second syllable; sometimes in the loud din of the dungeon I didn't have a clue what he was saying as his speech became ever softer almost to a mumble as his "fuck, fuck fuckity fucks" would grind to a halt almost falling over themselves. So I would usually wait until he was finished and say "Yeah, fuck yeah!" He was a chain smoker, a little pretentious, heavily into Crowley and high magick. He and his girlfriend had gone to the coven one Esbat and then a few times when I couldn't make it myself. I don't know what was said or done but he wasn't happy with the circle and had decided not to return. I suppose he probably clashed with Mags' easy going Zen-like attitude to magick. To Mags, it was the 'intent' that counted not so much the words or actions. However Paul, having trained himself as a proper magician was much more of a perfectionist and word perfect type of chap. He also had an open relationship with his girlfriend and was usually being followed around by a couple of woman, his girlfriend and some "female" protégée.

Mara and Mags had him down as a "cloak flapper," which was their slightly derogatory term for practitioners of proper high magick like Paul, which I thought was quite amusing, though I could see why he might not so think so. Mind you, I liked Paul very much; he seemed to have respect for me anyway and always had a bit of chat about him. He'd come over to me in the union and plonk a pint down in front of me, no questions asked, and seemed to genuinely want to be mates with me. He was a pretty intelligent guy and I sussed that (despite his high magical persona, charisma and girls following him about) he was desperately seeking approval, real friendship and just a bit of fucking respect from someone! He was the type of guy that got on the wrong side of people without trying and without knowing why. I suppose he hadn't realised that if you flaunt around with a couple of girlfriends in an environment full of young horny students, then you have to expect to be disliked. I suspected that he just felt that he didn't understand the human race and vice-versa and that probably he had been fucked over a couple of times. This is probably why he was drawn to high magick, to get a bit of control I suspected. The bottom line was that despite his pretensions, he meant well and I totally related to that.

Paul wanted to start up a Pagan society and get society status by the university. I went along to one of their first meetings. This involved standing by an old well and doing a bit of an impromptu ritual in a place called the Quad in the old part of the university. However this wasn't a randomly chosen place, but a well calculated action by Paul since it was right where the theology building was housed, including the theology library which was packed full of Christian philosophy students. So I decided to go along with it out of respect for Paul and the many pints we'd shared. We met in the St Machar Bar on the high street in Old Aberdeen. Paul was sitting there in-between his girlfriend Sophie and his other lover and "magical student" Gemma. She was a philosophy undergraduate, which made her interesting and deep. She looked very gothy with the trademark black eyeliner, dark cherry lips and attitude of focused non-attachment to conventionality, which emanated upwards from her purple swirly Doc Martin boots. Upon talking to her for four seconds I also realised that she had no time whatsoever for small talk; her acerbic wit was second only to her razor-sharp sarcasm. Of course, this was both a turn on and a minefield to negotiate. Gemma was highly intelligent and had not only read but had practiced nearly every magical grimoire available. I couldn't communicate with her on her level at the time very well. If she said *'goetia,'* I probably said *'bless you.'* She was though, in short, like the singer/poet Joolz Denby song describes: mad, bad and bloody dangerous to know!

I sidled into Paul's group and he introduced me to everyone. As was becoming usual for me at university, practically anyone Paul introduced me to did not utter a word to me or actually look me in the eye, which of course I took personally at every turn. Actually, this was the same for practically everybody I tried to talk to at university in the first year and by then I was getting used to it. Still, I found it strange and perplexing; I had come to the conclusion that it must be a middle-class thing that I just didn't understand.

Next Paul introduced me to a dreadlocked tie-dyed hippie in the corner, complete with weathered features, George Clooney grin and looks to match. This was Davie, who I learned wasn't a student but a bit of an acquaintance of Paul's and who had obviously been talked into this over a few pints rather like I had. Davie seemed to be one of those characters who was "just there." He would seem to be part of the furniture in whatever place he was sitting, a bit like Freddie, I mused, but hippier and even friendlier. I instantly liked him. He was easy to chat to, which I found comforting, in that I didn't feel too exposed socially or overly strained when talking to him and he actually looked me in the eye when he talked to me, which was quite reassuring. In fact, it was so unusual in this environment that I actually I found it quite unnerving. I also instinctively liked the fact that he wasn't manipulated by Paul's magnetism to become part of his permanent group, as if he was immune to such things, in a Freddie sorta-way.

So there we were, standing around this old brick well as Paul started waving this bloody huge athame around. I don't know how he could lift that bloody huge blade with one hand. It had the desired effect though; scores of Christian students emptied from the library and surrounded us in minutes, as if Paul's pointy athame had lanced an angry boil as they pooled around the quad around us. The situation suddenly became very hostile. They couldn't argue that we didn't have the right to be there or practice our spirituality; Paul would have made a good politician, I'll give him that. But they did claim Paul's athame was an offensive weapon and shouldn't be brandished in public. I actually agreed with them. It was a heavy fucking sinister looking thing. The sight of Paul gesticulating and appearing like, for want of a better description such a Charlie Manson figure; made me think that I should be concerned if he was brandishing as much as a breadstick in public.

Thereafter an ongoing debate started in the student rag about the affair. Paul's little masterstroke for publicity had worked. A Christian person had answered some critics that the reason they were against Wiccans practising there was because of a "comprehensive little book called the bible" and that if they appeared not to tolerate us it was because they were acting as good Christians. The tone was a little derisory towards poor deluded people like us. I retorted the week after saying something along the lines of "Wiccans don't want to persecute anyone, we just feel it's better to act as (or strive to be) good people!" I thought it was a definitive comeback anyway, though it appeared that to my Christian friends (actually my lab partners!) on my course when I spoke to them about it afterwards; that my response had been laughably simplistic. I still don't get it!?

I accepted their position on the incident and actually believed it was vitally important for me to see other people's point of view, to see what makes them tick and trying to put myself in their shoes. This was how they had been brought up, I suppose. They came to know that I was Pagan and were intrigued that I wasn't actually anti-Christian. They were really resolute about their beliefs and biblical laws. From my point of view, it was like they were quite conditioned by it. It suits me that Wicca has only one real chief tenet – 'Do thine own will and it harm none.' If you include yourself in that 'none,' then personally, I can't see how a person can go wrong.

I wasn't convinced about Paul and his actions at all because, despite all of his passionate and persuasive speeches, I suspected that it just came down to fairly simple, transparent attention seeking, as much as he himself would deny it. I felt rather uncomfortable, not because I didn't agree with standing up for your rights and facing up to religious intolerance, but because I really didn't think it would make any difference. My anarchistic leaning from reading and understanding much of the literature that came in with CRASS records, made me sympathise with the notion that change cannot be accomplished by force or by extension through ego posturing. This was evidently just causing a clash of egos between ours and the unswerving belief of their Christian sense of morals. Besides, Wicca for me, aside from gathering at Newmachar in a small group, was very much a private, behind the curtains kind of religion and we were ok with that. So finding myself exposed in the glare of broad daylight, surrounded by hordes of rather unfriendly faces and being passed by people that sat not too far away from me during Science or Psychology lectures, was embarrassing. I mean, it was just as well for me that there were not likely to be many people I had gone to school with here! Although I had come to terms with the psychological aspects of Wicca, for my own peace of mind, to allow me to keep investigating and taking part, I could never explain my involvement in the "occult" to fellow scientists.

Anyone can have a religious or spiritual experience, as my experience demonstrates. Wiccans can learn from Christians or anyone else for that matter and incorporate some teachings into their repertoire of beliefs. Wicca as a magick-based religion is actually eclectic and can borrow aspects from any faith. In nature, hybrids can create better offspring that survive better than the parents anyway and are usually more "fit" to survive. A religion, or for that matter any philosophy that doesn't move or evolve with the times merely represents an interesting record of the prevailing moods and accepted norms of the time, in my view. Philosophy does not stand still and neither does science nor art nor music nor prose nor fashion nor even for that matter language, nor does the way we actually perceive ourselves and our position in the universe. So why do we even tolerate some religious ideologies that insist on standing still?

Religion represents a large portion of the human experience. In this context, I believe, much of Christianity, although good in many contexts is a historical snapshot, a philosophy frozen in amber from over two thousand years ago.

So anyway, I felt pretty stupid standing there in the Old Kings building quad in the middle of a standoff with the irascible theology students. My advice in this situation would be exactly the same for wasps and large farm animals; do not bother them unnecessarily. If you don't annoy them, then they will not annoy you (surely!?). We didn't really seem to have any real plan and after a while Paul put his offending athame away and we quietly dispersed and wandered up the cobbled high street back towards the main buildings. As usual, all Pauls' university mates ignored me or obviously avoided my gaze and began hankering after Paul. Despite this I persevered and tried talking to one person, "Phew, pretty intense eh?" The third year social anthropology student, whose parents were probably disappointed because he hadn't chosen to study a law degree as they'd always hoped, kept walking and stared ahead pensively, although he must have heard me. I continued, "Those Christians, huh? Sheesh, thought it was going to get a bit hairy there eh?" Then I used the tried and tested Bill Hicks line, "But erm, you'd think they'd just fucking forgive us like they're supposed ta wouldn't cha?" But nope, no response, not even an eyebrow raise was forthcoming. My voice trailed away as he increased the distance between us. I shrugged to myself; if a Bill Hicks line couldn't get a response from these guys, then nothing could. It was definitely personal then, definitely something about me that people just didn't like. It was weird; it was as if I didn't have any personal social "force." Often if I spoke people just didn't hear it or I would need to repeat what I said a few times until someone picked it up. Conversation was exhausting sometimes. Often I would say something but only after someone else repeated it or picked it up subconsciously, was this then acknowledged. This was a depressing fact of life for me but actually very real, so I was used to this kind of behaviour from these guys. Students and *ergo* the middle classes avoided me like the plague. I didn't exist to them. I felt like a living example of the Radiohead song "How to disappear completely."

So when a voice started up right behind me my first response was to ignore it as I assumed that it was meant for someone else.

"So you're not quite into this making such a bold statement against the establishment then are you mate?" I casually looked behind me a few seconds too late to see the self-assured figure of the hippie stalking behind me along the pavement. Realising that he was the one who was speaking and there was no one else besides us, I suddenly felt embarrassed and a little flustered that I had been poignantly ignoring him (just like a fucking student). Not wanting to appear like another of Paul's studenty mates, I looked back and smiled to let him see that I wanted to engage him in conversation. I was a little curious as to whether this guy would know and understand counterculture in a way that my biases made me assume he would. After all, before university, sitting in the Prince with Freddie, I often had a notion that practically every third student would have deeply committed political views, including firm anarchistic beliefs and viewpoints. I thought I would have found friends and likeminded people in this academic ground of fertile minds and counterculture. But no, I walked among the student population even more isolated, ignored and misunderstood as I would have been in any place in Northfield. So I decided to retort with a bit of a tester.

"Yeah, yeah, well I'm a bit more Crasstafarian myself, I don't really see direct conflict achieving anything, I mean, I don't really think you can preach to the un-converted, especially these guys as they are far from ready to start any type of dialogue in't they? I mean, I just think this is just gonna cause a fight and I never got to be this good-looking by getting in fights." We both laughed and I congratulated myself on my wittiness and hoped he would think I was a veritable witty guy, but actually I was just copying the good-looking line, as it was something my uncle David always said. The hippie guy looked pensive as I spoke, nodding his head slightly and I began to feel a swell of superiority rising in my chest as I anticipated that he wouldn't know much about the band CRASS perhaps (which was the proper genuine article counterculture in my view). I half expected him to respond with some new-agey crap about violence being bad energy or some such nonsense, but all he did was smile with a twinkle in his eyes which then spread into an endearing grin. With his rollie still jammed in his lips, as if the sudden impulse to shake my hand meant he didn't have time to attend to it, he jutted out his hand towards me with an upwards nod of his mopped head telegraphing that he respected my response and was ready to engage a little more. "Name's Davie man, yours is Sean right? Blessed be to you and all that bollox!"

As he shook my hand his eyes widened in appreciation and after a pause to light his rather pleasant smelling rollie, he gestured towards me;

"Crasstafarian eh? Heheh; never heard it put like that before, 'Crasstafarian,' funny; only one way of life man! I can dig that all right, though I bet if Stevie Ignorant was here he'd be lambasting those fuckers. That's what punk is all about init?" He started singing in a Joe Strummer drawl. Although I guessed that they were lyrics from The Clash, I didn't actually know the words or the song very well. *"I wanna riot on my own, white riot! – Everybody's doin,' just what they're told to*! Y'know? Nothing wrong with stirring up the authorities a little sometimes, Seany old son."

It was one of those occasions where I'd totally misjudged someone and now I felt like a prat for mentioning CRASS in the first place, especially referring to myself as a 'Crasstafarian,' as I think he may actually have been taking the piss out of me a little for that one. Clearly he did know a bit more than I did about the topic of conversation; now the tables had turned from my slightly arrogant superior feeling to one of crashing inferiority (my usual frame of mind) and so I had to conceal my irritability and unease with the hippie guy. I grinned and said, "Yeah, fuck right; good old Clash" hoping he didn't catch on that I didn't actually know many Clash songs at all and wasn't even sure if he had sung one of their songs or not. If he did, I would be immediately ousted as probably "a student-wannabe punk" in his eyes, I'm sure. I somehow couldn't win; I'd moan to myself that most other students were shallow and a bit facile, but as soon as I met someone genuine, I immediately felt inferior as if I was the impostor. But as he passed his small reefer over towards my face it was obvious to me that he was enjoying talking to me and seemed to want to convey that he really quite liked me. I accepted the spliff gratefully as a symbolic kind of friend/peace pipe and toked a little as we walked up towards the central refectory.

Davie was a fascinating person to chat with, that much was clear. He had a hypnotic gaze with bright blue - grey eyes that shone with a keen intelligence behind them. His skin was bronzed and he appeared almost Adonis-like you would say. I suppose he was quite attractive to boot, being charming with a big dimpled grin upon manly but smoothly sculpted features. A lean, firm yoga-trained body radiated strength behind a flimsy hemp shirt which combined well with combat trousers, suggesting perhaps a heart that would fight for a cause. Finally the look was adorned with an almost obligatory jangly shark toothed necklace. I fathomed that he had probably travelled the world and perhaps killed the shark with his bare hands on a beach in Indonesia one summer, rescuing a dolphin or a small child or something like that. Nah, he didn't seem like a "regular" student at all.

We spoke a little about revolution, the point of studying at all and what it meant to be a real human being. I confessed that many of his philosophical references went right over my head. I was curious and quite impressed really, about how well-read and educated he appeared to be. I suspected that he must be spending his time sneaking into random lectures here and there, as he certainly wasn't a student of any particular course. He seemed far more widely educated than the average student that I had met. He kept smiling and slapping me on the shoulder in a gesture of genuine approval and friendliness; I felt quite taken aback that someone in this place seemed to positively enjoy my company and be so happy to chat with me and listen to my views.

"So what are you studying then?" I eventually enquired; the stock conversation starter in first year of university.

Davie just smiled. "Nahhh I don't study here, I'm more arty mate, but I'm not an art student or anything. I wouldn't really want to be mistaken for a student; I don't like universities mate, jump through hoops, do this by this time; be creative but do it between the hours of nine and five, y'know? They want you to be creative and inspired but expect you to behave and stay as straight as the fucking burned out staff that go there every day to pay the mortgage and stay on top of gas bills and car loans."

If I read between the lines properly it seems he was kicked out of art college for being stoned too much, which to be honest I did sympathise with to some degree, because if you can't be stoned and in a psychedelic trance during your art student years, then there wasn't really anywhere else you could be. Surely that would be the one place where being out of your box would be a help rather than a hindrance. Davie, it seemed, was already fed up with society at quite a young age. I guess he had a head start on most of us who had to wait until we reached a midlife crisis before we looked back on our lives and cried a little.

I realised that we'd completely separated from Paul's group and we were now hanging about outside the central refectory. I looked at my watch; I only had a few minutes before the next afternoon lecture at the Zoology building across the road. Since I was so close, I thought that I might as well go to it (I actually enjoyed them, when I attended anyway). I conveyed this conclusion to Davie, "Oh shit I was going to say we could grab a pint, but I have a lecture to go to now!"

Davie just shrugged; clearly, time and deadlines were not paradigms that concerned him. "No worries my good man, I guess you'll be joining the revolution with these guys at the next meeting, or are you going to give it a miss and listen to punk tunes instead, dude?"

I shrugged in resignation. "I'd rather not wind up like people who are that sexually repressed really; they already hate us because we get all the blow jobs!" Davie laughed uproariously, which took me by surprise, as I thought it was a bit of a desperately corny line, clearly just directly stolen from Robin Williams in the film 'Good Morning Vietnam,' but again he hit me on the shoulder and smiled broadly at me. He shot his hand out again to shake my hand, really affirming that he was happy to have chatted to me,

"See you then mate; don't sleep too long in the lecture now will ya?" and with that he turned away and walked back down towards the King's buildings, going fuck knows where. I had an inkling he would end up in some social studies female student's bedroom before the day was out. As I watched his hair bound over the road, he raised his fist in the air and loudly shouted "STUDENT POWER, WHAT A SHOWER!" and then laughed for my benefit as he went. I found out much later it was from an old Angelic Upstarts song. He had out-punked me completely, the bastard!

Davie, as it turned out also knew Don from some employment training scheme they had both been forced to go along to. Aberdeen is funny like that, you will find that people know people you wouldn't expect (it's Facebook in a town). Aberdeen still has a fishing village mentality about it, despite being an oil boom city. As this happened so fast, *i.e.* in only one generation, the slower moving 'spirit of the place' had still to catch up. Of course, it needn't have surprised me that Don and Davie knew each other. Don was quite a recognizable chap in Aberdeen and he just seemed to attract anyone who was slightly alternative, or especially those that were quite way-out. Davie seemed to shun work and was just doing his thing. I don't know what it was but he was doing it, much the same way as I was doing university because I was unaware of what else I could do. So I think we both got each other for that reason. He also liked New Model Army and the Levellers, predictably enough. To Don he was affectionately known as Hippie Davie, to distinguish him from two other unemployed Davids on the course. I guess the council were working their way through the alphabet! The moniker just suited him and so it stuck.

I had wanted to become a hippie traveller person at one point. I had decided that it would be the only way to live life honestly enough. However, in truth, like everything else I wasn't sure how to go about this and didn't trust my survival skills enough to just take off. I didn't have a manual for that, but I did know how to be a student and so that seemed like a nice stop-gap which wasn't working for the man, as it were, for the time being. Davie however, didn't need a manual; all he needed was a fluffy jumper, hair bands and a passion for the environment and some of its weeds!

Where there's one devoted hippie, there's another and Hippie Davie attracted a whole crowd of eco-warriors that overlapped with Paul's merry men of the student union. Now I've nothing against eco-warriors – I fancied myself as one as I really liked a particular eco-punk band called Oi Polloi – but these people were just weird. Not one of them took me on, looked me in the eye or even acknowledged my presence when I was introduced to them; it was so strange. Paul's little student circle soon became over-run with new-age hippies, which must have been a major disappointment to him, as he was at least at peace with his own human dark side, he didn't try to cover that up (Well, let's be honest, he did the exact opposite of cover that up). If you can imagine Darth Vader sitting in the pub, palm in face, trying to inspire a dark uprising among the Ewoks then you have an accurate description of Paul and his group! I heard from Davie that on one memorable occasion that the group met at a stone circle overlooking Aberdeen in a field near Dyce airport to perform a ritual on their concerns for the environment. The ritual involved burning MacDonalds cartons (which very probably released toxic fumes into the air – they obviously never thought it through) in a new age voodoo sort of way. I'm sure the marketing representatives of MacDonalds would have been shitting themselves if they knew. The ritual then culminated in them collectively baring their arses to the city of Aberdeen, as a mark of their displeasure with the policies of the City Council. If anyone could see them, then I suppose they would have only seen a bunch of hippie arseholes anyway!

Don, Hippie Davie and I spent a fair bit of time together for the next year or so and I started making good friends with people at uni as well, notably 'Neighbour John and a Catalan guy called Rogé (who gave up on British monolingualism quite fast and insisted we just call him Roger). I moved into a flat with an art student girlfriend who I had finally lost my virginity to and then had thought it was love. She promptly split up with me practically in the same week we moved in as she needed freedom to move between Dundee to do a Masters course and stayed at her parents during the week. I had the flat to myself which was pretty good for a student, given my mates at uni had to live in squalid halls. The flat became a good meeting point for relaxing and hanging out. I found myself often becoming relaxed in other people's company for once, mainly because I was now surrounding myself with people who I didn't feel were overly judgemental or acted in the text book alpha male fashion, making life so much easier and far less taxing.

One mate and neighbour John morphed into "John The Jumper." This wasn't an expression of his sexual strategies but was for his propensity for wearing John Craven-like big patterned jumpers (clearly a real proper Zoologist!). This morphed into "The Jumper," for Roger and me and often, affectionately, I'd refer to him as "MeOl'Jumpa." We'd often sing the Sultan's of Ping FC song, 'Where's me Jumpa,' if we spotted him coming towards us through the throng after lectures or in the ref (it had been a big hit a few years prior; well, if you were an avid listener of the John Peel show that is!). The Jumper lived along the road in a poxy little room but often would follow me back to mine, instead of saying cheerio and walking back to his flat, he would sort of hang about waiting for an invite until eventually he wouldn't ask but just follow me straight in. Hippie Davie and Don seemed to sort of move in as well. Since my flat was close to town it was the natural place to go after a night out. Since we had nights out every night, the lads just basically made camp in the living room, supping my home brew and watching Supermarket Sweep.

Actually MeOl'Jumpa had been known to me for ages, but we hadn't immediately been friends. He had been part of a social circle at university who kind of looked down on me for my obvious lack of commitment and bad work ethic. I didn't really like most of them either, as I considered them to be a bit dull. However, I had shared a room with the Jumper at a field course and we had laughed ourselves to sleep most nights. Since he lived on my street I often saw him walking up the long King Street home and started chatting to him and found him quite normal and friendly. He was obsessed about finding a girlfriend and upon finding out that I was a witch, wondered whether I could do something to help him in this endeavour. I decided to give it a try. I knew I could make some kind of talisman and charge it in the circle; also I was one hundred percent confident that it would have an effect. In fact, it would not enter my head that it would not. There was a definite cause and so I knew there would be a definite effect. This is perhaps the most essential ingredient in magick or prayer or any kind of mental wish fulfilment that involves and end goal—belief! In the case of Wicca, there is the addition of faith as a tangible principle of Nature; call it the Goddess and God or whatever shape that takes in your mind and imagination. Faith can equate to a powerful form of positive thinking and transform those who take part in it in a collective hypnosis sort of way. However, how rituals also alter fate takes a bit more explaining. Whatever the mechanics, let's be clear, magick works!

I told the Jumper to come to my flat that weekend. I was quite open to people who were interested and decided that he should attend the circle I was to cast so that he could contribute to the ritual I had devised. Knowing about all the pitfalls in magick and being aware that it would be hostile magick to impose any restrictions on what he was asking for, I tried to cover every clause I could think about. Charging the talisman I had constructed, I asked that the Jumper meet his perfect partner, regardless of their gender and so on, s'long as it was the perfect partner for him at this moment in his life. The ritual worked in spectacular fashion and speed. He began to shun the normal crowd of people he hung about with, almost rudely in fact, for no apparent reason in their eyes and started spending all his time with me. This actually happened before he virtually moved in, but the very rapid change in him was apparent to me. It had that flavour which one begins to notice as well, when things seem to reorganise. Behaviours alter to accommodate the will of the magick, which is "out there," as anyone who has practiced magick for any length of time begins to notice and recognise.

Obviously, as far as I was concerned, what had in fact happened was that I was his perfect partner for that time! Albeit not in a romantic way but then I hadn't stipulated romance or non-platonic love!! When I met the Jumper he was a little overly polite and repressed at times but that didn't last long. Within weeks, scenes in my flat with the Jumper might have looked like a real life scenes from *Men Behaving Badly* with the Jumper all but squashing beer cans on his head. He also found Don and Hippie Davie quite amusing, especially the former who would be quite suggestive towards him, which just made him laugh. I'll never know if he knew just how serious Don actually was.

You can argue that this would have happened anyway without any need for a "fantastic" explanation and I agree it would have happened. We got on well with each other and would be destined to become close friends anyway. However I know that ritual sped things up significantly and I document it here as an example of what to expect and perhaps as a warning to be very careful before venturing to use magick for your own purposes. Anyone doing magick will recognise this aspect; many times you get what you ask for – not –what you think you ask for!

Meanwhile, at the coven Don was about to get his second degree initiation. This was an acknowledgment that he had the skills to prepare a magical space, perform ritual and magick. However, just before this Don, Hippie Davie and I had started working together, ostensibly to practice and explore magick. Hippie Davie did not attend Newmachar, claiming he was not in keeping with Gardner as he preferred to think of himself as a Celtic sorcerer, which for him meant sitting under the full moon in the woods and dabbling in Druidery and drugs. Hippie Davie was sure that a Pagan would have originally been like the village Shaman and perhaps have been a bit of a loner, not messing about with circles and candles so much, though he was quite *au fait* with these methods as well. He was happy to work with us, though, as he felt the amount of dope smoking and lack of discipline was about right. Don was very relaxed and actually quite a powerful priest in these situations and we worked well together. I often felt that because of Don's complete belief in what he was doing, accepting the reality of spirits without question, for example, lent a great deal of power to the circle. I, on the other hand, was quite rational (of course) but we balanced each other well.

A new arrival appeared at Newmachar not long after Don received his second degree. This was a bloke called Michael, whose second name was actually Hutcheons! Everyone who ever met him found this very ironic; after all, he didn't exactly have good looks in excess; in fact, he was rather closer to the cretinous end of the spectrum as opposed to the sex-God-rock-star-end. He had quite pronounced lips, sort of chimp-like with his eyes hidden behind a little pair of spectacles which magnified his right eye to creepy proportions. His long, lank hair hung down each side of his head, which looked like it hadn't changed style since he was fifteen; his hair now given up waiting for a new style had just laid limply on his head and died peacefully. He wore an almost constant studied frown which he almost certainly thought made him look intelligent and thoughtful, but I'm afraid actually made him look like he was finding it difficult to comprehend everyday existence, which actually was probably the case. This look made him appear like a sort of fiendish trainspotter. Sure, he had the long hair, tattoos and a liking for the Goth scene but, even though he wore leather, he was still an anorak! If he heard someone use an expression which impressed him he would use it constantly, making it apparent he was trying to impress by over using it to death. His favourite statement was, "Aye definitely...definitely, without a doubt," or just "Without a doubt, without a doubt." This followed practically anything he said and became a bit of an 'in' joke with the rest of the coven, kinda thing.

Mikey had got in touch with Mags claiming he was an Amer-Indian Shaman. Apparently he had spent time in Canada studying this and had learned the old ways from a proper medicine man that introduced him to the underworld and thus accelerated his training in magick. He didn't waste any time announcing this to Don and I, in his characteristic slow and measured way,

"I was the only occidental Canadian-Scottish guy fully trained in the ways of the medicine man! (I had an inkling he was paraphrasing directly from the show 'The Master' from the eighties with Lee Van Cleef, but I let him continue). Oh aye, I was actually fairly high ranking in my Shamanic tribe of the Eastern Cree which means I'm actually at the same levil iz Mags 'n Ernest...Well, actually not to try to boast or onything, but in fact am definitely even higher, erm...higher aye, without a doubt!!"

That should have been a clear warning to us straight away, but perhaps I am naive about people. Don and I just thought he was a bit of a blowhard, but fairly innocuous and by the old Northfield standards to me he was a mate, simple as that.

Though he also wasted no time also in telling us that he'd played in many goth bands and had (unlikely) been a temporary bassist with the band Bauhaus! Apparently during a gig in Canada in which his band (The Eastern Death Cult) had opened for them, Bauhaus bassist David J

Haskins (or D.J. as he was known to Mikey of course) had a sudden injury. According to Mikey, there were so many bottles thrown at their gigs that D.J. copped one in the face one just after the first song. As Mikey happened to be standing just offstage giving them encouragement, he just jumped in amid all the confusion and took over the bass position. Luckily because he had trained a lot in kung fu back then, he had remarkable reflexes and so could dodge all the missiles; so they let him stay on for the rest of the tour! If you listen carefully to some of the effects Daniel Ash used on the album, 'Swing the Heartache' (the BBC Sessions) according to Mikey, you can hear many of the suggestions he had made being used. Then winked, "*And you know the song sanity assassin..? That was my riff, but I let 'em have it gratis*!"

He would also regale everyone of how he had also jammed with Neil Young in a coffee shop he worked in for a while in Montreal, cos he just lived over the road and used to come in disguised with a big coat and a fake beard to get cappuccino and a chocolate muffin. Luckily as he (Mikey) had been such a music aficionado, he recognised him and called him out on his disguise. I tried to point out that Neil already had a beard but he just tutted and said incredulously "Yeah…exactly…this was a fake one over his real one you idiot..! It was a different colour though, see…yid niver suspect 'at would ye!?"

Paul Alders' Goth protégée Gemma had started coming to the circle, but she hated Mikey, thinking he was extremely lecherous and a little bit screwed up. I feared for the man's life as she was quite aggressive towards him. She tried to warn us on several occasions that this guy wasn't right, that he had an appalling attitude towards women that was altogether un-Wiccan. Gemma would absolutely bristle with resentment in his presence, dropping caustic comments in his direction during conversations that would make a lesser man wither. Amazingly, Mikey never seemed to react to these comments, as if it all went over his head and perhaps indeed most did. I had a feeling that he was just screening them all out as he had such an over-inflated self-image. It was like he was thinking in the back of his mind somewhere that none of these put-downs could possibly refer to him. However this did not do for Gemma at all and she often wanted to make sure that he was clear about her feelings towards him.

In the university union dungeon one night as Mikey, Don and I were chatting to Gemma and her flat mates, I was hoping as usual to wangle at least a snog or cop a feel before the night was out but invariably the only offer I ever got was from Don on the long walk home, which was depressing. Mikey had tried to flirt with Gemma once before but only succeeded in getting a punch in the face. He acted like it was a joke, but I could see that it was really a fairly hard smack on the cheek. On that occasion one of her flat mates dragged her away to the toilets to calm her down whilst Don and I tried to conceal the fact that we actually found it totally hilarious.

We managed to get the evening going and just relax; I actually got on pretty well with Gemma and so acted like a buffer zone between them. Inevitably, not ten minutes had passed but Mikey could be heard trying to explain to one of Gemma's flatmates that he was in full control of his sex organs as he had practiced tantric meditation as well (though I think he may have been mistaking India the country with Canadian Indians…I wouldn't be a bit surprised actually). It wouldn't be so bad if he had said it with any flicker of irony, but the measured concentration on his face coupled with his almost unconscious cupping of his wedding tackle with his non-drinking hand to give them a quick jiggle around in emphasis was probably the defining moment for Gemma. Don and I were giving each other the 'here we go' look; free entertainment was on the way once again.

I could see Gemma eyeing him like a tarantula eyeing a cockroach as she called over, "Hey Mikey, do real men carry condoms about then?"

Mikey grinned, "Oh aye, aye I do as a matter of fact."

I had an inkling that this was not going to end well and tried to laugh it off and change the subject. However, Gemma just smiled and upped the ante. "Wow, I like a man who's honest and prepared, do you really have one, can I see it?" She got up and, using seductive body language to good effect, sat down beside him. Mikey flashed a winning smile at me and we all watched incredulously as he furtively wrestled with his wallet. The object in question was firmly lodged deep in an inner pocket and may have been there for some time. I also think this was one of the few times I saw him without a cigarette in one hand. He wrenched it out with an upward movement, as we all in turn stared upward in awe as he held it aloft for a second in what I mused was a moment of near religious admiration. It was an act that should have been accompanied by Also Sprach Zarathustra by Richard Straaus, like the ape-man scene from the film 2001. I mean, the similarities between that scene and this one are just too numerous to mention! The folded over tatty edges and lack of any discernible writing, due to aged fading, could not detract from Mikey's sense of pride in that moment.

But almost as suddenly the moment was gone forever as Gemma, now standing up, snatched the prize from his fingers. "Yooo fuckin' dirty bastard, you're absolutely unbelievable!" Mikey frowned, not understanding what was happening, but Don and I froze with embarrassment and intuitively began increasing the distance between him and us by slowly sliding backwards and leaning away. Onlookers became quiet as the entire dungeon turned to look at him and Gemma standing holding up his poor Johnny; a much less than fitting fanfare than Mikey had planned for it after its years in dark seclusion awaiting its call of duty.

Mikey looked up at Gemma open-mouthed; it hadn't quite yet filtered through to him that he was not going to demonstrate his tantric skills anytime soon. Gemma pushed home the tirade, "Fucking cheek to sit down here, take this out and says you fucking want it in the toilets ya dirty bitch, I can give it to ya! What the FUCK do you think women are mate? This is the 1990s ye know!?" I looked over at Don, who just looked down and shook his head tutting. I saw faces glower out of the gloom towards us all, scanning Don and I as well. Feeling rather like some Judas, I instinctively copied Don's example by shaking my head and mouthing *dis-gusting* with a look of contempt on my face. A member of the woman's rugby team who had been leaning on the bar spat on the floor and shouted over "Purrvert!" and I felt sure that Mikey was about to get strung up by the balls, as there were usually two or three from the rugby squad in drinking and chatting up the barmaids. Mikey, however, still looked confused and his mouth remained wide open, as if the tendons had actually snapped with shame. It now occurred to him that Gemma had stitched him up good and proper. It was a pretty good way to ensure he wouldn't be bothering her and her flatmates in there for quite some time.

I could see that she was just getting started and it seemed to me that she was invoking the Goddess Sekmet more and more into her psyche, as that is who Gemma strongly reminded me of. She could drink any of us under the table and had no apparent fear of any confrontation. As she stood in front of him mocking him, I fathomed that she was about to turn into a lioness and chew his head off right there and then. Mikey just looked around sheepishly grinning, as if it was just her little joke. He could never respond to direct criticism or confrontation. So I looked at my pretend watch, *oh is that the time?* We made our excuses and left, snogfree as usual. Outside, Mikey was chuckling and looking very triumphant. I couldn't help but round on him; I mean, he had started off with no chance, so he had just broke-even in real terms. I, however, had been sent right back to the start. Mikey was fast becoming a fucking large snake in this game of snakes and ladders.

I turned scowling at Mikey, "What are you so happy about Mikey? Seein' as it was your fuckin' unique brand of charm – which is like a cross between Benny Hill and a Rottweiler – that has, once again, fucked up our chances with females, you twat!"

Mikey just shook his head smiling. "Well, if that's no' a sign that she's totally gagging for it, then I don't know what is; fucking repressed as hell man, see how she fuckin' came up t'mi? Least now she definitely kaens I'm 'ay ready wi a condom!"

Don gave a derisory laugh whilst I sucked air through my teeth in contempt, "Maybe you want to go back in there and give her yer number gist in case, Mikey?"

Mikey waved the very notion away with the wave of his hand as he planted another ciggy in his lips, regaining his normal composure. "Nah, fuck she's always like that with me, coz she knows she just wants it fae me and she hates herself for it! I canna wait till I bed her, then she'll see!"

I was beginning to get worried; I could tell that he was actually serious.

Actually, Gemma had known Mikey from her acquaintance with Paul Alder, as Mikey and Paul had been mates from way back. Hippie Davie had known him briefly as well through that crowd; his response when we told him that Mikey had appeared at Newmachar was ominous –

"Oh fuck, not the fuckin,' Witch Doctor O' Torry!?" This was quite telling as Hippie Davie tended to treat absolutely everyone with the same chuffed carefree way no matter who they were; in fact, I don't think I'd ever heard Hippie Davie be that negative about anything really. Unbeknown to us, Mikey had actually been really lecherous to Gemma and a bit of a pest in the past. He could be very creepy towards women. Gemma warned us that he was pure evil really; 'bad fucking medicine' was the phrase she used (nearly spitting it out as she said it). She immediately appealed that he shouldn't be allowed into the circle.

She was annoyed that she hadn't had a say in his admittance in the first place. I always figured it was down to Mags anyway.

We had a conference about it in the circle. Mags could only see the good in anybody and I, feeling sorry for him, argued to give him a chance. I felt, at that time, that anyone who was genuinely interested in the craft should be allowed access to a circle and I also fathomed that the lecherous witch doctor would benefit from a very female centric religion for a while, maybe even learning respect. Gemma had left it a bit late anyway, as he was starting to be an established member by this time. Mags left the decision to Mara, who overruled Gemma. Gemma was gob smacked – I think she may have been used to getting her own way – and she stomped like a spoilt child and left the coven for a while.

Typically, coven politics are a total minefield and Pagans can be the worst subset of humanity for displaying bitchiness and manipulation. This is contrary to what many people think when they first get involved with the craft. They tend to think that Pagans are an enlightened and peace loving group of people, but alas nothing could be further from the truth. Mikey felt triumphant, he had felt really threatened by Gemma. Also, unbeknownst to me, he had also begun to resent me for having a friendship with Gemma but slyly managed to conceal that from me at the time. He was very good at pretending he was things that he wasn't.

Mikey, though, despite being a minor irritation, began to be more of a feature of our lives as he was also unemployed, or unemployable, who knows? He was therefore a perfect addition to our group of daytime layabouts, finding ourselves wandering around Aberdeen city centre in various cafés and pubs to pass the time. Hippie Davie acknowledged his presence on one such occasion with a casual "All right Doc, old son?" We all immediately saw the irony of this as Mikey was the last person you'd imagine had a PhD. Mikey's wide grimace telegraphed his internal discomfort with this moniker, thus we all, of course, referred to him from that moment on as 'The Doc,' or just plain old 'Doc.' This seemed much more fitting than the rockstaresque Michael Hutcheons anyway!

At twenty-five years old I only had one serious girlfriend. I had become a little bit more confident in my old age. I had a good bunch of mates, the Wiccan bunch, the Jumper, Roger and occasionally people I worked with in various part-time jobs. My other mates seemed to tolerate my weird magical mates and likewise they could see past their differences and were happy to hang out with them. We all had the same aim in life on a Friday night – to get out, to get drunk and to get laid. We were like any bunch of young guys together, horny and never getting enough, though never getting any is more accurate.

This was very true though, apart from Hippie Davie and of course Don. We were constantly amazed at how many women would crowd around Don at the Mudd Club or student union; they would literally mob the guy. It was the unusual gear at first but then on hearing he was gay they would become fascinated and inevitably at the end of the night, at least one of them would offer to have sex with him, so that he could 'find out' what a woman was like! This never failed to wind me up; the bastard was getting more action with women than any of us and it was totally fucking wasted on him. We all felt this was seriously unfair. Don could just amble into any park and get his rocks off if he really wanted too; Roger, Jumpa, The Doc and I had all come to the conclusion that we'd wished we were gay at times! Free sex and a better dress sense - all a man could want. Hippie Davie was all right; clearly the best looking of us all with his Adonis looks, bronzed skin, toned tofu cleansed body. The hippie women especially, loved him; he was a crusty Casanova. He would often give us the thumbs up with a smile before some nice looking woman would obscure his face by snogging him at the back of the union. We would smile back then crowd round and plot ways to kill the fucker!

Our desperation hung like an odour over the rest of us as we tried in vain to chat to women, get drunk and invariably plod home wondering why everyone else in the world seemed to be at it except us! I guess I wasn't that bad looking however; Jen and Gemma had insinuated that I was quite good looking, for a certain type of bloke anyway, but the main thing was that I was 'nice.' "Nice!" They said it in a way that was meant to sound like a defining characteristic, but I knew that this was a just a democratic way of saying they didn't really fancy me.

Although, I did find out that occasionally standing next to The Doc did the trick, his spotty, bespectacled face, snotty nose, lank haired 'children of the corn' appearance made for a useful contrast at times. I would also manage to get chatting to some of the women that tended to flock around Don. Roger and I hit upon the idea that if we at least pretended to be gay friends of Don's, then we might attract similar attention. However, all this seemed to do was to make us seem like a cute couple that girls seemed loathe to breaking apart; aside from also treating us in a very platonic, nonsexual way, which only further dented my confidence. As a result, Roger and I tended to end up dancing with each other, which may have cemented our friendship in many ways but started gossip around the Zoology building about us that became hard to shake off. Indeed, the rumour mill was so powerful that I sometimes started to believe it myself! Amazingly, I did manage to snog a couple of girls here and there and on those occasions I would give Roger, Davie, The Doc and The Jumpa the thumbs up from the back of the club, to which they would smile and wave back, clearly happy for me!

Consequently, I bumped into Gemma now and again in the union and now that I was single, didn't see any harm in walking her home from time to time. I had become more and more attracted to her, especially since I had started to work with her as priest and priestess on a regular basis at the circles. I don't know if this fact was strictly related, I'm sure a lot of Wiccan's would say it was. However, I just have to shrug and own up to the fact that I was just far too horny for my own good. As well as Gem and I did get on though, she never reciprocated any of my attempts at flirting and I always fell flat on my face. I consolidated my belief that I was just useless at 'the chatting up game.'

After one Mudd club Monday, I offered to walk her home, which was quite a usual pleasant stroll along the road, pausing only at Thain's bakery for morning rowies at 3am (Aberdeen's answer to the croissant – well not really, bread mixed with lard and salt and compressed into a disc…a disc that was fucking delicious at 3am after a night in the town). At her door I sensed a mutual attraction and just instinctively bent closer to kiss her. She looked a bit perplexed and stepped back, looking at me quizzically. 'Oh fuck,' I thought, 'I've totally misread this situation,' and I stammered pulling away. "Shit sorry Gem, got a bit carried away ye know, am cool am cool it's ok I'm sorry!" I was suddenly quite scared for the health of my bollocks, such was the demure and reputation that Gem had.

However Gemma merely smiled, somewhat quizzically and a bit victoriously, "Wait a minute…are you Bi' then?"

"Bye?…What you want me to leave?" I said misunderstanding and sort of nervously pointing in the other direction. However, seconds longer mental processing allowed the penny to drop. "No wait you mean am I 'bi' as in bisexual?"

"Yeahhhh," replied Gemma grinning. "Aren't you gay?"

I sighed, "Gay, me? Nah I'm not gay, hell I lived with Jen remember?"

Gemma shrugged, "Well I assumed that you going out with Jen was some kind of ruse, that she is just your flat mate. Aren't you actually going out with that Roger bloke?"

"Roger?! Ah fucksake no, well I did go out with Jen for a bit, but that's another story. No, no he's my mate, awh shit not you as well, that was a joke which turned into a persistent bloody rumour several months ago! How did you get wind of that!?" I couldn't believe that people were still going on about that; it was becoming quite depressing and was messing with my already minuscule love life.

Gemma shrugged. "Well Mikey Hutcheons strongly implied to me that you and Roger were very much an item!"

'The Doc!! The fucking basterd,' I thought, 'he's clearly been doing his best to sabotage any chance I had with Gemma.' "Fucking mates eh!?" I said shaking my head. "Ho, ho, ho, mates! What'ye gonna do?" I quipped, but at the same time I was thinking I was gonna fuckin' murder the little troll bastard when I saw him next!

Our relationship quickly consolidated and we started to become a bit of a couple. I got friendly with her flatmates and often spent time there. I bought her fish and chips, which to a girl from the Black Isle seemed to suggest that we were now legally engaged; however, I wasn't quite up to speed with their customs. To an Aberdonian, fish and chips were still only a symbol that your relationship was definitely still at the casual shag stage!

During the summer of 1993 I had signed up for a bat study in the Zoology department. The data would then go towards my own final thesis. This involved driving around the countryside trying to locate bat roosts, estimating their size and then plotting the location on a map. Roger was doing a similar study involving birds during the day. So I took out my first ever student loan. We clubbed our money together and bought a small clapped out car, which we shared. Roger had this during the day and then dropped it off at my flat. I used it all night and did the same at about two or three in the morning and then cycled back to mine. Since I actually had a summer job as a postman, this was a bit of a nightmare at times. Though mostly, I really didn't mind. I had a lot of stamina back then.

About a quarter of the way through my bat study Roger and I were called into the room of our supervisor, Professor Speakman, to discuss the progress of the project and so on. The professor announced that another student would be accompanying me for a while as she needed to find a location with a sizeable bat colony to study and I had had some experience driving around trying to find these. He searched around for a name on a bit of paper "It's...oh wait a sec' here it is, erm...Kim Murray!?" This was a woman who had joined our course in second year. Roger, the Jumper and I had spoken to her in the pub after exams at one time, both tripping over ourselves to chat her up before the other one could. We had all acknowledged that she was among one of the more desirable females in the department. As Professor Speakman read out her name, he looked up at us, for some sign of acknowledgement and recognition.

Roger couldn't help himself, he nearly fell off his chair, swivelling his gaze right around to try to meet mine, mouthing "You jammie fuckin' baas..."

I cut him off in mid-sentence though and cool as a cucumber, holding my gaze with the prof. "Oh right fine, yeah I'm not sure, but I think I know who she is yeah..!" I allowed myself a metaphorical thumbs up with a wink and smile at Roger who correspondingly looked at me with an intensity that showed he was really, really pleased with me as well!

So every evening I would pick her up and we'd drive around the Aberdeenshire countryside, looking for bat roosts. I was worried that I might not have much to say to her as I usually was the case with strangers, a residue of my old self-esteem issues. However, this now seemed to not be so bad for me with women, at least; I guess hormones had at last come to my rescue without me realising it. Like the old Smiths' lyrics, "Will nature make a man of me yet?" Yes...yes it had! I guess she had rescued me at that and now she was working overtime on my behalf to make sure I felt happy in that role. All worries evaporated, of course, on the first night, as we got on very well, better than I expected and we developed quite a good friendship.

We initially had swanky bat echo detecting headphones from the Zoology Department for our investigations. These amplified ultrasound to our ears and we wandered around old farm yards and derelict buildings like a couple of shot down pilots trying to find our way home in a strange environment. The world became a strange hiss of white noise where jangling keys and the swishing of grass underfoot became strangely amplified and vivid. As we crept around one old barn, I switched on a very powerful mag-light and directed it upwards to check the roof timbers for signs of bats. Suddenly, we were deafened by the terrifyingly loud sound of what sounded like thousands of wings madly flapping frantically around us, as a chaotic blur of pigeon bodies veered through the air searching for doorways and exits in panic as they were disturbed by the bright light. It may have been scary enough without the ultrasound, but through the headphones it was like Alfred Hitchcock's *The Birds* times a million. We ran out of the barn and headed halfway across a field before we ripped the headphones off and stumbled headlong onto the pasture. It was maybe five or ten minutes before my pulse settled down from mad psycho bastard speed to just totally fucking freaked. We looked at each other in disbelief, as we knelt trying to catch our breaths and then lay back laughing. Suddenly, I saw an opportunity as I felt I had to comfort her. I put my arm around her and instead of moving away she pulled in a little closer. I couldn't believe my luck; she was gorgeous and she started kissing me, as I quickly began to unbutton her blouse. We got a little carried away as we ended up naked under the stars; perhaps it was the nice clean air of the Aberdeenshire countryside and luckily the fields were deserted of people for miles around that evening. The mag-light came in handy for finding our clothes a little while later. Ye Gods, I loved being a student!

    Although I was seeing Gemma quite regularly, we hadn't ever discussed the ground rules of our relationship. Sometimes, because of my summer postie job and bat project, I wouldn't see Gem' for a week or so. I knew she went out a lot and she had dropped the hint a couple of times that she was getting a lot of male attention in the union, as I knew she would. She even mentioned during a quick coffee at Café 52 at the Green one afternoon that a first-year guy had tried to snog her and feel her up in the union. Funny enough, this didn't worry me at all, I had this image of a snotty nosed fresher just out of school and therefore not a great threat to me and I knew Gemma could handle herself no problem. I therefore came to the conclusion that we weren't seeing each other exclusively! I didn't therefore, also, really think that seeing Kim as well would be a problem! But in truth I really wasn't thinking with my brain at all. I hadn't studied any moral philosophy courses certainly, but my educated brain helped me conclude that it was probably ok as the two women didn't know each other! Right? (And what they don't know, don't 'urt em, eh? – said in true Alfie fashion). However to make absolutely sure, I eventually decided to go to the union and sound out Gemma about it. I suppose I might have felt, maybe, a little bit guilty at this point!?

The Jumper had stayed in Aberdeen working as a librarian for the summer and was happy to come out to the union with me, as I knew Gemma would be there as usual. We arrived there a little later and joined Gemma and some of her friends in the dungeon (yes, you see before widespread mobile technology, people just sort of met in familiar places). Gemma had a head start of a few pints of the establishment's finest watery bitter. I was having a good time and the Jumper for the first time ever was having some success chatting up one of Gemma's mates. This was a minor miracle, as poor old Jumper's chat-up technique inevitably involved him lecturing women on aspects of Zoology or birdwatching (usually both actually – in that order). In hindsight, perhaps having a bunch of mates referring to him constantly as "The Jumper" was a little misleading to some women. However, this woman was just too horny to care; also, a few pints of the student beer can sometimes have this effect on a person at a later stage in the evening in the dungeon.

I decided it was best to wait and choose my moment when Gemma and I had a quieter minute or so together, as I was enjoying the socialising. Eventually, I leaned over to her. "Listen Gem," I said, "We haven't seen each other in practically two weeks; I guess this means our relationship is starting to cool off a little, yeah?"

"Yeah I supposssse so..." she replied philosophically.

"I got to ask you then, Gem; I was wondering if you've y'know...been seeing anyone else or anything in the last couple of weeks or so?"

Gemma looked solemn for a moment. "Well yeah I've had a lot of interest from a couple of guys in here recently I must admit and I did almost sort of snog this guy who's been after me for ages when he walked me home last weekend."

I sat up and slapping my hand on my thigh I breathed a sigh of relief, as I reached towards my beer glass, leaning back and crossing one leg over my knee in a relaxed care-free manner; "Oh thank fuck for that! As I've been shaggin' the woman from ma' bat project for the past week now as well anyway!"

I quickly realised that this wasn't the response she had been expecting from me, however, as her face changed from sheer astonishment to sheer anger. I barely had time to dive out of the way as a she flung herself over the table at me and landed a hefty punch right into my cheek. My beer cascaded out of my hand and sloshed right over the bewildered Jumper and horny-girl, now locked into a passionate embrace. This seemed to cool their ardour somewhat. Drinks went scattering everywhere, as Gemma clambered to get another shot in, screaming abuse at me from the top of her considerably loud voice. "You absolute ARSEHOLE! You have no respect for people, you SELFISH FUCKING BASTARD! HOW COULD YOUUU? I'm gonna KILL YA!"

I was desperate for the floor to open and swallow me as the whole place fell silent and everyone now turned to watch the free entertainment. I could see familiar faces in the crowd, people from my courses, some of them smirking, as they watched me scramble about the beer-soaked floor, trying to get up while Gemma attempted to rugby tackle me back down again. I hid my face as best as I could, while her friends tried to pull her off me and tried to placate her. I had by now developed quite a mop of long grungey hair which cascaded over my shoulders. You can not believe how much you are rendered unable to move when an angry woman grabs a fistful of your hair and repeatedly smacks your face into a wooden table. You are completely powerless to retaliate. She continued her tirade against me, even after her friends had managed to prise her off of me. I walked away with my hands in the air in surrender, as that's just how I felt. Women lining the bar and corridor glared at me, as if I was some Nazi criminal leaving a war tribunal. My scalp was throbbing like hell as well, where hair had been tugged clean out by the roots. My face felt swollen and I thought there would be wood grain lines etched on my cheek. Fuck me, female fights really hurt!! I'd much rather just get a kick in the teeth!

Walking away, she shouted, "Just get out of my sight before I do you some real damage!"

I shuddered and felt my testicles literally shrink, as if to go into hiding; I'm sure she meant it as well. Meanwhile, my poor mate, MeOl'Jumper, hastily tried to speak with her friend to exchange numbers, but he never got the chance. Gemma rounded on him and I heard her shouting at him as I walked up the stairs, "What the hell do you want? If you value your testicles, you'll fuck off as well right now!" He caught up with me surprisingly quickly as I was heading out the front door. The bouncers smiled broadly at me, as I stepped onto the street; this had obviously given them a bit more entertainment than usual. I was thinking that none of them had appeared to my friggin' rescue, but then I didn't really blame them – they might have just made things worse anyway! The Jumper was right behind me and without turning around I said, "Stop looking at me; I just know you're fucking looking at me! Ok?" I knew I was going to have to make it up to him for a *looong* time to come. I thought of the one place I wouldn't be judged and where I could get away from everything. "I'm goin' down to Don's work to get stoned! Ye comin'?" By the time we got to Don's I thought the Jumper was going to start sobbing on my shoulder and it was me that had to comfort him!

I had been oblivious to the fact that she cared for me a lot more than I had realised. I hadn't read any of the signs whatsoever or had just dismissed them, as I was having too much fun and since she hadn't said anything…well!? I had thoughtlessly taken everything she had said at total face value, not understanding the mind-games at all. She had been trying to provoke a reaction from me, attempting to make me jealous. Obviously I had missed a few meetings on how to decipher women's signals. I felt that I just didn't have the common sense sometimes!

In that situation, you always have your mates, especially with the much appreciative Doc, who was only too glad to impart to me his vast experience of relationships with women. Clearly, this was probably karma for my schadenfreude of enjoying his misfortunes in the union with Gemma on too many occasions! If it was karma then I must have been really bad as, as it happened, very soon after the Gemma incident my bat project switched to focusing on gathering data on the bats hunting and feeding habits at one location only. So my new project involved taking a few measurements here and there like temperature and wind speed and then sitting in the car in the dark or on the swings in the middle of a pitch-dark play-park, waiting for cassette tapes to run out while they recorded the bat activity of Daubenton's bats feeding over the river in Stonehaven (a quaint little fishing town about twenty miles south of Aberdeen). So out of the passenger seat went the curvy Kim and in her place plopped the dozy Doc. Yeah, the same thought passed through my mind at the time as well; never dump a witch badly...just don't do it!

I must admit, for someone like myself, *i.e.* a bit of a goth and a Pagan, this was a very appropriate project to undertake. I found bats fascinating and before this project I hadn't heard of the Daubenton's bat, or the water bat as it is sometimes called. These bats are a little bigger than the common Pipistrelle bat and fly close to stretches of water, occasionally skimming insects off the top of the water with a special membrane stretched between their back feet. Long stretches of water, such as canals and rivers, were perfect habitats for them.

So driving out to the lonely park every evening would have been mind numbingly boring and a bit spooky were it not for the company of The Doc, who during these occasions was only too glad to impart to me his vast experience of relationships with women, clearly relishing my bad experience with Gemma. I suppose he was the one person who could truly empathise with me at this point, much to my dismay.

On the second day of the new project, I had driven to the park with Don, Hippie Davie and The Doc. As dusk fell, the three of us stood at the bank of the river awaiting the spectacle. Professor Speakman had taken me out the day before to show me the bats and I was amazed to see them skim the water and hear their calls translated on the hand-held bat boxes. Now as I stood at virtually the same spot with my three mates, I was acutely worried that the collective plume of dope smoke and whinging about the damp grass was going to scare off the bats from this river and ruin my project.

"Why are we coming all the way to Stonehaven then?" said Hippie Davie curiously.

"Well, this is a perfect stretch of river; it has calm areas and much riffled bits, not too big and all accessible from this park," I said in somewhat exasperated tones for the umpteenth time.

The Doc's thick-lensed spectacles trained on the water surface, his bulging, magnified right eye searching around suspiciously, like 'Mad-Eye Moody' off Harry Potter, in disbelief. "Are you ha'in' iz oan? Fuckin' water bats! I canna say av iver heard o' a bastard watery bat!"

"I've seen stranger things – who's to say what kind of creatures inhabit parks like this at night!" exclaimed Don thoughtfully through black lip gloss in my defence, a serious frown now exacerbated by the thick white make-up plastered over most of his face, the rest obscured by a large bat shape crossing over his eyes and temples. It was sweet that he had decided to mark the occasion by dressing appropriately.

"Well cunts like you for a start!" interjected Hippie Davie, alluding to Don's reputation for patrolling parks in Aberdeen to satisfy his voracious sexual appetite. We all sniggered, including Don, who acknowledged this eagerly as usual.

The Doc still looking puzzled and frowning deep in thought, speculated out loud for a moment, "I can see how a bat can be sorta-waterproof right enough, coz they do look a bit plastic onywy don't they? Nae hair or onything, like?...A bit like 'em chow-wa-wa things." Don looked in his direction and nodded in recognition, as The Doc continued, "But you'd think they'd get swept awa' in this watar though, right enough!"

Don promptly agreed. "Probably be ok if it's calm like that bit o'er there!" He pointed up the stream a few yards.

For fuck's sake; I realised that I had promised to take them out to see water bats feeding on the river! They had taken that to mean diving under it, chasing little fish like gannets or guillemots or something. I slapped my hand on my forehead.

Hippie Davie who was that bit more with it, despite smoking three times more dope than any of us put together, shook his head, "They don't swim in the water ya daft bastards! They obviously just fly above it! Don't tell me you were waiting for bats to start emerging from the water!?" He laughed condescendingly, but then even he contemplated this for a second, the dope obviously taking hold of his imagination, "They wouldn't though, would they?!"

All three of them then slowly turned their heads towards the water's surface in anticipation.

"Oh fuck, no, no of course not, Jeezuz, they just skim along the top occasionally dipping their feet on the top to scoop up insects with their membrane, a bit like swallows, you must have seen a swallow take an insect off the water surface?" I said.

"Really!?" said Hippie Davie incredulously, obviously finding this as nearly as unlikely as bats popping out of the water."

"Oh yeah," I said authoritatively, "the water bat is one of Britain's more common bat; habitats like this are ideal for it. I'd be very surprised if we didn't see any around here very soon actually." I nodded authoritatively, as I scanned around the riverside whilst looking at my watch with a knowing expression on my face, knowing full well that they were here about this time last night with Professor Speakman! "I'm surprised you guys have never heard of them, to be honest!"

Eventually, of course, the bats did appear and we watched them skirt a few inches above the water in regular beats up and down the river. Occasionally, they would veer upwards with expert flying precision and dart back along the surface again, sometimes missing each other by centimetres in the fading light of twilight. "This is better than the red arrows!" said Don.

"It's the red arrows for the nocturnal" said Hippie Davie, tuning into Don's mind.

I liked the feeling of twilight and the change of wildlife which occurs then. You can see the numbers of swifts and swallows begin to diminish and the odd early bat venture out as the two nightshift and dayshift species overlap for several minutes. Then the light fades and night takes hold. Night creatures often seemed more quiet and serene than their daytime counterparts and the bats were perfect examples of this, completely silent – or rather, to most they are – and perfectly adapted to the darkness. When you look at them closely, you can see they are clearly rodent-like and you can imagine their very distant ancestors being something like that. In this regard, they are the perfect examples of the wonders of evolution. Their flight is so sophisticated and fast, turning on a sixpence in mid-air, manoeuvring at speeds and angles no human machine can yet match. Coupled with this they have developed an astounding ability to navigate by sound in complete darkness. For them texture is their colour. They live in a world of texture and feeling that we can scarcely even imagine. And yet they filled me with a spiritual fascination also, as the dainty little bodies were associated with luck and protection in China, though filled people with dread and horror in this country. I had nothing but respect for them. I tried to tune into their spirit, as I used to on my forays into the countryside many years earlier; I would stand there trying to feel and interact with a group mind or essence of the bat on the astral plane. Well, you can laugh, but they were lucky for me.

Eventually, after setting the tapes on record near the river bank at defined intervals (by myself as the others complained too much about stingey nettles, midgies and rodents) we adjourned to sit on the swings in the darkness for a bit. Though, I think the unspoken consensus was that this just felt far too creepy as we gradually congregated on the roundabout. It was somehow just wrong to sit on a swing in the dark (they make a fucking eerier repetitive rusty chain whine for a start, which sounds like the prelude to just about any horror situation in any 1970s horror film that you can imagine. Strange when you think about it; as the same sound on a summer's day is more evocative of ice-cream and fun).

A midnight spin on the roundabout, however, was much more in keeping with our relaxed states of mind. All four of us lay down symmetrically, spinning softly around getting nicely stoned whilst staring up at the Milky Way slowly spinning above, which was quite visible in the dark of Stonehaven's park. Don would take it upon himself to perpetuate the movement of the roundabout with his trailing boots jangling with chains over the side. We watched satellites passing overhead and contemplated the universe's vastness. This is where we got to know Hippie Davie's philosophical notion of the universe, honed to perfect from masses of weed, smoked since his early teens.

"What do you think when you stare up at the stars then?" he said sombrely as we all lay plastered to a segment of our revolving habitats.

"Nuit the Egyptian Goddess!" exclaimed The Doc emphatically. "...And the underworld!" As always he mentioned the underworld. I think he thought of it as a sort of middle earth and perhaps there was a secret Shaman bus going there three times a week. If there was then he'd be fucking on it for sure! I looked up at the glimmering vastness of the spiral arm of the Milky Way spanning my vision ahead of me.

The obvious sprang to mind immediately. "The Klangers!" I said at once.

The laughter of instant recognition rang around the roundabout. "Aye the Klangers, the fuckin' Klangers! Definitely without a doubt!" laughed The Doc.

Don started whistling in Klanger fashion, which prompted the rest of us to follow suit. Pretty soon we were virtually conversing in Klanger, which we thought was hilarious. We didn't tire of this for some time, until Don decided to be the soup dragon which prompted another round of merry-go-round madness.

"It must be the play-park bringing out the kids in us," I said. "Were you often laying stoned on a roundabout as a kid then?" said Don.

"Aye," piped up Hippie Davie and we all went off again.

"Were they little pigs or something?" said The Doc; and we all thought for a second.

Hippie Davie retorted, with some authority, "Nah Klangers aren't pigs man, they walk on two legs and live in holes!"

"With dustbin lids for doors," I added.

Hippie Davie continued his line of argument, "Pigs live in pens! So I don't think they're pigs! Plus, you know, they live on a fuckin' MOON anyway!"

"Well they fuckin' look like pigs to me!" The Doc said defensively.

Don then piped up, "Could be jist a sort of Moon pig I suppose!"

I smirked. I had the answer. "Look, pigs canna whistle; it's anatomically and physically impossible for them to do so! So Hippie Davie is right, the Klangers are not pigs or even related to pigs for that matter!"

Hippie Davie turned his mop-like dreadlocked head towards me. "Is that a fact?"

"That is a fucking fact!" I said finally.

The Doc seemed pleased with this and Don made a "Hoommm!" sound in acknowledgement. I couldn't help but smile broadly to myself as I envisaged The Doc exclaim with confidence in polite company that he could tell that Klangers couldn't be pigs, as he'd researched it in some Zoology book! He often seemed obsessed about having "researched" something, which meant he'd seen it on T.V, read it in the paper or heard it from someone who he thought knew what they were talking about.

"Oliver Postgate," I said, "now there was a childhood hero, Noggin the Nog, Bagpus! Sheer genius!"

"Yeah," said Don in approval, those stories were out of this fucking world." There then ensued at least half-an-hour's conversation about Bagpus and the Klangers, the Klangers finally getting the vote as the most brilliant and imaginative children's show ever.

"The soup dragon!? The fuckin' iron chicken that lived in a nest in the sky!? The music tree!?" I exclaimed somewhat incredulously. "What were they all about, how did they come up with that stuff?"

"Never mind out of this world; out of his fuckin' face more like!" The Doc then piped up with a swipe at Hippie Davie. There seemed to be a bit of tension between the two, I never knew what had gone before between them within Paul's group. "You'll be writing the next series of Rainbow then, Davie?" quipped Doc.

This was easy meat for Hippie Davie, "Aye and I'll be typecasting you as Zippy the fucking gimp!"

I have to say, it was a very fitting put down; The Doc could definitely play that part and we all wished he had a big zip we could pull across his mouth!

Don was now in his happy zone and began to reflect, "Rainbow, that was such a deviant show, Rod, Jane and Freddy! There was a happy little threesome and Zippy was a definitely a little fucking gimp wasn't he? Couldn't be anything else. And I always wondered whether Bungle had an orifice of any kind?!

"Fuck's-sake Don!" I said, "leave it will ye? That's my childhood memories you're sabotaging! Bungle's orifice! Oh for-fuck's-sake!"

The Doc giggled. "Bungle likes it bungled right up the bungle bum hole!" Then he seemed to get animated. "Hey I bet in them old days the guy that played Bungle right, I bet he took his costume home and gave his wife one with it on, you know; I mean you would wouldn't ya?" He gurgled, a strange sinister sound in the back of his throat, clearly amusing himself, as he got carried away with the evil thought fermenting in his mind. "I bet he even used the same voice as well as he gave it to 'er Wwoo-ooh yes, George said I would like ladies!'" He then snorted and started giggling in a rather manic way. "Oh aye, I bet his wife has some real bad fuckin' mintal problems now efter that eh?" He laughed like a little evil gurgling gremlin a few feet away as the three of us kept silent.

Not quite knowing what to say and feeling a little sick actually, I lifted my head slightly to look at Don who was shaking his head and staring at The Doc. He looked like he wanted to bring his Doc Martins down and squash him like a bug.

Hippie Davie, thankfully, interrupted this line of thought "That's interesting! When confronted by the impossible reality of the universe our minds revert to childhood memories!"

I'd almost forgotten that Hippie Davie had initiated this line of thought for a reason. "Why so?" I said. "

"Well childhood is the time when we make sense of the world; our versions of reality are set in stone when we're infants eh?"

"Yeah," I mused, we learn our language and our roles in society, you could say that we're socialised from the word go!"

"Yeah, yeah man, like, that's it exactly," agreed Hippie Davie with enthusiasm, as I helped him underline his point.

"Without a doubt!" nodded The Doc.

Hippie Davie continued, "So our notion of everything is rooted in what we hold dear to be true, childhood memories are our most emotionally evocative!"

We looked up at the stars whilst Hippie Davie's words, fixed to one side of us, spiralled overhead into the majesty of the night's sky. "How we relate to the spiritual dimension is strongly linked to our social ideas of reality and what we are taught from a young age," he continued.

"Indoctrination!" added Don.

"Yeah," said Hippie Davie; "That's why they get us at a young age, coz it's linked to our emotions, our feelings about what we are taught is right and wrong, it's very powerful." Hippie Davie dragged on his spliff and blew smoke out thoughtfully in a long drawn out breath, kinda like his argument was. "But the Buddhists and Taoists were sussed when they realised that you can't make the divine fit ideas like that; it's too arbitrary! Our religion right? It's based on something you feel and we interpret the male and female, the yin and yang in nature as God and Goddess! But there are probably hundreds of Gods and Goddesses in the world, some lost to posterity, some rediscovered!"

"Yes!" I said "and some religions in the Pacific Islands may say the moon is masculine and the sun is feminine, whilst to us it's the reverse! It's all just a point of view, depending on the cycle of the crops where you live at the end of the day."

"I've often thought that!" Don further added. "The Romans just took all the Greek gods didn't they?"

Hippie Davie nodded, "And the Christians came here and labelled our gods as devils; as you say, it's all just a point of view!"

"That's obvious," I replied, "probably my vision of the gods differs from yours and every other Pagan! Let's face it, Pagans can't agree on anything!"

"Too true brother!" said Hippie Davie re-lighting another spliff, the shock of light glaring off the frame of the roundabout and the smoke drifting up towards the impossibly high twinkle of starlight. "My point is that *if* you are looking for a suitable pantheon, why borrow from stuff we know very little about or comes from a different age or even culture?! Go back to childhood, man. You might think of the Klangers when you look up there man, but it only means one thing to me and it's what I base my whole fucking idea of religion on."

We all looked up in wonder at the wonderful night sky above. What was he talking about?

"*Star Wars!*" exclaimed Hippie Davie in an awe struck voice.

I waited for the laugh which would have signalled that he taking the piss out of us, but it never came. "You serious?!" I asked.

"Never more brothers," he said quite emphatically. I was starting to realise why Newmachar, Mags and Erneh might not appeal to him after all. "Think about it," he urged, as he sat up now quite animated, feeling a sermon coming on, "Why try to conjure up some image of Dionysius or Osiris or Diana? I have only vague notions of them! Do you? I'm no scholar and I don't pretend to be!" I wasn't sure, but I felt the bastard was looking at me when he said that. "Coz we didn't get any of *that* at primary school, it has never been a part of our reality, it's all mere mythology to me...In the old days, people were brought up from childhood with the Pagan gods, but we have not! We've been chopped from the root from our own culture. The history was burned and re-written. We're fucking brainwashed into thinking Goddesses are evil! Goddesses mind you...! The soul of the universe is untrustworthy and evil. We're fucked brothers....However, we do watch T.V. and films! I rejected the old Sunday school con early on, thanks to liberal parents and common sense and I can replace that with much more modern and thus relevant notions of good and evil!"

Hippie Davie's new idea of using Star Wars as a source of religious inspiration seemed to me to be even more fanciful than Sunday school stories. "Oh yeah, with Wookies and Princess Leia thrown in!" I said a bit overly sardonically.

"Hey man, now you're offending my faith, that's not cool, I don't rail on yer horned god and queen of the fucking fairies now do I?"

I clenched my lips, accepting his point. "When you put it like that, Hippie Davie, then I suppose you don't...sorry dude!"

He forged on, "Think about it, the whole gamut is there, the force, nature centric religion and Yoda as an old Taoist priest! Good versus evil, people versus empire; look around, it's the perfect metaphor for today's world. Evil exists as a 'politically driven will' now, to hold us all down under the evil empire, with its relentless plundering of resources and slavery in the form of the capitalist model. Capitalism is the evil empire consuming the world, making a disturbance in the force with its evil technology. Their dominant religions waging wars with our personal freedoms and energies.

As he made his undeniably factual points, he became more animated and annoyed. "Don't you see, everything's commercial and economics rule the planet. The new religions are based on the consumer paradigm; we are informed through biased, controlled media, this is the new clergy, telling us what to do, how to think! Lucas, though, slipped the ideas of environmental-based religion and good against the evil imperialism right under the radar into mass consciousness and how? By using the very mechanism of commercialism: media, toys and mass marketing! It was a fucking master stroke to wake us up from childhood onwards!"

I pondered this for a moment. It smacked of a combination of excessive drug use, too much thinking and conspiracy theories. "Hippie Davie you have excelled yourself there!" I exclaimed.

Hippie Davie sighed, his voice making a last stand against the stars. "Think back to what was your first ever example in this society of any real emotive reference to the Tao, magick, a feminine warrior archetype, justice and a sense of aligning the will against the odds? What was your first ever kindling sense of a 'calling' to that 'inner-hero' part of yourself? How do you think these aspects lodged themselves in your subconscious long before the word Wicca hit your conscious brain? You talk about the goddess calling you Sean, well I'm betting *Star Wars* was the main catalyst behind that, whether you're aware of it or not!"

I shook my head; "Coincidence! It's a good story a modern day western, but all good stories have these elements, Hippie Davie!"

The silhouette of a hippie shrugging somewhere in the black of the night filtered through to my peripheral vision; "Maybe it is, maybe it isn't, doesn't matter. It's there, the mainstream religions are dying and they serve the system now, but their influence will always inhibit natural magical progression. *Star Wars*, on the other hand, can speak to us all! We Jedis have to fight this and get back to nature, resist the system! I tell you, you can spend your whole life thinking about what Lucas has created and you'll still find new meanings!"

I don't know if it was Hippie Davie's weed or the hypnotic revolving sky above, but it all made some weird insane sense. The Doc was first to acknowledge this point, "Aye, aye, course it diz, I mean chaos magicians have deconstructed the mechanics o' ritual now, for instance some magicians invoke the four spice girls for their quarters in circles for example, without a doubt!"

I had more than a sneaking suspicion that he been party to this conversation with Paul Alder sometime in the past.

"S'right," said Hippie Davie, "But they're mental of course!" he said, being intentionally ironic. "But that's the jist of it yeah; its power is in its emotional linkage to my notion of justice and the Divine. I can thank George Lucas for it, else I might have none at all and hence he is my personal prophet!"

"Is there a church, can I join?" I asked. "What are the holidays like?"

"The holidays are crap, but you get your own light-saber and the right to toss off to Carrie Fischer any time you want." He turned to Don "Or Harrison Ford," he said considerately.

I laughed. "Well I'm sold; you got me on Carrie Fisher!"

Then Hippie Davie's voice became curiously sober. "Seriously though, this film can unite the world, we've all seen it, there is nothing to fight over or have wars about and we all have the same link to its spiritual aspects! My dream is to unite the world through the church of Jedi; in fact I have further come to conclude that it may be our only hope as a species.A shared human interest kick starting global populations without borders or creed!"

Could I be sitting next to the future science fiction Martin Luther King? "I have a dream," I said and waved my hands in a mock evangelist way.

"I sure do brother!" he said somberly.

Don by now had stopped and was standing up and straightening his clothes; "Reminds me of thon Kenny Everett dude."

"Aye definitely, the boy wi' the big hands, the boy wi' the big hands," interjected The Doc excitedly, also standing up.

The next few minutes, much to Hippie Davie's chagrin, saw the three of us prancing around the roundabout waving our hands in the air like Baptist preachers singing "Brutha, Brutha, Brutha –lee-love!" at the top of our voices.

Later that night, Professor Speakman made an impromptu visit to the park to check in with me and see if everything was going all right. He just lived up the road and came by at times. As we spun around in slow motion on the roundabout, virtually oblivious to any other rhythm other than that of the spinning summer sky, we became aware of the car lights flickering through the trees and the car coming along the path. As I recognised the figure of professor Speakman lit by small lights on the side of a changing room building. Don slammed on the brakes with his muckle boots as we jumped up and made our way quickly back towards the car park. To my frustration, I found that no matter how hard I tried, I couldn't help but stumble into Don, as much as Hippie Davie or The Doc couldn't help stumbling into me and into one another. Being forced to jump up from a roundabout stoned in the dark of night seemed to have caused much confusion within unassuming brain cells at that time.

As we loomed into the triangle of light cast by the one lamp illuminating one side of the changing rooms building, Professor Speakman spun around to be met with the scene of four zombie-like figures staggering in uncoordinated fashion out of the darkness towards him. As we were all feeling a little ill by now, we were moaning and looking a little white-faced. It must have been like a scene from some Italian horror B movie. The bat-faced goth, complete with top hat and jangling chains reminiscent of Jacobe bloody Marley, the leather-clad, lank-haired bespectacled witch doctor looking like fucking Dracula's assistant 'Egor' in the dark, the taller dreadlocked stoner hippie and the indie/grunge-goth/punk dude in black combats and dusty combat jacket. Professor Speakman looked back perplexed, almost routed to the spot for a second. I heard him mutter "Christ!" and I suppose he was wishing he had studied tigers in some dark Siberian forest instead of this. Understandably he began to back off towards his car, his hand clasping the car keys, no doubt in readiness to decapitate Don with it if he had to. He needn't have worried, though, because the complicated one-person swing gate at the entrance of the play-park was proving far too difficult to co-ordinate anyway, as Don went first and began to wrestle with it, causing a bit of a bottleneck. After a few unsure pulls at the gate, Don then went flying headfirst over it in a spectacularly fast movement, his giant boots glinting in the moonlight, as they swayed up into view. At the same time, The Doc began to make retching sounds as he flailed helplessly backwards into a small bush. I was trying to catch Don's flailing feet and got a kick in the teeth; this together with The Doc's retching made me suddenly feel very ill as well, a veritable 'whitey in the nightey' was fast approaching!

"Ah Professor Speakman, I'll be with you in a minute!" I said before reeling sideways into a bush to be sick.

I eventually managed to explain about the roundabout, but to my eternal embarrassment I think he had made his mind up about how I passed the time doing nocturnal Zoology! Thus the batbox bunch, as we called ourselves, was tentatively born.

As the summer wore on however, neither Don nor Hippie Davie could make many evenings. The Doc, though actually insisted on helping; I think he had nothing else to do and felt this was a worthwhile endeavour. Hippie Davie had offered to help a few times but proved to be a bit unreliable; who knew a hippie would have no concept of time!? Actually, Hippie Davie had a habit of just disappearing off the radar for extended periods of time, two or even three weeks here and there. He lived in digs with a bunch of other hippies and nobody ever knew his whereabouts when asked and they never had a phone! Hippie Davie would just turn up in town after a spell, looking even more wild and carefree than normal. When asked, he would simply reply, "Just had to escape the urban jungle for a while!" The Doc and I suspected he was with some wild-hearted gypsy woman in her erotic caravan, having excesses of drugs and sex while we remained firmly bonded to good old mundane reality!

Don was working most nights so very rarely managed to come along with me. The Doc, though, was un-fathomly reliable, waiting for me most nights clutching a packed lunch, keenness lighting up his face as I pulled the car in near to his house. I suppose it must have been a boring life for the unemployed Doc, living at his mum's house watching *Eastenders* every other night and sipping tea. So he obviously looked forward to the nightly bat-watch, even though most of the night involved sitting in the dark in the car talking and smoking rollies. I suppose it was because I was prepared in these hours to listen to him ramble on and on. It was dark and lonely so I was very grateful of The Doc's company, even if it meant listening to him wax lyrical on many aspects of magick and the craft. Or sex and the craft, or magick and sex; or just bloody go on and on about sex. He often tried to convince me that, whilst Shamanic training in Canada, one of his female teachers would regularly select him during rituals and engage with him in various tantric sexual activities, right there in the magick circle. I couldn't imagine a worse sight; that would put me right off my potato salad and sausage rolls that would!

Of course, we knew he was full of it; The Doc simply didn't see the difference between bullshit and reality, or if he did, he ignored it. This is the problem with Paganism; it's very anarchistic but doesn't offer any proper guidance. There is no widespread formal training or study framework. There are loads of books and websites, but how does a person know which are useful or factually accurate and not just someone's opinions?

To his credit, though, he came out with me nearly every evening without fail; such was the schedule to get a large amount of data over the summer. Often Roger on day shift would be held up by the inadequate roads for the peak time Aberdeen traffic. Consequently, this meant getting the car late and so it became counter-productive to go all the way to The Doc's mum's house on the other side of town so I would go around to his girlfriend Pamela's flat, which was en-route and often wait until he got there. I don't know why he didn't live there, but it seemed she sent him away every morning back up to his mums. At first I couldn't believe that he had a regular girlfriend as he hadn't actually mentioned her before. So I was very intrigued to say the least and you could have knocked me over with a feather when I first met her. I was actually amazed that she was a real person the first time he introduced me to her! Pamela was strangely perfectly normal, bloody good looking and civil even, as well as very intelligent and polite. She was a professional, driven career woman with aspirations, working in a high-flying job for the NHS. She had a circle of well-educated friends that included doctors and various health care workers. At first I wondered how they could be a couple, as The Doc was; well, let's face it, the exact opposite of her in every way! So the idea of him spending time here with Pamela hosting very middle class dinner parties for her professional chums and reminiscing over the last Will Self interview in the Guardian was just not something I could readily imagine.

The first thing that came to my mind was that The Doc had used some evil Witch Doctor magick to hypnotise and enslave her in some way, or some awesomely powerful charm that made everything that he said be heard as witty, insightful and sensible banter. But then I realised that only a very select branch of magicians could pull off something as powerful as that and they were all employed working full time for the government.

However, it quickly transpired that Pamela was absolute gold-dust for me, as she was not in the slightest bit impressed or affected by Doc's bullshit. She very clearly was the dominant of the pair; she would enjoy shooting him down at any time he tried to boast about something, even scolding him to the point of bullying. It renewed my faith in Karma at every turn. The Doc didn't like this being on show and remarkably seemed to think he could conceal it from me. He tried at various times to change the arrangement and have me keep picking him up at his Ma's house in Torry. But this was way up the hill on the other side of the city, whereas Pamela's flat in Ferryhill was five minutes from mine by car and just next to the main road South to Stonehaven and the bats. Thankfully for me, she wouldn't hear of it, "No Michael, there's no point in Sean going all the way to Torry at rush hour," she said, "you just get yourself here on time."

I never understood why he was always late; all he had to do was get up around lunchtime and get himself into town. Yet he was always held up. What could a guy who was unemployed and living with his mother possible be held up by? He didn't appear to do anything at all except fuck about on his guitar and watch daytime T.V. The other thing that amazed me to the point of annoyance was his perpetual amazement that he was late. He'd come in and look at his watch with a studied look of profound bemusement. Then he would shrug, as if losing an hour or so was nothing worth thinking about. Perhaps he was being abducted by aliens on a daily basis; he certainly fitted the profile of their regular clientele. Mind you, I did appreciate him being late as I enjoyed Pamela's food and quite liked having a chat with her. I never liked eating food that The Doc had prepared, not even a cup of tea; he always seemed to have a snotty nose.

Pamela was very blunt and assertive and I certainly would not mess with her. She was quite strong looking, complementing The Doc's meek physique. When he came in, invariably late, he would act very cagey, "Yoo been here long?" At first I took offence, thinking that he was worried that I might make a move on Pamela but I very soon cottoned on that he was more worried about what our conversations might have been about, *i.e.* namely him and his antics with Pamela.

I was, as usual, sitting down to curry or some other nicely cooked meal when there was a knock on the door; it always amused me that he had to knock first. Pamela shouted, "Come away in Michael!" and he timidly open the door and then shut it very quietly, as if by training. He would mumble something like "Yes Pam," which sounded more like 'yes ma'am,' the way he said it (you've got to wonder actually!?).

Upon seeing me, he began manically motioning with his head that we should go, not even daring to utter a sound it seemed.

"I'm no finished ma curry." I shouted through. Pamela piped up looking down towards the hall. "Oh Michael stop bein' a pain and make us all a cup of tea." The Doc automatically headed for the kettle as if programmed to obey. It killed me that she kept calling him Michael in that way, it seemed like a name he was desperately trying to shrug off, a private moniker that exposed his true boy-like status.

"Aye c'mon Michael, make the tea," I chipped in emulating Pamela's command, enjoying his servitude.

The Doc sneered and gave me the finger, which made me smirk, triumphant at his obviously ruffled response. Pamela sensed an opportunity to reveal some of the real dynamics of their relationship and called through from the other room, "Yes you like to obey, don't you Michael?" There was an odd sexual satisfaction to her voice that telegraphed to me that this was a prelude to some sexual turn on for both of them. The Doc grinned nervously, but I could tell that he was more than complicit in this master and servant scenario, in a way that made me feel a bit awkward. It was becoming obvious just how dominant she was with The Doc.

Aside from the weird sexual antics, it was obvious that Pamela was the adult of the pair. She seemed more like his mother sometimes than a girlfriend as she had a career, paid all the bills and basically did everything while he just appeared and pretty much did what he was told. Now I have no problem at all with what people get up to; it's part of the human condition to indulge in such games and we're a very imaginative species after all. However, this seemed very strange to me as The Doc made it clear to all of us on a regular basis that he seemed to like to be the dominant one with females. So this was a strange topsy-turvy version of how he portrayed himself.

Out in the car afterwards, The Doc's whole demeanour changed. "Qui'ens, eh? Like to act like they're in charge aroond a hoose!"

"She looks like she's in charge a' right!" I smirked.

The Doc pondered on; "I da' mind helping' the lassie oot like, ye kaen, hoose work and stuff, she relies on me!" he mused, as we turned the corner from her street.

"It's her hoose tho' Doc isn't it?" I said.

"Wha' oh nut no, it's joint, joint; definitely without a doubt...Well...actually it is mair mine, but I canna hack bidin' wi' her twenty four - seven, you know how it is!? I have to have ma freedom, I like ma ain space too much!" he said resolutely and before I could raise any further point, "S'why I shack up at my ma's hoose, back te ma ain room, ma ain space! I fucking telt her straight; a sez, a man's gotta hae freedom and if you stay here with me…you hiv tae understand that I will come and go when I please, kaen? So I'm movin' oot for a while, a sez, I let her bide there though kaen? She kaen's the score! I let her bide there, it helps her oot, like!"

He looked thoughtful for a moment as he brought out another cigarette, now far more relaxed than he was indoors, clearly reading from a script he was inventing in his head.

"She didna like it, though, keeps begging me to come back like! She's the type o' lassie that needs a man aboot kaen?"

As always, I knew just to make the right noises. "Oh yeah?"

The Doc acknowledged this with a knowing nod. "Terrified!"

He waited for me to acknowledge this. "She is?"

"Oh aye, oh yeaahh; S'why I knock you see!? Coz when I just walk in, it scares her! And there's jist nae tellin' when I'm gonna come wandering back in onywy!" He continued in full flow now. "I keep an eye on her though. She has nae sense o' independence see?! Too spoilt by her ma, s'why I come in and do a bit of housework an' that, she's nae use on her ain!"

I couldn't help but assert my observations.

"She seems fairly independent to me Doc!" He turned his head far to the right and waved the very notion away.

"Naaaah, that's just an act like, the hale 'tough lassie' thing you mean? Naah, when we're alone she's like a pussy cat."

'More like a fuckin man-eating lion,' I thought.

It was a strange set up. The Doc didn't stay there and they weren't officially going out, but they acted like a couple. We had gone out a few times as a joint couple with my old art student girlfriend Jen. Although we had split up we were still friendly as she often appeared back in Aberdeen and stayed in the flat from time to time. Jen become quite friendly with Pamela. This meant there was plenty of cosy "coupley" things arranged like the pub or cinema and driving down to 'T in the park' music festival and so on. Occasions like these revealed just how much the "man of the partnership" The Doc really was as she'd often make him do her bidding, then reward him with a swift slap across the back of the head when he invariably cocked things up! It was most amusing to me and often I wished that Don and Hippie Davie could see it too, as this Stan Laureleque bitch role was the perfect opposite to how he always portrayed himself with us.

I often did feel sorry for him though, make no mistake. He told me that he had moved out after a big row during one of her dinner parties with friends. They had been an item way back when they were both students years ago, The Doc being that bit older than myself and the other guys. Pamela had clearly grown up and moved on; whilst The Doc, after dropping out of college, remained the same, with the same old made-up cool history and probably the exact same Bauhaus T-shirt. I guess she had been impressed with him once and lord knows, he might have been half-decent looking in the Eighties, but it probably had helped that the goth club (the venue in Aberdeen's harbour area) had been really dark inside. The Doc told me about the argument that led to him saying he'd had enough and now refused to stay there, but I could easily read between the lines.

I found out from Jen a bit later that Pamela had had a few friends around for a civilised meal and chat. She served two kinds of wine – red and white. Her friends also brought wine, of varieties both white and red. The Doc, who is not a refined wine drinker by any means, gulped glass after glass like a kid drinking lemonade (and if he mixed drinks he turned green and got out of his mind very fast, him being only a little guy of some five foot six). On top of that, he'd been to the pub to have a couple of swift ones to settle his nerves. Most people might have some semblance of self-awareness to anticipate what might happen if they did this all night. However, The Doc never seemed to learn; the practice of thinking ahead was not one of his strengths. By the end of the starter, The Doc was already slurring his words and the permanent frown on his forehead deepened, as he found following the conversation difficult. However, he desperately tried to conceal his confusion, whilst gradually losing the grip of the on-going social repartee. The burgeoning Mariana trench-like furrows on his brow, together with his bulging lips, must have given him the expression of a chimpanzee that had been just shown the solution to the Rubik's cube! However soon after, the aggression phase kicked in! On cue a comment by an M.D. on the opposite side of the table that homeopathy was "as much good as taking tap water for a broken leg" started to irritate him. The Doc retorted with what he decided was the most direct and appropriate response.

"At's actual *shite* by the way!"

The young doctor stammered, "Yeah, exactly, it's utter nonsense..!"

The Doc interrupted to clear up the point. "Nah mate, nah I mean, atz shite, aboot it bein'...shite, it's nay shite at a', ehhhh actually. It's..." He looked around in a drunken glaze and then appealed to the young female medical student to his right nudging her just a tad too inappropriately, "Fit would the opposite o' shite be onywy?"

Pamela was oblivious to any of this, pleasantly humming to herself, as she took the roasted potatoes out of the oven.

Another guest, feeling a little embarrassed and annoyed by The Doc's impertinence towards the young medic, answered his question, a little condescendingly, "Good shit I expect!" A nervous, conceited chuckle then rippled around the table.

The Doc felt further defensive as he sensed that these medical people were being judgmental not only of him but to alternative therapies and thus to all Paganism! That was what was wrong with the country, was why he couldn't get Bach flower remedies on the NHS to clear his snotty nose. He reached for his glass, raising it to his lips, creepily keeping one bulging right eye on the man who'd made the original comment as he slowly chugged the wine down.

The man shrugged. "Each to his own opinion, I suppose; that's what makes the world go around!"

The Doc plonked his glass down and put his hand on his chin in a thoughtful way, as if cogitating philosophically. He then leaned over jabbing an unsteady finger in his direction.

"Aye, at's the thing, the world goes around and around, but naaaaaeeebudy understands it, but it still happens! 'S same as the homo-opathy, it jist happens, but because you don't understand it, then...then people 'at believe and do understand have to suffer, iz a' I'm sayin'." He burped, as he nodded his head in a gesture of defiance then put his finger on the table to emphasise his moot point.

The young doctor looked down for a second a little embarrassed, trying to bite his tongue, but he couldn't help it, he wasn't going to sit there and listen to this spurious nonsense.

"Well that's a matter of opinion, I suppose, but I prefer to look at the facts. The fact is, it is quite well understood why the Earth spins, it's called inertia! And homeopathy has been evaluated a number of times now and the figures just do not suggest that anything resembling a proper cure has taken place or anything that is out of the ordinary is taking place at all, for that matter. I just think we need to be honest about these things. I personally think alternative therapies are very dangerous, especially if they are used in the wrong way, that's all I'm saying. Don't you agree?"

The Doc's head reeled; he must have realised he was a little out of his depth and the argument was sliding away from him. Any minute now, Pamela was going to walk back in and see him looking like a fool in front of all her friends. There was just no respect. No one cared that he actually once jammed with Neil Young or toured with Bauhaus; did these guys even own any of their records? Further these people could never understand the Shamanic training he'd had, that they were in the presence of a master magus. They had no idea whatsoever that they were sitting next to the only occidental Scottish-Canadian guy to be introduced into the advanced knowledge of the Eastern Cree tribe medicine culture. But oh no, all because Pamela was afraid for him, that he might attract negative attention off stupid Christian people and she had made him swear to keep it a secret for their own protection! But she didn't have to worry about him!? Yeah, if only they knew who he was and had some respect for the, as yet undiscovered, science of magick. He smirked knowingly and decided to let them in on it.

"Aye, aye mate magick is dangerous, dangerous in the wrong hands, if you don't have the skills like I do!" He supped more wine knowingly, waiting for them to realise that he had more to say if they were intelligent enough to ask.

Pamela continued whistling to herself and smiling; she liked cooking for people and loved socialising. She loaded a tray of salad and cutlery. It was bloody typical of Michael not to help her and sit bloody drinking, but she'd send him in to get the rest in a minute and she couldn't wait to watch him clean up in his little pinafore later. She walked into the living room expecting to hear the CD playing, but it was silent. Then she was met with the sight of The Doc standing upright, eyes rolling back in their sockets whilst murmuring some incantation. Sweat dripped from his head blurring a crudely drawn sigil on his forehead which he'd whacked on with a felt tip pen. "What on Earth..?" was all she could mouth.

Her boss, sitting closest to her replied, "I dunno, he said he was going to demonstrate using a lord of the underworld to move some pepper floating in a saucer. Then he just sorta...took off!" he said slowly pointing at the statuesque and possessed looking Doc. A large pentagram had been drawn on the table and three candles had been placed around a triangle with a small saucer with some pepper floating in some water in the centre.

Many of the guests were holding back smiles until the man who made the "good shit" comment quipped, "Didn't anyone tell him that's it's impolite to get possessed between courses?"

Pamela rounded on him "Michael for goodness sake!?" as she slammed the tray onto the table. Whether this startled the underworld spirit or whether it decided to show its presence in a more vivid way is unclear as The Doc's straining and swaying was effectively making him act like a giant cement mixer for the various alcohols and the prawn Marie-Rose starter, which he had consumed like a starved terrier, only several minutes earlier. Mind you, you could say that The Doc got his own back somewhat on the people that were mocking him as he suddenly began looking around wildly, eyes bulging like a circus freak with an alarming demented look on his face. Chairs scraped away from him as he, now looking quite possed for a few seconds, scanned wildly around the room as his flailing hands knocked over wine and water glasses. He lurched from table to the doorway and then back again before seizing the bag, of the poor unfortunate woman sitting beside him, by the handles. Spontaneously and without apology let loose a loud torrent of vomit straight into it. It sounded like it was a cracking homage to the film *The Exorcist* as red wine and pieces of foamy crustacean made their appearances again that evening. The real final insult, though, came as he continued to grip the bag wretching and periodically gobbing into it as the onlookers gazed with expressions of disgust mingled with disbelief. All he could do in response was to stand there, swaying a little muttering "Fauk, 'at's better!" Despite the protestations and shrieks of "Oh you horrible little bastard," ringing in his ears from the poor young medic who's only wrong-doing had been to sit next to him all evening.

So, yes, I actually felt very sorry for him most of the time, however. I couldn't help but be amused by watching the dynamics of his relationship with Pamela regularly play out before me. Pamela got on well with Jen though and I was a little concerned that her influence would rub off too much, even though we were just mates by now. "You gotta train men, Jen," she would say when Jen and I would spend occasional evenings at her flat, usually followed by, "Train them and keep them in line; you have to house train 'em; Michael here, is well-trained aren't you Michael!?"

The Doc just grinned, then turning to me winked, "Us Pagans know how to treat women, don't we, Sean, heheheh?"

Pamela eyed him like a snake eyeing a mouse before a devilish grin appeared on the side of her face. "And if you step out of line then we'll just fetch out the little strappy dress outfit again eh?"

Beer actually sprayed from his chimp-like pursed lips as he lurched forward in his chair. I laughed loudly in amusement as I didn't think people actually did that, thinking that such 'surprise - mouth spraying' was only ever done in Carry On movies. Jen and I looked at each other and smirked wide-eyed at the revelation.

"Aye very funny Pamela, very funny!" The Doc replied imploring her with his eyes and darting a glance at us. Panic in his face and his body language more than anything giving this away as something he desperately wanted to conceal.

Pamela gazed at The Doc, coyly raising an eyebrow, as a trace of devilment started to possess her features. "Aye, you look very fetching when your hair is in pigtails Michael!" she said, winking at him mischievously.

The Doc, who by now had gone an unhealthy shade of red, retorted with a fairly obvious fake nervous laugh; "Ha, ha, ha, ha, ha! Da'h listen to her, da'h listen to her; like every good Pagan I do believe in pleasing women, but I do draw the line...without a doubt!" he replied, but it was too late, the image of a pig-tailed Doc in drag, DM boots, smoking a fag and doing the dishes while Pamela kept an eye on him, was already dancing in front of my eyes. Jen later told me that this was all true and that Pamela had shown her the dresses and other objects including a painfully large looking strap-on dildo! Like all good mates, I just couldn't wait to tell Don and Hippie Davie! Well, if I was going to be cursed with this image, I was damn sure that I wasn't going to bear it alone.

Inevitably though, The Doc's constant bullshit was really starting to annoy the group at times, especially Don. Mara had graduated and now had left to go down south for work and the coven was a little scarce of members for a while. Don and myself found amusement taking the piss out of the Shaman, who we sometimes called Getafix (after the Shaman from the Asterix the Gaul comics) which also morphed into Getalife in the circle, much to his chagrin (one of Don's favourites was also Analdicks the Gaul). The Doc actually was also in contact with, and part of, another coven in Dundee where he apparently was teaching them all shamanism, as they had all become his Shamanic pupils.

As I also did the postie job during the day on the summer holidays, I actually delivered to his house (well, his mum's house where he lived) in Torry. On a Saturday, I would finish the round at his house and walk in laden with Aberdeen rowies fresh from the bakers for his mum, him and myself. One morning as I arrived with the rowies he ran to get his guitar; he had obviously been practising for a while that morning before I arrived, "Recognise this?" he winked and began to strum it. It took me a wee while to figure out whether there was a tune in there somewhere. I wasn't sure if he was taking the piss or not, I actually thought he was for a full few seconds but thankfully I held off saying 'fuck off, this is a wind up, now start playing it will ye!?'

I soon realised though, the longer he continued in earnest, that he was quite serious. He stopped and gave me a look of anticipation a couple of times, expecting me to guess the tune. I embarrassingly kept saying, "Maybe just a bit more, I recognise it but quite can't remember the name just now!" He then carried on with unabashed zeal, occasionally stopping and with studied concentration methodically plucked one chord at a time and then pressing on with the tune. I concentrated hard and remembering that he kept mentioning Bauhaus and the Neil Young incident, more than once, I began to focus on these. I then recognised a bit of a chord or two from *Harvest moon*, (thank fuck) and not wanting to hurt his feelings or incur a mad outburst and being a little scared by now, I clapped saying "Ah, *Harvest Moon*, well there's no mistaking that melodious piece of a genius tune eh mate!?" I was so relieved that I guessed it right. But fuck me, it was obvious he'd just tried to learn it that morning and had never played it before! I was worried that he was going to say he wrote it for Neil, as I was sure it crossed his mind.

The nights gradually became longer again and I now had become the "coven chauffeur" according to The Doc, as myself, Don, The Doc and other members were piling into my little fifteen year old VW Golf to get to Newmachar. Gemma had returned to the coven on very infrequent occasions. She now worked as a sales rep and I think she liked checking in every few months to keep an eye on me. She had mellowed a little with time and seemed not to bother with being frustrated by us anymore. She had even agreed to be present at The Doc's initiation to first degree. This was a little strange, as he was also initiated within the coven in Dundee. The Doc, it seemed, couldn't get enough of the craft, first trying the whole Shaman thing and now witchcraft squared! I enjoyed driving everyone out to Marget's, especially as I was in charge of the music, much to Don's chagrin. There was a good vibe in the car and I liked driving through the Aberdeenshire countryside on those nights, as the very air seemed charged with magick. It was also nice to be in the company of people who you could relate to and I was always comforted knowing Don was coming along with me, as Sherlock had said of Watson, "Where would he be without his Boswell?" (Whatever that meant!).

Sometimes I would daydream as The Doc droned on about magick and the power he had; often I would think about the little strappy dress outfit and the big strap-on dick that Jen had reported, which would make me snigger out loud. I wasn't sure whether to laugh or feel really sorry for him…it must have smarted a bit! I never let on I knew about the latter to The Doc, but Don, Hippie Davie and sometimes Gemma were all in on the joke. Incredibly all our comments seemed to go right over his head. It was an ongoing competition to see how many times we could sneak the word 'anal' into conversation in a matter of fact way. I have to add, without blowing our own trumpet too much that between the three of us, we were rather brilliant at it an'al!

## Chapter 5:

## The Green and the Grey

The practice circles that Hippie Davie, Don and I held were great. I liked working with Don as we had a really good intuitive understanding of what we were about. These circles were about just getting used to carrying out casting the circles ourselves, making talismans, healing, using tarot and dabbling with activities such as elemental balancing. We felt it was fundamentally important to improve our abilities to visualise and gain skills in the most basic of magical operations. Hippie Davie had told us that the Golden Dawn in particular insisted that initiates should have a good grounding in visualising and casting the circles. However, I also saw it as an opportunity to explore magick a little bit further, to satisfy curiosity and to try to apply a type of scientific methodology towards investigating aspects of magical reality. Basically being a "place it before my eyes before I believe it" type of person, I still craved definitive proof or some signal that magick was something more than current psychological understanding couldn't reduce to mere superstition. I had been inspired by reading more about shamanism and the uses of psychedelics for a direct route to an expansion of consciousness, such as books by Carlos Castaneda about the teachings of Don Juan or books by Terence McKenna, which were all available from Aberdeen's premier comic shop, Plan 9.

This was in no small part due to Hippie Davie's influence, as for him tripping out and spending time in the woods or a sacred spot was as normal as going to Newmachar was to us. He maintained that we would see the world with a different perspective and that the Gods were scarily real. This intrigued me. I had also read Aldous Huxley's 'The Doors of Perception" and "Heaven and Hell.' I appreciated the idea of experimenting in this manner to increase one's own understanding of the mind and experiencing an expansion of consciousness in this way. So, I basically resolved to take a fucking good doze of acid and use it in a circle to test the effects and basically see what happened!

We decided to let The Doc in on our little "training" circles, as he was a main member of the so called 'batbox bunch,' after all. We told Mags we met to practice now and again but didn't really bother mentioning the acid. We told The Doc about it and he was really up for it. Of course, he had great experience of this, as a Shaman he "had done this loads before," apparently. It was relatively easy to get the acid as Hippie Davie had a lot of sources that we were confident were reliable; acid wasn't actually that easy to come by at the time, as most people wanted E, or amphetamines and LSD was a little out of fashion. Hippie Davie got us eight "microdots," which were like little chalk-like capsules and were supposed to be fairly strong. Don also brought a couple of 'strawberries' with him; these were the more familiar little bits of card soaked in LSD with a little strawberry printed on them. Unfortunately, they didn't taste like strawberries at all, just a horrible little bit of cardboard. Who knew!?

We prepared the room for the circle in the usual way and changed into our robes. My flat had an old Victorian fireplace conveniently situated at the south, which in our tradition was the direction of the element of fire. We brought lots of food of course and remembering my bad mushroom experience I had a few bottles of beer on standby. It was also supposedly a well-known fact that vitamin C helped counteract the effects of a trip, so we arranged three large cartons of orange juice and various citrus blends, as a sort of "fire extinguisher" to the LSD if things were too much to handle. Hey kids, acid can be healthy! I also had a couple of disposable cameras and had them sitting near to the Altar, just in case anything strange happened, which might be photographable.

I cast the circle and Don and The Doc invoked the quarters. I then evoked the spirit of the God and Goddess into the circle as a means of guidance and protection. Then we did a quick meditation and then Hippie Davie in all earnesty paid homage to the spirit of ergot (the fungal infection of rye from which LSD was first extracted by Albert Hoffman in 1938. This was responsible for 'ergotism' and therefore was very probably responsible for episodes of mass hallucinations and hysteria in the Middle Ages, possibly the Salem witch trials as well). Hippie Davie asked the spirit of the ergot to guide us through a good trip and teach us its wisdom. This was far removed from drinking muddy brews in front of MTV and I felt that such a powerful mind altering substance deserved such respect. I also felt quite safe in this context, being sure that the Goddess would ultimately look after me. Her statue graced my altar, now sharing centre stage with an action-man sized model of Hans Solo which Hippie Davie had plonked down on it. Hippie Davie winked at me, aware of my trepidation; "He'll always get us out of a tight spot if need be!" So we were totally covered man, no worries. Most of all, I trusted Don, Hippie Davie and The Doc and this was the most important thing. It is a well-known aspect of a trip that the company you are in is a major variable to the trip's enjoyment (or lack of).

I wasn't sure how much to take and neither did Don, who had no previous experience with psychedelics. We also knew it was always prudent to ignore The Doc's advice on anything at all. However, the perceived wisdom from Hippie Davie was that it was always good to start with half at first. I reckon this is an accepted truth for any kind of first time experience with illegal pharmacological substances, actually, the length and breadth of Britain! So we each then divided up the two strawbs then sat back and waited. Before long we got a little impatient and decided to take the microdot as well. Well, we wanted real results. We were committed. As we lay about on the cushions staring at the fire, I suddenly realised that I might not have enough firewood and coal to last the whole night, a bit of an oversight. I decided what we had would have to do, as I had central heating as well anyway, but Don became quite resolute that we should have enough. Since Safeways was just a little bit down the road, Don elected to nip out and get the firewood and a small bag of coal. I was a little reluctant to let him go out, but we all felt ok and since it was only a little distance he should be ok. After all, I had walked to get food on mushrooms and knew it wasn't like you were not in control, only reality is a little perturbed.

Hippie Davie shrugged, "Ah, five minutes? He'll be fine," so we let him go!

While Don was gone, however, Hippie Davie, The Doc and I began to see the funny side of practically everything and before long we were laughing uproariously, bemused by the beginnings of strange visual distortions and effects. While this was happening, the thought also occurred to us that Don was, at the same time, quietly wandering around Safeways, in a fast-changing and ever weirder world. The thought of poor old Don's predicament had us gasping for breath on the floor with amusement. You could be forgiven for thinking that we were acting like a right bunch of unsympathetic bastards here and you would be right of course, but we were out of our faces, remember?

Don returned and I greeted him at the door with a knowing smile. His eyes were as wide as saucers. "Let me in let me in!" he said pushing past handing me a small chicken. "Fucking hell! Don't go out there; you will see the real world, like it really is...it's a fucked up world out there!"

He relayed to us that he had been wandering around the supermarket when he began to feel a little strange. After a few minutes, the Tannoy announced that "acid was now on special offer," with a nice friendly *bing-bong* tone and he definitely felt it was time to get going! As he attempted to leave, he realised that there was no obvious way out; aisle after aisle looked the same or seemed to change position and land him back, rather distressingly, at the same place. To make matters worse, he kept finding he was sauntering past the same poultry and meat sections. As he became incrementally more spaced with every passing, the sight of bloody slabs of slaughtered meat and dead naked chickens with their little stumps sticking up became increasingly surreal to him. Don wasn't a vegetarian, but he always believed in honouring the animal spirit that was being eaten. Being forced to confront rows of hacked up, blood-soaked pieces of meat and chicken bodies, clinically wrapped in cling-film on a white featureless surgical refrigerated shelf made him feel uneasy and nauseous. There was something sinister, almost vampiric about it all; the hum of the freezer seemed evilly "chilling" to him. Death, it seemed was accepted with callous indifference, dressed with a veneer of mundane happy *bing-bong* reality. Don realised he was wandering around in and I quote, "A supermarket from Hell in an alternate reality like if the Nazis had won the second world war!"

This Hell smelt strongly of butchery that stung the back of Don's throat, much worse than brimstone ever could. The most insidious thing was that it wasn't as obvious as hell should be! It was a disguised Hell where small children glowered at the slabs curiously, poking them almost to see if they could still feel pain, where people judged the meats of the poor animals, staring at their insides with a strange fascination and hunger. This made it seem all the more sick. People walked around in slow motion, smiling at death and ignoring the exploitation. Where could it end? It made Don feel like he could be next and this inescapable fact sank slowly into his brain without normal rational barriers to protect him. He vocalised this thought out loud as he watched a random shopper examine a pack of turkey escallops. "Bet you'd even buy a bit of goth meat as quick would you? If it was even cheaper than that!" Fortunately, the man either didn't quite hear him or just ignored him, as randomly talking to strangers didn't fit the script in here.

As he was empathising with animals in the slaughterhouse, Don realised he could even sense the animal's spirit, as the drug elevated his capacity for empathy to the telepathic level. He apologised to each slab of beef he passed and asked for their spirit to rest in peace. Doing this made him feel better and an avenue of light lit the way for him to escape from that dammed section. He thanked the spirit of the animal that helped him and made his escape.

He found himself careering around the aisles, being drawn by every item on the shelf, disorientated by the smoothness of the regularity around him, box after box in neat lines. It was an Alice in Wonderland weird world. He felt like a subject in a giant rat maze. It all seemed to be geared to stop people talking, the smoothness of the aisles and floor created an energy where people couldn't get attached socially. It was like a river; you had to keep moving and everyone pretended they didn't really see each other. He could feel the pressure, like in a race to keep going and not to get in anyone's way. Even eye contact was "smooth" like the aisles, with nothing to grab onto. It hit him – someone stole the conversation! He remembered his childhood in central Aberdeen, the community spirit that had been there, the conversations, the empathy and the buzz. People would go to markets as a place to meet, catch up and socialise. It was basically fun to go out and shop, as you got the gossip and the community updates. Now only the deathly silent freezers hummed, for the communities had been replaced by a cold silent machine that had stolen everyone's soul. This wasn't the calamitous fire pit that you'd usually associate with hell but was worse as it was sucking us all dry in plain sight; and it was ironically called Safeways. He closed his eyes and let the current take him, using magick he visualised the moonlight lighting his way home for him over the water. He thought that he would be swept out and break the magnetic link to all the items. It worked, as he found himself washed up by a queue of people.

As he stood in the queue, it hadn't occurred to him that he didn't actually have any produce or anything to pay for. Standing in the queue was now just a part of the script. He waited in line, trying to look as normal as he could, not realising that occasionally he was staring at people in the other queues, like a madman, grinning at them in their sharded 'queness.' As he stared at the checkout woman, fascinated by her robotic cyborg-like connection to the till, he became aware that he could read her mind. Don thought it was amusing to hear her real thoughts on all the people she was serving, while scanning through the goods in polite silence. This meant he was standing there periodically chuckling to himself, as if he was the only one in on the joke and occasionally agreeing, nodding saying "Yes, I agree, five tubs of ice-cream and a box o' Canderel, yeah totally, what is the fucking point? Ha-ha!" The real trouble began as, inevitably; the girl had to call for assistance. Everyone tutted and shifted about on the spot in annoyance.

Don turned to the person behind him; without even a word of introduction or sense of embarrassment, he spontaneously started talking to him. "It's like a whale isn't it?" Since he felt everyone was thinking the same thing, being psychically linked by the queue, he felt it was perfectly natural to verbally articulate this thought to the now confused looking guy behind him, who now shifted nervously and gripped onto the handle of his shopping basket a little harder. "They suck us in here through them gaping doors like a mouth, suck us in, they pretend it's random when we're in here, but those doors can suck in a whole street in one hour, I reckon! Nothing fucking safe about their ways eh? No danger pal!"

The guy laughed nervously, "Yeah!" he replied and looked over at the doors then unsure what to do next and started staring at his frozen peas with studied concentration.

Don continued with glee at his own insightful logic. "Then once we've fought our way out of the labyrinth, which saps all your strength, they stop you here and feed off your energy. I'm virtually paralysed I tell ya!" He shook his head, chuckling, looking for some empathy with his comrade. Upon realising how attractive this guy was, Don became intent on chatting him up. "What are you doing here then?" he said trying to stoke the conversation.

The guy held up his basket. "Jist th' spring chickens mate!" He shrugged nodding to his basket.

Don struggled hard to process this information as the microdots and strawb fraction danced their way through his chemically-confused cerebellum. "I see, I see, no worries pal!" he whispered leaning forward, eyes scanning from side to side. Don felt that he and this guy were fighting for the same cause, at the back of his mind he thought there would probably be a quick shag in it for him as well, if he helped him. Don had always admired Hippie Davie as well and now here was a chance to impress him later too (and yet further potential of a liaison with the man he had an insatiable and secret crush on). Don became a counterculture soldier of fortune "I'm wi' ye! You need any help brother?"

The unfortunately placed shopper tried his best to respond as rationally as he could to such a weird question. "No...no I've just the two of 'em yer a' right pal."

Don now was resolute; "Nae bother pal," he held his right hand aloft, Che Guevara style and exclaimed, "Spring tha fuckin' chickens! I'm nae feart of their unsafe ways. I'll help you spring the fucking lot right now brother! C'mon let's do the bastards!" Thus in an attempt to prove his worth to this new comrade against the might of the evil Safeways, he marched off to make a stand for cling-film wrapped animals everywhere. The guy, who looked a little perplexed, quickly jumped into his place in the queue; well, this was the more immediate benefit, as the whole queue gratefully shuffled up one place and virtually ignored the wired-looking goth guy purposely striding away.

As the guy eventually walked away towards those baleen-like doors, he was oblivious to the scene at the back of the shop, as a crazed-looking person was running around the aisles piling as much poultry as he could into a basket and heading towards the doors. A few minutes later as he started his car and pulled away from the car park, he was equally oblivious as a bunch of security guards desperately chased a crazy-looking goth, cape billowing in the wind, trying to run full tilt across a car park with a basket load of chickens that were bouncing out and rolling among the throngs of people, who were desperately trying to get out of his way, or in some cases stash them under their coats. He did, however, hear the fading sound of a lone voice shouting something about free chickens! Bastard, he thought and here's me just paid three quid for mine! He turned the corner and drove away thinking this place was too expensive and full of weirdos, *'am gonna start gan' tae Tescos!'* he thought.

"A fuckin' chicken!" said The Doc in disbelief, "we sent ye to Safeways for some wood and ye come back wi' a fuckin' chicken?!" Don stood in the hall wide eyed and looking really confused and upset, trying to hand him a chicken from his cloak pocket; "I...tried!?"

We all exploded with laughter. I seriously thought I was going to die when he told us the story. Apparently he had left a trail of chickens from the supermarket to my house; he was acutely worried that they would be able to track him down by following them.

"Don't worry! I said, "We're not too far from Seton...they won't last long out there.

After I calmed Don down a bit, we concluded that the chickens outside would have grown up by now and found their own way home, perfectly logical now. We each had a rant at the injustice of multi-corporations and then let our minds drift to other happier things.

The circle continued with much hilarity and all I can remember is a close up of the floor and feeling that if I didn't stop laughing soon, I was going to do myself an injury as my ribs were starting to hurt far too much. We gladly consumed the rest of the acid to hasten our trip. What I liked about it was that unlike dope, I felt perfectly normal except that I was hallucinating everywhere I looked.

Curiously Don, Hippie Davie and I were having the same hallucinations; looking into the fire, we all perceived a whole different world behind the flames. I knew instinctively that they were describing and seeing exactly the same as I was. As the flames whined, we became aware that the fire was breathing, the flames were captivating. The Doc, however, decided to summon a wolf spirit as a protector from his tribal familiars and started howling at the top of his voice, I was concerned that he'd scare my cat, but didn't have to intervene as respite came when Don thumped him on the nose and told him to go and lie down. The Doc then grabbed my bodhrán drum from a shelf (a small souvenier from a trip to Dublin) and started hitting it rhythmically while softly mouthing "hey-ya ho-a, whoa, hey-ya," *etc, etc* over and over. Hippie Davie let out an audibile sigh as Don and I creased up with laughter. The Doc momentarily stopped, looking over at us;

"At'z interestin'...this chant is supposed to clear negativity and create positive vibes. It's totally happening wi' yous two right enough init?" So he continued chanting on. "Hey-ya ho-a, whoa, hey-ya, Ho-a..."

I couldn't breathe and begged him to stop as it was making me so happy that it hurt and I was going to piss myself. Don also begged him to stop for similar reasons. However he carried on regardless,

"Hey-ya ho-a, whoa-ah, ho-ha, hey-ya, ya, ya, hey-ya...hey, that's amazing, look at you guys, so happy that you're actually writhing on the floor!!"

I'd never been in so much pain whilst experiencing so much mirth at the same time; it was actual torture. Fortunately Hippy Davie, who understood, made him stop in case the vibes rendered us permanently stupefied with a face permanently cramped into a big grin, ending up making Don and I look like dodgy car salesmen for the rest of our lives.

Hippie Davie obviously really took to acid; the trip seemed to enhance his physique and looks, making him look even more so like some bronzed Adonis figure. He sat with an almost regal look upon his face. We all understood that he was old friends with the spirit of ergot! After a while he picked up the bodhrán and began beating it in a rhythmic way. The rhythm seemed to echo with some pulse of the universe itself. It was amazing and for a second I seemed to snap out of my body in response. Hippie Davie was in a trance state, way ahead of us and he had forgotten to take us with him. My respect for Hippie Davie's Druidic practice rose instantly. Newmachar was nothing like this!

I have a little spiral tattoo which was whirling about and the little dancing figure was really dancing around. I was fascinated by it for ages. After a while, a strange draft swept around the circle and blew one of the candles, I tried to investigate but could find no real reason for this, as the doors were shut. The Doc then complained on being a bit chilly, which I thought was strange because I was sweating with the heat. I changed places with him. Immediately I was freezing cold, I was in the east now, air, it was cold and draughty, but only a few feet away. I stepped back into the south, it was roasting hot! I was quite amused by this and attempted to qualify if this was real by walking around the circle, "Ok guys let's sort this out...ok at the south...shit it's fuckin' roastin', a few steps to the east...I'm fuckin' freezin'!" I said laughing to myself.

Don, by this time was naked and just standing in the centre of the circle with his hands dangling at his side, staring upwards laughing and shaking with ecstasy.

"Are you all right there Don?"

"Oh aye...I'm just feeling the universe here!" He was experiencing extreme euphoria, which we were all feeling by this point. Hippie Davie stopped drumming, opened one eye and smiled. His work was obviously done.

At one point in the evening I thought it would be interesting to invoke the God. I went through to the bathroom, looked into the mirror and saw the Green Man staring back at me; it was a little perturbing but fascinating at the same time. The Doc also joined in this fun and decided that he must invoke an old medicine man of the Cree tribe, but unfortunately with all The Doc's histrionics, effort and straining he came across to us looking too much like some unearthly vision of Steve Buscemi in mid-wank. This freaked Don and I out a bit, so we had to tell him to stop-it.

Everything was in motion, bending and dancing, but it wasn't unpleasant, rather this just seemed like another way of seeing things. There was a sense of life, of consciousness everywhere, even in the sterile surroundings of my front room. I imagined what it would be like in the Amazon rain forest, or better yet, the sparse emptiness of a desert, where the white noise is turned down, allowing the internal environment to come to the fore.

Hippie Davie opened his eyes and looked at me, "That's why the Druids preferred the quiet woods; it's much better for faery or spirit."

We all agreed as if we were party to the same conversation, although a voice in my head was confused, saying *Wait a minute, didn't I just think that and he answered?* I wasn't sure, it was all too confusing! I watched his lips motion the word "*waaaatch,*" as he whispered. He sung a few notes of some old folk song I did not recognise; the sound was hypnotic and immediately made the back of my head buzz. Davie almost sounded female; it was very surreal. My head seemed to twist in my skull and it seemed like I was looking out of the back of my head for a moment, as if my body became still but my spirit body flung around. A faint light seemed to illuminate the wall around the fireplace; still, it was behind me, as I watched it. Hippie Davie's voice became louder and amazingly, seemed to be joined by the voice of a young woman singing. The thoughts danced in my brain that it must be Don or even Jen or someone else who had come in. However, I realised that the voice came from beyond the wall. The voice also sounded like the faint blue light. How I connected this I do not know, but the voice was that colour. It was a wonderful relaxing colour-sound. Then I saw her, at first fleetingly, the most beautiful face I'd ever seen, with long auburn hair and radiant blue eyes, glistening pools of eyes that one could get lost in. She was standing alone in a forest clearing, calling out to someone. I realised, after a moment that she was calling back to us, to Hippie Davie who sang to her from this room. Her voice was like nothing I'd ever heard before. The word Angel flashed through my mind, as that was the only description I could give her, both the sound and the effect that she had on me. She looked at each one of us and as her eyes rested on me, she smiled and I knew she could tell everything about me by looking into my eyes. I was staring at her in disbelief and she knew what to say to me. "I am Brigit-o'faery...and I exist here."

Every doubt I had disappeared in that instant, as I realised in that moment that she existed somewhere as real as I did, maybe more so. Somehow we were only waiting mere moments compared to her existence. I thought, 'Reality is relative; my reality in my head can experience information which I now shared with her, even if my body elsewhere experiences the room I was in now. My analytical brain seemed to break the spell and I returned into my kneeling body with a *thump!* I looked around the room; everyone looked a little freaked out.

Don looked startled, scanning around the room confused, "Wait a minute, Fa's that wifie spikin', I thought I jist heard a wifie – did you hear her anah?!"

The Doc looked positively worried, "That's right, I could hear a woman talking, far wiz she? I da'h kaen far she wiz!"

Then he looked at Hippie Davie, as we all did "Is...is that you fucking aboot wi' oor heeds ya Hippie bastard?"

I stared incredulously at Hippie Davie. The fact that everyone had a similar experience was conclusive evidence for me; I didn't question it in that state of mind. I knew it was real because I could feel it. This seemed much more positive proof than merely seeing it!

Hippie Davie knew also, "We're lucky. She's an old friend of mine, but you never know if she'll answer, faery are entirely unpredictable that way!"

We each lay down and tried to conjure up her image again, but it seemed that it needed Hippie Davie's magick, not just the power of imagination. It was like Davie had found a key at some point and we either had to find it, too, or have him do it for us! I realised it would take a lot more meditation and effort to uncover a doorway like Hippie Davie had and so I had a new admiration for his druidic abilities. We stayed in the circle until early morning, until the fire was dying out. We each took some large glasses of orange, ate some chicken and then bedded down for the rest of the night.

The next day, I went for a walk into town. This was the single strangest day of my life. I felt like I had been catapulted into space and had returned as a very different person. Walking through the bustling crowds, I felt like an alien wandering through a strange place. I recalled the Castaneda book, *Return to Ixtlan*. I knew better what it meant now; I had changed a little and felt like I couldn't return. I felt like I had "woken up" and was walking around an ant colony with everybody busy walking around in lines, unaware of the real world. I also felt very calm and strangely refreshed.

In another universe, almost parallel in fact, a T.V. anchor-man read the headlines, "A psychic goth was being sought for questioning regarding the liberation of a flock of former chickens. You are advised not to approach this man nor challenge him to a game of poker. And finally, four guys had a really good night on LSD, they opened their heads in a Druid-Shamanic ritual and realised that we are connected in profound para-social ways!...Now here's Heather with the weather!" Whereas the front page of the paper in the corner shop should have been; "That will LSD nicely."

The four of us continued to meet in our circle, ostensibly to try path-workings and do little spells, balancing the elemental forces within us. We even tried experimenting, invoking Egyptian gods. When I performed an invocation on Don, I could really *feel* the atmosphere change in the room and see, quite clearly, the change come over his posture and persona. On one occasion, my mind was blank, as I was sitting in a path working with Hippie Davie and The Doc, Don liked to practice talking us through them. I was supposed to be awaiting a gift from the Goddess, but I was just lying there as usual, wishing I was better at it. As clear as crystal, the eye of Isis appeared in my vision, without any contribution or fantasy from me. A large light blinked from the eye and seemed to fill me with happiness. I considered this a triumph and that I was getting better at using my magical imagination, as opposed to idle daydreaming.

Being a student worked well for me, as I had the time to meet up with the guys quite often. As Don worked nightshift and the other two didn't work any shift, we would invariably meet in town. Aberdeen is a little bit small that way; there were only a few places we would go during the day. Our favourite haunt was a café (café 52) on the Green. This was a large cobbled area (ironically called the Green) that lay down a long flight of stairs from Union Street. It was called the Green as in years gone by women used to collect down there and do their washing at the burn which now flowed out of sight, underground. Now we four wasters smoked dope – the main reason Hippie Davie liked this place and it was his place before we knew him – and listlessly put our feet up on the chairs outside the café and watched the occasional shopper walk by.

Consequently, I found myself meandering towards it once again. I had nipped out to get a breath of fresh air and relax over a beer with my friends. I fathomed that essentially that was what life was all about anyway. When you work in some workplace, an office, for example, you find yourself spending many hours with workmates more so than with your family. In this situation, which we find is imposed on us; we adapt and bond with people, finding some common ground and mutual respect. Most of the bonding is done around the actual job, which is why it's always boring and a bit awkward going out with a friend or partner's work colleagues as "the job" is all they talk about! However, sometimes, if you're lucky, you will find like-minded people and that's great when that happens. Now people like me? A person that, as it turns out, was born with an affinity for alternative psychologies such as witchcraft and what might be termed "the occult"? Then like-minded people are really quite thin on the ground, especially in "Ae-bir-deen"! I mean, most people would think me weird, insane or dangerous. Not a hundred years ago or so around here, the ancestors of these people who now casually and politely side-step me on the pavement would have been chasing me around the Castlegate with pitchforks and flaming torches. Many of them probably still would if they knew more about my extra-curricular activities and had half a chance. So, I quite appreciated that I did have a bunch of mates who really were like-minded. I could be completely and utterly safe and able to express myself with them. I definitely wouldn't be this much myself even with my closest family, but then I've never met anyone who could be their selves with their families either, so I suppose that is normal (unless your dad is David Bowie or something!).

I smiled to myself thinking this as I walked around the back of the tech-ie college feeling a pang of nostalgia for a brief former life there, topping up my school qualifications in the dusty classrooms and for the girl who dressed in black and got me into the band The Fall! This was the time I could think more clearly, the time to drift away, as I hiked up the hill and meandered past the gothic spires and grandeur of the Marschial College, down through Schoolhill and the townhouse out towards St Nicholas Street and on past the Prince of Wales on the quiet old cobbled St Nicholas lane. Nothing changes here very much – I used to think it never will – the dappled light from the tall trees of St

Nicholas kirk graveyard whispered quietly of days gone by, of the people who also stood here, not understanding the futility of time. Watching the busy Union Street a mere twelve feet or so above rattle past, unaware of them. The shops came and went up high there but the little old Correction Wynd, leading to the arch beneath Union Street, looking like a backdrop from some gothic vampire movie scene; continues underneath towards the cobbled little Green retaining its almost medieval character. A conduit that eventually leads to roads which all too soon open out to the next world of waves and the harbour nearby. The Green sleeps in cold stone, unchanged for years such is the spirit of the place, like the heart of older but never forgotten Aberdeen.

As I neared the end of the tunnel towards the cool stone-grey light of the Green, I could sense my mates' presences before I saw or heard their tones. I knew they would be sitting, out of time, passing the day in the cool, moist North Sea breeze. As a kind of amusing icebreaker, I sang aloud the last lines of the tune tingling in my earpiece, "Outa ma mind on dope-and-speed!"

The Doc, who was sitting with his back to me, carried on with "Outa my mind on jam and breed!"

Hippie Davie smiled his broad unshaven grin and slid a chair with his long booted leg towards me, "Well in that case you'll fit right in here, have yerself a sit doon."

The usual slapping of shoulders was done, not too hard, but not overly soft either. "Julian Cope eh? Man's a genius," said The Doc.

"Yep;" interjected Hippie Davie. "A bit loopy though!"

The Doc pushed his point. "Nah eccentric genius; wouldn't want to challenge him to a drug smoking fest, though!"

"Well why not?" said Hippie Davie. "Though, I don't think I could keep up with his mind, it's over-stimulated I expect!"

"I doubt Julian Cope could Cope with you, Hippie Davie!" I said tongue in cheek and to keep him from going off on one!

The Doc giggled and Don smirked out loud. "His grave would say 'Julian, could no longer Cope, Cope.' Here, sounds like the Shoop, Shoop song doesn't it? The Cope, Cope song!"

The Doc jumped in grabbing his groin and with a startling unconvincing Glaswegian accent, "Aye couldna cope with ma big coa-ck up 'ees erse min!" He then spluttered into laughter as we all glanced at each other in a quite perplexed manner and shrugged. The Doc delivered up his latest thought.

"He Collects Dolls...? That's weird, even for Julian Cope!"

I looked at him, "Why is that so bad?"

"Well, maybe it's no bad, aye, but he's no' even gay is he? He's normal!" exclaimed The Doc with a thoughtful frown on his face.

I looked at Don, embarrassed, shaking my head in disbelief. Don just regarded him as one might regard an offensive insect crawling across your cheese sandwich on a picnic. "Well I'd have a better conversation with dolls than with you, you fucking dip-stick!" said Don.

I piped up, to regain the point of the conversation. "Well Hippie Davie, you'd have to be careful, you know about the Bill Drummond story!? How Julian Cope chased him across the Yorkshire Dales with a shotgun."

"Why?" said Don.

I shrugged, "Coz he was off his face and took issue with Bill Drummond saying the Teardrop Explodes could boost sales dramatically if Julian were to do himself in, in a Rock 'n Roll suicide thing," I exclaimed.

Hippie Davie mused for a moment. "Fuck me! I guess he was trying to make some cynical point about the music business – but that's fucking ignoring the years of genius Julian Cope has left. That's a bit shit really! Bill Drummond? Aye - I always remember him saying that the reason why the North of England produces so much talent, music-wise, is because of the convergence of major ley lines that cross in those areas!"

Don raised his fingers to his chin, stroking his face, conceding the point for a moment; "Makes sense, I suppose, when you think about all the great bands that seem to come from there. You have the Beatles from Liverpool, of course, as well as Julian Cope himself, Echo and the Bunnymen..."

I thought for a second. "Yeah funny, all my favourite bands seem to be from around the north of England. Christ you have The Sisters of Mercy and the Mission from Leeds, The Wedding Present; Leeds again, I fuckin' love them! Pulp from Sheffield, erm..." The Doc cut in,

"The Cult from Bradford!" I nodded acknowledging this, before continuing,

"Yeah, yeah and erm, Robert Smith from Blackpool and then there's Manchester! The list from there is quite an impressive C.V. There's, Joy Division and New Order and Vini Reily and all that from Factory records, The Smiths, of course..." Hippie Davie pointed over,

"Yeah, the Buzzcocks of course and Magazine and, eh, erm John Cooper Clarke, the people's poet, yeah?" I smiled but the word poet made me remember my obvious favourite,

"The Fall! Simply one of the greatest bands ever and now there's the Happy Mondays, The Stone Roses and that new band Oasis!"

The Doc scoffed. "Oasis!? Pfff they'll come tae fuck all, just you wait and see, their time has passed, it's too late for all that indie stuff, same as that Blur. It's past its best, indie's dead!"

Don piped in, "Aren't New Model Army from around Bradford or something, somewhere north of England, too? And then just down the road you've got Depeche Mode – the Basildon boys – the rest of Cure from Crawley." He nodded in approval towards Hippie Davie;

"Yeah you're right Hippie Davie! I mean, why do all the good bands come from England!? Why isn't there a French Cure or a German Beatles or a Scottish Rolling Stones, come to that!? I mean let's face it; it just wouldn't happen would it? It's weird that? Must be the fucking ley lines, yeah!"

I sighed and mocked Don's voice in a high pitches silly voice. "Must be the ley lines, must be the fucking ley lines!"

Don tutted, "Well how do you explain it then, Mr. Fuckin' Scientist?"

"Oh for fu–!" I gasped. I could barely form a coherent sentence I was so annoyed. "Well, it's probably more to do with socio-economic factors, init? Poverty and hardship, or the culture of the north of England, a strong Irish Influx, or Welsh migration with cultures that sing all the fucking time! Plus the music business is geared and biased towards the English language, thus ignoring most of Europe's talents; sheesh, my mate Roger would give you a three-hour lecture if he heard you say that. I mean, I don't know why a lot of good bands hail from there, but there's no need to invoke the magick of ley lines as an explanation!"

Don scoffed a little and muttered something into his coffee cup. Hippie Davie shrugged and said, "Well it's only a theory!" defensively, a little put out.

Predictably The Doc just looked around at everyone giving them that, 'we know something he doesn't know' kind of look.

I felt the need to press home my point and justify my annoyance.

"I'm sorry, but it just smacks of 'gap-fill' logic, you know? That's not proof, that's just making stuff up to fit the facts, just because the real facts have not been properly established; there is simply no evidence for it! I'm sorry!" I turned to Hippie Davie.

"By your logic then, Aberdeen should have a lot of talent up here, as there are huge concentrations of stone circles here, more than anywhere else in the world probably!"

Hippie Davie shrugged, obviously not really all that interested in the conversation that much, his mind elsewhere. "Annie–"

I stopped him in his tracks "Apart from Annie fucking Lennox!" The Doc was about to say what I knew he was going to say, "The Shhh" I shot him down, too.

"I know, I know, The Shaman...Jesus loves America! You only like it for the words! Ever tried dancing to it? It's a bloody awful tune! I tell you. Hippie Davie shook his dreadlocks from side to side. "Nope! The stone circles have helped them go techno...Eees are good, Eees are good!" We laughed as Don interjected, "Fuckin' poetry, sheer poetry, most subtle writing since....Mudd exclaimed they dug neat tiger feet!"

Don thought for a second, "Imagine if the Rolling Stones or the Beatles had come from Aberdeen, the world would be a different place eh?"

I made a hoarse sound in concession; "Mmm....yeah, Paint it Black would just be about the clouds! And it wouldn't be Strawberry Fields Forever would it?"

Hippie Davie smiled, "Maybe the Dirty Auld Green For-ever!"

I raised my coffee cup and we all clicked our drinks together. "I'll drink to that!" I said and we sang the chorus together, but it sounded a bit silly out loud.

These occasions were most relaxing and we were happy just to talk bollocks and think of things to try out at the next magical meeting. I, however, kept finding myself arguing from a logical point of view, which was opposite from the other three who shared a more accepting notion of the nature of witchcraft and magick. For example, I had a problem with the flippant use of the word *energy*, which everybody used from hippies to magicians, but especially hippies. This was a word Hippie Davie used a lot; he talked about the energy of a person or energy of an action. I had to admit I was not convinced. My tirade of scepticism had clearly annoyed Don as he put on his hat and left to go and get more baccy. I really knew he was taking a break because he was finding me irritating. We had that married couple kind of understanding between us.

As he strode away jangling, I thought about that, about Don's energy leaving the group. I resumed the conversation, now just looking to moan and pick a fight. I leaned over to The Doc,

"I'll tell you what, I don't like this use of the word *energy*; it seems to me that people are borrowing this phrase from the discipline of physics but not bothering to ever quantify what they mean!" I had had a similar moan to him in the car a few nights earlier.

The Doc sat back, "Och you're just being too scientific as usual! You just don't get it! Anyway, we medicine men call it *power*…maybe you witches have a problem feeling that right enough! Though you use that in circles, don't you? Therefore you must know it exists right? S'all you need tae fuckin' know then! Definitely, without a doubt!"

I hated the use of "you just don't get it." The Doc's continual use of that phrase was like a red rag to a bull to me!

Before I could launch a counter-offensive, though, Hippie Davie joined in on the attack. "Power is everywhere, it surrounds and imbues every living thing, us Pagans are that bit more attuned to it, y'know? Have an instinctive sense for it; to use it, all we have to do is ask Nature for it."

I was becoming more irascible by the minute, "May the force be with us, eh, please?" I said in response, but my clever little play on words seemed to be lost on them, much to my disappointment.

Hippie Davie looked up and shook his head, back to task, "Uh? – oh aye – well aye!"

Oh fuck what had I said? Mentioning *Star Wars* was going be a big mistake; I was my own worst enemy sometimes. "Aye ok Yoda!" I replied signalling with a wave of my hand for him not to go there.

But Hippie Davie felt the need to defend the faith (or force). "Well where do you think George Lucas got the idea for Yoda and the force from eh? Yoda is modelled on the Taoist priests of old, keepers of the old wisdom, uncontaminated by the new masculine dominance culture whose legacy is war and rape of the natural world. Annnnd what about the force? Fuckin' midichlorians!?" He looked challengingly at me, eyebrow rising in a condescending arch.

I shrugged in resignation and at the same time repressing a sneer, I didn't want to reveal any trace of annoyance. I thought it was important not to let Hippie Davie think that he had the upper hand in the information war! "Dunno, but I'm sure you're gonna tell me," I replied in sarcastic tones, thus ensuring that he knew I thought he was talking shit from the word go anyway!

"Well you're the biologist, what about the biochemical evidence?" retorted Hippie Davie.

Oh fuck's sake! I hated it when he tried to lecture me on Biology or science. Who does he think he is? Probably doesn't have two standard grades to rub together. "Yeah, *Star Wars* biochemistry let me think….Nuh, I maybe slept in for that lecture, you'd better enlighten us Hippie Dee!"

Hippie Davie sucked at the top of his latte, making triumphant little ripples on the hot milky surface coinciding with a content, smug look spreading over the lines of his face. This often preceded one of his lectures, which strangely usually always involved *Star Wars*! George Lucas has a lot to answer for where our generation is concerned! He proceeded,

"All living things to my knowledge create energy right? They absorb the raw materials from their surroundings and produce the energy of life, that's why all things have an aura yeah!?" Hippie Davie spoke with an enthusiasm and eloquence on these matters that made you feel that he was spouting from some fountain of secret knowledge. He was quite compelling and one felt quite pulled along for the ride.

I went with the thought. "Energy that has its origins in the Sun and ultimately the universe?" I said, instantly regretting my apparent support for his argument and feeling a little deflated for lacking the will to stay true to my scepticism; a little embarrassed that my weakness was exposed.

Hippie Davie leapt on it, "Yeah, exactly, exactly!" His eyes were wide with appreciation, jabbing the point home with an eager hand towards my position. "The law of conservation of energy, man; it's true, it's like a big fuckin' snake weaving through the known universe, changing shape and form but always connected, always going somewhere."

The Doc nodded his head in appreciation, "Laws of thermodynamics, ancient laws!" he stated emphatically nodding with a smile on his face that seemed to convey he knew where Hippie Davie was going.

"And are you going somewhere with this?" I said. "What have snakes and ladders gotta do with the force anyway? You saying that all the energy in the universe is like the force?"

"Wha..? Oh yeah sorry brother yeah ok, yeah as I was about to say, think about your metabolism, you know? Where does all the energy in your body cells come from?" Hippie Davie, obviously now, had something up his sleeve and was trying a new tack which clearly involved probing my knowledge or ignorance on Biology.

I grimaced slightly pressing my lips together. "Mitochondria!" I said emphatically to stress that this was obvious and shrugged, there was no mystery there! A felt a bit like he was insulting my intelligence now.

However, Hippie Davie presented me with his hand, indicating that I had neglected to consider some obvious point which was right there in front of me! There was a pause while he eyed me with his expression of triumph. "Don't you think that sounds way too similar to 'midi-chlorians?' You know, the particles which convey the force?"

The similarity struck me for a second. "Mmm..." I thought midichlorians were supposed to be particles or something!? Is that no' just a coincidence, Hippie Davie, brought on by your joint-addled thinking?"

Hippie Davie smiled, as if to feel sorry for me; I was unenlightened, after all. "Joint-assisted thinking." He winked, "You could use some inspiration man. Just fuckin look at the two words!" Hippie Davie used his hands to carry the idea of the two words by plonking the invisible words on either side of the table for me to imagine. "Mitochondrion, Midichlorions. Lucas is tryin' to tell us something, man; it's the energy that makes everything possible – moving, building civilisations on one level, but it's also what powers the mind, dreams and our thoughts. Mitochondria *are* particles onywy dude, like little living nano-particles creating energy, cycling it from the Big Bang and making our thoughts possible right now." He pointed his index finger on the table in a manner which reminded me of the pompous Oliver Norvel Hardy, except with very dirty finger nails.

The Doc chuckled, "Nanoo, Nanoo!..." mimicking Robin Williams as Mork from Ork.

"We don't need any other science fiction references just now, Doc!" I said and he laughed contentedly, feeling happy that he was joining Hippie Davie to annoy me.

I momentarily scowled at the offending dirty finger and then it occurred to me that the Hippie might have a point, or George Lucas had! Was I becoming a believer?

"That's an intriguing thought," I started. "In the case of sentient creatures, some of that blood sugar in the brain is being converted to supply energy for dreams and abstract ideas..." Then I thought a little bit more. "But that's a 'personal,' subjective experience, that's all. It's not like you could represent it with an equation:

$$C_6H_{12}O_6 + 6O_2 \longrightarrow 6CO_2 + 6H_2O + E_a$$

Where $E_a$ =Classification of neuron activation energy (of type astral).

Hippie Davie seized on the idea, "Why not, dude? The type-astral part of your equation right!? Can be likened to a portal to another reality being expressed, something emerging from little stuff, just like all other living things on the planet come together to create an ecosystem. Except imagination forms the basis for the astral planes, man! An astral or imaginative ecosystem" Hippie Davie implored with palms up, like we'd all missed the obvious!

The Doc looked very serious for a second, "Thi astrill planes, astrill planes min, collective unconscious min, aye definitely, definitely without a doubt!"

I fought on with my analogy. "But you can liken that to a computer! It's powered by DC current and a picture is produced but the picture is an illusion created by pixels. A picture does not have any other meaning other than a representation in the real world. It's a bunch of pixels, only we can see the picture. You can just represent it, encode it but shouldn't be confused with reality."

Hippie Davie was one step ahead, "Well the Buddhists would say reality as we perceive it is an illusion. The picture is an emergent property, another reality that transcends the physical! See, electronic pixels, T.V. like you say are not reality, aye, but human imagination, that's different. Imagination, the mind work *is* part of the fabric of reality! Fuck this conversation needs to be re-fuelled by more dope brother!"

"Am not yer brother!" I exclaimed, he always called me brother in the context of dope, or *Star Wars*. I don't know why, but it got on my nerves the first time and continued to do so. I mused on his words while he frantically re-rolled.

"Ah I suppose that Plato argued that the only true reality is mathematics didn't he?" I conceded, "That all perceptions were limited to biases in what we can know?! Funny, talkin' of computers, that's all they know as well isn't it maths? I'm sure that's ironic somehow."

Hippie Davie rolled furiously but with a deftness and precision that you had to admire for a few seconds. "Philosophical conversations man, boy I love dope man."

The Doc nodded, "Plato's *Republic*! Can't say I agree with everything he wrote!"

Hippie Davie and I both paused for a second and looked at him curiously. The Doc looked back defensively, "Well there's a lot of time to read when you're unemployed!" I looked back to Hippie Davie. "Anyway, you're the only one that's stoned Hippie Davie, am no'!"

Hippie Davie's eyebrows rose and his mouth drooped conveying his hurt. A familiar contortion at the left corner of his lip together with a momentary flash of mischief in his gaze, however, conveyed his lack of seriousness. "Awwwh c'mon now, that's some unjust aspersions to be firing at me when yer in my company brother! That was it; it was because it made him sound like some kind of spaced out evangelist preacher! That was why I hated it; I had just figured that out.

It was an astonishingly risky reefer for public consumption; I supped at my cappuccino and looked around; the staff didn't bat an eyelid as Hippie Davie's head momentarily disappeared in a cloud of dense slow motion smoke that seemed to make the entire café slip out of phase with the errant pace of life just a few feet away on the street.

Hippie Davie, now happily less sober, was again content to resume the thread; "The material world is based on numbers, isn't it? Increase something in a food web and something else is affected, that right? Action, reaction, eh?"

For a non-biologist, he was annoyingly right sometimes. I resented these intrusions into my realm and I always felt uneasy that he knew more than I did. It made me feel like he was trying to get one over on me all the time.

I conceded again, "Well yeah, I mean, population dynamics conform to statistics like most things in life – chances of getting heart disease, run over or eaten by a crocodile, all depends on where you live and how many risks you're willing to take I suppose!"

Hippie Davie contemplated this whilst already rolling another, having passed the first one to The Doc. "Heavy man, that's like a kind of fate isn't it? Well, numbers become more complicated, equations grow from simpler numbers, emergent properties are an intrinsic property of maths, growth and complexity is a real artefact of a universe based on numbers. I mean, I think the sciences have missed the point a little because since the industrial revolution everyone thinks about entropy, the law of thermodynamics that The Doc mentioned a minute ago. Coz basically everything is reduced to states of 'heat.' That dictates that everything crumbles doesn't it? Everything must flow towards the lowest energy state over the arrow of time."

I had some notion of what he was speaking about, though I hadn't heard it put in simple terms quite like that before.

He carried on, his mind obviously like a library of interesting facts. I must admit I was very impressed with his scientific mind-set which just seemed to come to the fore all of a sudden, I had no idea that side of him lurked within that art student/hippie dreadlocked head of his. This was making me feel even more insecure, as he continued unaware of my growing unease.

"They thought that up back in the day coz steam engines break and stuff blows up, it's true I suppose, but what about the numerical reality of the universe that underpins everything, equations emerge and reality changes? And time, time alters reality, think about that, reality isn't a fixed construct. Time messes with it, morphs it and bends it. Time and energy go hand in hand much like time and space do. I mean you can't have one without the other can you? Think of that! What does that mean for reality? Energy is actually packaged, quantified, so that scales up to discrete steps in reality, *i.e.* like numbers. Reality changes numerically! DNA, right, started replicating. That's a numerical property as well and then things get ever more complex. Reality changes gear, transcends from simple to complex. Energy flows, numbers change over time and therefore you need an ever more complex brain to perceive it...and perhaps reality is infinite, just like numbers! So reality really isn't like a slow decay after all, it's the opposite. Decay may happen, yeah, but reality constantly recreates itself out of that destruction. There must be a physical 'law' for that, call it 'God' if you will!"

I was actually quite impressed and he had some sort of point in there somewhere. I liked it, 'the God law,' that Physics hasn't found yet! I felt the need to take a few big tokes of what Hippie Davie was on. I was conscious of trying to get just enough to tickle the same centres of the brain that was stimulating Hippie Davie, so I could share his insights but not overdo it and forget basic maths like two plus two. A sort of, can-I-have-what-he's-having scenario. I puffed and waited almost as if to wait for a magical thought to enter my head. It didn't! So I gathered the thread again.

"I like the emergent properties analogy, a well-known thing in Biology to just invent a rational explanation for cells magically emerging out of primordial mush or thoughts emerging out of massive neural networks!" I said. "It's where we diverge from creation scientists; they say God is involved there and we – correctly in terms of science – say it's not useful or scientific to invoke a second non provable variable, so we say it may be something to do with mathematics and the weird properties of co-operating non-living parts giving rise to life, as a sort of accident of physics almost. But neither of us really knows." I mused aloud in order to let him know I could follow his train of thought.

I continued on with that kind of thought to Hippie Davie and his assertion that non-physical planes of existence and extra realities (astral planes) could "emerge" from the basic biochemistry in our brains.

"Hippie Davie, I reckon you're using that as a convenient leap from the physical world to the spiritual, but you cannot prove it. It's mere philosophy. Unfortunately, it doesn't help me feel any better with the nature of the universe and reality!" We paused, drank and drew smoke in synchrony and I continued another line of thought. "Though I suppose most things conform to numbers right enough, like that guy showed, Fibonacci, the number sequences guy."

Hippie Davie paused for a second as he put the finishing touches to another big spliff. He looked up at me, quizzically; "Fibonacci Dude?"

Brilliant, unlikely enough he hadn't heard of him! I was back in the driver's seat. "Aye, this Italian mathematician found repeating number sequences all over the place in nature; look at that plant over there, there's a regularity that occurs in the way the leaves are organised etc. The number is probably a Fibonacci sequence. Nature obeys mathematical principles!"

The Doc looked from one to the other, "Atz like fractils int it, aye was he the guy that invented fractals!?"

Hippie Davie was intrigued, "Yeah, like fractals dude, trees are like big fractals, who tells 'em to do that, dude?"

I felt the need to answer this, it was in my court. "It's in the DNA I suppose, probably an artefact of dividing cells in the embryonic plant.

Nature is numerical like you say, Hippie Davie. 'Division or actually multiplication of one cell into trillions is a numerical process! So, it happens in the embryo. Come to think about it evolution works at that level too, mutations at the embryonic not the older organism and that gives rise to changing statistics and chances going up or down for life and death for the individual also."

Hippie Davie interjected, "Fuckin wow and DNA is like the recording device charting the throws of the dice as the energy constantly changes and goes towards its home back to the Godhead."

I looked at The Doc and then back to Hippie Davie. "What the fuck does that mean?" I snapped.

Hippie Davie explained, "Since the big bang the energy of the universe has been expressing itself, as matter, stars, planets and life. Then consciousness and especially the insightful human consciousness was the *second* big bang! Eons of time being the essential variable for endless possibilities! With that humans have been born and the conscious possibility or potential is the godhead that we are moving towards, the ultimate expression of love, total, one hundred percent universal conscious awareness!"

I looked back at The Doc who just shrugged and said, "Fuck's sake Davie, for a Hippie you can be quite eloquent sometimes!"

I picked up the thread of the conversation again.

"Well DNA is a binary code right enough. It's a better way to store information!"

Hippie Davie looked surprised. "Binary code? Holy O.B.One-olay bro! Like, I've never heard DNA expressed like that...Binary code...Shit DNA might be like a giant living computer man!? Oh my God, Douglas Adams in Hitchhiker's Guide may have been onto something. Fuckinell, I bet if Plato knew about computers he would have been fuckin freaked right out man, he would have travelled the earth looking for the giant plug!"

I nodded. "Well it means that natural development conforms to numerical equations at some level, just like I said, spookily like the progress of computer software man! We, all things in existence seem to have that in common!"

Hippie Davie seemed to freeze, smoke falling at its own pace from the corners of his lips, his eyes lit by the sunlight glinting off the table and his dirty face made him all the more like a backdrop from a Black

Sabbath concert. "Waaaaait a fuckin' minute; waait a fuckiiiiiiiIIn' minute...!"

'I think I know where this is going,' I thought to myself as he passed the joint over, as if to share his joint meant sharing his thought.

"AtzzIt!" he exclaimed at once, having an eureka moment. "The universe is a big computer and we're awh inside it and once we all realise it totally, the program might stop and reset or something!" Hippie Davie bit his lip and looked genuinely worried. He hugged himself and looked like he was about to cry, "I'm nae real, I'm not even real. I don't even exist!"

It was extremely good timing as two older shoppers who'd strayed down from Union Street looking for a rest had been hanging about outside perusing the menu and trying to make up their minds to come go in or not, having clocked us three weirdos sitting there puffing away next to the front door. They had finally decided to venture in just as Hippie Davie started hugging himself and exclaiming out loud that he didn't exist. I watched them in synchrony stop in their tracks and then in unison swivel around and head right back out the door without even having to confer with each other. It was a moment of sheer comedy brilliance, but no one else saw it but me. I was becoming more sober as time passed, plus Hippie Davie was always way ahead of us in terms of brain THC content.

I decided to hand him back his joint and throw fuel on the fire. "Or maybe we're all in an experiment and the people in the real world somewhere are running a simulation and watching us. You ever think of that? I do sometimes!"

"Simulations!?" Hippie Davie's expression changed from genuinely worried to positively frightened!"

Bingo; it worked and I tried to suppress a smirk. I was enjoying watching the birth of a brand new psychological complex!

The Doc then interjected going the extra mile. "Or perhaps our bodies are somewhere else and we're imprisoned in a virtual world where advanced artificial intelligences farm us and control our every waking moment through virtual reality!?"

We all looked at each other momentarily and then spluttered into laughter!

I shook my head in resignation. "Awh fuck, now we're really are going too far, Jeeeeziz, the shite ye think up when yer stoned eh?"

Hippie Davie, though, looked somber for a moment, "Nah, nah, hey though! Thatz no' a bad idea, Doc, maybe we could write all this doon man, write a short story or even make it intae a film script or something! I mean it's a sort of modern version of Descartes monsters idea, but yeah....I like it!" We all stopped for a minute, alone in thought.

"Nah!" I said finally. "Naebody wid buy that idea, it'd be boring; it'd be pish! Trust me, no point in even thinking about it, it would never work!" I regarded Hippie Davie and his very stoned and now slightly confused expression and smiled; "Descartes! Now there was another guy that just smoked too much weed!"

We had a laugh about it, but it the conversation hadn't helped me organise my thoughts on problems I had with magick and the craft. I clasped my drink and looked into the coffee cup, "I still can't reconcile power or energy with anything actually physical, hence measurable!" I mouthed in resignation.

Hippie Davie empathised with my dilemma. "If enough people or enough emotional input is involved in a rite then the feeling of power one person has can affect another person or situation! You know that!?"

I did. "Yeah, healing, remotely affecting other people, yeah I have experienced that like numerable others."

"Well then stop trying to rationalise what you do know with knowledge that is currently inadequate to describe it," Hippie Davie said. "For a scientist, you are in good company of some real visionary scientists using magick like you do!"

I felt quite touched that Hippie Davie acknowledged me as having such worth. I had sensed some antagonism between us and had thought perhaps he thought I was a bit naïve or uneducated!

The Doc, meanwhile had been thinking things through as well. "Don't worry, you'll get it mate, someday!"

"Get what?" I rounded on the condescending little titmouse.

He then tried to do a Hippie Davie on me.

"You're always looking for evidence or proof of magick; that's the one thing that will unbalance the nuances of ritual magick. We Shamans have long understood the relationship between the living world and energy. In fact, Shamans have always used the force. Actually...Yoda's a sort of Shaman!"

I couldn't help but make an exasperated sigh.

"Yoda is a fuckin' muppet, all right!? A fucking muppet! Ees got a hand up ees fuckin' arse a-right!? Just like your heed's up yours!"

The Doc grinned, as he always did when he wanted to avoid confrontation.

Hippie Davie looked a bit offended. "Yoda's more animated than your little clay Goddess statue, that you paid over the price for on some new-agey shite stall, will ever be!"

With that, Don strode into view returning from a bit of random retail therapy and therefore much more upbeat than when he left. "All right boys, what have I missed then?" he said.

"Shamanism and the church of Star Wars were collaborating to overthrow the current mechanistic scientific paradigm," Hippie Davie said, sardonically whilst nodding towards me.

"Yeah, just the fucking usual, ye know Don!?" I said smiling whilst putting my face into my coffee cup.

"Well then, I've got something here to help the cause!" said Don and in dramatic fashion he pushed away a flap of his coat and wielded, in an arc and flick of the wrist, a large green Luke-Skywalker plastic light-saber complete with movie sounds! We all gasped as our faces were lit by an eerie green glow; an electric hum droning from the handset kidnapped the centre of attention. "Twenty two quid from Plan 9!" he said triumphantly.

I shook my head in disbelief. "Oh for fuck-sake!...Not you as well!?"

Don was a security guard, rather fittingly working at nights and sleeping by day, which matched his goth-like persona. Remarkably, when I first met Don at the circle, wearing his priest's cassock, large boots and white face, I asked him what his favourite Goth band was and he replied "What's a Goth?" Amazingly, he didn't deliberately follow any band or trend; that was just the way he decided to leave the house each day. No one understood why he chose to wear the priest's cassock! When I asked Don about it, he just exclaimed that it was a cool thing he found in a second-hand store and felt comfortable in it (Paul Alder had rather amusingly christened him "The Vicar of Wicca" in the dungeon one evening!).

Don had always been the person who we considered was the one that was most sensitive to spirit. Before finding his vocation as a witch Don had felt compelled to sit around graveyards of an evening, opening himself up to the spiritual impressions that he felt there. I had always been a little sceptical of mediums and talk of the departed. This wasn't really a large part of Wicca, except at Samhain (pronounced *sow-ain*) where the lord of shadows took us beyond the veil to the other side as it were. Actually, necromancy was the one aspect that I could never have any success with. I would sit there trying to scrye into a glass or something, desperately trying to contact my departed grandfather and so on, without ever a bloody single impression or anything. It was most disappointing to me and I had come to dismiss this side of the craft as wishful thinking.

Working alone at nights suited Don well, especially in this rather spooky building. The second floor in particular was supposedly haunted and many a night watchman had run out of the building never to return. There were all sorts of stories about people hearing voices on that floor, seeing moving shadows or feeling that someone was following them. A receptionist had heard someone walk down the stairwell from that floor, had heard doors swing open, footsteps and even what sounded like a ring scraping down the chrome banister, but no-one had come out of the doors below. Three chairs were often pulled out in the small canteen on that floor as if people had been sitting at a table. During the subsequent night-watchman's rounds they were replaced, but they were found to be pulled out again at the next walkabout. Don attested to this himself, but frankly I failed to believe it!

It was a spooky place to be sure and very quiet at night. I had poked my head into the quiet stairwell after hearing that story but elected not to go too far up. I don't know how Don managed to patrol that place himself at nights; it scared the hell out of me, but he seemed to quite like it. He had seen the apparition of a man and had even decided that his name was Harry. He would chat to him up there during his walkabouts as if he was addressing a work colleague! Whether he was totally fearless or just totally fucking nuts, I could never decide. Windows also had a tendency to open on the second floor by themselves, despite Don closing them on his rounds. It was weird. I experienced this myself and the lifts would spontaneously come down from the second floor to the reception where we were sitting chatting and open, empty. On one occasion while I sat in reception chatting away to Don, a loud bang like a door being hammered shut echoed through the building. I looked at Don startled – we were supposed to be the only people in the building – but Don didn't blink an eye, he just casually rolled a cigarette and without looking up said "It's ok, it's just

Harry, he often slams the door, I'll hae tae go up in spik to 'im later, I hivni' spoke tillum for a wee whilie, he's just wanting attention."

That was a little bit too scary for me to take. "He often slams the door?? Just wants attention?? Fuck me Don, cats often just want attention, mate, this is not normal man. I think you must be the only person in the world who has a fucking pet poltergeist! I do hope he's neutered!"

I knew which door he meant because I had walked with him sometimes and we often went into the conference room to play his Sony PlayStation PGA golf on the big screen and to help ourselves to the coffee and biscuits. I also knew that that door actually had a combination keypad lock on it and was a really big heavy door. This was just a bit too fuckin' much really. I had always thought Don was perhaps just a little impressionable when it came to ghosts and such like, but here he was talking matter-of-factly about weird poltergeist-like activities in a big lonely building in the middle of the night, things that had made other bigger, hairier security guards leave the building white faced and trembling, never to return.

After leaving us at the café 52 The Green, Don plodded onto work. Later that night, the unsuspecting Goth security guard sat in the small pool of light in the lower reception of a harbour building in Aberdeen, watching an episode of *Star Trek: The Next Generation*. He had an important night's work ahead of him and had the complete set of videos in front of him with box two laying open on top of the small television that sat atop the counter. He looked at his watch, 1:30 am; he picked up the handheld bar-code reader on the desk in front of him, "Central stairwell...right...about...now!" He pointed the reader to a photocopied A4 sheet of barcodes in front of him and with a beep, he relaxed, slid the paper back into a paper folder hidden under a book and then turned back towards the T.V. As the credits of episode two rolled, Don decided to make himself a cup of coffee and have a bit of weed before settling down to the rest of the night's work. As he stood up, he glanced along the wide, quiet streets that led down to the quay just in case his 'beat driver' was going to make an unexpected visitation. Fraser was getting good at mooching any weed and Don was trying to put a stop to that. A cursory glance at this street usually revealed it to be very quiet save for the odd sailor going back to their boat, but the ferry wasn't in tonight. You could almost hear the sound of the cushioned wings of the gulls gliding through the cones of light spreading to ground from the regular rows of glaring orange lozenge-like lamplights. A lack of sailors meant Don had to find other means of entertainment and fortunately he knew a guy who avidly collected sci-fi and had lent him the videos in exchange for other, ahem, small favours.

However, as he glanced along the street this night, Don hesitated. Something made him stop still before even straightening up from his chair, as he squinted along the long row of lights from the building. Across from the entrance, a lone figure stood motionless, facing the building. Don blinked, it was definitely a person. This was odd and he reached behind him put off all the lights and then switched off the T.V. to get a closer look through the large glass doors. Was this going to be some sort of raid? He glanced at the radio on the counter. It wasn't his job to confront aggressors. The company policy was to radio for aid and not give resistance. Don was quite clear on the last part. This wasn't fair, it wasn't part of his job, as security guard his was quite certain by now that his job involved sitting on his arse, watching sci-fi and porn all night, having to put up with a possible break-in wasn't in his personal job description at any rate.

The figure remained motionless and Don could see better through the glass. It wore a large cowl, like a monk dressed in black. Thinking of the ghostly companion in this dark place, Don naturally began to speak loudly towards the figure outside, "Harry is that you?" then speaking softly to himself, "No wait...Harry disnae wear a cloak!" He walked forward and pressed his face closer to the glass. The figure, whose face had been bowed all this time, slowly began to raise his head. Don could not make out any features within the blackened shade of the large hood. The figure slowly raised his arm and an outstretched finger beckoned towards him. He cast a long shadow across the road from the street lights behind him. *'Mmmmm so it is an actual person,'* Don thought, *'not a phantom monk at all!'* He realised he was applying a scientific rigour to this that Sean might have been proud of! The monk-figure strode across the road with much deliberation and with the same outstretched hand began to reach into his cowl.

Don at once understood what the figure wanted. It cared not for the company secrets in the many files or the thousands of pounds worth of office equipment. It was here for him. It was here for combat and Don realised that he had only a few minutes to react. He backed away from the glass and ran towards his seat, nearly slipping on the marble floor, as he rounded the desk. The figure strode purposely up the steps fixating on the furtive movements of its quarry inside. Don's hand reached behind the desk, his night-stick was over by his chair, a precious few meters away but with barely enough time Don's hand plunged into his backpack as he heard the door swing open a few feet away from him. Fumbling around for a weapon, his fingers found the lightsaber he had bought earlier and with an arc-like movement honed from watching many late night action films, he wielded the plastic toy and flicked on the movie sounds as he spun his body round to face his attacker. The green light flickered onto the hooded figure looming in front of him.

"Yer valour is most commendable! Bit yer gan ti need mair in jist that tae defeet me!" the figure said in a voice recognisable to Don before the strike came!

The marble entry way of the building echoed with the din of movie-sound lightsabers as the red glow of the monk's weapon collided with the green of Don's own one. Don could see the determination on the red-lit face of The Doc underneath the hood as the two danced circles around each other striking and parrying as they went. He was every bit as ugly as the emperor and then some. Don recounted in best Errol Flynn style, honed by a lifetime of watching old films on Sunday afternoons, "Have at you sir, ye canna defeet me ya bastird, I'll jist become more powerful than you can ever imagine – you ugly, poxy little cunt!" Who knows what films Don watched?

A quarter of a mile away on Market Street, two drunk old guys made their way on their long walk back to Torry after being kicked out of the pub, long after closing time. One of the pair stopped and peered towards the flashing green and red lights of the duel now in full swing. "What's the fuck's happening doon there?" he said pointing towards the darkened harbour building with the red and green lights arcing and clashing in strange rhythmic regularity.

His unsteady companion squinted and walked forwards a few yards, looking back he said "It's the security guard mannie, fighting aff some monkie lookin' boyh wi some kind o'...laser sticks!

Lines of confusion deepened across the other man's face, etched with ages of bar side philosophy. He shook his head in disapproval, "'Laser stickies is it now!? Monkie boys and iv-ery thing? They keep a' this stuff secret fae uz eh din't they?"

His pal wobbling on the spot put his finger in the air, "I ken fit it is! It's that Star Warsie thing thit Reagan started, I seen sumink aboot it on the news a while-ie ago!"

His pal still staring over at the building slowly nodded in agreement, "Fuckin' aye richt enuff; it must be one of thon American companies!"

And with that they shrugged and carried on walking home, safe in the knowledge that they had it all figured out; it would be the topic of conversation in the Schooner at opening time the next day.

In the evenings, I would often find the other three a good distraction from actually doing any work, as I was now well into my first term of year four. We would often drive out to stone circles at night and hang about, doing Pagan stuff, such as eating crisps and smoking rollies (occasionally we'd try to astral project and commune with nature spirits there, but mainly, it involved the former activities). The doc told us that as a Shaman, he knew the secrets of stone circles and how to "activate" them. Sitting in the Prince one Sunday afternoon, the four of us resolved to make a serious attempt to invoke any presence's which might be there. The Doc was doing his best to convince us with every breath, but mainly just convincing himself.

"I'll open the portal of this circle and it'll link us to other realms, definitely...definitely without a doubt."

Out of curiosity and a hankering for crisps, we thought we might as well let him have a pop at it.

We sped out later that evening in my VW Golf headed for the East Aquorthies stone circle close to Inverurie; Don had the night off, so we were good to go. The Doc had us take positions around the circle, annoyingly pushing and pulling at us until he was satisfied we were in the right place.

"Right, now what you've got to bear in mind is that this circle is just dormant at the moment, with the appropriate words and enough focused energy we can raise and talk to the ancestors." The Doc walked off and stood in front of the large recumbent stone and started making random Amer-indian sounding chants. "Hey-ya - ho-ya – Hey-ya – ho-ya..." I looked over at Don, my face frozen in a manic grin as I repressed the laugh that wanted so much to escape. Finally I couldn't resist,

"Hey – ya who you callin' a ho?" This was met with an immediate:

"Fuck you! – bloody wiccans!! Shut up!" He carried on regardless, albeit a little less loudly, muttering something under his breath as he went. My eyes were just becoming accustomed to the dark when it I noticed the main stone glowing red. I gasped for a second in awe, before realising what was happening,

"Oh my God, wait...Doc? Is that a fucking lightsaber you've got in your hands? OH For FUCK'S SAKE!!"

The Doc put a finger to his lips. "Sssh we're nae going to wake this dor-mint circle wi' your attitude!"

"My attitude!" I exclaimed. "Look Doc, the only dormant thing here is your brain. You think the ancestors used battery-operated fuckin' toys? Are you lot taking the piss?" I turned to look at Hippie Davie who just looked away, a little embarrassed. I was aware that Hippie Davie used a toy lightsaber as an athame in all earnest at times; he had reasoned that objects were all items of the mind and that this was as relevant to him as the concept of a knife to project imaginary circles for ritual purposes anyway.

"What is this all about?" I turned to Hippie Davie.

"Look Sean, why not? I know I've been using toys like this to conjure up my imagination since I was first able to hold one. It is easier to use an object that the mind is used to for imagination purposes. Since power is bent and created by the will and imagination, what better to guide it than something that is relevant to the imagination, why should a big knife represent the direction of power? In 'real' faery lore metal is supposed to drain energy away anyway!"

The Doc cut in, "Exactly, exactly, magick is all aboot imagination and using that bit of the mind, jist like fin we were kids, yiv jist got to believe, thatz the key to making magick work, so it makes sense to use summing fae childhood, so why nae? Besides it's fuckin' pitch black oot here, fit better thin an athame wi it's ain built in torch?"

I muttered in reply loud enough for everybody to hear, conveying my disappointment and scepticism, "Aye, it helps if you've got the mentality of an eight-year-old then Doc!"

Hippie Davie cut in, "I would have thought you of all people would have understood that we're just being unconventional, anarchistic even! Fuck all that crap about athames, circles and doing things according to some fucker's fuckin' law. Some wanker's just made it up anyway, it's all Golden Dawn stuff that, they made up lots of stuff. We are Wiccans, Shamans and the official Sorcerers of Britain. We make the rules, we have power of mind over matter, there *is* only one way of fucking life and that's our own."

He glared at me, a power in his eyes. I felt an empathy with his words; quoting from CRASS and the Levellers was a cheap trick, he had me there. "Ok, ok save your Jedi mind tricks, it won't work with me young Padawan," I said in order to break the spell that Hippie Davie was casting on me.

Hippie Davie smiled and grabbed my shoulder, "The force is strong in this one." He patted me on the back.

"I get it, magick is in the mind, we four are a coven of the mind, cool, but maybe my mind is different from yours!" I said. "Ok, ok, Doc, do what the hell you want but if you start chanting anything to do with the Darth Vader, I swear to god, I'll kick ye so hard in the nuts that we'll huv' tae start calling ye O.B. Wonky Knobby!"

We all had a bit of a laugh before The Doc insisted we should get started again.

The Doc turned around and again and muttered something about me being too scientific for my own good. The recumbent stone again glowed red and I had to admit it looked very eerie and pretty like that. He assured us that he had to walk around the circle three times clockwise alone. As he walked around us waving his long red torch, I mused that if anyone were to guide in a UFO to one of these circles, then The Doc was the main man. He went off murmuring an incantation under his breath as he went. He wouldn't tell us what the words were, but he could well have been singing "I'm a lumberjack and I'm all right" for all we knew. Time passed and then passed some more. Fuck all happened! It was a cold November night and frost lay all over the ground, even with layers on I was starting to shiver.

"Fuck this for a game of soldiers!" I said. "I don't care if a bastard UFO is about to land, I'm getting back into that car, putting the heating on before hypothermia sets in, or is that too scientific for ya?"

The Doc shone his torch over his hand and two fingers lit up at the other side of the circle, their shadow poignantly skimming over the frosted ground to where I was standing. "Fuck off then, I'll dae it masael!" he replied from behind a large stone, I knew any lack of success would be put down to me with much griping in future. I didn't care; it was freezing and I knew he'd have us standing there like prunes all night if he could. Anyway, I knew Hippie Davie and Don knew that he was a twat as well.

"Getting too much like close encounters of the twat kind around here!" I uttered. I was a little bit pissed off to say the least. "Standin' in the freezin' bloody cauld...pitch black...three times roond for fuck all..fuckin' lumberjack and I'm all right."

The Doc not to be defeated had set off on his way round again, thinking maybe he had missed a bit perhaps or that he had been one hey short of a heyahoya.

Back in the car with the heater on full blast, we did the usual stuffing our faces and enjoying a bit of a smoke. Looking dead ahead into the dark towards the circle, we were all stunned by the sudden bright flash coming off one of the legs of the little metal placard that had all the information about the circle for tourists and visitors. This lay over the fence just beside the circle in front of us. "W'tae fuck wiz satt?" we collectively said in total surprise, as it was quite dark and there were no lights about for miles. I turned around to check whether Hippie Davie had his light saber with him.

Hippie Davie looked innocent, "Nuthin' to do with me," he said.

We slowly climbed out of the car.

"I knew it, I knew it," exclaimed The Doc. "There! You see, did you see that? That's energy being emitted from the charged circle; from my ritual...believe me now?"

I must admit I was a little lost for words..."Nah, surely not!" But try as I might, I couldn't find an explanation for it and couldn't conceive of how a metal post could spontaneously flash. I thought of reflected light, but unless some bugger was pissing about in the adjacent cold and dark field with a torch, then I didn't see how it could have been. It couldn't have been The Doc; it just didn't fit with his toy red light, as the flash was quite white. I even ruled out planes and helicopters and there were no cars anywhere near the small dirt-track farm roads surrounding us. 'Bizarre,' I thought!

Meanwhile, little big man was dancing about "I've activated the circle, wow I've actually done it...see if there had been more people, we could re-start this now dormint circle *etc, etc*."

We went back to the car, but Don elected to stay. After sitting for a while, we started wondering where he was.

"Switch on the bloody lights," said The Doc, "see what he's doing."

I switched them on. The car was facing the circle and the headlights illuminated the ring of stones. There standing in the middle of the cold circle, grass white with frost, was Don, naked as the day he was born.

The Doc started pissing himself laughing, "What the fuck'see dee'in...he must be freezing cauld o'er 'er...quick get the camera." He went rummaging for the camera I usually took with me on these occasions, but I had it in my pocket and didn't give it to him; I had noticed that he tended to whip out a camera when people were exposing themselves in outdoor rituals and it was starting to worry me.

I had to admit, it was quite a funny sight, though, Don's cold dimpled buttocks lit up in the dark night. We hadn't expected it to see his shiny naked ass reflecting the car lights like that and as it was such a bitterly cold night, it was a strange thing to do, but that was Don, he just got the urge to do that and he didn't care. I guess that anomalous light had convinced him as well that something was going on there and perhaps thought that the ancestors might be honoured by the sight of his bare penis swaying about defying the cold Aberdeenshire night air; after all, he had had a few compliments about it in the past didn't he? I suppose he was quite proud of it. The Picts, come to think about it, were renowned for running into battle naked covered in paint, hence the name, Pictish (c.f. pictogram) and Don did have his fair share of tattoos – a big scarab beetle on his chest, a dragon on his legs and large goddess on his arms. I suppose he looked the part. However I couldn't believe the flash had originated from paranormal reasons. The metal had felt cold, but I was beginning to feel sure that we had perhaps witnessed a form of St. Elmo's fire. I believed strongly in Conan Doyle's 'Sherlock Holmes' dictum; "Once you eliminate the impossible, whatever remains, no matter how improbable, must be the truth." To me some natural phenomenon still ranked as a more probable explanation, I just didn't know what it was; but there was no real reason to invoke ideas of ancestors or Shaman power.

## Chapter 6:
## The Doors of Reception

I went for a drive with The Jumper a few nights later and ended up at Easter Aquorthies again, ostensibly because he hadn't seen it and I figured night was the best time to go, plus I was still intrigued and bugged about the strange "astral light" that The Doc was going on and on about. As we wandered around looking at the stones close up and so on, I headed back to the car to get a packet of mints or something and as I was heading towards the fence I happened to see again a flash emanating from the same metal leg of the information plaque of the time before. This time I looked around wildly, determined to find the source of the illumination and was just in time to spot car headlights blinking on a very distant hill turning away on full beam on a faraway bend. "AAhha Watson," I cried in triumph, I'd discovered the key to the little riddle. The hill must have been a good thirty miles away or more, very far away. But there was nothing impeding the view from there to the stones. You'd never guess car headlights could travel all that way, but on full beam apparently they did. It obviously happened only occasionally as that seemed to be a very lonely little road on that hill, perhaps the car of people who lived there. It was too far away to light up the stones, but was just enough to reflect off that much shinier bit of metal. I felt that Sherlock Holmes himself would have been proud of that observation and I couldn't wait to tell The Doc, Hippie Davie and Don but especially The Doc.

Spurred on by this bit of deduction, I decided that we should investigate the second floor of Don's workplace. So the batbox bunch minus one Hippie Davie (who had warned that Yoda had advised against such things) assembled at the building one evening soon after. The truth was Hippie Davie didn't really like Don's work and had heard the stories too many times, not to mention see the lift coming down for himself. Also, he was probably 'spending time' with the older married woman he was currently seeing (and as it happened worked at the blumin' Prince Of Wales – If we were jealous of him before...!?). I was very envious at that one and tried to refer to him as "Alfie" after the Michael Cain character from the Sixties. However, he just told me to fuck off and mind my own business, or else he'd shag me as well. I tried to bitch to Don about Hippie Davie's lack of morals, but he wouldn't hear a bad word about him, as I suspected he was madly in love with him. That did grate my nerves at times, though The Doc and I, at least, could bitch together about Hippie Davie's lack of morals and sexual exploits.

So on this intrepid evening facing the bottom of the infamous stairwell we contemplated hiking up into the dark and haunted abyss. The Doc actually held out his hand and grabbed mine (what's worse was, I didn't let it go) looking all brave and fearless he nonchalantly said, "C'mon then, let's go, let's definitely do it, without a doubt." I was buoyed by his apparent confidence; however Don waved his hands and stood between us and the bottom step.

"No, no, no, you canna go up like that, it's only gan tae work if go up one at a time...erm...that's the only way that he appears to people!" he resolutely informed us.

I looked up the stairs, I didn't fancy it one little bit, but Don was calling the shots here, so I relented. Besides, this would be a good way of facing what was surely an irrational fear, as no ghost in history, to my knowledge, had actually hurt anyone so surely it was in the mind! Therefore, if I could control my mind, then I would prove something to myself. I mean, Sherlock Holmes would never be scared to walk down a fucking corridor at night now would he!?

I lost the coin toss and had to go first. As we watched it land heads up, I shook my head in disdain, "Oh, that's so fucking typical that is!" The other two then, without so much as a pat on the back, fucked off straight away to go and have a smoke and a cup of tea. "Bastards!" I exclaimed as they disappeared from sight into the small corridor and suddenly I felt a bit weak at the knees as I became hypersensitive to every little sound around me echoing in the stairwell, such as The Doc's relieved voice and Don's jangly boots.

I walked up the stairwell; it was quiet and quite frightening. I had to keep my nerve, but all I could think about was the story of the noise of a phantom 'someone' walking down this very stair from the second floor. The sound of the ring scraping on the chrome banister and the phantom footsteps were playing on my mind. It was also very fresh in my head, as Don had very kindly reminded us of the story right before he sent us in. "Might as well have shone a torch underneath his bloody face to freak us oot, I mean, fuck me; what an actual fuckin' bastard!" I said sardonically out loud to comfort myself. Also, I thought if I maintained the victimised persona, the ghost may have some sympathy for me. It was worth a shot anyway.

The stairs were lit, but that didn't help much; it was a spiral staircase and so after slowly traversing the first floor I quickly found myself truly cut off from the reception and felt quite alone. I kept stopping to look up the middle of the banister towards the ominous second floor, feeling almost sure that a figure was about to lean over the rail and peer down at me at any moment. Perhaps a white ghostie's face, grinning like a nutter gazing down onto a white fearties' face grimacing upwards!? The adrenaline coursed through my arms, as I gripped the metal banister hard with whitening knuckles, pulling myself on, trying to dispel those types of thoughts and think instead of Sherlock Holmes; "What would Holmes do?" I muttered to myself, egging myself on. I put my head down and plodded onwards and upwards, trying to make it feel as natural as possible, purposely whistling like a window cleaner in Dracula's castle.

Entering the door to the second floor, I found myself in the small reception of the oil company that operated on that floor, together with a couple of silver lift doors, a small black PVC chrome couch and a large model of an oil rig in a glass case, which had been randomly placed in the middle of the floor. Taking some time to gather myself, I made a point of studying the model oil rig in detail. 'People work here,' I thought to myself, 'this is stupid.' I thought about the receptionist, the people who walk past here every day amid the hustle and bustle of office life. All those work facts and figure-fixated minds, the inevitable boring golf conversations colouring the atmosphere with caffeine and sexual tensions. I then turned to the large doors to the left of the small reception desk and duly punched in the numbers, which Don had given me, onto the little silver push buttons on a small black combination lock. The large heavy door swung open like a crypt entrance as I stepped through into darkness. The door eventually swung closed behind me and I stood motionless waiting for my eyes to adjust to the darkness. If you've ever played *Alien* on the Sony PlayStation, then you'll know just how perturbing this situation was.

The plan was to walk right down the long dark corridor, which stretched away to the right. To the left was a short walk to a window that overlooked the harbour. I walked towards it and stayed there for a minute or so staring out into the harbour, occasionally looking around, staring towards the penetrating darkness until my eyes became accustomed to the darkness. I began to see the corridor very dimly lit by a row of small rectangular windows running along the top, lit by the lights from the road and harbour. Eventually I looked into it and collected myself. I allowed myself to get a little pissed off, even aggressive so I could make myself move along the corridor. I was a witch, after all, so I called the horned God and invoked him into me. I then withdrew my athame from my back pocket and pointed it forward. This was a great comfort to me as on initiation, we are told that the athame is a witch's tool for controlling spirits. Casting a circle of self-protection around myself I felt my Qi/Chi/Ki energy (or as a witch refers to this: my power) balloon and expand then illuminate, going around and ahead of me like a snow plough.

I continued on down the narrow corridor into the darkness. I passed dark offices where red lights blinked on fax machines whilst photocopiers hummed in the silence. I only occasionally glanced behind me. I had moved a fair bit along and darkness now enveloped the corridor behind. Eventually, I came to a short sort of chicane in the corridor and I stopped and looked forward, feeling a little more perturbed here than anywhere else. I felt cold and a prickly chill raised up my spine to my neck and spread all over the back of my head. Suddenly, the air became very much colder and just as I was processing this fact with a feeling of dreadful anticipation, I presently became aware of some movement next to me and my heart jumped in response. Suddenly, out of the quiet darkness, a human-like movement cut in front of me from the corner to my left to the corridor in front of me. It was tall, three dimensional and man-shaped and appeared to be blocking my way in front of me. It was so solid in appearance that the corridor which had been empty now seemed blocked. I would actually have had to push it out of the way to go forward. Forward, however, was not a direction my legs wanted to go, or any other part of my whole fucking being come to that! The air was very cold and the hair was standing up on the back of my neck. I had stopped dead in my tracks, every fibre in my body was shrieking for me to turn back and run back to reception. I was terrified and it seemed that I was all of a sudden no longer alone!

However, this is what I came for wasn't it? I also reasoned that this was perhaps my only chance to ever prove something to myself; 'what would Sherlock Holmes do now,' I thought? And so I peered through the darkness towards the figure that appeared to be in front of me. 'I must be sure, I must make sure, this must be my imagination and so I must prove it to myself one way or the other,' I thought to myself and so I dug in my heels, gulped and raised my athame towards the shadow in the corridor.

"I mean you no harm; I only wish to communicate with you," I said and willed myself one step forward.

To my utter horror and amazement, the shadowy figure seemed to actually jump backwards and run down the corridor, jump behind the chicane in the corridor and then seconds later appeared to pop its head around to watch me (course, if someone accosted me brandishing a pointy knife claiming he only wanted to communicate with me, I might fuck off sharpish down the corridor as well). It also appeared still to be quite three dimensional. I really wish at this moment that I had just run up to the bloody thing and made one hundred percent sure this was no trick of the light, or just imagination, but my inner dialogue was computing at break neck speed, 'Is what I'm seeing real? Yes it certainly seems so, it looks three dimensional and it is there watching me...do I need further evidence? I don't fuckin' think so. Right that's it, it's a wrap, now let's get the fuck out of dodge pronto.' Indeed, my legs were already carrying me towards that big door even before this flash of inner dialogue had come to a conclusion. I left the great detective's skills there in the dark, now more Scooby Doo than Sherlock Holmes. I didn't bother with the lift; I bolted down those stairs, about six at a time and emerged into the foyer and ground floor reception.

"Well Doc old son," I said, as I neared the front reception, very relieved to see them both sitting with the normality of coffee cups and conversation, "It's your turn, on you fuckin' go son, he's waiting for ye!"

I wouldn't normally have expected anyone in their right mind to go upstairs after that, but The Doc had been regaling Don and I for a good week or so on how a Shaman at his level had power over spirits; in fact he said, "Av nothing to fear from ghosts n' stuff me, those type of things can perceive 'my' power on the astriil. They're actually really scared of *me*!" So off he went upstairs, brandishing some kind of wooden rattle with manky looking crow feathers hanging off of it and I began taking bets with Don on how long he'd be up there for. Maybe he'd go right to the end of the corridor, who knows? But before we even had a chance to debate this, the lift started down and out strode The Doc looking just a little distressed, loudly rattling his rattle.

I smirked in amazement. "What the fuck?? Ye couldn't have been in the lobby mair'n' two seconds min! fit are ye deein' doon here already?" I said as he made his way back to the desk.

"Oh I don't know aboot this like lads, there's a funny 'atmosphere' up there, I dae like it one little bit…Am, am getting danger signals! I…I can feel it in my water, I get warnings like that when there's hostile spirits aboot, without a doubt!" He was acting a bit like Basil Fawlty with his war wound excuse to get out of doing any work.

"Warnin' signals? Huh, heheh, that's just palpitations ye big fearty!" I said laughing.

Don cut in smiling wryly, clearly enjoying himself, sounding like some evil Victorian school master; "Well, well, well; so this is the high fearless medicine man? You never even went into the lobby yet did ye? Fuck's sake min! I da kaen." He shook his head, a wide smirk on his face. "Tut tut, what do you think, Sean?"

"Right enough," I said picking up on the pincer movement, "seems like a total cop out tae me like, least us witches can hack it eh Don? But you witch doctors, well ye seem to have fuck-all power over spirits after all!"

This was too much for The Doc. Here was the man who had started to believe he could make Don and I his pupils in witch-doctery if we wanted. In fact, he had been boasting of this down the road in Dundee, just as he was coming up here and telling all of us that they'd converted their coven to a proper Shaman tribal group and hence they had all become his pupils and disciples. He seemed a bit obsessed with having pupils and I suspected he was desperately trying to emulate Paul Alder, as they had been mates in the past. Now The Doc lauded Paul as being reckless with high magick and incompetent to boot, which definitely meant that Paul had slapped The Doc's wrists for something and so they were no longer friends.

After a wee respite, The Doc stood up.

"Awright, awright I wull go up jist you watch, am nae scared" and off he went again, rattle in hand. He knew that Don's smirking face would be all he would see for the next few months or even the rest of his life and no-one could take that. You'd rather walk into Hell for twenty minutes than put up with that.

Don called after him, "An' 'mind now, you have to go through the doors or it disnae coont, Harry won't go out to the lobby tonight."

As he disappeared into the stairwell, Don and I just smiled at each other. I smirked, "I like how he's already got the rattle, so let's club in and get him the massive dummy to ram in his gob for good!"

Shaking his head, Don said "He's the only massive dummy aroon' here. I kint it, ah kint 'at would happen, I kint he wiz full o' shite, an' that's why I got yez to go up one at a time!"

I looked at him a little exasperated; "Bloody hell Don!" I was a bit miffed that I had endured that on my own, "I wiz fuckin' terrified up there!"

"Well" he said, sounding a bit thoughtful and even surprised, "at least you went right into the corridor."

I regarded him for a second, reading the look of this on his face. "You didn't think I wiz gan tae did ye?"

"Wellllll," he replied sounding a little condescending, with obvious contradiction in his voice, "I did think you might open the door and look in, but I didnae think you'd...be awa for so lang!"

"You cheeky bastard!" I said thinking out loud.

But our conversation was soon cut short by the earth shuddering reverberations of the security doors above us on the second floor slamming shut with tremendous force. I jumped and looked startled at Don. "What the fuck's he dee'in up there?" I mouthed a little unnerved by the ferocity of the exploding door sound still emanating around the building.

Don listened on, looking curious, one eyebrow contorted Roger Moore-like, lighter poised at his spliff now still in front of his face, which was quite unlike Roger Moore. As the echo of the big bang was subsiding and before I had finished my sentence, there followed the fast squeaky-scuttling sound of Doc Martin boots near catching fire on a stairwell. Our heads then spun around in synchrony, as the stair door burst open accompanied by a low terrified moaning sound. All we could see was a confusion of tattooed arms scrambling through the door followed by the sound of "fuuuuuuuuuuuuuuuuuuuucccccccccccccckkkkkkkkkkkinnnnellllllllll," as The Doc shot out without even looking in our direction. And in a scene reminiscent of the lion from The Wizard of Oz taking flight down the long corridor as the wizard boomed at them and diving out of a window as he went, he ran straight past us, tore open the front doors and scrambled out into the street.

We turned to look at each other quizzically as the Shaman shape left the building before us and was fast disappearing into the fresh air outside. I could almost swear that he was leaving cartoon style puffs of smoke in his wake. Then with a double take, we leapt into action and began to give hot pursuit. This was partly out of concern for him, but also more especially out of my resolute sense of self-preservation, which was now at full mast. When we eventually caught up with him about a mile and a half up the road, he was hysterical and as white as a sheet.

"No way, No way," he cried, clutching at his chest and shaking like a leaf. "It's too hostile up there," he continued, between gasps for breath. As a bit of a chain smoker, his little sprint had been really quite impressive for speed and distance. "You must have aggravated them far too much, Sean! Tears had streaked over his cheeks. It was a little while before we could get the full story out of him.

He wasn't joking, either. Apparently the poor bastard had just got to the top of the stairs and into the little reception when he was met with the sight of the doors in front of him now improbably standing wide open. As he was debating to himself how this could be – *i.e.* had I not shut them correctly or had they just drifted open to reveal the pitch black lobby behind it – something he described as extremely cold and sickening and big and black, slammed into him, almost knocking him over as the two doors, pulled or pushed by invisible hands, slammed angrily with great speed and with a deafening boom right in front of him. It must have seemed like a scene from a hammer house of horror film come to life and damn near sent our great champion of Shamanism on a one-way ticket to meet his ancestors.

"You've aggravated something up there; yes, yes that's what it is, without a doubt...***without...a...doubt!***" he said barely having enough breath for the last *doubt*. He was shitting himself, clearly in shock and I really couldn't blame him. Wild horses wouldn't drag me back up there. I couldn't explain that, I knew I had shut the door. I don't believe The Doc even went near the door on his first visit, besides the building was never windy or anything and I doubted air could suck those heavy security doors anyway! I was genuinely freaked and perplexed by this. However, I was even more perplexed as to how Don could just amble back in there and do a night's work! He actually walked down that corridor later and just had a laugh about it with that particularly inhospitable spook.

To my mind, this door slamming was a little bit more inexplicable than seeing just an apparition. Psychology informs us that perception is, by default unreliable as the brain can process things differently in different situation; that's just common sense. On the other hand, a bunch of people hearing a loud bang occur in a spooky building coinciding with someone seeing the doors apparently move on their own, now that was a little bit more difficult to explain. This included a physical element that seemed to concur with the visual experience, which was very hard to explain away.

This resulted in genuine cognitive dissonance for me, as did a strange but much less scary apparition that occurred out of the blue a few weeks after this, one evening in my flat. I owned a black cat, which I agreed over the phone to have from the cat protection league. (I hadn't specifically asked for a black cat, but that's what they came with and I fell in love with him instantly, as he went exploring my flat meowing intermittently. I elected to call him Darwin, as this was the first name that I saw as my eyes perused along the bookshelf).

One afternoon I was sitting chatting to The Jumper when, from the corner of my eye, I saw Darwin walking through from the kitchen. From where I was sitting, I had a view of the hall and kitchen beyond. I turned and began to call to him but as I was doing so I noticed that he was a little smaller and looked different. Also, I began to get a little confused, as it dawned on me that I was sure that Darwin was actually out and there was no way he could've got in himself. The cat then turned and as he did so he brushed against the tassel hanging down from a small lamp table that began to sway with the contact. I then watched the little black cat head towards the main door of the hall and then simply vanish into the closed door! I sat mouth agape and The Jumper, realising that I was a little stunned broke off from his conversation. I jumped up and ran into the hall, the tassel was still swaying and it never did that on its own. I tried almost obsessively over the next few days to replicate this motion by causing draughts in various directions, but the motion had been too strong to be a draught and besides I could not reproduce the rhythmic swinging unless I pushed them. Eventually I concluded that something genuinely strange had occurred.

Pondering this with the other three one afternoon, Don informed me that it wasn't unusual for phantom cats to be seen in a flat where there are cats going about. Naturally, we tried to bring it to materialisation in a circle but alas nothing of any note happened. I fancied I saw the outline of a little cat sitting curiously at the edge of the circle but dismissed this as pure fantasy. Afterwards, I remarked to Hippie Davie, "Funny, it seems that when I really try to conjure up spirits, I see fuck all! But if I'm sitting talking to a buddy or something, wham, a fuckin' apparition walks through a wall! It's exactly like trying to watch wildlife."

Hippie Davie leaned forward, animated. "Yeah, exactly! Because it is wildlife in a way! They are not aware of you, particularly, either, unless you catch them off guard, like walking into a clearing in a forest as a herd of deer run by."

I was still not entirely convinced. I thought that it was not an illusion of some sort. The best and most rational explanation that made sense to me was that perhaps, subconsciously I had become aware of the tassels swinging and to explain it, my brain had "painted in" the black cat; like when you think you've seen a flying insect, for example, when in fact it's just a piece of fluff or something caught on your eyelashes. A few more split seconds of perception and you are aware of the error and actually catch yourself "updating" the perception experience. I mean, our brains do this all the time, constantly painting in our fovea spot or blind spot on the retina. We become conditioned to expectations as well; it saves on processing time. So it wasn't a leap of imagination for me to accept that my perception processing had just enlarged the blind spot painting and my expectations filled in a "black cat," and perhaps my imagination just enjoyed the scene or indulged that scene for a second longer then was realistically practical. My hallucination had to be based on this type of error! I still couldn't explain the swaying tassels, though.

I put that to Hippie Davie in the student union dungeon with Don one evening a few days later; he mused for a second and then shook his head, the dreadlocks moving in synchronicity as one nodding affirmative mass. It made me wonder, for a second, whether hippies used copious amounts of hairspray, which would be a gross disappointment to me if it were true. He trapped me in his gaze, which was always weirdly electric, sending a slight shiver down my spine and a genuine pleasant sense that I was looking into the eyes of someone that actually genuinely liked me and thus made me lower you guard. No wonder he got so many girls!

"Well, you see Sean," he said, "When you start doing magick in a purposeful way, you set a ball rolling. You, eh-um...start a process of transformation. I mean, you begin to externalise parts of yourself, perhaps and the universe kicks in to help you on your way."

I didn't know what he was talking about! "What do you mean by 'externalise parts of myself?' I've not done that! I wouldn't know where to start!"

Hippie Davie smiled and searched his word bank for a few seconds; I watched the mental processing drift across his expression and I thought I saw a slight glimmer of triumph. I wasn't sure if it was over-confidence or condescension that was the cause of his self-satisfaction at times!

"Think of it like this, Sean - you made a kind of oath back there in the circle several weeks ago, remember? A serious oath to learn the ways of magick and develop your third eye and 'develop psychically.' I think those were the words you used. Well Sean, mate, you did that in a circle with real intent. I do sympathise with that aim, of course but you don't actually know what you're letting yourself in for brother! I mean that's the problem with Wicca, in my opinion. It exposes people to this, this amazing technology, this system of changing your very reality and nobody seems to mention it! Nobody seems to acknowledge that aspect; you just act out the Sabats and have faith that the Goddess is a light in your life. In some ways it's just being like a Christian having faith in a God. Yeah, you're more focused on the feminine and nature herself and that's fine, that's good to get that consciousness going again, I mean God forbid, the world, the Earth really needs it. But you're playing around with magick and mind-altering technologies and these things are the doorways to real alchemy!"

The first thing that came to mind was some old renaissance period Da Vinci-like character hovering over a chemistry set trying to make gold out of lead, mercury and a host of other chemicals that are probably bad for you before the days of fume cupboards. I turned the sage's face into a demented looking Wally Fraser in my head, just as desperate for his amphetamine-gold that would never come. I screwed my face up at Hippie Davie, telegraphing that I wasn't following what he was saying and was beginning to get hacked off by it.

"Sorry, I'm not with you, how is Wicca a doorway to alchemy? You mean coz they share a root in pre-science or something?"

Hippie Davie scratched his face, rubbed his chin a little and I fathomed that he didn't even know what he was talking about.

"Naaaah, brother, what I mean by alchemy is just a form of mental exercises or meditations that help you forge yourself anew in the cauldron of your own body and energy." He looked very animated as he spoke and his eyes shone with enthusiasm. "I mean, like yoga or something, or like the Tai Chi that I've been trying to do for years and only just getting to grips with now. Magick is alchemy in that you can really transform yourself, your mind, in ways you don't know yet. Trust me, I know it can be very big, very sudden and erm...and this is equated with basically, enlightenment in stages!" He pondered and shook his head from side to side as if wrestling with two opposing views, vying for a compromise of explanations." Except in magick you don't call it enlightenment, it's known as illumination! So when you said that, in the circle, I think, you basically asked the powers that be, that you wanted illumination! And that has probably started you on a path to fuck knows where my brother!" He grinned and patted me on the shoulder, in a manner that was one cult member slapping the back of another cult member who'd just received their white robe in the post after giving up all their worldly riches. Except I didn't have many riches to give up anyway and we weren't in California. We were in the student union dungeon in Aberdeen.

Sometimes speaking to Hippie Davie just messed with my head a little, especially as you tended to end up being stoned halfway through. This had the effect of everything seeming rational or even like some divine revelation at the time. However, in the cold light of the next day, I was desperately trying to work out what it was that seemed to make sense just a short time ago. I mused that it was funny that my friends really did make me feel like I was visiting a strange land that they inhabited. Hippie Davie made you immerse deeper and deeper in his strange inverted philosophical land where scientific rationalism didn't seem to stick as much, much like wrestling with quantum physics phenomena. Strange because he lived in the same universe that I came from, but I definitely didn't have the answers in mine (Maybe he was me, from a distant galaxy in a different time frame). Don lived in a fantasy land where nothing mattered. The mundane nine to five world didn't exist to him and aspects of medieval times overlapped with Victorian England which overlapped with PlayStations, videos, coffee shops and lightsabers. And as for The Doc? That poor bastard was from a galaxy of chaos and illusion and just general bad luck that ran hand in hand with poor personal hygiene, it seemed! I obviously just preferred life in the company of zany or "different" people. However, I steadfastly refused to be completely converted to their way of thinking. I knew they probably thought I was the odd one out because I kept emphasising rational explanations and scientific rules to spoil their fun; I was like Toto from the movie the Wizard of Oz, peeling back the curtain and ruining the illusion of real magic. I really was in a strange technocolour alternative universe with these guys.

I shrugged and considered what Hippie Davie was saying, as he drew to a close while regarding Don and I in a kind of pontificating manner that made me think that he had been spending far too much time with The Doc for his own good. Don was tutting and I knew he wasn't happy about Hippie Davie's sudden little tirade against Wicca. He'd never said anything before like that and we'd always assumed that he was a fellow nature-magician like ourselves. All about getting back to nature and not conforming to established orthodox religions. But here he was coming from a different angle, talking about magick in a way we didn't quite follow. I regarded him for a second, just what the fuck was Hippie Davie anyway?

Don was giving Hippie Davie a blast of 'how can you say that, Wicca goes back to the stone-age and is the first real religion.' In many ways, although we were both of the coven and both shared those dreams, Don and I were of one spirit. I had to admit; he was much more passionate about Wicca as a religion than I was, as he really felt it and lived his life in a faith-absorbed manner. I on the other hand prided myself on questioning everything. I considered myself quite grounded, but he never actually needed to be. He was completely free from doubt and any need to question his faith. I was getting tired of the conversation but happily watched Don wade into Hippie Davie and make him back-track. Quickly rolling his cigarette furtively, Hippie Davie nodded and bowed his head in a kind of submissive gesture of apology and 'I-didn't-mean-that-exactly' body language. To give him his due, he could have been a prick but I could see he was going out of his way to appease Don and not try to condescend to him at all. Listening and smiling, as I drew a few tokes of a special rollie of my own, I nodded in agreement with Don and smiled at the squirming hippie. A natural lull in the argument allowed me to throw in a small wedge that each of them seized on to get out of the potential escalation that was on the cards.

"I still dunno what the fuck this has got to do with fucking cat hallucinations anyway!"

Hippie Davie leaned back and pointed over towards me with a long fringed sleeve.

"Once you sign up to be a real magician brother, the world becomes a strange place. Things are revealed to you, things will be revealed to you. You begin to skate the world of synchronicity and weird coincidences. There's an...*intelligence* to all this somehow." He looked about the air wildly and gesticulated in small circular motions. "An intelligence that you've just plugged your subconscious mind right into! You see you needed to see something with your eyes; you always say you're a 'put it in front of me kind of person.' Well there you are, you see something weird with your own eyes and then, the tassels swing like mad in way that you can't then dismiss as a figment of your imagination! Or those banging doors and that poor trapped astral geezer on the second floor shows you his reality. Of course, you being a confirmed materialist have found a way around that, but I bet deep down you know you saw that fucking cat! You saw it. It walked through a door and it moved a piece of your furnishing. You were shown a bit more of reality. Other planes of 'being' are as real as this one and *alllll* you have to do is use your imagination to perceive them and engage with them too!"

This was a challenge I'd been waiting to put to Hippie Davie. Theorising was ok but could he put his money where his mouth was?

"OK then, I should be able to do it again then should I? Simple if it's real, we should be able to test it. I mean, if it's real and therefore is based on some kind of energy or mass, then we should be able to get a 'signal' of this reality 'as it were,' and present this to myself and maybe even the rest of the world!?"

Don mused, "Mmm aye like take a photy-graph or summing?"

I shrugged. "Yeah like call it into a circle and make it walk over ink and get its feet prints or something like that!? Make it ring a bell or play with a stuffed mouse!"

Don looked at me in a critical manner, getting carried away with the scientific process that he usually chided so much.

"Aye bit fit aboot yer ain cat, he'll make prints in the ink and that!?" I cocked my head at him, my mouth falling into the shape of an open bag of scorn, "Well I think I kaen the difference atween ma ain cat and a ghostie cat! I'm nae gan tae sit in a circle and then take photies of my ain cat and then run roond to the papers and say I've got the world's first ghost pictures now am A? Ye think am fuckin' stew-pit or summing!" Don tossed his head away to one side to shield himself from the verbal barrage and held his hand up in defence, "A'right, a'right; I'm jist sayin'!"

So we resolved to challenge Hippie Davie to show us a proper high magick circle more in keeping with something he'd had experience of before. This wasn't Wicca, per-se, it was what Hippie Davie referred to Solomaic magick, magick with a "K," Hermetic Qabalah, "real Golden Dawn shit" as he put it!

A few days later, Hippie Davie arrived at my flat and we started to prepare the room. Or rather we spent most of the time preparing the room while he seemed to spend a large portion of the time flirting with Jen and The Doc's girlfriend Pamela, much to the chagrin of both The Doc and myself. We gave each other knowing glances every time we heard girly giggling, which seemed to be every ten seconds. Even when we managed to coerce him to leave the kitchen where the girls were hanging out sipping tea and smoking joints, Jen kept happening to pop by, giggling and seeming to act like I didn't even exist while she asked Hippie Davie some inane question like how did you get your hair like that and didn't you go to art college at some point? Although she was an ex-girlfriend, it still felt a little bit weird to me. Of course he had, but it turns out that Hippie Davie was also a fucking life model at the art college from time to time! Jen and Pamela were talking about the size of his cock, as The Doc and I busied ourselves lifting furniture to make a circle area in the living room. While Jen joked to Pamela aiming at Hippie Davie, "Ooh that's what it is; I didn't recognise you with your clothes on!" These types of comments went on and on and on; they were clearly going overboard in sheer lust! I hated hippies; I was going all Bobby Gillespie on him, I wanted to kill all fucking hippies!

As the area was cleared we all turned to Hippie Davie who stood in the centre of the circle. "So show us some of this Solomaic stuff then?"

He shrugged. "Yeah, but what do you have in mind?"

"What about a materialisation of the horned god in the circle?" I asked, like I was choosing from a catalogue, not asking for much!

He shrugged, like it was easy if you know how. "Sure, just gimme an hour or so and I'll prepare something."

Filled with a sense of anticipation, I was sent into the garden to collect some greenery and some twigs, which I duly did. The Doc and Don were dispatched to ready the room for the evocation as Hippie Davie sat devising a suitable chant. Later, he instructed us on how to project it and focus this in the circle. I was quite excited! A small triangle was constructed from candles, which marked the spot where the horned god was to appear. I had read up on this a little since Hippie Davie had mentioned it and was fascinated that I was taking part in such a ritual. I felt it was ok to call on the horned god, since we had invoked him many times. This however was evocation, calling his energies into a confined and safe place, separate from an individual's psyche and therefore a bit more interesting in terms of a viable visible result. I was sure that the horned God wouldn't object to our experimenting like this.

As the ritual began, we all took our places and Hippie Davie started gesturing and reciting strange qabalistic incantations. It was a whole new language and I didn't know what the hell was going on. He would mutter sometimes then suddenly rush forward with his hands out like he was about to go for a swim booming out strange biblical sounding names and words. It was quite loud at times, I mean "High Priest Erneh" kind of loud and we could hear Pamela and Jen in the kitchen commenting and saying, "What the hell is going on in there!" They weren't allowed in despite their protests that they could just sit quietly in the corner. As we had prized them out the living door Jen remarked to Pamela that we did our rituals naked and the pain on her face was very real as we all had to physically prize her out of the doorframe and make them swear that they on no account try to open the door. Hippie Davie had said matter-of-factly that it wouldn't be a big deal to have them sit in the corner quietly if we wanted, to which The Doc and I simultaneously asserted "No!!!"

We all took part in the chant to follow and filled our minds with the images of the horned god. We then sat and watched the triangle. I wasn't really expecting to see anything, but I wondered whether I would feel anything of note or see an anomaly of some kind. Suddenly the triangle of candles appeared to be linked as if there was a strong optical illusion connecting all three candles, creating a triangular border. This, along with the candles at each corner appeared to go like a photo-negative effect. After a few seconds of staring at this phenomenon, the whole apparatus appeared to sink down into the floor, as if the floor was becoming a sort of hill which we were looking over and into. To my amazement, a horned face clearly morphed into the centre of the triangle; it was green and looked like Pan. Occasionally, though, this would morph into another type of horned face more akin to Herne the hunter. I watched this happening for some time, instinctively, though I don't know how, I knew Hippie Davie was watching the same thing. It reminded me of the acid trip which had occurred a few months prior to this, when Hippie Davie, Don and I were experiencing the same trip. I looked around the room. Don it seemed hadn't liked it on this occasion and wasn't with us, as I had expected him to be. Instead, he had his eyes closed and palms flat on the floor, which I recognised meant that he had felt a bit too much power for his liking and was grounding himself, disconnecting from the group mind. Hippie Davie watched the triangle with a happy expression on his face. I knew he was seeing what I was seeing, again I just felt it. I glanced at the circle and the green, leafy face seemed to smile and morphed into a kind of Yoda face! I glanced at The Doc, who looked momentarily quizzical and then back at Hippie Davie who was now looking right at me, smiling. His eyes were like saucers and a cold feeling swept down the back of my neck. He was aware of what I saw, he knew and what is more, I understood that he had made it happen somehow. I realised at that moment just how easily magick came to Hippie Davie.

I glanced around. The Doc just had his usual frown set upon his face and I actually thought he was a little perturbed, maybe even scared, although he would never admit this. He'd been swaggering around desperately trying to convey to everyone that this was all old hat for him. When Hippie Davie had requested that Doc perform the lesser banishing rite of the pentagram, he made a face and body posture like Norman Wisdom thinking through a complex plot, before asserting that Shamans don't like banishing. They prefer to make requests but he'd have to travel to the underworld first and 'oh is that the time? Probably left it a bit late for that..!'

I watched on a little longer, I don't know how long it took, or how much time had passed - that was irrelevant. At some point the figure faded and the triangle began to move upwards again. The floor was slowly bending back into place; this seemed exactly like an acid hallucination, but no one had been near strong psychedelics of late. The floor snapped back into place and I knew that this was a signal that the ritual was over. I knew Hippie Davie had been aware of this also, for at that precise moment he stood up, walked over and snuffed out the candles.

We talked about it afterwards. Hippie Davie wasn't surprised at all that we had seen the same effect and easily could describe the morphing face to me. Don admitted that he hadn't been properly prepared and taking the safe option, due to the unknown element of the ritual for him, he had bowed out. This was characteristically sensible for Don, who always acted with suspicion in situations he had no prior knowledge of. I on the other hand, was like Aldous Huxley with the needle in hand, bring it on, I want to have my eyes opened! This was science to me and that meant investigation. I became a bit more respectful of Solomaic magick. I must have looked a little bit dazed as Hippie Davie walked over to me and handed me a spliff. "You see brother, there is more than one way to see reality and try to work with it. There's science yes; but that's not enough, you need the science of the saints, not the science of a clockwork dead universe. You try to measure reality with rulers and compasses, but the alchemy of the adepts and masters bend your reality to your will. Magick offers keys to make the universe come alive! Wake up man! That's what this technology is really all about. If you direct that power towards yourself you will find your own true will, basically.

Despite being a major part of my life and spending a lot of time with the other three, like other Pagans I never spoke of my interest in Wicca and magick to my colleagues, except of course to my close friends. My best mate Roger was a very sceptical person, the kind I would have been without the subjective experiences I had had. We had many discussions and arguments about these matters. I understood where Roger was coming from. There was no real proof, just an awful lot of charlatans who had been ousted and plenty of evidence from psychology to demonstrate that people will believe what they want to believe, especially certain personality types which I may actually belong to. My argument ran something like just because you can find an alternative explanation doesn't make a genuine experience invalid.

I felt like Hippie Davie when he argued with me! I tried to explain to Rog' often in the university refectory; "My experiences regarding my finding an emotional and mental/spiritual connection to the Goddess may be delusional. It may be a product of my unconscious, projecting an alternative way to express a suppressed feminine aspect to my nature. Or it may be true that such a Goddess exists in some collective unconscious realm, from where she reaches out to me. From a Freudian point of view even, a calling from the Goddess may represent an unconscious desire to supplement some grownup need for a childish parental love!? I don't know. The point is, is that it doesn't matter; the experience has affected me, affected the way I view life and the choices I've made throughout life. Thus it has resulted in what is my true nature asserting itself in my life."

Roger nodded. "Yeah man, that's ok for you. The problem I have is all this talk of spirits and such like. This is 1994 man! Physicists would have found something like that by now; don't you know that Einstein has interpreted the 'ether' experiments as proof that the ether does not exist? There are no subtle planes, no ectoplasm, no ethereal entities! No evidence of astral planes. Whose right man, new-agey floaty people or modern Physics?"

Talk of spirits and the concept of the astral plane, I admit to an educated person seems to be a very naïve and primitive expression. The magician, however, perhaps realises that these things are "clothed" by the mind and when we talk about spiritual energies or presences, we are talking about mental energies, given a vehicle for expression. I could see the quality and type of mind my friend possessed, but also realise that his rigid scientific thinking somewhat barred him from considering such things before dismissing them completely. I came to conclude after such conversations that quite simply these phenomena belong in the domain of psychology and anthropology studies. Roger was probably correct. It may never be corroborated with hard science and Physics. Although I feel that the problem is simply to do with the arrow of time, the true nature of reality which we cannot yet measure and cause and effect. So we simply need a new scientific and philosophical approach to explain why people can be healed at a distance or perceive definite and accurate flashes of precognition, for example.

## Chapter 7:
## Never Mind the Bollox

Now the circle, it seemed, was dominated by boys, The Doc, Don, very occasionally Hippie Davie, myself plus Mags and Erneh. We might as well have swapped the ceremonial wine for lager. I suspect Mags was wondering where it all went wrong, but if she did she never let on she seemed to enjoy our company anyway, chuckling as we mocked The Doc.

As the new year of 1995 got under way, Mags received a letter from a young girl who wanted to meet with a representative of the Pagan Federation in Aberdeen. Her name was Patricia Day. The Doc wasted no time in volunteering to go with Mags to meet her, at the Prince of Wales. I opted not to go. I had too much coursework to do, which I had let mount up as usual. The next day though, The Doc burst into my flat, obviously highly excited. Apparently this girl had come on to him in the pub. He was going for a drink with her later that evening. I was sure he must have been exaggerating. You could have knocked me down with a feather duster when he turned up at the flat some hours later with a rather attractive young brunette in tow. She was all over him smiling and he was continually putting his hand on her leg. I couldn't believe it. I kept staring at her trying to figure out exactly what was wrong with her. She didn't have a guide dog or thick glasses and when she spoke there was no evidence of severe brain damage. Just like Pamela before her, she seemed lovely and intelligent. I will never, ever figure out the female sex. It was obvious to any guy after five minutes that The Doc was sexist, a compulsive liar and somewhat sad and deluded, but she seemed to think he was the coolest thing since sliced bread. As The Doc went to the toilet, she smiled enthusiastically at me. "Ooh he's so cool, you know he played guitar with Bauhaus?" she said wide eyed and impressed.

I leant forward, putting my fingers to my temples. "Oh for fuck's sake!" I muttered as I turned away towards the door, as if to look towards The Doc in the other room. Patricia looked at me, not quite understanding my reaction and frowned quizzically. "Yeah, yeah, so he tells me Trisha, so he tells me as well! Remembering the Roger-Gay slander by him, I nodded towards Trish;

"Aye, well actually the true story of that is Pete Murphy did keep him around as a roadie coz he liked the fact that Mikey was the only guy he'd ever met who had a smaller penis than he did!" She looked at me quizzically as The Doc padded back towards the living room.

Taking my bitterness as friendly sarcasm, she laughed nervously and then beamed at the door as the would-be rock star graced us with his presence again. I was, however, becoming a little concerned with The Doc's behaviour, as he seemed to be using his position in the coven to try to impress naïve girls. To us, that was an abuse of his position. Especially as we'd heard him on more than one occasion proclaim to some young goth, with an interest in Wicca and magick at Pagan pub moots, that the key to real magick was control of the sexual energies and further that his Shaman training made him an expert at it. Hippie Davie had by now told Don and I that The Doc had preyed on some student girls that hung around Paul and had been working on turning them into a little harem for a while, where he was their High Priest. The Doc had told them, among other things, that he had played with Bauhaus a few times and continued to be good mates with Daniel Ash. (Although he wasn't that good mates with Pete Murphy; far too much ego you see!? Course they'd ended up fighting one night, after which The Doc put him in a kung fu death hold and six bouncers had to pull him off of him. Unfortunately, he was kicked out the band for that, though Daniel Ash and D.J. secretly thought it was hilarious, as Pete had had it coming for years!). Hippie Davie had talked the girls out of being The Doc's groupies but he was still very angry at The Doc.

Hippie Davie had been rather uncharacteristically angry when he told us about it; "He abused his position, no question in my mind. They were quite upset. I swear karma is going to catch up with that cunt soon enough!" However, I was more annoyed that he thought he could take on Pete Murphy! I mean, he was a wirey, coke fuelled king of goth rock and I'd bet that he could take The Doc no problem, even on a bad night.

The Doc though, right at this moment was giving me the puppy eyes. How could I refuse a face like that? It was too canine-like for his own good sometimes.

"Can you like, put us up for the night Sean? Mate?" He said, imploring me with his eyes, the right eye especially magnifying the request to creepy new proportions. I forgot; the great rock star wasn't going to bring her home to his rat-infested coonical hoose bedroom at his Ma's hoose in Torry was he? That left my flat or paying for a room and as the dozy bastard had no money; that just left my flat as an option for his sordid little plans! I sighed, "Sure, sure I suppose so, but I've got coursework to do, so I'll be doing an all-nighter on the kitchen table!" I was acutely aware that The Doc was planning an all-nighter all of his own and this was a hint for him to be as discrete as possible, to avoid any unnecessary embarrassment. Alas discretion was not a word in The Doc's rather limited dictionary, definitely, definitely not without a doubt.

I could hardly work, with the sound of The Doc shagging and moaning non-stop. It was probably the worst thing a man could hear in the early hours of the morning. This was compounded by the occasional screech from Trisha. As I put my Walkman on to near full blast and as the pounding Prodigy drowned out the moaning mad Doc, I fathomed that the last screech I heard was due to the drugs wearing off and she had probably just put the light on!

Hot on the heels of Trish, The Doc appeared, with another new potential disciple. This was a neighbour who'd had the misfortune to have found interest in something Doc had mentioned to him. Apparently he had been a neighbour of Pamela's who'd met The Doc in the garden one night, meditating...or something. They'd struck up a conversation about the paranormal and this guy was scared of something haunting his flat. The Doc had gone round to perform a little bit of exorcism. (I could just picture it, him walking about fag in mouth banging a drum and making Amer-Indian sounding vocalisations that he would definitely be making up on the spot – without a doubt). Apparently it made the thing ten times worse much later, but that was beside the point. The Doc sensed a couple of prospective students in the making.

The latest addition though, seemed extremely wet behind the ears and a little naïve. We referred to him constantly as ThaNewboy. He had become quite fascinated with Shamanism due to The Doc's continual boasting to him about it and had requested a demonstration of magick and Shamanism. This is something that strangely enough, none of us ever thought to ask him. The Doc was only too happy to oblige and a batbox bunch meeting was arranged. It was to include ThaNewboy and to consist of some Shamanic ritual which The Doc was to devise for the day. Don, Hippie Davie and I waited for the day with bated breath.

The day arrived, present was myself, Don, Hippie Davie, Trish, ThaNewboy and of course The Doc! We all assembled in my flat. The Doc talked us through the ritual which was to be an invocation of Lord Ursio, a bear God which The Doc had dreamt of (and had tattooed on his arm). This obviously had some special significance for him. The Doc informed us that this circle would be different, as this was more like a Cree tribe Medicine circle, not like the mere *low* magick of Wicca! In a high magick circle, everything had to be right, there didn't seem to be any room for error. I turned to Hippie Davie who didn't seem too happy to be there, "Seems everything has got to be just right for old Lord Arse-io to be summoned up fae the underworld!?"

Hippie Davie whispered to me. "Aye, if a guy fae a successful techno-band appears at the door, one of us had better be ready to let him in!" I smirked. Hippie Davie turned to me with a serious expression,

"Nah, dinna let him in, he'll drink all yer lager lager, lager, lager..." I laughed out loud and then covered my mouth and Don who was standing nearby chuckled with his characteristic shoulder bobbing. We were all fucking loving taking the piss and it was going to be fucking hard not to laugh. We knew if one person did then all three of us were gonna blow like an exploding pressure gauge.

The Doc who fortunately was out of earshot at the time came prancing back in, loving being the director. He told us he was to invoke Lord Ursio and let him speak whatever wisdom he had for the occasion. I was given a quarter to evoke and was happy enough with only a small part to do. Soon after the last circle was cast however The Doc walked into the middle of the circle and all of a sudden pointed at me and requested that I do the invocation. I was a bit pissed off at this, as he hadn't given me any warning or instructions and I wasn't sure what to say or even how to visualise the Lord in question. I thought, 'Doc, you utter cunt!' and looked at him, wondering what the fuck I was supposed to say! I put my palms in the air in resignation. I asked him, not concealing an obvious air of annoyance in my voice, "What?"

All eyes turned to watch me in the circle and I felt a little foolish. So much for the *Cree tribe medicine circle* and its exacting high magick structure! I was starting to wish I was high myself. The Doc covered his face with a huge brown hood, the voice from underneath impatiently informed me just to invoke him like the horned god but visualise wise Lord Ursio a great Bear God instead. I glanced around at Don and

Hippie Davie with an expression of disbelief. Hippie Davie replied by smirking at me. I shook my head, shrugged and then I knelt down and pointing my wand at him. Feeling just a little conspicuous I just made some stuff up and hoped for the best, my heart by now not really in it. I don't remember what I said but it had all the sincerity of "Lord Ursio, fancy coming over for some pizza, son? We have beer and we can rent a good film if ye want?" I was no expert on shamanism myself, but I was sure it wouldn't be anything like this at least.

To my amazement and some amusement, The Doc began staggering about a bit and after a few seconds of this 'reeling' he stood upright with his arms up in front of his chest, with hands quite relaxed and paw like. I had to bite my bottom lip. The hooded figure stood in silence for a moment before murmuring in a low growling husky voice,

"*I am-Lord Ursio,-what do you-ask of me?*"

My face contorted with the effort of trying not to burst out laughing at this spectacle. Lord Ursio must have been on at least sixty fags a day, I reckon. However, even ThaNewboy couldn't control himself; he began giggling uncontrollably and I had to quickly bite into the sleeve of my robe not to do the same. The robed arm of the hooded figure, in response, shot upward pointing at ThaNewboy.

"*SILENCE! cheeky boy! – have – more – respect.*" It came back to me then, that was it, hadn't Lord Ursio taught Maths in my first year!? I couldn't take it anymore. I collapsed onto ThaNewboy's shoulder and laughed freely. With that Hippie Davie's face, now contorted in a very broad grin, seemed to leak a high pitched whine which he couldn't restrain. Don, who usually tried to be ultra-respectful and serious in a circle situation, was going redder and redder suddenly opened his mouth wide and a loud unmitigated "Pahhhhahahahah" boomed forth into the room.

We all started laughing, but The Doc stayed resolutely still in the centre of the circle. This unresponsive hooded figure just standing there made the ridiculousness of the situation all he more pronounced. You had to wonder what was going on underneath that hood (We often wondered just what was going on underneath the hood!).

"Oh for fuck's sake," I said laughing and shaking my head, "Shamanism's fuckin' magic fun!"

Hppie Davie nearly fell backwards he laughed so hard! We giggled for a few more minutes.

"*SILENCE!*" shouted The Doc/Lord *Ursio*! This was so funny but somehow incredibly cringey at the same time. The hooded figure spoke again,

"*SILENCE!...Cease this-impertinence! Or I shall-remove myself-from thy presence.*" I loved how he soldiered on in Lord Ursio mode; it was just beautiful to behold. At this point, I saw Don shake his head and turn his back pointedly and walk to the corner of the room, his head in his hands. 'Oh shit, maybe we're going too far,' I thought and set about composing myself. Also, I knew that if I interrupted The Doc now, I would never hear the end of it, plus he was using words like 'thy' and so must have been serious!

So I apologised and made some shit up about mirth being acceptable in a Wiccan circle. We were new to Shamanism and that we had some questions. This seemed to do the job and Lord Ursio continued in his characteristic gravely fashion –

"*Who – has – the – first – question - for Lord – Ursio?*"

ThaNewboy then cleared his throat and looked around. "Erm, I would like to ask one small thing, sorta on behalf of someone else who wants me to ask it?"

We were all intrigued about what he might say. Lord Ursio shrugged under his hood and robe, ThaNewboy looked at me and I nodded, "Yep, Lord Ursio will answer your question now." I was finding this amusing but was also quite livid that The Doc had promoted me to be Lord Ursio's P.A. without so much as pay rise.

ThaNewboy then spoke quite nervously and politely to The Doc.

"Erm, Lord Michael, eh I mean Lord Ursio, my girlfriend wanted to ask of the spirits, is it always absolutely necessary to be nearly unclothed or dress in *that way* during Shamanism practice? And I mean, would it also be possible to raise the spirits without the great rite?"

I immediately looked over to Hippie Davie just to check if I was actually hearing what I thought I was hearing and I hadn't got the wrong end of the stick. Hippie Davie looked back at me with a knowing look of disapproval and scorn. I think we can guess what had been going on here all right.

ThaNewboy continued, "I mean, she thinks and I kinda agree, that the black robe is a little skimpy, and could we at least....do the great rite in....private?"

Lord Ursio coughed a little nervously and then held one hand out as if to shush him.

"All – things – are lawful in nature – and those – that want – to gain truth– and be truly free of the spirit – must give up old, Christian-repressed ways. All – I can council you on – is, –  is that it is better to enter the temple – without the clothing – of the everyday world...It's really as simple as that my son!"

ThaNewboy shrugged and nodded, obviously not wanting to cause a fuss among so many people he didn't know too well but I could see he had reservations. He nodded in resignation. "Thanks O' Lord Ursio, I see what you mean, thank you."

The Doc was about to move on but I couldn't help but interject,

"Ehhhhh, wait a wee moment there, Lord Ursio, but doesn't the querant have a point here? I mean if his girlfriend is not comfortable with anything, surely that's fine!"

I tried to accentuate my opposition to this and to telegraph to The Doc to make it right by the tone of my voice.

"Isn't that RIGHT ye Lord Ursio?"

The Doc, however, didn't seem too keen on committing and invariably tried to squirm out of a direct answer and fob me off.

"Now...peace be with you O' brother of the craft, – hear ye, for it is not so that thy Gardnerian Magick – insists on nudity– for some good reason, – it is nothing to be ashamed of...!"

I became quite angry now; this was nonsense.

 "No! Lord Ursio, no, this is not so, for how could one millimetre of cloth make any difference at all to energy when it is supposed to be able to travel the whole universe? C'mon on now Lord Ursio, Wicca does not insist that people be uncomfortable!"

Lord Ursio's voice suspiciously became a little bit more like The Doc and a whiney annoyed voice made its assertion from under the hood.

"All should do as they will, – yes, yes, but – please bear in mind – that it is often wise to listen to the council of your teacher."

I couldn't take it anymore, so I rounded on him; I would have no part in him basically manipulating young women to get their kit off and I was now very pissed off.

"No! No right Lord Ursio...fuck off!" He tried to blurt out a response, but I talked over him, "No, No just stop talking, just...shut up a minute! You're right about one thing – you should do your own will and nothing more than that." I looked over at ThaNewboy. "There's no spirit, no teacher, no prophet, who can tell you or your girlfriend what to do, what to wear or who to agree with. Wicca is about 'And it harm none, do thine own will!' And what is more, I wouldn't be comfortable if I had a girlfriend in the same room wearing a duffle coat next to this cunt." I motioned over to The Doc under the hood, the Lord Ursio now seeming even more ridiculous and out of place than ever before and incredibly he stood there maintaining the posture with arms bent out before him like some biblical seer prophet/ great bear spirit, who had just been called a cunt.

Eventually, after a lull he groaned,

*"Lord Ursio – does not like being addressed as a cunt – by impertinent Wiccans..!"* His voice had become characteristically huskier again.

I retorted, "I was actually talking to The Doc, but if that's your opinion as well, well then you're both a pair of cunts!" I felt encouraged by the fact that I knew that both Don and Hippie Davie were definitely on my side here. I'm not the type that usually is confrontational in most situations. However this was too much and I felt I had to speak out for the apparently meeker ThaNewboy here.

Don giggled to himself and Hippie Davie who had been laughing all the way through our dialogue exploded with uproarious laughter at the concept of me calling both The Doc and Ursio both a couple of cunts to the same ridiculous looking figure who now stood motionless and clueless under the hood. Clearly, all semblance of magick or mystery had left the room completely and now, quite simply, we were arguing with The Doc standing quietly with a large piece of fabric draped over his head, hands out like he was possessed by the spirit of Max Bygraves.

Then The Doc spoke after a pause, considering his next move.

*"Lord Ursio – agrees with you and respects this is a Wiccan circle– and not a Shamanic portal, therefore I respectfully concede – that you are correct to council thy pupils – as you please."*

Then in an astral Shamanic go version of wow, is that the time, right I must be off then, he raised his head backwards and whimpered,

*"I must now leave this place– to be with my kind."*

He fell to his knees and then let out a soft moan and taking his hood down looked confused and scared.

I patted ThaNewboy on the shoulder and shook my head.

"I'm sorry, I would have suggested that you should contact the Pagan Federation and do some reading up on the craft before trusting people you don't know very well." I motioned over to The Doc who knelt panting on the floor.

"And trust me; you don't know that one very well!"

When the circle was closed, I went straight over to Don who was shaking his head and looking quite pissed off "Are you ok pal'? What's up?" I asked him.

Don looked serious and nodded once, "The Doc! He's going too far; Mags would be furious if she knew. He's giving us all a bad name!"

I didn't meet ThaNewboy again after that until sometime much later on Union Street. He told me The Doc was trying to encourage them to use sex magick, as this was the best expression of natural energy or some such nonsense. Unsurprisingly, his girlfriend became suspicious that he was just trying to get into her knickers.

I tidied up apologising to the others that this was not a Wiccan circle. Hippie Davie and Don were talking in the corner and as I neared I heard them say something about having to postpone the initiation and rethink the whole thing.

"Rethink what?" I asked as I drew near.

Don looked a bit unsure how to react and Hippie Davie just sucked his lips in a gesture of contemplation.

I wondered what seemed so difficult to convey. "Spit it out guys," I said.

Don glanced over at the door, The Doc was getting changed in the other room and Trish had gone through to speak to him.

"Eh...look Sean this iz nithing ti dee wi the batbox bunch...we were spikin aboot The Doc and Jedi stuff sorta thing."

Hippie Davie looked at me; I looked from one to the other,

"Jedi stuff?" Hippie Davie explained;

"Look ye know my views, my religious practice, the sorta technocoloured jedi magick I promulgate...I'm nae one to spread the word."

"Prom-you-what now? Spread the weird s'probably more accurate!" I quipped, as a kind of afterthought.

Hippie Davie and Don both laughed, a little bit more forcefully than was necessary. "Heh, yes good one, good one, weird that's me heheh," Hippie Davie conceded nervously, "Yep, heheh."

I looked at them both, from one to the other! "Weird yes, but you're clearly in the right place." I gesticulated towards where The Doc had been standing.

Hippie Davie shook his head and leaned forward as if to conceal his conversation; instinctively Don and I leaned forward in response. "Yes there's weird and then there's also clean aff the top shelf, fuckin' psycho-mintal so far from reality that only strong medication and a padded cell are yer only options left!"

"The Doc 'n Lord 'Ur – so' fucking full o' shite-io!" I replied.

Don rolled his eyes upwards and made a *tsk* sound that morphed into a *skfuck*, as he shook his head slowly in annoyance.

Hippie Davie continued, "Aye The Doc!? I used to think he was funny, but I'm getting scared!" He motioned with his index finger to and fro between his chest and Don, "We...are getting scared!"

"Yeah, I dunno," I said, "Maybe I'll ask Mags to have a word with him, s'difficult you know? I dunno what's up with him...anyway what initiation? Doc's?"

Hippie Davie relented. "I'm talking about Jediism; we were thinking of letting The Doc join, but after tonight's performance, I reckon he needs to just ground himself a little first, do a bit of reality re-hab."

"Join?" I said. "You guys running a Jedi school now?"

"Just a bit of formal recognition," said Hippie Davie slightly defensively.

"I thought Jedi was a state of mind," I said, "kinda like being a hippie. One doesn't need a license!"

"Aye well, you could say that about Wicca, but you need an initiation when you affiliate yourself to a group. We're not running a school...just providing a bit of support and guidance with our codes."

"So you got The Doc in on this as well?"

"Well aye," replied Don, "but maybe's he's not in a good place right now though eh!?"

Hippie Davie looked slightly apologetic, acknowledging my own distinct lack of invitation. "Sorry, we just didn't think you'd be a' that interested! Anyway, we're worried about The Doc; perhaps he doesn't need another religion to commit to!?"

We all turned around to face the door as The Doc wandered in, holding his head, "God I can hardly remember anything, what time is it? What went on?"

Without even turning to Don and Hippie Davie, I whispered, "Don't worry, he's all yours, take him, you can have him, I won't be offended, definitely, definitely…without a fuckin' doubt!"

University was becoming more and more stressful; the pressure was on to go to the library, work hard on my honour's thesis and get my coursework done. However, enroute to university I invariably would cycle up to Union Street and like on some kind of guided missile, find myself under the bridge and into the Green. There the lord of the green as it were, was sitting by the open doors of Café 52. I rattled over on my bike, Hippie Davie, half asleep, lay stretched out on a chair; the barmaid, Becky, who was sitting beside him, looked up at me and smiled; she went to get me a coffee. I liked getting handed a brew without asking; it made me feel like this was our place.

I kicked Hippie Davie on the sole of his boot. "Shoulda let him get it, Becky!" I said.

"Can't disturb chilled out customers!" she said smiling back as she wafted past, her nice lithe frame registered with the relevant recognition units of my brain.

"You mean he doesn't actually work here then? Jeezaz!"

She laughed and I noticed how her body nicely reverberated as she bent down to get the nutmeg and cinnamon for my cappuccino. 'She really is very sexy,' I thought, but then didn't go any further with it, for there was no point, as she was practically in love with Hippie Davie, of course.

Hippie Davie grunted, opened one eye and stared over at me, like some psychedelic pirate. "Who is using the 'W' word around here!?" he said then acknowledged my presence with, "A-right mannie?"

"A-right Hippie D!?" I said as I sat down.

This was a typical Aberdonian conversation. It could have stopped there! Everything we wanted to know about each other had been said. We were both still alive and a-right mannies!

I sat down and sighed, looking over I pushed my lips together in resignation towards Hippie Davie in response. "Canna seem tae dae any work worth-a-fuck jist now! Thought I'd come over here and stop you chattin' up Becky the waitress for a while."

Hippie Davie smiled and looked over. He caught her eye and she smiled back.

"Ah well, too fuckin' late then I see...for fucksake Hippie Davie, fit iver ye dee dinna upset her, she maks a fuckin' good cappuccino!"

Hippie Davie turned to look at me. "Dae worry, wouldn't want to see you not getting yer fix, you might become dangerous!" he slowly replied raising an eyebrow, in a manner more characteristic of Johnny Lydon.

I wasn't sure if that was a compliment or a piss-take of my fairly unthreatening persona, so I let it go. I would mull it over later and perhaps ask the cat his opinion in the evening, though the cat would usually just shake his head and say I was just being paranoid! On occasion, though, he would walk away with his tail in the air in derision, "Yeah, everybody hates you, you twat; what'ya gonna do?!"

Pretending not to acknowledge any possible ambivalence whatsoever, I changed the subject. "Yeah talking of dangerous, where is our deranged witch doctor?"

Hippie Davie eyed me curiously, a small almost imperceptible smirk taking shape at the corner of his mouth. I realised he was cogitating over my lack of response to his cheekiness, perhaps experiencing a small victory, but more likely a small internal nod of some confirmation. "He's rehearsing today – thank fuck – I canna be done wi' that gobshite the day!"

"Rehearsing for what Davie? - He finally get a gig with Underworld?"

"Nahhh!" said Hippie Davie laughing. "Him and Trish are starting up a band...seems she's a good singer apparently and The Doc reckons they're gonna be the next All About Eve!"

I snorted. "Fuck'n hell...he tell you that?"

Hippie Davie winced. "Aye, fuckin' wanted me to play bass, but I couldn't imagine spending time up at his Ma's messing about in his room, while his Ma makes the tea and crumpets...very rock and roll! Besides I can't stand to be in the fucker's presence for any length of time these days, especially after Lord Total and complete Arse-io made an appearance the other night, the dozy fucking twat!"

I smirked. "Maybe Lord Arse-io will duet with Trisha!"

Hippie Davie laughed, now imagining this as well. "Give Carl McCoy a run for his money!" He put his arms out in front of him mocking Doc's possessed stance and impersonated the silly gravelly tones of Lord Ursio from the night before,

"*Moonchild – lower- me –down...*" It was a great rendition of the Fields of the Nephilim hit and we laughed uproariously. For all his faults, The Doc was proving very useful – there's nothing like taking the piss out of a mutual twathead to bring two mates together.

We spoke about The Doc for a while, until time passed with the changing light and walking people gave way to bellowing seagulls and billowing crisp packets on the breeze. This was the in-between time, a time when people like Don strode the Earth. Just as I watched a lesser black-back gull screech across the empty Green, blissfully unaware of all the ghost women who washed their clothes there, Don emerged from the darkness of under the bridge. Emerging as if he had been just born at that precise moment; walking in from another reality. In fact, if I hadn't been to his house many times I would suspect that that is exactly where he came from. Whenever Don appeared he always seemed to be walking in slow motion, perhaps the large forty holer Dr. Martins and jangling jewellery slowed him down so much. People would stop and not say anything, regarding him for a moment, thus a hush always seemed to precede the arrival of Don. I would find it amusing at times, from a bus across the street, spotting Don walking in the town. Union Street, the main thoroughfare of the town, was always jam-packed on a shopping day. The fairly narrow pavement, although ample in 1801 when it was constructed, was now obliterated from sight as many shopping bag laden people negotiated its width, snaking in unequal rows in both directions; making impatient feet step out on the road in front of cyclists and crazy bus drivers here and there. I would see his top hat glide along over the heads of the throng, occasionally stopping, weaving and bobbing along, as if having a mind of its own. Of course I knew the actual mind beneath was complaining and cursing as his path to the tobacco shop in Aberdeen market had been rendered much slower. People would slow down to stare at him for a second or just dive out of the way, creating a little slow bubble in the throng.

"Here he goes, the hep cat in the hat," mouthed Hippie Davie, as he neared the coffee shop.

"Just thought I'd look in," said Don, striding over and sitting down taking off his top hat in an elegant fashion, like a gentleman should, "Kint erd be sumbody doon here." He alluded to the fact that during the day neither of us seemed to do much else.

"Just waitin' for the harbour coffee shop to open!" I said. Invariably, I would end up at Don's workplace smoking spliffs and chatting as I escaped my books staring up at me from where I left them several days ago. "It's true, we never do that much these days, just sit aboot here eyein' up Becky an' spikin' shite."

"Speak for yourself," said Don, "I sit here 'n eye up the baith o' you twa spikin' shite!" He had a great knack of making you feel totally vulnerable.

I smirked. "We should do something, get some fresh air."

Hippie Davie and Don exchanged glances, "Well funnily enough we were spikin' aboot that jist the ither day!" said Don smiling.

"That's right," said Hippie Davie leaning forward, "I never got the chance to sound you out about it yet; I was thinking of getting away from the concrete and clay for a while, before the weather starts getting much colder and I was wondering if you and Don wanted to come along?"

"Nae Doc?" I said.

"Nuh!" they replied in synchrony.

"Well I'm there then," I said and smiled. "Where are we going then?"

Hippie Davie nodded his head in acknowledgement, "Cool my friends! That's what I like to hear, we're going to get outdoors and see parts of Scotland which are far from the beaten path and seldom visited...even by the great Tom Weir."

I liked the idea of exploring the countryside like the great Tom Weir. That guy was an inspiration; I was just starting to get into his programmes and it was weird that Hippie Davie mentioned his name. I often wondered about morphic resonance and suspected that between magical colleagues coincidences may be more pronounced, the para-social effect again. "So is this where you get to when you disappear for a while Davie?"

"A lot of the time, aye!" replied Hippie Davie.

"Will we meet any gypsy women?" I said, starting to fantasise.

Hippie Davie looked at Don quizzically, "Come again?"

"...Oh nothing," I said shaking my head, "it's nothing, forget I said anything!"

We arranged to go that weekend, so I resolved to get some work done. I went home and actually made some headway on an essay I was working on about predator prey relationships. I had almost as much as a whole paragraph typed up when the phone went.

It was The Doc's girlfriend Pamela. "Hi Sean, is Michael with you, his Ma says she thinks he's with you!?"

I thought for a second, "No...No he's no, haven't seen him for a few days, Pamela, not since the weekend, when we were doing a bit of a ritual here!"

"Oh yeah, he did mention that, seems to have taken a lot out of him, said he needed to go and recuperate for a while. I don't know what you guys have been doing but he always seems totally knackered when he comes around here these days!"

I felt a little awkward; I knew full well why he was so knackered all the time! But what could I say? I automatically took the side of the bloke. It was in my nature.

"Yeah I dunno, guess all those nights bat watchin' has caught up him. He's not used to working after all eh?" I grimaced as I realised I was slagging him off a little bit to his girlfriend; I was used to talking about him to Hippie Davie or Don, my mouth had forgotten to change tack!

Pamela acknowledged this with a short affirmative noise as an afterthought, clearly still computing where else he could be.

"He said he was going to be crashing at yours, meditating and doing some Abramelin rite for several days while you're at uni' and stuff...and his Ma seems quite adamant that he's at yours as well...Do you think he could be with Don or Davie then?" she reflected, "Bit strange of him to be out of touch for so long!"

'Oh crap,' I thought, 'nice of The Doc to drop me in it!' I fumbled with the ball momentarily. "Yeah well I said he could stay here right enough...but he's eh, no here, canna think where else...oh wait Hippie Davie mentioned he wiz gan tae go into the woods for a while, Him, The Do.., I mean, Michael and Don, on some Jedi quest I think. I bet that's where the fucker is, Pamela!" Touchdown! I was so convincing, I now believed that's where he was as well!

This seemed to satisfy her. "Ahh that's it, they not letting you play in their little gang this time, Sean? That's unfair!"

Pamela had obviously heard The Doc wax lyrical about their Jedi brotherhood. He probably enjoying the fact that I was left out! I was starting to feel sorry for myself as well.

"It's ok Pam, am busy anyway with essays and things, I canna be a Jedi just now, nae a guy fae Northfield, there are no vacancies. Hell if Luke Skywalker lived round my Ma's way, he wouldn't be a Jedi either!"

Pamela laughed clearly cheered up now, "Wouldn't've got very far in Northfield eh?"

"Are you jokin'? he would have got a right fucking kickin' if he walked into the Lord Byron (a well-known inn in the area, where Sandy Rourke now hung out!) waving a lightsaber and askin' where at fat boy Jabba ran his operation! Actually he would have got a right fuckin' kickin' jist if he walked into the Lord Byron full stop!"

We said our goodbyes and I put the phone down, eventually making my way back to the small desk propped up in the middle of the room, strewn with books and papers. I sat, put the CD player back on, tapped out the beat to Dodgy's; 'Staying out for the summer' and cranked the volume up. It was such a catchy tune that I had to sing along! The open books lent themselves well as a makeshift drum kit. I then put the sound down a bit, looked back at the books and regarded my pen. As I was alone in the flat, I couldn't resist making it into a space ship! The pen top made a cool lone fighter. It seemed to make the sound of a "Star Wars" imperial fighter as it zoomed around the room at arm's length from me, a few feet above the books and notes now a backdrop to an intergalactic scene. I say again, George Lucas has a lot to answer for when it comes to my generation! A few minutes later, as an eraser shot missile-like at a candle holder, knocking it off in slow motion from the window sill to the ground, the phone rang again!

The Doc's voice erupted in my ear "Hullo, Sean?" He sounded a bit panicky.

"Doc!" I replied a bit sternly, "I'm busy trying to write an essay here man!" I said irascibly, as if every second counted! "What's up wi ye?

The Doc's furtive voice leapt down the phone at me,

"Hullo!? aye Sean, fitlike? lus'in; I'm at your hoose if Pamela asks ye a'right? At your hoooose if she phones, but say am or oot or hae-in a shite or summink, so canna come to the phone...obviously. Kin ye jist tell her 'at? At yours, definitely ok? Coz I suspect she will ask you...probably soon! No wait, say deep in meditation, coz you kin still technically answer the phone wi' a shite kint-ye?"

I stopped him from a further tirade of his deep logic which was depressing me.

"Doc...for fucksake, she called me ten minutes ago! Where are you?"

There was a silence of realisation on the other end of the line, the slow plotting and the whirring of worrying wheels. The Doc sucked air, he actually hadn't thought she would have phoned here after trying his mum's, despite him telling his mum that he was here. The mind boggles, but never mind, there was no point in trying to figure out what he was thinking, or why he didn't think of that.

"All right...shit, ten minutes ago?"

"Ten minutes ago pal," I said. "Well you were'nae here, fit was I gan tae dee? I didnae kaen where you were!"

"Right, right, am at Trisha's, we've been, eh, rehearsing!"

"I bet you have!" I said in sarcastic tones which as usual seemed to go over his head, I could actually hear his face muscles contort into a massive grin over the phone.

"Aye – we have! And lots of shaggin' as well; it's fuckin' great min. Inspired me to write some songs anaw. Trisha is a good singer, really good, a jist need a bit mair practice wi' my guitar and well maybe get some gigs!"

I felt he was wandering away from the important issues here so I helped guide his thoughts.

"You'll be writing your fuckin' own obituary if Pamela finds out where you've been, ya dozy prick!"

"Oh aye, shit, aye, fit did ye say tae her?"

I thought he'd never ask. "It's a'right, I bailed you oot, sez you was away wi' Hippie Davie and Don on their Jedi quest!"

The Doc sighed with relief on the other end. "Cool, cool...here; fit gave ye that idea?"

I became tongue tied and a bit at a loss for words. It seemed that I was a natural when it came to lying to women, but words escaped me when I was trying to bullshit a mate. I stammered a little, feeling myself going red.

"Well, Hippie Davie does that all the time doesn't he? And Don mentioned something aboot it the other day." I grimaced and swung around on the spot holding the top of my head in my hand, as if to stem the flow of words pouring out from me, but The Doc was onto it.

"Man, that would be a good idea. I need to get awa, need to get awa for a whiley...Don say when they were going?"

I was right on the spot here; I just couldn't bring myself to lie to him outright! I found myself fumbling with the ball for the second time; my stats weren't getting any better!

"Ehhhh, Hippie Davie said summing aboot afore it gets cauld like, even mintioned it tae me like...I dae kaen tho' dae kaen if Hippie Davie's actually gan tae go, aye maybe it's too cauld like?"

But it was too late, the idea had taken seed.

"Aye Hippie Davie did reckon it was too cauld last time I spoke tae him, bit it's nae is it? It's fine...I reckon they must have changed their minds. I should get in touch with them...I need tae get awa! I need tae get awa fae here for a bit. I kaen far Hippie Davie will be later, I'll catch up with him them, you spik tae Don for me and then get back to me will ya, cheers min!"

Interception!! I put the phone down; oh bollox, I thought, 'they're gonna kill me!'

"...And I may have just let the weekend slip out tae The Doc," I blurted out down at Don's work's reception later that evening.

Don raised an eyebrow at me. He paused, rolling for a second and then re-started rolling the joint. "By 'may,' I take it you have virtually invited the cunt?"

I was offended. "No...No! I have not...I said I would speak to you first!"

Don looked really pissed; we never ever fought or fell out, but he did tend to get pissed from time to time and I hated it as usually, it was my fault and he could make me feel guilty for days, even just by the disapproving way he rolled a joint!

"Look, what was I to do?" I said. "Pamela put me on the spot, then she phoned his Ma and his Ma swore blind he was away with yous. I couldnae deny it, but I never actually told him we already had arranged it. He's desperate to get awa, he got the idea into his head and he's awa tae pester Hippie Davie the night! So it's nething tae dae wi' me really....it's a' The Doc's Ma's fault really!"

Don eyed me suspiciously; I'm sure he saw through me. Damn those coven mind sharing morphic resonances!

Meanwhile, Hippie Davie and Becky were cuddling up at Under The Hammer folk bar on Justice Street, listening to now ex Lorelei singer Martin strum his guitar and sweetly sing folk melodies. This was against a backdrop of candles flickering over candle wax shapes which had been sculpted by time and many previous evenings; wine bottles buried in dripped wax and soft lights fell about the cosy room. The Guinness was thick and excellent, almost as good as Dublin, which was a mean feat for a Scottish pub. Hippie Davie felt comfortable with Becky, had grown fond of her company; strangely, he hadn't felt the need to go to the student union and chat up other women for some time. Davie started to feel a bit more grown up; this was the most romantic night he'd had since he could remember. Becky snuggled close as Martin waved and said, "This next one is for my good friends Davie and Becky." He winked. It was very astute of him to notice their closeness over the last couple of nights and he started strumming a Lorelei hit which he had wrote, "Hooooold onto youhhhrrrr love!" Hippie Davie smiled his broad grin and waved back, it was perfect. As Martin closed the song and the crowd clapped in eager and uncontrived appreciation, Davie slid away to the bar and a toilet break.

As he stood at the urinal, a strange feeling of almost foreboding came over him. It was more of a slight annoyance than foreboding, a niggling presence, like a pesky fly, but he ignored it.

When he returned and looked over to smile towards Becky, there smiling back at him was The Doc sitting next to her, chatting freely and holding the last few centimetres of Hippie Davie's Guinness. A voice in the back of Davie's head smugly chimed, "...told you so!"

Hippie Davie waved over and The Doc waved back as he held Hippie Davie's glass to his mouth before downing the remainder, then he motioning into the empty glass before pointing to himself and Becky. Hippie Davie made eye contact with Becky to show his utter disapproval before turning to the bar, muttering "For fuck's sake" loud enough for everyone around him to hear and regard him suspiciously for a second. As he made his way back through the crowd with the three drinks spilling Guinness up his arm, he overheard Doc's conversation. "Aye he's some boy like, yer lucky there, disnae Muck aboot oor Davie, many a night at the union–"

Hippie Davie cut him short. "Doc! Becky doesn't want to hear aboot our sad nights at the fuckin' student union...anyway, that sounds more like Sean to me!"

The Doc, not to be undeterred in his attempts to big up his mate, pressed on; he had also missed out on Gemma because of the aforementioned Sean. Hippie Davie, though, was the king in his eyes.

"Nah come on you fanny rat ye! Dinna be shy...you've had tons mair women than Sean and the rest of uz put together!"

Hippie Davie was usually quite sympathetic when slagging off Sean, so The Doc knew he had a confederate here and he wasn't going to let him down. Hippie Davie slammed the drinks on the table, getting more Guinness on his arm.

The Doc homed in, "Whoops a daisy, well that will be your one then!" He immediately clasped the fullest of the two Guinness's with his non-smoking hand and then lent back purposefully, making himself very comfortable. "Guinness in here is fuckin' excellent min, fuckin' excellent; without a doubt!"

Hippie Davie sat down waving drops of Guinness from his sleeve before sucking excess foam off his thumb, "Yeah, well we're trying to enjoy a *quiet* evenings drinking it ourselves!" he said motioning to Becky with his eyes.

The Doc carried on regardless. "Love this place, don't know why I don't come more often...Trish would like it, quite romantic really. Hey, we might get a gig here iz well!"

Hippie Davie looked at Becky and looked murderous for a second. "Ya think, romantic? How astute of you Doc!"

The Doc smiled; he loved it when people recognised and appreciated his keen observant nature. He watched Hippie Davie wipe his hands on his thighs sternly. I bet he thought, *'Davie's all right; I think we're actually getting closer!'* He saw Becky give Hippie Davie a funny look, which telegraphed some disappointment from her. The Doc further pondered *'Yeah, trouble in paradise, well that could only be good, maybe I could move in after she dumps Davie, which would be great. I saw her first after all, it's just unlucky that Davie spent so much blooming time at the Café 52 and stole her from under me.'* He watched her for a few seconds, noticing how her body giggled under her top as she leant forward a little to get her drink. Bingo, there was the lovely cleavage. He took the opportunity to prolong his gaze there, pretending that he was scratching his chin as he craned his neck. This was the gentlemanly thing to do and he was subtle like that.

Hippie Davie sat down and tried to placate Becky; she was clearly getting uncomfortable. This isn't the nice evening it was meant to be. "I'll get rid of him!" he said then winked.

She ignored him in a gesture that spoke volumes and reached for her drink.

"I hadn't invited him!" Davie whispered and then looked over at The Doc, who was craning his neck like a man possessed to look down Becky's cleavage; it was obvious to everyone in the pub! For fuck's sake that was it! "Doc!" he snapped, "look I'll be blunt, am trying to have a date here. What are you doing here anyway?" He implored him with his hands; The Doc had never come here that much, if at all. Was he trying to cock things up with him and Becky?

The Doc held his hand up.

"Relax, relax, act-chew-illy am here cos I need tae spik tae ye, first a need yer advice coz I kaen how good ye are wi'...um...certain...situations!"

Hippie Davie continued his gaze. "What?" He shrugged, not disguising that he felt, by now, quite harassed.

The Doc pressed on, he felt that his best strategy would be to appeal to Davie's ego here and acknowledge his prowess in front of his little girlfriend. Plus this was important mates stuff, man talk; the girl would have to wait.

"Well I've goat the two burds going at the moment like and Pam seems to hiv gotten wind am rehearsin' wi' Trish." Although the fact that he made a prodding motion with his ring finger of his right hand into a curled hoop of thumb and index finger of his left rendered the whole premise of his euphemism quite redundant. "Fit kin I say tae keep 'em awa fae een an ither?"

Hippie Davie put his hand over his eyes, as if he was going to weep. After a second, he slid his hand slowly down his face to cover his mouth, his eyes fixed on The Doc, perplexed, not for the first time and he shook his head. "How does a guy get to be you?" he asked in all honesty.

Becky also looked a bit perplexed, "Rehearsing?" she said out loud.

Hippie Davie's pupils dilated in response, 'Oh God no!' he mouthed to himself. He instinctively knew any further enquiry was a bad move.

The Doc's face lit up, happy to impress Becky with his sexual prowess.

"Oh aye, she canna get enough o' me jist now, were at it a' the time, she's a wee bit younger, an 'ats good coz I've got so much stamina for shaggin...a' o'er the hoose. It's fucking magic like! I divna give a fuck; dae anythin' me, she even lets me put it up the arse an iverythin' if I want tae!"

Hippie Davie's hand clenched into a fist; there wasn't a hippie in the world that could take this kind of provocation!

Becky tho' was fit for him, "Yes Doc, we've all heard about yer up the arse antics!" She grimaced with a condescending smile and waved over at Martin. "Oh look there's Martin," and with that she got up and walked away!

The Doc looked confused, contemplating her remark but before he could finish making a mental note to get her in line, a large hand clasped on his chest just below the throat and nearly knocked the wind from his beleaguered little lungs. Hippie Davie's eyes were aflame and boring into The Doc's head. The Doc gasped at the sheer intensity in those big grey eyes, caught like a rabbit in their headlights.

Hippie Davie sneered in menacing slow motion "You little fucking shrew, I've got a good mind to slap your fucking head off. Get out of my sight will ye!"

The Doc whimpered and looked confused; years of bullying at Torry Academy made him go on auto-pilot in such confrontational situations. Doc's submissiveness almost instantly made Hippie Davie lessen his grip. The Doc stammered, "Sorry, sorry mate, didnae mean to spoil yer evening, without a doubt, eh aye...doubt! I'll apologise the now to Becky, I didnae realise she was...so sensitive pal!"

Hippie Davie baulked at the thought, "No you will not, you'll fuck right off now!"

The Doc nodded. "Ok, ok nae buther, I'll leave ye to it, but afore I go I've got to ask ye Hippie Davie, go'an let me come wi ye's on the jedi weekend yer gan awa tae!?"

Hippie Davie looked suspicious for a moment. "What makes you think–"

The Doc looked up, all puppy eyed, "Ah c'mon mate, Sean mentioned it. I kaen yer plannin tae go awa withoot me, tiking Sean withoot me an' aw! I'll be alright mate, I just need time to sort myself out, jist hang oot wi' mates and get awa fae aw' these fuckin' needy women."

Hippie Davie was a little embarrassed and repulsed by this image before him; no doubt thinking that he was much like Russell Hunter as the character Lonely in the Sixties T.V. show *Callan* with Edward Woodward and he probably wanted to remove it from his sight as soon as possible. Hippie Davie paused, he was about to tell him to fuck off completely, but as he glanced over he saw Becky chatting to Martin.

They were acquaintances and Martin was a real charmer, he had to be quick. He regarded The Doc for a moment. "Tell you what, if you fuck off right this second, Doc, you can come along ok!?"

The Doc stood up and downed the rest of his pint in several large gulps; his composure was right back, as if Hippie Davie had never so much as looked at him angrily. "Ok mate, ok, you've got yourself a deal, a deal!"

With that, he slapped Hippie Davie on the shoulder, gave Becky a wee wave and strode out, muttering triumphantly under his breath; "Mission accomplished and I am one intelligint muthirfuckar!"

One by one I herded Hippie Davie, Don and finally The Doc into my car on the following Friday afternoon. I had just handed in a half-assed dissertation, which I knew was enough to pass. I was a bit sleep deprived and addled, but I was relieved to be going for a wee break with my mates. Hippie Davie in the passenger seat gave directions as we drove far inland, further than I was used to on nightly excursions. The Doc spluttered on about his problem regarding Pamela asking about Trish and his "rehearsals," and apparently she was looking for him! We all smirked at the fear in his voice, as he recounted his problem.

Don was enjoying it. "Phoned my work three times over the last few days. I kept getting the beat driver to say I was away on some trip! She's closin' in boy, the dragnet is getting tighter!"

We all laughed, enjoying his worry, especially Hippie Davie, who I thought I saw an almost satanic glee cross his usually hippie-benevolent face as he teased him. "She'll put nails in yer dildo and shag you to death with it, man. Wouldnae like to be you when she finds oot, 'ats if she doesn't already know right enough!"

Deeper into the countryside we were hurled, as the Grampian Mountains loomed ever closer into view, cold inhospitable looking grey giants awaiting our presence. Finally, after what seemed like an age, we turned off the road, in the middle of nowhere and drove for many miles down a dirt track snaking through the shade of a thick forest. Eventually we saw the thin plume of smoke from a camp fire and the white material of a makeshift tent through the trees and minutes later we arrived into a large clearing dappled with sunlight filtering through the trees. Light twinkled through various pieces of coloured glass hanging spinning on branches. Wind chimes tingled peacefully here and there, giving a constant lulling chime that heralded the end of stress and civilisation. Tie-dyed banners flapped in the breeze and a large psychedelic canvas, now very faded, almost entirely lay draped over what looked the remnants of an old caravan. It may have been there since the Sixties or had been magically transported by mistake from Woodstock. I instantly loved it as I stepped out of the car and stretched my weary legs. I knew that I would be able to do this, live like this and just forget about the clock, time and the nine to five...it seemed so easy after all. A tall and very bearded man lay stretched out on a chair in front of the caravan; he put a hand over his forehead and looked over.

Before Hippie Davie even climbed out of the passenger side, he spoke over in a perfect impersonation of C-3PO, "Ah, I say, is that young mastir look?"

For a second, I was really worried that the people here were all Star Wars nuts like Hippie Davie, which might very well drive me round the bend! However, he was actually being sarcastic to Davie and so I began to quite like this man.

Hippie Davie climbed out. "Wolf!" Wolf?"

I thought, 'Either Hippie Davie is channelling Lassie, or this guy is actually called Wolf!' Ah well, it wasn't unusual for Pagans to give themselves animal names, 'Wolf' sounded kinda cool! Again I thought, 'I'd never have the balls to do that!' Hippie Davie threw his stuff into Wolf's caravan and gave this Wolf a big hug; Wolf was obviously quite fond of Hippie Davie. He was tall, sinewy and weathered and I couldn't tell whether he was twenty five or forty five years old. It could have been anything under that beard.

He came over and purposefully grabbed each hand in a warm gesture of welcome. As he held my hand he smiled, the bearded face revealing bright twinkling big brown eyes beset by laughter lines. It was a face you could trust; if he wasn't a hippie, he would have made a deadly insurance salesman! As he looked into my eyes, I felt a surge of something, like an electric arc had passed through the air between us; the very air seemed to rise, as if my body responded by an almost imperceptible altered state. As he clasped Don's hand I noticed Don take a breath; I knew he had experienced the same thing as well as an element of affection at first sight. I glanced at Don as Wolf strode over to welcome The Doc.

As usual, Don said what I didn't have to confirm, "I Kaen, I felt it an' a' this place has an amazing vibe." Don looked up and around. "Afa lot o' coloured glass and bottles hing-ing fae the branches!?"

Wolf who was standing a fair distance away by now smiled at us, "That's there to keep the woods people happy and in a good mood with us!" He called over and winked.

Don and I looked at each other; we thought of hill Billy types with axes and banjos. Then Don reflected, "Oh right, he means faerie!"

I nodded back sarcastically; "Of course, how stupid of me!"

Hippie Davie was obviously happy to be there, ecstatically bouncing around, "C'mon guys I'll show you around!" We passed beside the fire where nice carved benches were set around it, an ash-strewn barbecue sat not far in the corner and some hoses lay on the grass, snaking their way down to a small clear bubbling burn. I have to say that the place was amazing; there were showers which were hooked up to a boiler housed in a small brick cubicle, large sooty curls told of the method of heating the water within. Hippie Davie led us to a long shed-like building almost obscured by foliage at the back of the site. Like everything else, it had clearly been there for as long as hippiedom had arrived in these woods. A familiar smell permeated the air around it and was very pleasant. Inside were large bins filled with what looked like dark frothy fermenting ales. Glass jugs were stacked in rows along shelves, the little thistle funnels gave them away as wine fermenters. We jumped, as in the dark a figure moved. As our eyes adjusted to the black interior a small plump man with black beard and impressive looking beer belly with a big dragon motif T-shirt stretched as tight as a drum skin over it, wiped his hands on his apron and extended his hand toward us. He looked up at us over half-moon glasses. His looks and demeanour reminded me of Wally Fraser, the intellectual type tinkering away, creating brain altering chemicals for the good of mankind. I half expected his name to be "Owl" or "Peregrine" or something.

"Albert Hugh Harellson, department of Biotechnology at your service!" He followed this with a strange series of chuckles ending in a low sort of "ich-hooo!" like an owl with a sore throat. What made this all the more endearing was that his shoulders shot up quite automatically as he chuckled, making his head seem to tuck down onto his body at the conclusion, in an owly fashion. He seemed to me to be not a real human being at all, but like a strange woodland character from the Wind in the Willows! 'Wow, he has a very normal name,' I thought to myself; I was acutely worried that everyone had some sort of nickname – Hippie Davie, The Doc, Wolf and me plain old Sean. Albert continued, "Most people call me Alchemist-Al, Hoppy Harellson, or Wee Hughey the Hughey! Depends on what you need me for at the time ich-hoo, hoo, hoo!" He grinned at us with such benevolence that I instantly liked him. I knew that he was the type of intellectual guy that would give you the time of day anytime in a non-judgemental way.

'Oh well,' I thought, 'not one nickname but three; I know when I'm beat. I don't know how to earn one nickname, never mind three!' The Doc behind me snorted,

"At's funny, cuz you're ca'd Harellson...and you live in a Wood! Eh?" The woodland-like figure of Alchemist-Al stood with his hands hanging at his side, clearly bemused, squinting at all of us with confusion and mirth as the conversation momentarily ran aground with The Doc's painful observation. We all wrinkled our faces in silent confusion. Finally Alchemist-Al broke the deadlock, "Ah, yes....well you must be The Doc! I've heard about you....Yes, could you kindly take your cigarette and your awful puns out of here please! Either is liable to upset the balance, awfully, in here!"

As we all filed out, Don and I locked eyes with each other telegraphing our mutual embarassement with The Doc. A tall auburn haired woman emerged from the trees carrying a small bundle of sticks. She was barefoot, wore a long green coloured smock and her red hair cascaded around her shoulders with flowers popping over her ears and fringe. The Doc and I shot a glance at each other and smiled knowingly.

Hippie Davie shouted over, "Hey Arianne, c'mon and meet some friends of mine!"

'Arianne!?' Again Doc and I caught each other's eyes. We tried to suppress our smiles like a couple of schoolboys.

She walked over gracefully, her hand trailing on the grasses smiling. Her voice was lovely and caring with a discernible Northern Irish accent, "Hi Davie, good to see you my love and I see you have brought new friends with you!?"

As we introduced ourselves, two more people waded through the grass from the trees – a young, lithe-looking punk-type called Peter, who had affectionately become known as Quiet Pete, on account of his obvious disdain for small talk or any apparent conversation, smiled and shook hands. He communicated mainly by smiling, nodding and laughing at other's jokes. However any jokes which his own mind manufactured, he just kept to himself. I guess that in 'normal' society over there, behind the trees and hills he would be overlooked or seen as a little bit abnormal. Here however, in hippiedom, he was quietly accepted as one of the group, without question. Also present was a woman called Amber, who I had seen working at Café 52 a few times and had, perhaps predictably enough, gone out with Hippie Davie for a while. Amber now looked more like Mara, complete with shaved head and red braids of hair flowing back to a large bunch tied at the back and ended with metallic looking beads. The Doc was almost salivating, though my heart was sinking a little; all these people were far too cool, I wasn't Hippie Sean but plain no-nickname Sean. I wished I could think of a really original inventive nickname!

We began to get our stuff tp pitch our tents, but The Doc just stood around smoking and looking sheepish. Don eventually noticed that The Doc appeared to be just standing watching us.

"You've nae got a tint wi' ye hiv ye, ye stupit-lookin'-fool!" Don snapped. The Doc just grinned back at him in a 'whoops' kind of fashion, shrugginh his shoulders apologetically. Hippie Davie, who seemed rather pissed off for a hippie, rounded on him,

"Oh for fucksake! Why would you come on a campin' trip in the woods without a fucking tent, Doc?"

The Doc baulked a little at the venom of Hippie Davie's inquisition.

"Look, I thought this place was a commune o' some kind wi' heaps a' caravans 'n shit!"

Hippie Davie just looked away with his arms at his side, shaking his head. "Honestly, Doc, ye dinna think man, just dinna think!"

Hippie Davie seemed to be taking the whole Lord Ursio thing pretty badly, I thought, 'not like him to be so aggressive.' As always, I felt sorry seeing The Doc under fire.

"Ach he kin sleep in the car!" I said.

The Doc agreed, "Aye in the car, definitely!" He raised his voice towards Hippie Davie in defiance, "Car…without a doubt!"

We pitched our tents and made our way to the fire which was now crackling and looking inviting as the cool twilight settled down on the campsite, the new smoke spreading and circulating among the woods like a spirit exploring its surroundings. Food was sizzling on the barbecue and Wolf and Arianne produced fresh bread and stew from their stove. Ales were poured into wooden cups and we chatted and ate as night fell. It felt a bit like the coven after a ritual. I found myself chatting to Arianne, "Nice stew, do you get all the provisions from around the area?"

"Oh yes," she replied enthusiastically, "we get quite a lot of eggs and fresh vegetables from the surrounding farms, but the Tesco in Braemar is very useful as well. Might call upon your car in fact, as Wolf's motorbike gets a little dangerously over-balanced at times!"

'Oh well,' I thought, 'even hippies need toilet roll and tea bags!' We spoke about the campsite. Arianne explained that they had been coming there for about six years now. They had met a bunch of people touring Scotland and they decided that this was a good spot for settling and creating a permanent site, hidden away in these woods. The others had gone on to Ireland and the west of Scotland, but Wolf, Arianne and Alchemist-Al had decided to stay. They had got to know Hippie Davie and his mates from university. Anyone was free to stay there, as long as you fitted in and did your fair share. In the autumn, they would take their bikes, go far away and head for the Balearic Islands. I glanced over at the large shiny motorbikes parked in front of the caravan. They all had large Celtic looking swallows painted on them. I understood the significance now.

"And you keep being drawn back here?" I asked.

"Yes, it's a favourite place, plus with all the stone circles around here, this part of the country is quite a vibrant place for Moon rituals, you can feel it in the air! The forest seems alive!"

I smiled. "I know...I often feel like that, I actually used to feel compelled just to walk about places like this till dark, with no idea of what I was looking for...that was before I discovered Wicca!" She nodded, obviously seeing a kindred spirit in me.

Night fell and the effects of Al's ales and wines lit a strange fuse in my head. It had been a long day and everyone parted to go to their tents. The Doc had been chatting to Amber quite a lot; they seemed to have changed positions a few times, as Amber moved seats and The Doc had edged closer again. Don and I tripped along giggling to our tent, after much hilarity. We quickly removed jackets and jeans and slid into sleeping bags.

"Goodnight Don brother!" and then absent mindedly I said, "Don't let the bed bugs bite!"

There was a slight pause, before his voice broke the silence again as he mused, "Mmm Fitza bed bug onywy?"

I shrugged; I didn't actually know that much about them. "Well, I think it's a sort of five pence piece-sized bug that sits on your face at night and feeds on your blood."

There was a slight pause again. "Well then, why the fuck would you say that to me right before I go to sleep?"

I shrugged in the silence, smirking in fun. "I dunno, it's just a saying for fuck's sake! I never thought about it!"

Don suddenly made a disgruntled sound in the dark, "Fuh-ucck me!" Moments later I drowsily fell into sleep.

At some point, though, I awoke and found myself staring at the roof of the tent, listening to the murmur of Hippie Davie and Amber and Alchemist-Al chatting next to the now smaller fire, my head still spinning from the effects of Al's wine, which he informed us had a dash of mushroom from the forest mixed in with it. I chuckled to myself; surely The Doc was thinking he'd get it together with Amber, but he'd have no chance – Alchemist-Al was one of those guys who could just chat forever and he had new companions to talk to now. I smiled as an 'ich-hooo' emanated from the fireside right on cue.

As I lay there I felt disorientated and floaty, the motion effects of travelling through the day were making me feel an almost seasick, bobbing feeling oscillate through my body. After a little while of lying there, for I don't know how long, I heard the soft sound of feet on the grass next to our tent. I got onto my elbows and the figure stopped moving outside. I slowly and very quietly slid out of my sleeping bag. Then I heard the sound of somebody or something tug at the ropes of the tent and chuckle a bit, a voice was whispering very quietly. 'There must be a couple of people pissing about out there,' I thought, 'probably The fucking Doc playing some prank!' I reached out, unzipped the tent quickly and popped my head outside. There wasn't a soul in sight; the quietness of the cool clearing and the eerie wood beyond felt very foreboding. I decided that the bugger was hiding nearby, so I slipped on my DMs and stood up. It was dark, but my eyes appeared to be perfectly adapted to the night. I could see quite clearly in the dark, which was strange but welcome and the light from the fire seemed very bright and strangely more vivid. I turned to glance over at the car, again gleaming really vividly bright white and metallic in the night, parked over by the caravan and motorbikes. I walked over and looked through the window; there was The Doc curled up asleep in a sleeping bag on the back seat like a dozy dark little dormouse; so that ruled him out. A bit confused, I turned to look towards the fire and Amber had got up and was heading over to her tent, not far from where I was standing. As she walked past, I held up my hand in a wave and nodded. She barely acknowledged me as she looked away from the car where I was standing and hurried the last few steps towards her own tent. 'Typical of one of Hippie Davie's friends,' I thought, 'did I emit an odour de Northfield or something that these middle-class types seemed to pick up on?'

I glanced back towards the fire. Alchemist-Al, Hippie Davie and Quiet Pete were now joined by the figure of Wolf. He was standing by the fire and was looking over at me smiling as he waved me over. Al and Hippie Davie were deep in conversation, whilst Quiet Pete sat thoughtfully staring into the flames. When I reached them, Wolf slapped me on the shoulder and smiled, "I see you've got the hang of Al's wine already?" The friendliness of his touch spread from my shoulder all over me in a wave. His smiling face seemed to lift my spirits. I realised that all trace of the self-doubt which had been hanging over me, as a result of Amber's snub of my presence, had evaporated. I thought, 'Wow the effects that a human being can have on another, purely through physical contact was immense!' I looked at him aghast for a second, acknowledging my instant emotional lift, when he began to chuckle.

"Come with me, I'm here to show you something!" he said.

I followed him through the camp and out towards the woods. Curiously, I didn't feel intoxicated at all, merely light and happy, my feet deftly traced the steps of Wolf in the dark, barely making a sound, as we strode ever further through the dark canopy. I mused at the level of visibility we both enjoyed, thinking that the range of human night-vision was really excellent once your eyes became properly dark adapted.

Wood anemonies positively glowed with an eerie white brilliance as we passed them; I could swear I could hear electrical buzzing and humming from various forest plants, as we brushed past. Strange animal noises echoed through the forest and life seemed to crackle everywhere. Suddenly, I heard in the distance the distinctive sound of a wolf howling. I froze; it was spine chilling and worrying as there were no wild wolves in Scotland anymore. "What the hell is that!?" I said to Wolf, who now stopped and crouched in front of me.

"A distant lone spirit, nothing more," he remarked, matter-of-factly. "Come here."

Though confused and a little concerned, I did as he asked.

"Look." He pointed through branches at a large moss-covered boulder in the centre of a clearing. There slouched along the top of the stone lay the figure of what looked like a child, with strange spindly legs, one which swung nonchalantly and care-free from side to side. I watched mesmerised and curious as its head rested on two long arms slung behind its back. What looked like a long pipe jutted out several inches from its head, with smoke slowly spiralling up out of it gripped in its mouth. Wolf was laughing to himself.

"They came to see you tonight; only fair you have a wee peek at them...they don't much like it mind, being snuck up on!" He grinned.

I turned to look at the figure again and a feeling of recognition flashed up my spine as I struggled to comprehend what I was looking at. I slowly stood up, wanting to get a better look. As my head came over the top of the bushes, the figure stopped and in slow motion the head moved round towards mine. Dread filled my heart and mind, as the misshapen features, once eclipsed, orbited into view. I stood rooted to the spot, heart pounding, as the face that now appeared green with piercing black-angled eyes fixed down upon my position like an insect predator considering its prey. A long ripped-looking misshapen mouth sneered down at me. There before me loomed an alien intelligence, with strange unhuman features and with who knew what morals hiding behind that visage.

I tried to let out a scream as my body fell backwards. With a twist in the air I landed expertly onto the forest's ferny floor. With a kick of my heels and a superhuman charge along my back and shoulders I whipped through the foliage and into the protective darkness of the woods. Far I ran, as I put good distance between me and whatever I was leaving behind. I hurled myself through the night, hurtling over burns and fallen logs, instinctively twisting on my trail so that it would be hard to follow me, under bushes and over more marshy ground. Eventually I came to a road; hearing dogs barking in a nearby farmhouse spurred me on again, frightened of what those horrible hounds could inflict on me in the dead of night. I instinctively bolted through a hole in a fence and found myself rushing headlong through the long grass of a field of wheat. I felt hidden in the grass and I stuck to a long rut for a while, but then feeling exposed dipped my shoulder and careered into the grass towards the woods again, scared that the rushing sound might give my presence away. I ran through more woods before slowing down to a walk.

I found myself walking downhill towards a complex of old huts. I stopped and paused quietly transfixed as a vixen and her cub slowly ambled out. Their presence and the quietness of the scene made me feel safe and at home. She sharply looked over and stopped also; I felt their company was good and reassuring but she looked at me suspiciously and made a sound that I knew was displeasure to see me. She wanted me to keep away from her and her cub, feeling protective, not wanting anything to do with me. That is when I knew, when I realised how I knew the vixen's mind. My shape, my body, I wasn't walking at all, but springing along on four stilt-like legs, panting, I was frightened. No wonder the vixen was afraid, she could sense or smell my fear; I was a fox...but I was still me as well. I crept around the hut, a smell beckoned me. I looked over towards a fire through the trees, attracted by the smells but not trusting the glowing embers and rustles of activity, the fear still pumping in my chest. I lay my triangular head down in resignation and slept behind a shed. I started to visualise more hounds after me and had nightmares. Seconds later, I was aware of Don's voice, "Sean, Sean, what the hell is wrong with you?"

My eyes snapped open. I was back in my sleeping bag, drenched in sweat and my concerned friend's face hovered over me.

"You're having a bad dream, it's ok!" he said.

I told Don everything, excited; I wanted to bound out of the tent and go to see if Wolf was sitting by the fire. Don assured me there was no one there.

Don thought for a second, "Sounds very shamanic, have you ever dreamt of be'in' a fox afore?"

I shook my head. "I've never, never had an experience like this in my life. It was real. I'm telling you it was real, I got up..." I was still very confused about this part. I had got up. I had gone to the woods with Wolf. It was real and how could I be in bed? I couldn't comprehend how I could have been dreaming all this.

Don lay back in his sleeping bag. "Well maybe if we could get any sleep around here we could all get a go," he said disgruntled.

"You're a right moody sod when you're tired Don."

"Love you...Goodnight," came the reply.

"Sweet dreams my brother, sweet dreams!" I murmured before closing my eyes.

The morning came suddenly, as if by turning the page and finding myself on a new paragraph. I had had no further astral experiences, but I felt refreshed and alive. Don was, as usual, way ahead of me, chatting to people around the site, who were emerging hair on end to splash water on their faces and clean furry mouths. The morning had a texture of dappled light and ageing tie-dyed fabric, with a slight hint of fermenting ale. It was peaceful and wonderful. It smelt of the woods and echoed to the tune of chaffinches and robins. I half expected a cartoon robin to land on my shoulder, as I made my way over to the wash area. As I turned the tap, which connected to a large length of hose that snaked up to a large rainwater collecting drum, I thought, 'these hippies are kinda civilised really.' I heard a large splash and some laughter. I followed the sound through the trees to the small river where the sound came from further up. I heard the sound of a woman's voice; I thought I shouldn't investigate any further but was too curious to see what was going on, so I decided to stealthily walk forward to try to get a quick peak. I walked further along a small path by the river going uphill while the river swirled, cold looking and brown, to my right. Then I saw a flash of skin through the light of the trees and realised that I was looking at three figures splashing in a small pool of water. I peered closer, Arianne, Wolf and the dreadlocked Hippie Davie were swimming around in a large pool of water fed by a small waterfall gushing in a torrent of water from a ledge about five feet above the pool. Hippie Davie had just dived in from the side and Arianne was trying to swim away, giggling, from the now unseen figure under the water, like a hippie torpedo going after her legs. Wolf stood under the water fall, the power of the water flattening his hair and obliterating his features to a happy frown.

Then Wolf stepped forward as water dribbled from his beard and eyes. He arched his head back to shake water from his hair and as he did so he caught sight of me standing transfixed on the bank.

"Ah morning, c'mon, the shower's free and very bracing it is this morning!"

I was a little bit embarrassed, I had been slightly transfixed by the naked giggling frame of Arianne, but fortunately they didn't seem to mind. "I just wondered what the splashing sounds were, sorry!" I stammered.

Hippie Davie, who had come up for air, smiled at me, "Come on man, this is the only way to freshen up after a night of Ally's wines!"

I hesitated for a moment; what should I do? I felt a little shy being invited into a pool by naked people whom I didn't really know that well.

As I was debating this, I was forced to stand aside as Don ambled past me, tattoos danced past my eyes on cold wrinkled skin, "Mornin!" he said. "I'm gan tae get ma towel I said!"

I tentatively removed my boxers and exposed myself to the cool morning air. If that wasn't chilling enough for my anatomy, then the searing strength-sapping shock of an all over freeze plunging into the pool was orders of magnitude worse. The pool hadn't looked as if it could be that cold, glinting in the morning sun, pretty like a shortbread tin painting, the kind you fantasise about jumping into whilst romanticising about the beauty of our country. But we (us Scots) often fail to remember that we're a stone's throw from the Arctic-Circle don't we? Yes, suffice to say, it was freezing, I mean, bollocks numbingly freezing. It took your breath away as well as wiping away any trace of manhood you had. Soon we were joined by the unflattering body of Alchemist-Al, the welcome body of Amber and finally Quiet Pete. Yes, a strange fact of life in the North East of Scotland is that whenever the weather is even the least bit clement, Aberdonians will go on picnics, strip to their underpants and immerse themselves into the iciest pools of water like this. The trick was to just jump in quick; after a few minutes of breathlessness and numb pain, the body becomes quite numb and anaesthetised to the cold. As a child in Northfield, we would head down to the seaside, grab an old tyre inner tube from a nearby truck depot and head for the North Sea. We would dive bomb off the harbour jetties, enjoying the waves produced by the big boats like the ferry in sub-arctic cold water. We would dive underneath the waves and touch the sandy bottom or body surf along the picturesque sandy beach. Whilst perhaps not twenty miles away offshore oil rig workers were being warned in training seminars that they wouldn't last ten minutes in the water without a survival suit!

As we languished in the cold water, I caught sight of Wolf regarding me curiously. I was almost sure that he was aware of the events of last night, but in the cold light of day my experience of being a fox the night before now seemed unreal, had all been a dream brought on by drugged ale!

"That was a strange brew richt enough last night eh, that's a weird power it has?" I said.

Wolf nodded. "Only gives you what power you already have Sean!" He grinned. I wasn't sure what he meant, though he carried on quite matter-of-factly, "That was a cool disappearing trick you did last night, what did you do?"

I was a little confused. The water glistened radiantly, as a ray of sun struck the pool and golden looking pebbles became more visible along the bottom. I thought perhaps Wolf meant Don and I leaving the party early due to tiredness.

"Well, we were tired."

Wolf pressed water off of face and beard with both hands and looked at me earnestly. He leaned a little closer and the sounds of laughter and splashing fell away further into the background. He smiled a little and looked me in the eye.

"Your spirit animal came to your aid last night didn't it, when you felt threatened? - It is an honour indeed to receive such an ally without any real attempt from you to do so!" He was talking almost as if he was in awe himself, or jealous. "You obviously have one foot in the realm of spirit, to react as easily as that!"

Wolf's words seemed to caress my thoughts. The whole scene seemed to freeze as I was both shocked and excited at what he was saying! My heart thumped in my cold numb ears as a realisation sparked somewhere in my mind and tears welled in my eyes at the mention of such an ally. A strong pang of emotional recognition spread across my face and dripped from the corner of my eye. However my mind also raced with confusion. Did I get up and was I confusing a dream with a conversation I had while tripping in the woods with Wolf? At what point did the dream begin? Why had I no memory of walking back to the tent and getting into bed? It didn't make any sense. I looked back at Wolf, words failed me, I began "Did I, did we...how?"

He smiled and slapped me on the shoulder; his friendliness was warm and encouraging. With that, the large shadow of the arrival of a scary, fleshy asteroid momentarily filled the sky above us as Alchemist-Al dive bombed from above the waterfall. The sight of his bulbous naked body and the mega-tsunami of brown water that filled my mouth and nostrils was enough to wake me up completely; I certainly wasn't dreaming this.

We dried ourselves off, the towel feeling exceptionally rough against hypersensitive chilled goose bumped skin with little feeling and with arm muscles almost too chilled to coordinate effectively. The only benefit was that even the faint cool breeze permeating this part of the country now seemed almost warm. We had some tea and porridge and I was voted to go and get provisions with Hippie Davie and Don. The Doc was sulking because no one had thought to wake him for a swim. In truth, it was an unspoken agreement that he would have been just too creepy and would have made the women feel uncomfortable. Driving to the store felt really surreal to me, as the confusion of the previous night's proceedings was still wrestling with my rational side. The store was a reminder of the civilisation to which I belonged; I saw that the store and everything that was associated with it relied on a consensus of opinion and beliefs. Though I no longer felt this consensus was one hundred percent adequate to satisfy my perception of reality – that and how cream eggs always looked smaller these days.

As I strolled around the aisles of the Co-op, I began to see how thin a veneer reality actually was. People busied themselves stacking and tidying, gossiping and re-ordering. It was a cycle of normality, a mere consensus that kept the other, quieter world at bay. Perhaps animals lived in this other world of quiet contemplation; they do not distract themselves with such separation of mind and environment, possibly we humans used to be like that as well in our ancient past. This world is not as far away as you think; for me, it seemed like it was a mere car ride into a road that disappeared into a wood. A few doses of some local herbs and fungi and I would be stepping into that other world, just as surely as day becomes night. I stared at the rows of items on the shelf; they were half in that world and this, too.

Quietly, everything that exists has inputs or ripples in the otherworld, like an echo. "Like an echo," I said out loud, making my thoughts physical and I mused how on this occasion my words were the echo of my thoughts in the waking environment now, while during the previous night, my dreams had been the original environment, a reverse mirror reality. Perhaps this was how schizophrenic or highly artistic or eccentric people felt about society at large. My only consolation was that pioneers in thinking also faced this type of insecurity, from Darwin to Jung, or Galileo to Descartes. However, I felt grounded while shopping and talking about mundane things like how much of a twat The Doc could be with my buddies for a while.

Later in the day, after a lot of lazing about and reading papers and munching of pork pies, we prepared to go for a ramble with our hosts Wolf and Arianne. This was to include a short ritual or some kind of dedication in the woods. I was looking forward to this immensely; as I was sure working with these people would be fascinating. As we walked through fields and woodland, I was filled with admiration by just how vast Wolf's knowledge of the natural world was. Every bird that made a sound was identified, whereas I could only identify about two or three if I was lucky. Wolf would stop and wait and invariably an animal would reveal itself like a more common wood pigeon, or a less seen wren or stonechat. Every now and again he would stop, "Ah, this is a good herb for sore stomachs!" or "This moss is so acidic it is virtually sterile, good field dressing, used it in the first world war you know!?" I was amazed when he would reach down and pluck wood sorrel from the ground and munch into it, or select certain mushrooms and carefully put them into a muslin sack which was slung around his shoulder. Occasionally, he would bound like a predatory animal into a thicket after "power plants," as he would refer to them. He would remove these very carefully, digging with his hands around a large area, completely removing the roots and lifting them like a new born baby into the sack. He would then murmur something inaudible and sprinkle what looked like tobacco onto the spot.

I was a little embarrassed, as I was studying Biology at degree level and I couldn't identify shit! I nearly trod on a small toad, which Wolf spotted far behind me and gently lifted up, whispering to it like Dr. Doolittle! I'd never seen anything like that before. On ecology trips with the university, (the very inspirational) Professor Martin Gorman had caught shrews in a trap, although he was kind to the pulsating ball of life in his gloved hand and regarded it with some awe, there was never any question of an empathic sense of equality. It frequently annoyed me that in the nineties, on a Zoology course, the objects of study weren't afforded any proper "alive" status. One professor even talking about "growing marine proteins," where after several minutes I realised he was talking about fish farming. The living animals were described in terms of yield and economics, much like arable farming, which was rather telling. It was wrong! Anyone who owned a pet intuitively realises how wrong this is! It seemed to me that anyone with a brain can identify that Wolf's relationship with the natural world was much more positive, beneficial and a more mentally healthy way of interacting with the world and its other inhabitants. This is regardless of whether you think humans have a right of superior sentience or not. All that we can say is that we possess human sentience and likewise other animals will have evolved their particular kind of sentience which might be better or less than ours. Language is not a sign of a "soul" or a superior place in the living world; it is particular to us, as echo location is to bats, an evolved attribute for a particular way of life and existence.

Eventually, Arianne called us into a circle. She'd decided it was time to indulge in a rite of thanks and acknowledge the gods of our ancestors. We all held hands and were led through the woods. Arianne led the chant which we all began to reiterate. As we carried on, her voice took on a very lovely lilt, which became a song, I don't know what it was, but it reminded me of Scarborough Fair and I began to wonder about the roots of that song, did it have this psychic quality? The lull and the effect reminded me of Hippie Davie's druidic song to Brigit. As I walked, I felt a little like felt during the chants for healing we did at Newmachar. The pace quickened and gathered momentum. The God of the wood began to fill my consciousness. I felt a little like an Ent from *The Two Towers*, rolling through the wood. I felt such love for life while the energy of the woods pulsed through us. It was so joyous I burst out laughing and many others did, too, almost in synchrony. There was no sense of fear or retribution from the gods which filled our consciousness; only love and a sense of freedom. Arianne was like some kind of elven goddess; as if we were picking up on their presence, like an antenna and all we needed were Arianne and her song. These gods were all about life and the land, of good times and healing. I understood that this ritual and frame of mind was valid as it was only right that we should be aware that our world provides so much for us, now we needed to heal it in return!

We eventually got back to the camp and I spent much of the time lazing around with The Doc and Hippie Davie, while Don went for a walk with Quiet Pete. As the afternoon wore on a little, though, The Doc gave me the heads up that the small but ever-burgeoning tribe of the religion of Jedi had arranged a quest in the woods and that I was invited as a spectator. After finding out that neither Wolf nor Arianne were taking part, I decided to sneak away instead, to speak to Wolf, intrigued with what had gone on the night before, as I wanted to clear that up. "I'll leave you to polish yer light-saber!" I said sardonically, "...And then after that ye'll be wanting to get ready for yer Jedi thing!" With that, I ambled away with my hands in my pockets in the general direction of Wolf's caravan.

I knocked on the caravan door which embarrassingly made it reverberate in its hinges, shaking the caravan impatiently. "Come in," replied Arianne who was bustling about inside. Wolf was avidly staring into a small television screen with studied concentration, slapping the sides to no avail on the white snowy screen.

I chuckled at the sight, "I thought people came out here to get away from all of that!" I said sardonically.

Wolf looked a little agitated, "Nah, you jokin, T.V. is an amazing place to surf and see; here be the dreams of the sleeping human race man.

I regarded him for a second; his capacity for turning an everyday remark into a philosophical springboard reminded me of Hippie Davie. Why doesn't he just admit he was looking for the Flintstones or maybe some sexy scenes in a foreign film? I considered saying this out loud, but stopped myself; I was his guest and didn't know him that well, sensing it was perhaps a little impolite. He continued to stare at the small screen, as he backed away from it slowly and sat down carefully, reaching for the remote, as he did so. I thought him just a tad rude and it made me feel a little bit stupid and uncomfortable.

He motioned for me to sit down opposite,

"Sorry, sorry just a minute; I have to do this, I've had a bit of a sign you see; the cosmos is in the right kind of mood to interact with me, if you could just bear with me a second or two." He broke off a little from his sentence and turned to regard me sitting looking quizzically a few feet away. "Actually, you're probably here to watch, this seems to be your turn to watch this weekend!"

With that, he sank back into his chair and let his head fall slowly backwards. As he did so, he slowly raised his hand with the remote control towards the television set, the tragic lantern flickering like a new age crystal ball in the corner of the room, set to mute. He murmured some incomprehensible incantations under his breath, which sounded like Greek or Latin and his eyes rolled back in his sockets as his trance-like state descended, he spoke,

"Let me hear the answer I seek?" As he spoke, he started flicking through the channels in a random manner. Suddenly he hit the mute button and a few words from an advertisement rang out in the room:

"Seeking paradise?"

He pressed the mute again and started flicking through the channels again, then suddenly he hit the mute button again, this time he rested on an old western as an older U.S. marshal type was talking,

"Bo'y a advise you ta."

Then mute and flick and unmute again; this time the screen rested on an excerpt from the T.V. series *Kung Fu*, where the old priest with the weird eyes was talking to the boy Caine,

"As we must eat to sustain the body, so the mind must also eat. What you eat makes your body and what we learn feeds our minds!"

Slowly Wolf lowered his head and nodded. "Always a bit weird to actually hear your answer being spoken out loud to you in the room and beats having to decipher tarot cards don't it?" I was thinking that it was pretty cool to have the master out of Kung Fu speaking some wisdom directly! What were the chances of that? I nodded and looked over at Wolf,

"What was the question?" Arianne, who was in the background, smiled over.

"Should he stay vegetarian or not!?" I thought about the apparent answer he had just received and widened my eyes in admiration, nodding. All I could think to say was, "Fucking cool grasshopper!"

I looked over at the glowing screen in the corner.

"I suppose T.V. is on just about twenty four hours a day these days and probably represents a sort of collective unconscious being played out all the time? I would never have thought to do what you just did though!"

Wolf stroked his beard and motioned over towards the flickering screen. "Yes, it's a real otherworldly reflection of life, a continuous tickertape recording of human history. We're so gonna be judged harshly in hundreds of years' time as archaeologists try to debate just how fucked and primitive our opinions were on the eco-system and the development of our own species!"

I smiled, "Yeah, I've often thought that and they'll probably have professors searching for ages on how something like 'Noel Edmonds House Party' was deemed to be big entertainment!"

As Arianne handed me a welcome cup of green tea, he looked into the distance for a second and then continued;

"Nah, don't knock Noel man, guy gets a lot of stick, but he'll always be a childhood hero for me!"

"Multi-coloured swap shop?" I conceded in return.

"That's it!" he nodded in acknowledgement. "And every morning on radio one: '...Start you're day with No-El-Edmonds!'"

I nodded. "God yeah, my Ma used to listen to that every morning an aw,' must be a seventies and eighties thing!"

Wolf nodded almost absentmindedly. "Yes that's right, before breakfast T.V. you see. It was like the whole UK used to wake to these guys!" I agreed,

"Yeah, I suppose the mighty No-El-Edmonds was like yer best pal for a while there...but the whole Mr. Blobby thing...he's like the annoying twat of a mate that you dread meeting now...wonder if he's a medicine man as well!?"

We chatted about television for a moment or two and I began to feel completely at ease. Before knocking at the door I was concerned that I would have nothing to say to Wolf and that he'd quickly work out that I was pretty boring and uninteresting, which was always embarrasing. I mean, I still tended to feel insecure with myself in social situations. I would feel ashamed upon realising that I was creating social disharmony and awkwardness around me, because of my social inadequacies. However, as we chatted freely about radio, DJs and television programmes of our youth, I became aware that it didn't matter. He wouldn't be thinking about me like that, that was a concern that existed in my own head. You didn't have to be wind swept and interesting all the time, people just want to chat about anything really, that was the key, to be relaxed and prepared to go with whatever the situation demanded and just keep it real, kinda thing.

I found that in this place I could easily be relaxed and just be myself. Arianne came over with a pot of tea, "Why is it that whenever men get together they invariably tend to start talking passionately about Mr. Blobby or kids T.V programmes?" She laughed; Wolf and I sat speechless for a moment. I loved her soft Northern Irish lilt, it made her sound quite intellectual to me.

"Coz I haven't got around to asking him what team he supports yet!" Wolf said factually.

"Yer all just a bunch of daft kids underneath it all!" she smirked and as I looked at her Celtic goddess features, I fancied that this is how the goddess viewed the entire male complement of the planet. She turned around and nudged Wolf with a playful smile. "And you with yer Noel Edmunds fixation!"

I joined in, "Ye winna hear a bad word against him!"

She sniggered, "I know, what *is* that?"

Wolf had that philosophical look on his face again. "We talk about T.V. coz we're getting older and it's good to reflect on these things. Television viewing is the stuff that binds the nation together. Communal watching is a real social phenomenon that people take for granted nowadays, but T.V. allows people to experience a real sense of 'group mind' far more than any other means of doing so. Far better than any other media, it's very powerful magick."

"Aye, it's just so quick and accessible…and visual. We humans are very visual animals," I said.

Arianne cut in, "And a very social one. People are very easily persuaded to conform to the social norms, just something else that is ingrained by natural selection!"

I nodded, said "I suppose," and then looked up at her a little surprised.

Wolf whispered from the corner of his mouth knowingly and nodded in her direction, "Anthropologist!"

We talked further about American T.V. and the superiority of their sitcoms. Finally, after a few sips of chateau du-lally kindly supplied by Alchemist-Al, I brought up the subject of out of body dreaming;

"Hey guys, I wanted to talk to you about an experience I seemed to have had last night, I'm still confused about it and the more I think about it the more confused I get!"

Wolf smiled a little and ran three fingers through his beard. Perhaps appreciating the look of genuine bewilderment crossing my face he went straight to the point.

"Sean, what you saw last night was real; all the wine was able to do was help you salvage your memory of the night. It was a real time out of body experience. What you saw in the woods was a real look at how they are now and how they have been in the past. Time has a tendency to slip a little bit…more freely in the spirit realm!"

I regarded him for a second, allowing his words to penetrate. *'Real-time* and *spirit realm.'* How come I had only just seen this now, if these phenomena were so apparent? I had many questions.

"Last night and in the woods; that was real?" I started to feel a little chill of apprehension and the memory of the previous night's fear crept back to me. The blood started pumping again in my ears as my heart pounded at the implications of Wolf's words. I had felt more secure when I had convinced myself that the whole experience with Wolf in the woods had been a vivid dream. Now it was as potent a fear as finding out vampires and werewolves actually existed in the woods beyond. Wolf looked hard at me for an instant,

"...Yes! Surely you have understood by now that there are ways beyond the norm that link us all together!"

I still found this a little hard to take and looked a little dumbfounded at Arianne and then back to Wolf, I suspected that last night I must have talked a bit to Wolf, then passed out and confused this drug-induced hallucination within a dream. I asked again,

"But that wasn't as real as this is and how did I get back to bed and anyway...how do you know what I saw last night, or think I saw?"

Wolf sighed a little, he sat back looking at me thoughtfully. "Sean, I know because I saw, just as you did...what we saw may not have been exactly the same, down to every detail, but we saw it together, because I was waiting for you by the fire...I watched the faerie tug at your tent and saw you emerge, but I knew by the way you appeared through the tent that you were there in the same way as I was. I knew then I was there to meet you!"

I regarded him silently, still trying to come to terms with what he was saying but simultaneously becoming more and more excited by the reality of the implications of his speech. I regarded him for a second,

"But...but if this is so normal, I mean, why hasn't anyone else seemed to mention it, I mean, how come science hasn't caught up with it?"

Arianne cut in smiling, "In our cultural understanding, it is very difficult to accept that separate people can experience a similar or simultaneous out of body dream sequence...or that events can be glimpsed days before they occur. I think it's perhaps difficult for the waking mind, which is so dedicated to experiencing the immediate physical environment, to come to terms with the notion of a non-physical environment that changes and is bent by the will!"

I nodded, still pondering the concept. "Yeah, well I certainly don't quite accept it myself."

Arianne continued, "You must remember that Western science and philosophy is still relatively in its infancy in some respects. Take the Hindu universe, for example; it's much older. The comparison I make here informs us that better models of the universe can still be arrived at! There's a quote I like which will help you here – have you heard of the Indian scientist J.B.S Haldane?"

I nodded. The name was familiar from somewhere, perhaps one of Carl Sagan's programmes on the cosmos that had captivated me as a child, "Yeah...I thought he was Scottish though, for some reason?"

Arianne smiled as she mouthed the words, "I suspect that the universe is not only queerer than we suppose, but queerer than we *can* suppose!"

Wolf suddenly leaned forward clasping hands over his knees; the sudden movement impregnated the room around him with an air of expectation. I waited for the sermon. "Science may be the best kind of enlightenment we have of the world, but unfortunately it is limited, in that it is blind!"

I regarded him suspiciously, having heard similar arguments promulgated from the Christian right.

"Science is like a mole brother, ploughing on short-sighted through the substrate, making a burrow in a straight line, like linear logic building up on the last thing discovered. But despite its many insights it can only ever be the most probable mathematical description of anything. So, don't you see that if reality and the universe or whatever is actually beyond that is indeed, infinite, or that rules can change, such as within black holes or...or frogs raining from the sky then science at present can only ever be a best guess, never having one hundred percent clarity!"

I shrugged; he had a point, "Well, you said it, it is our *best* guess, therefore our only reliable tool; well that's good because one hundred percent knowledge would mean there would be no mystery left in the world and surely that would probably be boring anyway."

Arianne cut in smiling a little as if in some kind of sympathy. She continued; the soft lilt of her northern Irish accent further conveying intelligence and a sense of erudition unrivalled to me...it was also of course, an extremely sexy combination!

"Science for all its power is only as good as the lens it creates. Newton gave us the mechanistic clockwork universe, as that's because he and people like Robert Hook and Christopher Wren were immersed in that mind-set. That's where seventeeth and eighteenth century technologies had got to. Now what? Everyone talks about software and programming and algorithms, as that's the dominant technology now." She became suddenly more animated. "But the universe doesn't exist as a clockwork whirring programmed machine, neither is it a virtual reality in a computer...it is 'original' reality in all its glory with life and wonder in it. A computer program depends on time running in a certain way, with a beginning and an ending algorithm. The universe chews up our notions of time. Why do we insist that the universe follows our very limited human perception of chronology and reality? That could probably well be as illusory as a flat earth!?? Just because no scientist can understand how Wolf, or you, or I, can leave our physical bodies and witness events ahead of time, doesn't mean it cannot be possible. Not if we, and enough other people, know it to be true!"

Wolf chimed in at this point, his brow furrowed in earnest, "Look, you mentioned Carl Sagan's *Cosmos* programme before. Do you remember by any chance his analogy of flatland to represent how action can be perceived across dimensions?"

As a matter of fact I had, "Aye, if you consider a table top world populated by two dimensional beings, like shadows, they would have no concept at all of height, the third dimension. I remember Carl then placed an apple with ink on the bottom on the table; it would appear to those in flatland that four small points made by the base of the apple appeared in space before them. However, the two dimensional flatlanders would have no concept of the rest of the apple nor that the points were connected to and a part of that three dimensional object." Wolf nodded quickly acknowledging that he didn't have to explain further.

"Well, using that analogy, simply substitute the third dimension of height for the fourth of time, which is a dimension which we are limited by (since of course we're physically limited by the speed of light)."

I pondered that for a second, "Yeah, right it's known as the arrow of time, cause and effect - all that sort of stuff!" Wolf nodded approvingly, as I pondered that fact, however before he could go on, I had the light bulb moment he was getting at.

"Ahh, wait so yeah, if anyone or anything had the ability or potential to step out of the constraints of time, then that being or discarnate awareness could look down from a vantage point and see all of time and life's experiences laid out in a long continuous line, like a flowing river branching and searching across the fabric of a space-time table top. Further, such a being could interact with any point in space-time, along the branching river of a lifetime in an instant, just by reaching down to any point. Just like a three dimensional person looking down on flatland as they would be kind of above or apart from the restrictions we refer to as time! Both ahead, the past and present would all be visible and all accessible from such a position."

Wolf's broad smile and glinting teeth beaming from his bearded face, assuredly dimpled with satisfaction, conveyed his pleasure at my understanding of his analogy. He put his hand on my shoulder. "Yeah and what is that awareness?" he said, further imploring me with his eyes.

My mind raced, "The Goddess, my higher self?"

Wolf creased his brow in response and bowed his head into a slow motion nod of affirmation, "Yeah, yeeeah all of those and actually your own self, your own subconscious mind and your own holy guardian angel! It, whatever that is, could look at any point of your life-time in an instant, it would be able to nudge and guide you, hoping you'd discover more self awareness along the way, hoping you would find your own will!!"

Arianne chuckled, "Seems easy when you talk it through does it?" She smiled over at her unassuming but greatly talented husband.

I wandered whether it could all be a as simple, as he made it seem, that an aspect of mind could really be separate from the body and that it could act in an independent way from the physical body. I muttered out loud, seeking to consolidate and clarify,

"S'the ultimate in Cartesian body and mind duality then is it? The mind leaving the body, it's a shame coz neuroscience and parapsychology at the moment are pretty much refuting that with more and more studies. Monism, I think the word is, is pretty much the dominant and accepted paradigm among evidential sciences right now is it not?"

Arianne merely smirked, looking a little triumphant as she ran a hand through her long auburn hair. Her arms conveyed sinewy strength, which made me think that actually she was a fair bit older than the early thirties age bracket I originally had placed her in. I suddenly felt a pang of jealously, I thought, 'It's not fair, she was like a perfect woman, wise, mystical and logical all at the same time. Maybe that's because she was from an earlier and wiser generation like Wolf here and Alchemist-Al. Maybe there were no people like them anymore in my generation.'

However, as I gazed at her that train of though was interrupted as she parried my point. "Ahh, but who says there's a need for such duality between mind and body?" My face contorted in confusion, as she continued.

"If you can glimpse the future while lying in your bed right now, there's no duality, your mind is still here... only it has information from the future, therefore an aspect of your mind is also there as well, simultaneously. There's no real 'duality' as you put it..." She made the inverted comma sign with her fingers. "...only an 'as well', as your mind hasn't separated from your body in space, but only separated in time, much like the Copenhagen conclusion of quantum behaviour, that quanta of your mind is everywhere at once, until it's 'collapsed' into information at any point in time; so monism could equally be correct!"

I began to see the point as Wolf helped guide the conclusion.

"Well, if that's possible and remember that there's no doubt to me and you and plenty of others that it is, then the conclusion is that once you exist, you exist forever in a state of superposition outside the arrow of time, with the ability to interact anywhere you wished, but not quite physically, more as information. Maybe if an out of body experience happens to the scientist who actually witnessed ball lightning, then it will become a topic worthy of investigation to others!"

What was painfully obvious to me is that the laws of the universe did conform to this reality on a quantum level (and on the grosse level at various speeds). Therefore, *déjà vu*, ghosts, premonitions, God, Gods, action by prayer or at a distance, magick and all paranormal events including life after death – all of it – was explicable once you factor in that aspects of mind of every conscious person can at times leave the confines of straight time and pop up anywhere and interact with reality at some superpositional-level of information, if not matter itself.

So, for example, a ghost really is the 'ghost of the information' about what was physical at one earlier point. It was a simple theory, but such a powerful one, with much explanatory power, I liked it. This also meant that our sensibilities, aspects of our awareness, call it what you will (soul?) that once this exists, then ultimately this exists forever. So, Liam Gallagher wasn't quite so full of shit at all was he? *Ergo* not life after death as such; but death of the ego or 'eternization' of awareness after physical death.

All I could think to say was, "Wow! But wait, so what are the astral planes and such like?" As I looked towards Arianne for more minblowing insights.

Arianne looked thoughtful, "Well...I tend to think of it this way; when someone gives you information, you make a representation of it in your head so that you can consciously 'look at it,' as we're a visual species. So if information arrives internally via the mind, we just do the same, make an image so we can look at it. So ghosts, gods, premonitions of the future are our minds recreating the information for us to see and mentally represent."

Her words seemed to help fill a void of explanation I had for my experience. This sounded like the beginnings of a theory, one which could provide a satisfactory working model. I attempted to clarify,

"So what you are suggesting is a brain-generated imaginary construct outside of physical reality, overlapping and bigger, containing information not accessible to only one person and outside of time as we know it, but a reality nonetheless!?"

Wolf pursed his lips and shrugged; "Yeah!"

Arianne nodded pensively, "Yes, in a sentence that is what I think can explain it for you. The astral planes are a reality, because people can exist within them and explore these with their full waking conscious awareness. Therefore these realms are more real than mere fantasy and dreams, because if you can interact with people and a place whilst awake and they have the same experience, then that place does exist, at least philosophically if not physically! No one could deny that!"

I sat back, allowing the information to insert itself into a new shape within my schemata of the world. I smiled, these notions fitted perfectly, as I already had a gap where these explanations were needed. I was content at that moment in the knowledge that I both finally felt comfortable with myself and the way I saw the world. I felt the need to thank Arianne and Wolf for revealing this fantastic truth to me about the nature of mind and matter.

"Geez, I really appreciate you explaining all this to me, it's just...I can't understand why more people don't have these experiences, or that the astral planes are not more widely known!?"

Wolf's large benevolent dark eye's twinkled with knowing as his beard creased a little, betraying the smile beneath; "Well you'd be surprised just how many people can perceive these things. I actually think most people can, except they choose to just ignore it when it happens! It's like dreams with premonitions and meeting people you're fated to meet. Many people intuitively realise the greater reality behind everything, but don't consciously acknowledge this!"

Arianne brushed fine strands of hair from her face, before quickly and urgently hooking them behind her ear in a down-to-business manner. The furtive motion, it seemed to me, corresponding with increased amplitude in cognitive speed. She concurred with Wolf's train of thought.

"Personally I have had experiences where I know for a fact I've seen the future, thus personally the notion of cognitive processes or mirror neurons is not satisfactory for me, so I need a better model!" I was leaning towards agreeing with her; I had great sympathy with her attempts to reconcile a psychological approach with her spiritual experiences. It was such a relief to hear another Pagan person taking the same position as myself, only much more wisely. She continued;

"That's the problem we all face in this culture. Magick, Wicca, Shamanism all works, we know it does, but there is no satisfactory materialistic model to explain it. Eastern cultures, though, have no hang-ups about this. Magick is a part of what we are, part of being human, a talent of natural influence which we have that is a vital part of us which should be embraced, because if we ignore it then we are not 'being all the human' we can be!"

I felt she was right; in fact, I was sure of it! I knew magick worked, divination often works, and people have premonitions. There has to be a slightly better theory other than 'it's all an error of perception.' Religion, spirituality and even magick are very much part of being human, just as an appreciation of art, music and poetry are also distinctly human. The human mind has developed an awareness of aspects of mental experience which are not directly related to survival. Magick, divination, religious and spiritual experiences then, are akin to this level of awareness. Hippie Davie's words came back to me; perhaps reality changes gear due to emergent properties.

There was a short pause as we all cogitated the conversation. I thought about what Arianne had just said – "Drop out of work, take drugs, do magick, be all you can be!"

We all chuckled, "So, fuck...there are faerie people in the woods!? I can leave my body and travel. I can experience the future?"

Wolf smiled at me, "S'right...not so hard to believe is it?" He grinned at me then went on almost solemnly, "Pretty much everyone can leave their bodies that way, but if people do, then most don't remember at all when they wake up! Not many people can maintain the conscious mind with the imaginary body. But here's the most bizarre thing; it is possible!" He stopped for a second or so, as if in contemplation. "It's like no-one informed the subconscious that it isn't possible, so it goes ahead and does it and it seems entirely consistent with how the universe 'is.'"

I nodded, I must have known this deep down, but my scientific training made me question this at every angle and seek a more coherent explanation, in keeping with what we assume about the semantics of our description of time, space and hence reality.

"If you're saying that you saw me somehow when I was in a shadow state and you were as well, then it can't have been coincidences could it?" I said. "Can't have just been a shared dream; is this really possible, I mean, why have I never done this before?"

Wolf smiled and his eyes bored into me as if he was reading my soul. "You have done it before, Sean; seems like you're trying not to remember. Odd how you try to exclude parts of your own reality. Maybe it's time to wake up, Sean."

I slumped back in my seat and began to beam with a sense of happiness. All my life I didn't fit. I knew I had never been fully satisfied with everyday social interactions or expectations. Now as I began to compute what Wolf was telling me, a sense of "told you so," crept up from the back of my mind and a feeling of contentment and kind of self-assurance settled down across my shoulders. Also, the universe suddenly came to life in my mind. I had always been perplexed and intensely curious about how things came to be and how the laws of the universe accidently collided to produce form and individuality. In a sense, I had thought "time" was God, time enabled all phenomena and we were the idle but grateful spectators. I, like Carl Sagan and those demi gods of science from Darwin to Dawkins, had been a grateful spectator; now my viewpoint shifted from "time" being God to "life itself" being God. Life, consciousness was perhaps a fingerprint of something else from another dimension outwith the fourth dimension of time and thus, perhaps created itself. The ancient image of the

Ouroboros, the snake eating its own tail came to my mind. If my mind could step out of the constraint of "space" and then indeed "time," then <u>time was not the bedrock of reality at all</u>. Like Arianne had said, this was a human assumption which ranked alongside the false assumption that the earth was flat. Einstein had showed that *semantics* (*i.e.* how we think) had dictated to our perception that space and time were not indistinct. His genius was to see beyond this conditioning, to properly describe and understand these, demonstrating that they had to be linked. To me, now the lesson had to be further contemplated and extended to life and reality. Life itself, reverberating across time, can favour an outcome out of chaos. If you think about it, if the big bang contained within it all the fields, energy and mathematical constants; perhaps aspects of life and consciousness had to be also already present, just as time itself began at that point.

The universe is full of laws, equations and what I would call "gelling" factors that favour symbiotic relationships and cooperation, be it biochemistry or cooperation among living organisms. A consequence of Darwinian evolution may be that complex consciousness is not wholly governed by 'accidental time' and so life could accelerate and favour various beneficial outcomes. "Will" is a key and I also began to realise that the strongest "will," will succeed. Will was like a subtle physical law, similar to the gelling factor in the universe. Will enables building, creation and evolution. Further, if all humans want/willed for love and freedom at their deepest core, no matter what their religion, creed or desires, I couldn't see how human beings could fail! Will was magick and magick is everywhere, magick is for all.

As I contemplated all this at some pre-articulate level, Wolf continued, "The etheric plane offers a world of possibilities, as those that can walk it and those that can send their will through magick to influence them have much influence in the real world. It's like, for instance, having the ability to hypnotise people over large distances. Through magick we can gain good allies on that side, to walk with your allies and communicate with them. These are the shamans, the striders between the worlds. It is an honour to be given such a role!" He looked at me intently, checking whether I followed.

"So you are a shaman then?" I asked prompting him for further info.

He smiled wryly, "Perhaps yes, we're healers, we use craft learned to heal the people whose spirits call for us. At other times we may be sent to aid a situation by turning up at the right place at the right time; spirit lets us know when it's time to do something like that."

"How does one become a shaman then?" I asked;

The lines on Wolf face creased into a concerted frown of concentration. "Usually one doesn't just become a shaman; rather, the spirit realm chooses you. You see, a shaman is born to be a messenger for spirit. The person can ignore it or embrace it, but if you do you will see wonders you never dreamt of and see the world from a different perspective. Yeah...things you will see, other places, the future, the past; but it takes courage of course."

I loved sitting there in this small magical caravan, peacefully placed in the woods under the safety of a wavey canopy of leaves. This was the outdoors, the woods, the original reality of our species. Maybe that was why I felt so 'real' and happy here, listening to what Wolf and Arianne were saying.

I was used to being around people who were very matter of fact about the existence of other realms and of the practicalities of magick, but I had come to learn to partition these thoughts in my mind. I was now faced with a reality that was both daunting and inspiring at the same time; a merging of the two sides of my personality. Contentment had fallen upon me, as if something which had been separated, congealed into a tangible fact in my mind. Further, this was connected to this whole positive experience right now in my life. The wheat was being separated from the chaff so that only relevance and that which was good for my soul was left. To think all I had to do was spend a few days in a hippie commune in the woods dosing myself with all manner of dodgy psychoactive herbs and weird home brews. I was aware that it was getting late and I began to gather myself and my various bits and bobs when I heard a bit of commotion outside. Instinctively we all stopped and listened to the voices drifting our way. It sounded for all the world like someone was shouting for The Doc.

# A: The Ordeals

## Chapter 8:
## Get a fix on Getafix

As the voices grew louder I became able to discern Don's exasperated voice bawling imploringly for The Doc. We stepped out into the, now looming darkness and shadowy quietness of the woods. Don drew nearer, looking expectantly in our direction. I shrugged to answer his gaze, "Doc? Av nae seen 'im, have you checked with Alchemist-Al? Mibee?" But there was no sight of The Doc; he was long gone into the night.

As I had sloped off to share a rollie or two with Arianne and Wolf, the Jedi gang had made for the heart of the woods for a vision quest. I understood this to be a sort of "chaos magick" ritual which tapped into their early childhood wonder of the universe and its possibilities, according to Hippie Davie. That was about all I heard. The Doc had excitedly droned on about vision quests to the unconscious and the various qabalistic sephiroth as well, high magick stuff I wouldn't particularly know much about.

The six of them went traipsing through the night, lit on all sides by their glowing plastic sticks, getting more into character with every step. They had that right. Magick, Wicca, ceremony all relies heavily on acting and transpersonal psychology. Any result relies on expectation and a real belief that something ultra-mundane can manifest. Hippie Davie had that well sussed; the people he had with him had a real ready-made childish acceptance of the situation that was perfect for success. Alchemist-Al trotted along with them, with an air of amusement and just sheer happiness to be in the company of people. He may not have been quite as *au-fait* with Hippie Davie's star wars pantheon, but being an old Hippie himself, he had seen stranger things before this! Who knew what strange thoughts and philosophies whizzed through that alkaloid addled old brain of his. It was hard to tell. His expression rarely changed from a kind of "Know it all, been there done that, happy." Quiet Pete walked along happy to be in company, whilst magically feeling no pressure to express his ego externally. I fathomed later that life was one big meditation for Pete.

Hippie Davie led the way, slowly treading through the dirt path that lead into the darkness. There was a slight sense of foreboding among the group as the darkness of the forest closed in and seized them one by one. The woods could easily now be filled with unknown monsters out there, for all they knew. Thoughts of faerie and weird unhuman saucer-eyed paranormal creatures easily entered the imagination in this environment. Trying to remain unaffected by such fantasies was almost impossible for a sane person. All except Don, who strode unperturbed into the darkness; feeling practically more at home with every step. In Don's mind there were no monsters, merely Ewoks and Wookies chattering in the tree tops, like little teddy bears singing and frolicking around. He hummed to himself smiling as he joined in with their happy attitude to life in the Empire.

Meanwhile, The Doc, whose eyes were darting in every direction, felt a sense of unease about being led into the darkness. The Doc looked on spitefully as he watched Don jauntily stride along the quiet dark forest track. 'What's that fuckin' bastard smiling at,' The Doc thought to himself, '*fuckin Wiccans, oblivious to the threat around them!*' The Doc considered himself that bit wiser about woods and trees, being a Shaman, the forests were his domain and faerie was his to command. In the cold light of day all that seemed fine, but here, in the dark, he began to have second thoughts.

What was it Alchemist-Al had said to him earlier at the camp fire, on a conversation with faerie? "Ahhh, but there's a *reason* why our ancestors broke contact with faerie! Once upon a time, in our early agricultural existence, in small nature dependent and social personal lives, the two worlds were closer and mutually beneficial. As people began to acquire possessions and money took over, our selfish impersonal way of life contaminated faerie with ill intent. You see, as our societies grew and became more urbanised, the rage, the frustrations of modern life spilled out of our subconscious minds and into the faerie realms. What once was the source of lore and myth became defiled and corrupted by the Christian mind-set that created devils, monsters and demons everywhere you looked. The wise woman or wise man with a foot in the otherworld became a cavorter with the unseen, a dangerous ally of the infernal. It was a fear of all that was once revered and part of the framework of the living environment, a basic fear of the dark and all the worst imagining of what lurked there. Fear robbed us of part of our core humanity, our link to the land."

The Doc now thought about this, Alchemist-Al's words now becoming imbedded in the darkness as an irrefutable argument in his mind. He had really spooked him. The Doc mulled it over, 'True us Shamans once commanded those realms, but now...right enough it has become contaminated. Faerie was neither good nor evil, it was completely amoral; they didn't understand the sanctity of life or pain or death. It was all very well for his Shaman ancestors in the good old days but now he had to contend with all the demons and evil that the Christian mind-set brought over with them, with their foul notions of hell and torture. It was sick.

A vague memory from some school lesson on Shakespeare or something sprang into his mind, "*Like flies, they kill us for their sport.*"

'*Bloody hell,*' thought The Doc, they will toy with us, hunt us in here, kill us for their sport! A layer of sweat formed on his back making it clammy as frog skin under his T-shirt. His eyes darted around, trying to penetrate the darkness. He felt sure he was being watched. Demons now gathered around him. He could feel their presence, long-necked subhuman forms loomed towards him just out of range, big saucer eyed demons in the dark, he thought, or long necked lumbering beasts...maybe even long necked, saucer eyed beasts! He shuddered and swallowed hard, those were the worst kind! The creaking of the trees in the dark sent his nerves jangling on edge. He peered over at the other faces, everyone else looked slightly on edge and he could sense it, sending him further into nervous turmoil. A large spruce cracked in the wind a few feet away from him in the impenetrable darkness.

"What in fuck's name wiz that!?" he yelled out as he instinctively grabbed a tight handful of Amber's top in front of him.

She shrugged him off impatiently. "Just a tree cracking in the wind, calm down."

He stared into the gloom, "Fuck me really? Do they always fucking do that? I didnae kaen they did that, fit a fucking noise too? D'ye hear it? T'wiz lika big beast or some-ming...fuck me!" Though to his frustration, no-one answered him as the group walked on as he stayed a bit closer to the back of Amber, his head darting to and fro.

He glanced again at Don, smiling and humming something to himself. '*Fooool,*' he thought, '*no fucking idea of the evil hunting him. Well if something attacks him and drives him insane with fear, then it'll be his own fuckin' fault! And if he expects me the Shaman to help him, then fuck it, he's on his own. I can't be expected to defend everyone all the time now can I!?*' The thought of Don taking his Shaman protection for granted pissed him off further. "Arsehole!" he snarled under his breath, as Don oblivious, smiled merrily on!

Eventually they came to a clearing surrounded by rocks and roots. Hippie Davie lit some lamps and placed them around the clearing, marking out a convenient circle. An upturned tree stump, glistening with fungus and moss waving slightly in the cool breeze, gleamed under the flickering light of the lamp hung from an old branch. Davie unfurled a cloth with a symbol of the rebels from 'The Empire Strikes Back" printed on it. Everyone took a position around the circle. Some final large gulps of Alchemist-Al's brew were quaffed as it was shared around. Hippie Davie took a few swigs before handing it onto The Doc, "Here ye go Doc, might as well just finish it mate!"

Hippie Davie then took the lead in the centre of the circle, invoking the spirits of the force and that which unifies all life and existence! A strange sensation whipped around the group, exerting a collective pull which seemed to emanate from the very ground itself as everyone took a deep breath and gasped in unison at the feeling of the power.

"Let the force surge within us, Jedi disciples, Saber wielders. Let our human spirits merge with your spirit, Lords of justice, Princess of Power, chaos Goddess, god, je-die." With that they all joined hands and felt the force gather, Hippie Davie lead them through a rune which they'd all had to learn:

*Jedi Knight and Saber light, smash the evil Empire's might.*
*Of all the stars, life we share, the force is here and everywhere!*
*East and West and South and North, here we are to call the force!*

*Gods of Old and Spirits new, come to us, us Jedis, few!*
*Gather here and build the force, the centre of our universe!*

*Queen of tatuin, princess Peril, lend your power unto our spell*
*Shamans, skywalkers, Jedis bold we call ye forth as Lucas told!*

They then quickened the pace and started to walk in a circle, getting louder, quickening with every word and repeating the last lines until it became a crescendo.

*Here we are to build the force, fill us build it round and round,*

*rise around us from the ground,*
*From rocks and roots and stars and oak*

*our Jedi power we do invoke.*

There then was a pause and everyone instinctively knew exactly when the end point had arrived. Power surged through them making everyone dizzy with sensation. All hands were raised and pointing to the centre of the circle, which seemed to now be imbued with a shade of lightsaber green. Hippie Davie then gave a short dedication and asked the allies of the force to aid them in their lives and help free the spirit from the shackles of the evil empire which threatened the environment and the liberty and true will of every person. Everyone then knelt in front of the altar and pledged their Jedi vows and asked their holy ally to keep them happy and guide them through a proper path in life. Amber asked for peace and protection for a loved one and a more energy was built up to send them a healing through the force. Quiet Pete's smiling face gleamed green through the dark wood dappled shade.

Then came the part of the circle that The Doc was waiting for; his initiation. He loved a good initiation. Hippie Davie pointed to The Doc.

"Now we have a person in our midst that wishes to follow the path of power, to take the quest to see if he could become a Jedi Knight!"

The Doc reeled a little, clearly feeling decidedly odd and a little giddy from all the power and chanting. He looked a little over anxious, like he knew something wasn't quite right, though he didn't really know why. However, this is what he had been waiting for, a vision quest was sure to increase his magical power. Soon he would be a credible voice and part of this growing Jedi movement. He intended to become grand master Jedi and supersede Hippie Davie in no time. He'd then break off and form his own religion, a brand of Shamanism and Jediism. He had so much experience now and such a lot to share. He had always known that he was different, destined for something greater, a prophet of the new age, a new Jesus with twenty first century wisdom…and spare batteries for his light sabre.

The trail of light flooding from Hippie Davie's light saber was so brilliant that The Doc could scarcely look at it. A large green ark brushed across the scene and remained like a slow motion sparkler against the darkness. Hippie Davie's words were hypnotic, splitting into The Doc's mind commanding one hundred percent attention.

"The quest to become a true Jedi is indeed perilous...you must face your greatest fears, lose all trappings of greed and lust for the Empire. Is this truly what you seek traveller in the darkness?"

The Doc stood facing Hippie Davie, the throng of people standing as silhouettes behind him. "Yes...yes, I do!"

Again Davie's voice loomed austere in front of him, a large black cowed figure lit magnificently by the green of the force, now not Hippie Davie, but talking green lit features emanating out of the dark circle, now OB-1 himself.

"This is no idle promise you make, it is better that you die and return and be reunited with the great force, than to fail and know ruin!"

The Doc didn't seem to compute what was said, he answered again, "I do...I do...I want to be a Jedi!"

"Then hand over your weapon, you must pass this test unarmed!"

The Doc held out his light saber, which was removed. He must have felt naked without it in this dark setting.

All lightsabers flicked on and were now held aloft to create an archway of multi-coloured lights which lead a way out of the circle towards the trees. It was amazing and as blinding as the pearly gates might be, except perhaps a bit more colourful. It was astounding; The Doc was drawn towards them and he gawped at the sheer brilliance of the rainbow swimming in front of him and all around him. It was heavenly and hypnotic and did indeed seem like a tunnel to another world. If he had been able to take his gaze and attention from it for even a second he might have begun to realise that he was tripping far too much than he should be and was beginning to slip into a place of no control, but he didn't.

His heart fluttered as he walked through the tunnel of light leading him to his destiny with the drone of lightsabers and John Williams's theme tune playing in the back of his mind somewhere. Finally, with the words of "May the force be with you!" ringing in his ears and a hard but friendly slap on his back from someone, the night suddenly fell silent and black.

He stumbled forwards towards the trees along a path in the darkness; he knew what he supposed to do, follow this path for a few hundred yards until he came to a widening in the path and then head for two Yew trees that grew together, creating a domed circular spot underneath them. He wasn't looking forward to it; it had been a little bit too quiet and spooky during daylight hours earlier when Hippie Davie first put it to him that this was part of his first vision quest.

He squinted back towards the direction of the circle but could see nothing, no lanterns, no movement; no voices came to comfort him. He was completely alone. He began to wonder just how long he had been standing there. His thoughts whirled around his head and he began to feel completely lost and vulnerable. The cracking of the trees and rustling leaves rang at him through the long black shadows that protruded from the menacing blackness surrounding him and enveloped him as he walked. Creaking trees now screeched quite loudly with human-sounding voices penetrating the black silence while leaves hissed warnings in the dark as ungodly winds passed between them.

Fear gripped him. His heart began to pound in his ears as he again stopped dead in his tracks, he felt like he did not know what he doing there, where was he going? He couldn't think straight, nor fathom whether to head back or keep going. He had become disorientated and lost; he knew he had to meditate on why he wanted to become a Jedi and to discover an ally of the force that would help him face his fears, but what if they could not protect him from all the evil that lurked in these woods? He slowly began walking again, now on full alert, the wind carried strange mewling and snuffling, sometimes a little bit too close for comfort. He could hear stalking all around him and felt as if something was hunting him, searching for him in the dark. His heart pounded in his ear as panic swelled inside him.

The Doc then realised that all the power raising and ritual work would have lit him up like a beacon on the astral plane. Everything that was everything in the spirit realm could see him now. He was a walking target in the dark. He realised this to himself, *'Oh my God they're hunting me, to intercept me before I join the light side.'* Of course, it made sense, they never warned him about that, curse them, the bastards have made him as an offering out here alone. He has been offered up as human prey to the forces that didn't much care for human beings. His whole body trembled as he listened to the footsteps behind him and around him. His head shot from side to side as he crouched down in the bushes, muttering incantations to himself and crossing himself with the qabalistic cross. He concentrated hard, asking for protection from every God, Goddess and power he could think of. The quietness surged around him, draining him of courage. *'Did everyone really do this? Had Amber, a slim younger girl really done this a mere few weeks ago?'* He wanted to turn back, maybe he could just say he went there, but Hippie Davie had mentioned that it was important that he go there to begin the next phase of the quest! Fuck, probably got somebody waiting there to scare the shit out of me or something *'The bastards, the bastards...!'* 'he thought and then, *'Ye buncha bastards!'* He muttered to himself bitterly and then looked around wildly trying to think of a way out of there.

He looked back in the direction of where he thought the circle had been. They should have known better than to mess with him. He closed his eyes and quickly muttered through clenched teeth,

"Never underestimate the dark side, never underestimate the dark side!" He knew it; he always knew that he was fascinated by the dark side, fascinated by black magic, by power. Healing was all very well and so were nice chants to gain happiness and good fortune. However, that didn't get you respect; the allure of black magick, however, that gave you some power. The occult community would only take you seriously if you had a mastery of black magick that was for sure. That was reaaal magick; the lesser Gramaticon, the Goetia "The Howlinggg!" he mouthed to himself. "Abramelin the mage, Enochian magick, having a command of Demons and Angels, real stuff like Alistair Crowley!" Where Crowley had failed, he The Doc, once he had mastered all the various systems, would integrate them and reveal a new way for mankind to be and to follow him! It was easy; he just had to try to stem this crippling fear of the dark first.

The wind got up a little and the forest seemed to shake with rage; almost goading him for thinking such thoughts of grandeur. His stomach churned with fear and his bravado leaked away like water from a colander. Black bat-like shapes circled overhead, skirting though the air like silhouettes of his very fears come to life. That was it, he'd learned, the dark side might eventually take his soul, torment him, he had to stop thinking bad things, ok! "Ok, ok!" he spluttered through tears, "I've had enough, I've learned I've learned, please let me go." He had to get back to the security of the circle. He made up his mind to just run. He picked himself up and darted towards the darkness of the path. Leaves angrily whipped his face and legs as he sped forward, towards the yew trees path, where he felt sure someone was waiting for him with his light saber.

Eventually he came to the widening in the road, the sound of leaves suddenly increased in amplitude as if getting louder as if to accompany his arrival. His heart raced and he gritted his teeth and stood still, perhaps he could just stay here for fifteen minutes and then slowly head back!? But he didn't feel particularly safe standing there, in fact he felt more anxious here, more exposed than at any point on the path so far. The hairs stood up on the back of his neck and he felt a strong presence of someone watching him. He felt as if he had walked through a thin wispy spider's web and his foot nudged a small stone. He looked down on the sandy path in front of him, his eyes squinted to make out markings in the river sand beneath him, apparently fairly recently drawn. He walked a little further and bent down, sure enough there were symbols he recognised as runes and combinations of runes joined together, drawn out in a triangular shape all around him. Surrounding them was a small circle of neatly placed stones. As he was pondering this curiosity, he began to feel light headed and slightly spacey again. He put his hands to his temples. His head buzzed with the cocktail of Al's wines and spliffs and he almost felt as if he would just float away if he didn't struggle to keep his feet on the ground.

The feeling of someone watching intensified and he snapped his eyes open and looked around, almost expecting someone to be standing there. His eyes fell upon a flat stone with strange symbols on it, a sharp pain jabbed him on the shoulder and instinctively his hand shot around his head and he grabbed the cloth of his robe. Something came away in his hand and he brought it round to his eyes to look at it. It was a small piece of card with some symbols carved onto it, symbols which now looked strangely similar to the runic symbols scraped on the flat stones.

The Doc did not like it, he did not like it all, something wasn't right. A confounding feeling of peril swept over him as the howling winds intensified around him in the forest. He swirled around, looking around for the source of the ill feeling and decided that it was time he was getting out of there. The adrenaline flooded his mind and muscles and he drew a deep breath preparing to sprint back to his companions. He didn't care anymore; he had quite enough of their little games, it wasn't funny anymore. However he found himself not running, but frozen to the spot as, as he looked ahead, the path, it seemed, was blocked by someone!

Or something ahead of him was standing quite motionless; a wizened, vampiric looking figure, dressed in black, with a large hood and a partial face showing through. The Doc blinked a few times unable to believe he was looking at something actually real, something apparently "there." Sure, he had been practising magick now for years, since school where he scrawled hateful spells in his jotter, as sigils to gain revenge for those that teased him (The Doc went through a lot of maths jotters per term). However, he'd never actually seen something "real" or permanent enough that if you didn't blink it would remain. It was very frightening indeed to take in such a ghostly image as real as anything else in the clearing. He wanted to run screaming, as the hair on the back of his head again stood up and the air froze around him; but he couldn't. All he could do was keep staring towards it, transfixed as if hypnotised to the spot as his stomach churned in adrenaline frenzy.

The figure moved very slowly, in slow motion, as if it was standing in a different medium to his and experiencing a slightly different passage of time. It could have been that, or it could have been the massive pulses of fear hormones that were focusing his mind and jolting his nervous system to react about three times faster than usual. The figure slowly raised its head to reveal it's features, as it did so a strange eerie predatory-like howling filled the air, seeming to come from everywhere all at once around him, as if this thing's presence had wounded the very air.

It was the face that frightened The Doc the most. For apart from the drawn white cheekbones and the large un-human eyes, it was recognisable as resembling his own face but with a strange cat-like quality and an evil malignant gaze with an open yawning mouth, as if held permanently in a screaming moan. The Doc was literally looking his own ravaged demon in the face. As he was still trying to accept what he was looking at, tears streamed down his face and all energy or fight seemed to leak away from his body as the physical equivalent, a widening stain patterned the fabric of his robe. The figure had him held in its gaze like a hawk staring down at a mouse as it slowly pulled from its cloak a long bony arm with something glinting in its hand. Again The Doc could only stare in disbelief, his eyes glued to the scene as his body would not obey the command from his will to run away. He choked back tears, as he tried in vain to shout for Hippie Davie, but only a shrill croak whispered out of his mouth. He started to cry freely as an ominous deep red laser light spread down from the glinting handle in its hand. The air was electrified to the soft hum of a menacing lightsaber which bathed the scene in a hellish deep red. The Doc understood immediately what this meant, knew that he was about to die, as he stood there motionless and defenceless against the evil sight before him.

Seconds later – an eternity of fear for The Doc – the figure screeched an agonised hateful scream, as loud as the howling wind and flew straight towards him. Horribly, The Doc's worst fears came to light, even though he still couldn't believe this was actually happening to him, as the slash of red light burned down across his chest. The Doc screamed and fell back with his arms in front of his face, as the figure slammed into his chest. He reeled in disbelief and abject fear as he felt the sickening and very real physical sensation of the thing's wizened frame hit into him, knocking him further backwards and pinning him to the ground. This was very, very real. He could see it, smell it and feel its horrible presence in the air around him screeching and howling like a betrayed, tortured animal. Now he could feel it, as its mass knocked him back with another painful blow.

He panted hard scrambling for several seconds and rolling back and forth in the undergrowth, crying, kicking, screaming and lashing out with flailing arm, defending his face and body from the evil in front of him. To his frustration and alarm his kicks and punches fell into thin air, like a nightmare, offering no resistance or defence against the repulsive evil tearing at him. He heard the swish of the weapon occasionally increase in volume and his body tensed in rediment for more blows, as he cried out loudly, tears streaming down his face, begging it to stop. Eventually he lay face down mouth gurgling in the mud with arms outstretched in defeat waiting for the final blow to come and end his pain and torment. He could hear its movement about him but couldn't see it; he didn't want to see it. Finally, he could feel its presence closing in and the horrible cat-like squeal rose to almost deafening pitch in his ears. He trembled uncontrollably as fear penetrated to his very soul. All he could do was sob in self-pity and resignation.

The blow never came, but the howling continued to ebb and flow about him. He cautiously crawled forward; his body on remote control to get out of danger despite feeling it was no longer useful. He turned around, hardly daring to look as the sound receded a little, as if it was far away; perhaps he could escape after all.

He scrambled to his feet and to the path in the darkness and started to run along it. His unbalanced, uncoordinated lurch broke into a sprint but he could still hear the siren-like scream somewhere in the distance, though he couldn't figure out which direction in the darkness it was coming from. He hoped and prayed that he put some distance between him and it. Terrified, he could hear the demon now screaming after him. He ran and ran, onwards, his body and legs aching under the huge demand he was putting on his physique. Occasionally, his loose robes would snag on a branch sending him reeling into the air and smashing his body down onto rubble or roots but he didn't feel it, as he scrambled back up and kept moving. The more he ran the louder and more frenetic the screams became. He couldn't take it anymore, couldn't run any further. Sweat and tears obscured his view as he veered helplessly into thorns and bushes stumbling off the path. He twisted through the bushes trying to get up, trying to see behind him. Pain shredded at his consciousness briefly before being blocked out again as thorns and branches tore angrily at his flesh and flimsy robe.

The Doc could hear the screeching again but this time began to realise that it was near him, becoming ever closer to him in the foliage. Pausing, he looked at his chest and saw the fabric was torn there; he also saw a large red mark and it began to dawn on him that the figure had somehow entered into his very being and was now inside his head like a parasite. The screaming he realised, with some horror and revulsion, came from his own lips. He crawled out of the bush, dripping red from various wounds and his head spun. As he walked along the path bewildered, he fought with tears the urge to scream again, wrestling with the demonic force inside him, screeching with pain, bitterness and emptiness which he had stored away all his life. It was too much; his will had been drained by the cocktail of drugs and his reason hung by the feeblest of threads. As he staggered out, he knelt, looking up, placing his palms together he prayed to God and Jesus. "Please help me God, oh God have mercy on my soul, oh Jesus help me." But the very words just seemed to anger the darkness nestling inside him and inhabiting the inside of his skull as it roared out of his head. His hands clasped his face in an effort to stop it. He sobbed freely, as it roared and spat and howled with all the mad energy The Doc had left at his disposal. There was not a thing he could do about it. His hands ineffectively clawed at his face and chest in an effort to rid himself of the foreign entity to no avail. He staggered forward in resignation before hurtling zombie-like and in silence over a fence and into darkness.

As The Doc disappeared into the trees at the camp, the lights were snuffed and all fell quiet. Hippie Davie then busied himself closing the circle and the rest of the party busied themselves eating and drinking, lighting more candles and cigarettes. They sat around while Davie, with a wave, left to walk towards the trees, "Right I'll take the short cut to the grove!" That should have been it. They were secure in the knowledge that the night was all but over and after a little relaxation they would head back to the campsite. However, it wasn't long before a series of distant screams shattered the peace of the party.

Amber climbed to her feet, as they all listened, the scream continued and sounded exceedingly frightening and terrible in the distance. "I'd better go and see what's going on!" she said finally.

Don glanced up, a frown of concern spreading across on his caring features. "I'll come with ye!"

Amber looked down at Don's huge forty holer Doc Martins. "Sorry, but with all due respect, you're not going to keep up, besides I know the way!" and with that she sped, gazelle-like along the path.

Don took a step in her direction and stopped, as she disappeared from sight almost instantly. He turned towards Alchemist-Al and shrugged. Alchemist-Al responded with a smile, a shrug and an *ich-hoo!*

Amber sprinted through the darkness towards the grove. As she came to the widened path she saw Hippie Davie standing there lighting up a joint and aimlessly kicking stones into the trees in frustration. There was no sign of The Doc, "What's up?? What was the screaming? Is he ok?"

Hippie Davie shrugged, "Christ, I dunno, I was just getting to the grove from the other side when I heard him screaming, I ran up here but he was nowhere in sight by the time I got here. He could have gone down any one of these paths but I'm not sure which one he would have taken. I'm just listening to see if I can work it out; he can't be that far." Hippie Davie looked annoyed and short tempered for a second, "Dozy bastard, the way was well signposted as well-look!" He pointed up to a wooden stake with a little cardboard cut-out of Yoda pointing down along the paths to the grove site.

Amber regarded him for a second, "You could be a bit more sympathetic Dave; it's very spooky down here alone and he's a bit delicate I think! Something must have given him a really bad fright, I'll try to catch up with him this way and you try the other one." With that, she ran off down one of the paths and Hippie Davie, taking a toke on his spliff, grinned and whispered out of the side of his mouth, "Well, he's possibly be a bit more fucking delicate now that's f'sure!" He then started off; hands in pockets, ambling down the other path.

Amber never caught up with The Doc; he had long gone, veering off the path and into farmland. Wandering over fields and dales, the lone mad medicine man roved, snarling and occasionally stopping only to howl up at the moon, regarded only by an indifferent tawny owl staring down at him from above; meek-yes, vulnerable-check, too big to be a mouse…awwh bugger! His mind and morals were in tatters as he stumbled over muddy ground, his cloak snagging on everything higher than his ankles, making him spin around and tug at his skirt behind, fields spanned out all around him. "Never underestimate the power of the darkside," he muttered quivering like a child. He could see in his mind the broad snarling grin of a triumphant demon within him, like a mouse with a large cat glaring down at him, toying with him with one large paw on his chest. He stumbled into a small depression in a mound of earth and slumped down onto his knees in prayer. In complete resignation he lifted his eyes to the Heavens and implored Jesus and Lord Ursio to help him. Saying the Lord's Prayer over and over provided some comfort, while the power of the bear gave him more stamina and courage. As he said the words, most assuredly it did seem to keep the dark power at bay, easing it from tormenting him, with flashing images in his mind or screaming loudly in his brain. Eventually, physically and mentally exhausted he slumped down into the damp cold earth and lapsed into unconsciousness.

Back at camp zero, we sat around and waited for Amber and Hippie Davie to appear with The Doc. Don and Alchemist-Al relit the glowing embers of the fire, with Don stating that The Doc may see the smoke. I was about to point out that he couldn't in the dark, but decided to let him carry on anyway as sitting by a fire would be quite nice actually. I was sure The Doc would return. It didn't surprise me that he would make a song and dance about an initiation and I surmised that it was just him being his normal attention-seeking self. We sat and talked until the dawn began to break; quickly it spread and daylight started to rapidly expand the horizon of vision around us. Hippie Davie and Amber returned one after the other, shrugging.

I could see Hippie Davie looked a little worried, "He's just vanished!" exclaimed Davie in exasperated tones.

Amber, the voice of reason spoke, "I think the poor dear's had a scare, ran off and gotten himself lost!"

We all thought for a second, there was a pause. I chipped in, "So he's just dressed in his Shaman robes then?"

A grimace instantly spread around the group as this recognition compounded the problem.

"And...he doesn't even have his lightsaber with him!" added Don sounding even more serious and everyone glanced towards him, thinking their own thoughts on that statement.

Meanwhile, dawn was also breaking across the mind of the now slightly sobering brain of The Doc. Shivering as he sat up, he drew his knees close to his body. He felt a little better for seeing the daylight and he felt as if the grip of the Demon had lessened a bit, though his mind still hung in tatters as drool dripped from the side of his mouth. A bedraggled spectacle with ragged torn robes hanging off his punctured marked body and dried blood caked on his arms and quivering legs, emerged from a hovel in the field, like the walking dead, sending sheep scattering and bleating in surprise in all directions. He scanned the area and spotted a farm track. Delicately, he limped his way towards it, feeling nauseous and dehydrated, a headache beginning to pound with every footstep and the brightening sun searing the tops of his eyeballs.

He could still feel the entity's presence within him and became aware that he was missing little bits of time as he walked across the field. He stopped and looked back, realising he had been completely unaware of two or three scary seconds of time. He was sharing his body with something else, something that wasn't him. He began to cry, as he walked. "I'm evil, I am the dark side," he whimpered to himself in resignation as he neared the end of the field. At the edge of the field the ground dropped off a few feet into a gully where a fence separated overgrown boggy mud and sheep shite from the main road. The Doc stopped and gazed down on a few sheep that trotted along nibbling at grass growing through the fencing. He sneered at them as he stood there, still fuzzy and unsteady on his feet. '*Look at them, innocent, unaware of my power to destroy them at will, just like people, sheep the lot of them,*' he thought, as he watched them silently from above. He watched a young ewe, in confusion, run in the wrong direction towards him rather than away with the others as he began to walk along the ridge. The Doc towering above lapsed into predator mode as the thing inside him chewed away at his sanity. "Never underestimate the dark side," he whispered under his breath between clenched snarling teeth. With that he seemed to lose all self-control as he threw himself down towards the hapless animal intending to satisfy the urge to kill and do mindless bad things. The demon inside him, it seemed, at this point may have just been an expression of his own stupidity.

The Doc, whether or not fully responsible for his actions, although indeed never underestimating the dark side, had quite underestimated the power of a frightened herd animal. The animal, in fright, had tried to run into the end of the ditch in front of the fencing where it could go no further. In panic it thrashed around and, for a few seconds, The Doc looked like a rag doll on a rodeo. He slipped off the sheep's back and found himself being squashed into the wire of the fence, a deft wrestling move which he was powerless to overturn. He turned his head to the side, trying to push himself onto his feet and avoid a close up of a thrashing, muddy and manky, matted sheep's rear end. He was definitely now regretting deeply the decision to ambush a sheep in this manner and as he fought with the flailing, confusing and smelly rump end of it, he made a definite mental note to never try this again. Mind you, on the up-side he had found a very quick road to sobriety and to taking his mind off of his current possession issues, which were now on hold.

Of course, he was to regret this decision even a hundred fold more as the animal, also hemmed in, bucked and kicked feverishly bringing both hooves smashing into his groin with unexpected force, twice in succession in quick repeating bucks, before hurrying off bleating loudly in defiant annoyance. It wasn't the only thing bleating loudly as The Doc slowly keeled over sideways in the squatting position and remained in that pose as he hit the tarmac of the road on the other side of the fence, before wincing softly.

Mere seconds later, a car stuffed full of middle-age ramblers in bright coloured walking jackets, slowly came to a halt on the road in front of him. They had prepared sandwiches and Thermos flasks of tea. They had prepared for the changeable north eastern weather. They probably had not prepared themselves, though, for the sight of The Doc in a tattered looking dress laying there clutching his red bruised genitalia and crying like a baby, after apparently trying to have sexual intercourse with a sheep. Aberdonians do have that reputation in the rest of Scotland; this defintely was not helping to destroy that myth.

"So what were you doing Mr. Baraclough up in Mr. Mason's fields in the first place, tell me again, how did you arrive at the scene?" The stern but sympathetic sounding voice of the Grampian Police sergeant spoke again.

The Doc grasped the cup of tea, hands still a little shaky. "It's Bearcloud actually..!" He had had a couple of hours sleep in the cell downstairs and was grateful for the hot sweet brew that helped him gather his thoughts. He looked ashen grey and a bit silly, dressed in an oversized shirt and blanket. The blood had been washed off his skin and numerous plasters were scattered apparently randomly all over him, making him look like a human version of the Wile E. Coyote. His face and arms were scored with a variety of ridiculously horrendous looking cuts and scars. "An' I wiz practisin', Just as av sed!" replied The Doc, irascibly.

The officer flicked the page in front of him, clearly irritated. "Bearcloud aye? Really, listen you little shit, give me your real name or I'll book you right here and now!"

The Doc was about to protest but the sergeant cut him short; "And I don't mean your Indian name, or whatever, I mean your Christian name, pleeease! Just indulge me, for the sake of my records?"

The Doc relented, having little energy left to argue with someone who really wouldn't understand; "Aye ok, ok, it's...eh...Michael." He politely waited, allowing time for the sergeant to complete the writing before continuing, "...Hutcheons!"

The sergeant started to write but then stopped dead, looking up with an expression of disbelief and annoyance rolled into one. "Don't you try to take the piss with me my lad! I'm in no mood for this this morning!"

The Doc held up his hands in submission shaking his head, "Fit?? I'm tellin' ye, am tellin' ye, that's my fuckin' name mate....er sarge!"

The sergeant slid back his chair, before suddenly and aggressively lunging over, grabbed The Doc by the collar and angrily lifted him up out of the seat! The Doc's hot tea cup, rudely wrenched from equilibrium, splashed successive little bouts of hot liquid onto his already traumatised arms and leags, making the cuts sting. The Doc yelled and started sniffling in fear; he really couldn't face a good kicking from an older, stronger and more aggressive adult right at this moment in time. Through teary eyes he implored the sergeant not to hit him,

"Naw, ma Ba's, naaaw ma baaa's!! Nae sudden movements please ma ba's, mind ma ba's!! Ahhhhhhhhh, please min ma fuckin' ba's are still agongy! I'm nae kiddin' that is ma name, ye kin phone my Ma... jist let me phone ma' Ma then, please...my ba's are agony, oh for fuck's sake, please!?"

The sergeant relented and lessened his grip. Apologising, he handed The Doc a paper towel to wipe the tears and snot from his face and the tea from his arms and body. Sitting down again slowly and carefully The Doc dusted himself off, "Fuck me..!"

"Right, err...sorry and sorry about your...erm...ba's. Yes, let's recap on your statement then, Mr. Hutcheons. You were practising medieval battle re-enactments, on your *own*." The officer's voice became a little drawn and he looked over at the squirming Doc raising an eyebrow. "After getting separated from your, erm, associates..." He raised an eyebrow again scornfully and secretly he was worried that more of the same were running around the hillsides. "...You were practising attacking the Christian hordes and you, as a local Shaman in berserker mode, were single-handedly driving all them evil Christian bastards off this shore." He looked over at The Doc, who was going over this statement in his head, his head a little fuzzy about any statement he may have made a few hours before.

"Yeah, yeah practisin', yeah practisin', 'ats ah, no law against that is there?" The Doc interjected defensively, a little concerned that the officer could leap across and grab him again at any minute.

"Annnd you didn't quite realise that it was a sheep when you jumped onto it this morning as, to quote you, it looked like a 'Knights Templar' hiding behind the wall at the time, before it kicked you right in the, erm 'fucking goooooleees!?" He drew out the last phrase in an exaggerated John Cleese kind of way, in an effort to disguise his own embarrassment with the silliness of the phrase.

"It was dark!" protested The Doc, the officer maintained his stare and continued looking incredulously at the stammering, more confused looking than usual Doc. This prompted The Doc to proceed with some further defence.

"I just seen the white, like it was a woolly coat and the big horns and that and big fuckin' goatey fuckin' staring eyes, you know?" The Doc was gesticulating to emphasise the size of the big fucking eyes with his hands, to help build the picture of his assailant!

The officer sat back and sighed a little, usually on a day like this he'd be reading the paper, or summoning up the energy to drive around and hassle some local youths before setting back with a coffee and a bacon roll. This mad little scantily clad lunatic from out of nowhere was starting to make him just a little bit more on the displeased side at the moment.

"I'm afraid that I don't really know what you mean, Mr. Hutcheons, no! I'm no expert on medieval warrior monks, but I would expect perhaps...oh for starters...armour! A sword! Maybe a shield properly emblazoned with a Christian motif, a big cross or something like that. Those might be things that would make me suspect that I was indeed faced with such a mighty crusader in a sheep field in the middle of the night and not a random sheep! Oh and one other thing..." He raised his voice sarcastically. "It would have to be 1195 and not 1995, that would be another major defining factor, I feel!" The officer's sarcastic tones drew to a spiteful close, as it almost hissed from his lips, his face twisting in an impatient scowl to emphasis his growing annoyance with the tattered time waster before him. "Horns and big fucking goatey eyes, as you say, might not at first glance make me think of a Templar knight! As I'm not aware they were known for big eyes and horns now were they!?"

The Doc shrugged. "A-right 'en, a vikin' could have been a vikin'!?"

The officer lost all patience and spluttered, raising his voice and gesticulating wildly, "I don't care if you thought it was the Devil himself, Mr. Hutcheons; it doesn't give you the excuse to run around half-naked interfering with animals and alarming ramblers! The tourist trade has suffered enough setbacks up here coz of the fucking midgies, we don't need the likes of you as well!"

The Doc arrogantly slumped back in his chair, "Pah, The Devil is just made up nonsense, there's far worse and powerful things than the Devil. I would have no problem taking him out with my lightsaber!" He was reflecting on the ghastly image he had seen the night before and to The Doc indeed this was very true. He shuddered and began to weep a little at the thought of the dark side of the force that had attacked and then entered him. He was going to be forever in its power, he didn't know what he was going to do.

The officer looked a little surprised at his reaction and The Doc's sudden tears "Lightsaber? Shamans use light sabers now?"

The Doc retaliated defensively, "Well it is the nineties mate!" he replied to his own satisfaction. The office scribbled the word lightsaber on the bottom of a long list of words in his note book, which included "bestial pervert, fantasist, annoying little twat, Satanist or really crazed?" and "danger to himself, public and livestock?" He had underlined *really crazed* twice. He paused, where to go now with his questioning. It could, he suppose, go anywhere; he could see The Doc was clearly distressed and had been quite scared at the mention of the devil for some reason. Hedging his bets he pressed on with a question. "Well, did you see Satan last night, Mr. Hutcheons?"

The Doc gave a derisory smirk. "I dinnae believe in such medieval concepts!" He said, defiantly shaking his head from side to side in disbelief.

The officer replied, somewhat confused, "But you do believe in medieval knights, Mr. Hutcheons?"

The Doc shrugged and pursed his lips. "What have I got tae tell ye?"

"But you did say you'd kill Satan if you saw him?" The officer pressed on slightly annoyed and still none the wiser.

"Aye well, ok! I dinna believe in him, but, if he was real, I wouldn't be afraid of him. You see, he's a recent god; my gods would smite him, oh, aye! If he was real, which he isna'...so it doesnae matter...onywy but if he was real...then; actually...killing Satan's no a crime onywy is it?"

The officer shrugged, he'd never ever thought of that; "Well...I don't know actually, he'd probably get great lawyers!"

Rather than laugh at the joke The Doc lit a cigarette which he'd taken from the pack offered to him and nodded approvingly,

"Good point actually!"

Then realising that he was getting pulled into a stupid argument, the police sergeant shook his head in annoyance and decided to get this apparent charade over with. He hadn't even had a proper breakfast yet!

"Anyway, can you explain how you could have mistaken this animal you were caught molesting for someone else, given that you were on your own?"

The Doc looked checkmated for a second, "Aye, aye I was on my own then, I mean, I'm on my own here now, but I did have some mates the night afore, I just got a bit lost that's ah!"

The sergeant scribbled down more notes, finally getting somewhere,

"Ah so where are these people now, may I ask?"

The Doc pointed behind him, "Up the hill, camping in the woods, it's a little errr...battle re-enactment society."

The policeman looked very stern towards The Doc now, holding him in a prolonged and angry stare.

"Oh, your little 'battle re-enactment society' is very well known to us here Mr. Hutcheons!" He said almost sneering now, "This is alllll starting to make a lot more sense now, just be honest then sunshine, were you really 'playing soldiers?' or something else Mr. Hutcheons, because let me tell you something young fella me lad, weak excuses like that are not going to do at all, not at all. It'll be far better for you in the long run to just admit what you were up to."

The Doc shrugged. "Wisane daein' nuthin', just a bit of confusion due to hyper-thermia that's a'."

The sergeant scribbling down some more notes casually corrected him as he did so, "Hypo; as in hypo-dermic!"

The Doc regarded him for a second, not sure why he'd asked that. "Na, I don't use hard drugs, just a bit o' blow now and again and mushrooms and stuff, all natural, that's not against the law is it?"

The sergeant looked up, incredulously, giving him a long hard stare as The Doc's confused expression mirrored the officer's movement, returning the sergeant's look blankly back in response, his magnified right eye bulgingly conveying innocence and confusion with the officer's further annoyance. In exasperation and in anger the sergeant retorted,

"Yes! Yes it is against the bloody law, laddie. That's the trouble with you hippie lot, you've no real grasp of reality; running about up here out if it, causing a danger to yourselves and others and getting up to weird bloody stupid Satanic acts with our livestock, look at the state of you son! You think your mother would be proud if she saw you right now?"

The Doc straightened himself up suddenly, "Satanic!??"

The sergeant drowned him out, "Yessss Satanic! I know all about your weird bloody sex cults and naked witchy stuff going on with all you hippies up there!" He leaned forward now pointing. "And we're not going to put up with it I assure you."

The Doc folding his arms sat up, grimacing badly as he slowly lifted one leg exposing a horrible, skint knobbly knee and padded bandages where normally boxer shorts should be (which did nothing to aid his sense of self-righteousness). Despite the fact that he was becoming scared, as he thought there was a very real chance that the sergeant was about to pounce on him again and give him a good kicking, as clearly he was making him more angry for some reason, he had to defend himself.

"How dare you call me that? I am a Shaman, a Witch and the only occidental Canadian-Scotsman to be initiated into the Eastern Cree tribal medicine society and thus I demand some respect! You have no right to religiously discrimate against me!"

The officer put his hands to his temples and began laughing in response. Until now, he hadn't been sure if The Doc was taking the piss or had actually been serious but his latest display of being offended made him think that, in fact, he was serious and it was dawning on him how hilarious this situation was. They'd never believe this one back at head office. He'd have a story to tell at the Xmas party now for sure that would rival the U.F.O anal probing and abducting complaints from the Blairgowrie Abductee Society (comprised of only one person).

The Doc scowled. He hated not being taken seriously. "I don't know why yer laffin,' I have a perfect right as a citizen of Albion to exercise my religion and as such I will be lodging a formal complaint to my M.P. This is typical of the discrimination faced by us tribes folk, it's like General Custard all over again!"

The policeman merely grunted as he stood up and planted his hat back on his head with a surly back to business sweep of his arm, resisting the urge to grab The Doc again and give him a slap.

"Aye, aye, just shut the fuck up sheep shagger and get back in the fucking cell for now, before I stop resisting the urge to pan yer stupid fuckin' face in!" The Doc limped away, keeping a watchful right eye on the officer just in case, as he shuffled past,

"Any chance I can go to hospital now!?" he pleaded.

"Oh, you'll be going to a hospital alright!" The officer replied and he watched the pathetic spectacle slowly depart, shaking his head before finally smiling, "General fucking Custard…fa-ckin-'ell!"

We had decided to drive into town, thinking that we may see The Doc stretched out in the local park or hanging around the shops like the local junkie, although I suspect the local junkie might complain there wouldn't be room enough for two in this town. Alas, though, he was nowhere to be seen. We decided to split up for a while and walk around to see if we could find him. Don and I toked on some blow and ambled around in the warmth of the morning sunlight. We were tired and just a little bit lethargic. I was more concerned than the night before, as I had visions of The Doc wandering the Highlands forevermore, growing long lank hair, a beard while muttering to himself and scaring backpackers.

Even Don, normally unruffled, as if he knew absolutely everything was going to some sort of plan that only he and the gods were in on, seemed a little perturbed.

"Where the fuck has the dozy bastard got to?" he said irascibly, "I blame Hippie Davie, he should have known better than to let him wander about on his own."

I agreed, "Christ I would be worried about lettin' the cunt wander about a fuckin' shopping centre on his own, never mind the middle of the bloody woods!?"

"Well you know how annoying and insistent The Doc can be, with a' the bloody bullshit he says, easier just to give in and let him get his own way init?"

"Yeah, yeah I know, Christ I never thought I'd say this, but I think I'm actually worried about him!" I mouthed, slightly incredulously at my own admission.

Don nodded, "I kaen he's a bit 'feil' and a right pain in the erse, yes even a wee bit, well…evil as fuck at times, but I do feel quite protective over him sometimes, it's how ye are with mates I suppose!"

We stopped at a street corner. "Could be anywhere!" I shrugged. "If only there was some kind of medicine man tracking device we could buy outa the camping shoappie or something!?"

"We-lllll," crooned Don out of the corner of mouth, an idea forming. "We could do a quick finding spell!"

"If only it would work," I opined, motioning back to him.

Don looked thoughtful, "Mmm works ok for keys and glasses...never tried it out on medicine men tho'!"

'Why not,' I thought, anything is worth trying at this stage in the game. "Go for it!" I replied.

Together we stood at the end of the street facing each other in concentration, as people ambled past. More than a few people raised an eye as it was fairly unusual for two grown men to be standing holding hands in the street in this wee north east village and more than a few hurried past at the sight of the jangly top-hatted Don, as I imagined many of the older residents that dominated the pavement at this time of day could have probably mistaken him for Death himself. Don mouthed some incantations to his spirit helpers and a "Goddess of finding stuff," his cool hands limply folded over, grasping onto my fingers.

Eventually he opened his eyes, "Mmmm that's strange, I just had visions of him being kept prisoner by Darth Vader, glowering at him from under his black helmet!"

I nodded. "Well, if I didn't know better, I'd say The Doc *was* Darth fuckin' Vader! C'mon lets go get a cup o' coffee man!"

We strolled around the corner to the wee coffee shop and stood outside looking at the dessert tray, my mind now far away from The Doc and concentrating at the job in hand. "Look at that Don, £1.50 for a fuckin' biskit! Just coz they gie it an Italian sounding name!"

Don nodded in mute agreement.

Just then the doors of the nearby police station swung open and an officer purposely strode out to meet another policeman climbing out of the car in front. "No dangerous is he guvna?"

"Would be if he had any fuckin" brains!" the other older man replied.

With that Don and I stopped and looked at each other with a look of shared recognition between us.

The older man continued, "Just check him into the nut hoose, I think this guy's going to need to be assessed by professionals before we can be sure, says he was staying at some holiday camp in the woods. Bet it's those bloody hippies again, if I told 'em once I've told 'em a hundred times!" He shook his head in frustration. "C'mon you, out you get Bear-bum, Officer Sinclair here's going to take you somewhere to get fixed up and have a nice wee chat to someone."

Don and I looked on silently as a ragged looking Doc, limped past by within a few feet of us looking ahead with total resignation, solemnly getting into the waiting car, almost I thought, a little too willingly. The officer watched the car pull out onto the road and hurl away with our priestly quarry; he then turned around and caught our bemused faces looking in the same direction. A second of eye contact seemed like an age as all our brains in synchrony whirled around gauging the situation. Don and I turned our heads back towards the café window and studiously began contemplating biscotti. The officer's eyes dawdled over Don's top hat and cloak and then swept over my combat jacket complete with New Model Army, CRASS and Leveller's patches. We kept staring into the window trying to look innocent;

"Coffee and biscotti then Alistair?"

Don peered behind him for a second, clearly looking for Alchemist-Al, my eyelids dropped a little in despair. Don righted himself as the penny dropped,

"Oh right! Yes sir! iffffff that be your desire sir!" he drawled and bowed taking off his hat and pointing towards the café door in a long low exaggerated servile swoop.

The officer's eyes rolled and muttering something about "They're all out for the fucking weekend," strode back inside to the safety of his desk, doughnuts and cells. Perhaps also he thought that real anarchists wouldn't be so fixated on coffee and biscotti, like normal people.

I pushed Don on the shoulder, like the three stooges minus one. "What the fuckinhell are you playing at?"

Don looked a little perplexed and hurt, "I thought you were pretendin' I was your butler with the 'Alistaaaaiiiir and all that!?"

I sighed. "I just didn't want to use our names in case The Doc had blabbed, especially in light of the half ounce of resin in your waistcoat pocket! Anyway, Butler!? Have you looked at what I'm wearing? How many punks have butlers, Don? You think Johnny Lydon employed a finely tailored man-servant to polish his chains to maybe spit on people on the front row of gigs for him?"

This image ran through both our minds for a second, "Be good though, wouldn't it?"

259

Don responded sniggering, "Pogo-in' butler flickin' snot with a silver spoon at the crowd? Shoutin'; one' is a proper cunt sir...and a bounder to boot!"

"Maybe, maybe!" I said chuckling at Don's image. "But you do realise that guy'll now be thinking we're in some weird sexual 'master n slave' type scenario now? Thank you very much!"

Don's face lit up a little and a smile slowly stretched his lips, pressing them together with smug satisfaction.

"Well there's no need to look so fucking happy about neither!" I snapped. I looked back down the road towards where the car had been. "Fuckinhell Don, I don't how you do it, but your spells certainly bastard deliver do they? Remind me never to piss you off!"

Don smirked, "The nut hoose? That will be the Royal Cornhill Hospital in Aberdeen! And did you see the fucking state of him? Looks like they gave him a real good fuckin' kicking in there, what a bloody shame!"

"Yeah," I replied in resignation, "I've heard the police can be heavy handed with hippies and stuff, like the levellers song 'battle of the beanfield' has documented, but that looked a bit severe I have to say. He probably told them he was an arch tribal Shaman and they had better not piss him off or something!"

Don mused, "Mmmm, well actually you don't need an excuse to want to give him a good kicking do ya? Just talking to him can make you want to do that...it has crossed my mind many times!"

I laughed a little. "Yeah, but Cornhill? Once *they* get a hold o' 'im, they'll never let him oot! There's enough material there to keep 'em busy for a lifetime!"

Don chuckled, "Did you hear the boy as well gan on aboot the hippies? Reckon they'll be visiting soon; I reckon the party's well and truly over now mate!"

The realisation hit us; we hadn't thought for one moment that our carefree lifestyles in the freedom of the woods might create problems for us with the law. Seems that we weren't free at all!

## *Chapter 9*:
## Out of the woods and into the frying pan

    The news that the fuzz were likely to be popping around any minute seemed to galvanize the group, especially Wolf and Alchemist-Al; he especially going a little quiet. Hippie Davie looked stressed for the first time since I had known him and kept asking questions about The Doc's condition and anything else the policeman might have said. I almost thought he looked a little guilty. When I told them that they'd obviously given The Doc a right severe hidin;' Wolf and Alchemist-Al visibly gulped. Alchemist-Al was a big man, but was obviously the type of person who would far rather opt to talk his way out of trouble; which, only knowing him for a mere couple of days, was something I was in no doubt he could do most of the time. Quiet Pete who had been standing close when I broke the news suddenly exclaimed,
    "Oh shyte, not tha foockin' pigs!" We all swivelled our heads in his direction in bewilderment at his unexpected outburst as he returned our gazes with the usual mute smiley expression.
    "Fuck me, I didn't know you were Irish Pete!?" I said in amazement, he replied with a nod and a smile.
    Arianne spoke for the group, "It's not going to go down too well is it? I mean they tolerate people here at the camp. S'long as we keep our heads down and not bother anyone, but a bedraggled guy in robes, tripping and wandering around the main road in a daze may piss off a few people!"
    Wolf interjected, "Yeah George isn't going to like this if he finds out he was part of a ritual taking place here!"
    "George?" I asked.
    Alchemist-Al looked over at me, "George is the police chief here, a friendly enough guy; we've got a sort of understanding with him..!"
    I contemplated this for a minute. *'An understanding!?'* It seemed to me like George was the "Daddy" keeping an eye out for us. We could be as free spirited and anarchistic as much we liked, s'long as we didn't annoy George. Don't annoy 'tha man' – 'tha man' now had a name and it was fucking Geoooorge! I thought about a new badge for my combat jacket, 'Freedom from George!' Or just simply 'Fuck George!' Course I

ran the risk of people confusing this sentiment with the bloke out of seventies sitcom George and Mildred, which would upset me a bit as I'd always been really fond of actor Brian Murphy…for no specific reason.

After a while, we reached the consensus that we would pack up and go home. We had had a magnificent time. It was hard to believe that we had just been there for a few short days. It felt like we had been there for ages, settling into the pace of life and the rhythm of the woods around us. Maybe it was the company, or perhaps the drugs, but it seemed that we had been away much longer; I thought of the Leveller's song 'So Far From Home,' I had indeed both learned and 'done' so much.

I didn't really want to leave at all and had contemplated just staying there, building a more permanent dwelling for myself with Hippie Davie and Don. The idea was quite appealing; it offered a way out of the mundane march of city life and towards a more ideal, honest way of living. At the same time, I knew deep down that I couldn't stay there. I did, after all, quite like some of the trappings of life – a proper bed, running water, cable T.V, electricity, street lights and coffee shops. I was weak and I knew it. I liked possessions, comics, books, records and these things *did* define my life somewhat. It was all I had to go on in those days of council bedroom drudgery. I cherished these things…I liked sitting down to *The Simpsons* with my dinner on my lap! Why not? Technology gave us comforts, distractions. I realised that sitting here forever tripping out and smoking weed would kill me; I needed constant electronic stimulation, T.V, movies, cinemas, computer games, a local video store and pizza on speed dial to make me happy. That's what this spiritual junket in the woods had taught me, who I really was. I'm the fucking cable guy! I was brought up on a diet of T.V. morning, noon and night.

My family tended to only communicate during the adverts or bond through telly. We laughed together as Uncle Albert dropped the chandelier along the corridor on the floor along from Del and Rodney. I learned all my spiritual teachings from watching fucking 'Monkey' and 'Kung-fu' with David Carradine. We gawped at wildlife from far-flung places as creatures unseen, scuttled and swooped passed us outside. We ate, drank and lived through our T.V.s I understood a little better now why Hippie Davie probably clung to Star Wars to guide him spiritually, the poor bastard was like me, he had nothing else! That's why T.V. is both a friend and a dangerous ally. It provides information, a society, a tribe, a family, which was a huge draw, but it could also tell you how to think, what to think, what your politics were, what to wear, buy and even feel! That was very powerful medicine, as it were, as Wolf had intimated; and who were the few people who used T.V. to cast its spell to their advantage?

We packed the car quite quickly and almost in silence. I couldn't help noticing that Hippie Davie looked quite anxious, which I found strange and I figured that he felt guilty about getting The Doc into that situation. However, as much as we all tried, none of us could come up with a satisfactory explanation for the turn of events that would have sent even The Doc obviously quite so spectacularly off the rails to just disappear screaming like he did. We said our goodbyes, hugs and promises to see each other at a later date, Don adding poignantly, "When the time is again right!" I shook Arianne and Wolf's hands. I still had many questions and facts that I needed confirmed. I still had some doubts as to the validity of Wolf's claim that he shared a dream with me and that our shared vision took place in a 'plastic' environment; a simulation of the real world with added extras and beings who appeared to have their own conscious existence. This made me ask, what exactly was consciousness? I knew that I was conscious and that I existed and therefore tended to think that I was unique. However, I had a feeling that the "astral" type of consciousness was somehow of a different quality, but a definite type of experience just the same.

I felt the need to probe Hippy Davie's views on all this, as it was now obvious that he must have experienced these types of shared experiences before, on Alchemist-Al's brews, in this environment. I just couldn't quite accept this still; however, Don was quite content with Wolf's explanation but that was no help to me coming to terms with these concepts!

"How about it Hippie Davie, have you shared an out of body experience with Wolf or anyone else before?" I asked as we sped along the lonely tree-lined tarmacked skin of road, like skimming the back of some never-ending fossilised snake riding between the reality of dark woods and humans.

Hippy Davie grinned a little. "Hell yeah brother, yeah I have that." He smiled, taking a puff on the for-the-journey joint! "And you know, I had a feeling you would as well, Seany boy!"

I became a little annoyed at his apparent pre-cognitive level of insight! "Ah c'mon Hippie Dee, you expect me to believe that?"

Hippie Davie blew a long bilious stream of THC-laced smoke into the volume of the car; he frowned and looked out of the window in thought.

"Well, I know because I've seen you man, in dreams, actually just days after we met I saw you in a dream. We stood together at the university quad and I recognised you. We shook hands as mates and spoke a little. As I woke I knew that we had met in spirit and that our dream selves had even arranged for us to meet. You were checking me out in a different space and time to the concrete one we age and live in now. When I awoke I knew it hadn't just been a dream, that we had spoken and hence I knew you were the sort of person that could send your dream-self ahead of you! Just like Wolf and I!"

He looked me in the eye, appealing to me to affirm that he was genuine and shrugged. "So I had a pretty good idea that you would probably have an experience like that in those woods." He thought for a second, clearly deciding whether to reveal some more. "In fact, Wolf and I were planning a proper ritual, to call you down some allies, but it seems you already have them! Wolf said that as soon as he shook hands with you, he could feel them, feel the force of your allies behind you. He could feel the force of your spirit helpers." Hippie Davie nodded in admiration; "You're a lucky man, having those kinds of forces around you!"

A tear welled around my eye and a tingling feeling shot through my chest and up my spine as he spoke, reminding me of the surge leading to my shadow body fleeing as a fox spirit. I could feel a surge of almost ecstatic happiness and energy welling up and collecting in my abdomen. It was a feeling that I wished everyone on the planet could share.

"Allies!?" I said out loud, mulling over the word and the implications. I needed more confirmation from Hippie Davie. "Assuming that is true, that I have acquired allies, where on earth did I get them from? I mean why me, why us?"

Hippie Davie smiled a knowing smile, "Why indeed eh? Why indeed!? Well I suppose what we all have in common is an awareness and sensitivity to the possibility that such things exist. Think about it, not everyone is good at maths, or excels at art; only some people have those predilections. Perhaps we're just lucky, but surely a poet feels lucky to think of the world in the way that he or she does or a painter or even a mathematician!?"

As we hurtled through the wild and rugged Grampian landscape, all of us were aware of the absence of The Doc in the car; it was far more pleasant than it should have been. Eventually I turned on some CRASS and put my foot down and as usual Don started to complain that it wasn't fair to listen to my stuff all the time and so we compromised on The Cure. Hippie Davie giggled in the background "You're like an old married couple heheh!"

As we arrived in Aberdeen it was still early, so I parked the car and suggested a little conference to discuss all the events of the preceding few days. We headed off to the Café 52 and Don tried to phone The Doc's mother and Pamela to see if he had been let out yet!

I sat down with Hippie Davie and thought I could use the time to probe him further. I felt on the eve of acceptance of what I already felt, that my conscious self was only the tip of the iceberg and that unconsciously I was trying to arrange people and events somehow ahead of myself. "What about the faeries then Hippie Davie? Was that creature I witnessed real, as real as you and I are?"

Hippie Davie shrugged, "Maybe, yeah, they are there, they don't have a shape or a face unless your imagination provides it I think…but they are there, their influence can be felt and their image conjured up by anyone who can and they are, for all intents and purposes, independent from you right now. If some other people were to walk through the same area, they would feel them too, perhaps even see them!"

"But would they see the same thing, same independent thing as I or anyone else saw?"

"Aye there's the rub, thing is they would see something similar. I don't know who first dreamt them, how they got there, but yes, they are there!"

I was itching to pass on my thoughts. "Maybe it's like, just down to more natural laws, if some kind of environment exists (and let's call this shared imaginary experience 'some kind of environment') and autonomous creatures exist within it, then 'any' environmental *niches* within it will be filled. So our imaginations interact with some hitherto unknown aspect of space and time and thought forms become items in that environment. Eventually, they become independent and evolve and fill the niches, 'existing" in their own right!"

Hippie Davie paused for a second, anticipating my next thought.

"Yeaah, it's a chicken and egg scenario isn't it? What came first, people or faerie? Hippie Davie paused and thought deeply, he looked across at me, frowns deepening across his brow.

"I've thought about this actually, since you spoke about it before and I reckon I have an explanation that you will like! If you think about life and all the wonderful symbiotic things, life-forms that have sprung up...where does that drive come from? You have to admit there seems to be a field or physical law which dictates that co-operation will occur between living things!? It's what causes things to stick together; like the first primeval pieces of dirt stuck together and grew in complexity!"

"Exactly! exactly yeah, I know this, I sorta think about that, too, Hippie Dee!" I exclaimed in agreement remembering the conversation from before. The notion of a mathematical 'god law,' that dictates complexity and thereby new instances, like 'big bangs' of newness, the original physical big bang and then, more recently, the mental consciousness big bangs coming into being, effusing the universe with consciously aware beings and imagination. So the universe isn't just 'there' in the cold and dark anymore, it is realised and enjoyed!"

"Well," Davie continued on smiling, maintaining a patience and acknowledgment that we were on the same page.

"Seems like things that exist, co-operate and if you think about it, that's what our subconscious can also do! Co-operate, arrange things and reach out in symbiosis!" He leaned forward to finalise his argument, as I gawped nonchalantly at the roof of the coffee shop, as the ideas of his theory gently made their way through the tissue of my brain unimpeded as he pressed home his point.

"Our brains right, are imagination machines...aaaand a cooperation device! We can't be individuals, not totally, because we'd be starved, unstimulated and go mad. It's one of the worst forms of torture to a human being, absolute solitary confinement."

"Fucking Genius!" I exclaimed, as I started to grasp what he meant. It seemed plausible; well, at least I liked to think it was. Imagination, this shared superposition of mind stuff obeys the universal drive to co-operate and gel like everything else in the universe. It was genius, almost so straight forward it had to have a basis in truth! I pondered it for a little while.

"You Might be a fuckin' Hippie genius, Hippie Davie; maybe we should all be taking regular doses of cannabis. You have a way of sounding fairly convincing; I mean I know what I saw and I'm pretty sure Wolf described what I saw without me telling him...so how the hell can he do that unless what you suggest is true? You might be right; it's a symbiosis between minds!? Our powers of empathy occasionally gain information about other people, other minds also in a superposition of states. Perhaps there is some kind of field or physical/universal law that living conscious material can exploit and utilise. Just like Arianne said, it doesn't become information until a brain recodes it back into imagination, sorta like a modem reconverts a signal back into thoughts!? Gawd, the computer analogy again."

I thought about something Don had said a few weeks previously during one of my many visits to his work. "Well maybe a better analogy exists; just the technology hasn't been invented yet!"

Hippie Davie laughed and pointed a triumphant finger at me. "You got it Sean, spot on and the proper analogy probably doesn't exist yet, simple as that!"

The conversation, however, took a back seat as Don re-appeared and sat down, plonking his hat on the table, to stake his claim to take over the conversation. Don's eyebrows rose a little. "I just phoned Pamela!"

"And?" snapped Davie imploringly, as we both gesticulated in suspense.

"She's going down to Cornhill later; he's in there right enough. Apparently he's sedated right now, had some sort of breakdown they say, might be suffering some sort of psychotic episode. He's quite upset apparently. Pamela's fuming, practically shrieking down the phone at me demanding to know what was going on." Hippie Davie sank back pulling his hand over his mouth, causing his top lip to bulge like a red rubber aneurysm. I regarded his expression for a moment; I sensed his concern and something told me he felt responsible.

I decided to strike while the iron was hot. "What the fuckinhell did you do to the poor bastard, Hippie Davie?" I looked at Hippie Davie and then Don. I could see Don looked perplexed.

Hippie Davie became immediately defensive, "Look! It's not my fault if the daft bastard fucks off, is it and then ends ups in the nuthoose? Fucksake, he's always been doolahlay! It was just a matter of time!"

We all pondered this for a second and sat back. I huffed, "Yeah, we should have known, should have seen it coming right enough!"

The realisation hit me that perhaps we had been a little blasé allowing The Doc to attend rituals and invoke spirits. Perhaps what we should have been doing was making sure he was well grounded. Mags had always stressed this point to us – get a job, make sure you are grounded; Wicca is about being a part of things, a part of life, not existing in some separate higher realm divorced from reality and society. I knew what she meant now, one could get carried away and think that magick could offer a better alternative existence; The Doc was a case in point. I glanced around the table at my compatriots, the dreadlocked hippie who never had a job, the top hatted goth who wanted to retreat to some Neil Gaiman-esque Victorian London and me the biscotti and cappuccino-loving armchair anarchist who was coasting through university and probably voted by my peers as the one most likely to drop out! In the silence, I suddenly felt quite unimportant and a little bit stupid.

Don had to go to work. That was our cue to hit the road. I elected to visit The Doc the day after and Hippie Davie said he would meet me there. I went home, slumped onto my bed and slept for twelve hours. The next evening I regained some motivation and phoned the hospital to find out which ward The Doc was in and whether it was ok to visit. I imagined the poor bastard lying salivating, heavily sedated and chained up to a sturdy metal 1960s style hospital bed.

"Mr. Hutcheons has left the building!" the receptionist said.

'Oh well,' I thought, 'he'll be off home,' but neither Pamela nor anyone at his mother's house were answering the phone. I thought about phoning Trish's place, but as I punched the number I paused and put the phone down...later! At least he must be ok now, he's out and I'll get him later! I had, after all, loads of work to do. I made a cup of tea and a sandwich and watched an episode of *"Star Trek: the Next Generation"* to procrastinate, the books now a little dusty still lay in the same place calling for my attention from the table in the corner of my room (can you hear me?). I made another cup of tea and regarded the pile of textbooks and photocopied pages from various relevant sources. I sighed; this is what non-students don't understand when they go on about students not working or having a great life. When they come home from work, they switch off and watch T.V. or go to the pub, take the dog for a walk. But for a student the work is always there, always at the back of your mind, there is no escape from it, morning, noon and night.

Eventually, I slumped onto the uncomfortable chair, propped up on many well placed cushions and began to read. After a mere ten minutes, and as I scribbled a few lines of notes, I jumped as a loud wrap (predictably) echoed through the flat from the front door. I sighed and put my head in my hand, sighing out loud; "fuck-in-hael." I swung the door open and wasn't completely surprised to see The Doc standing there agitatedly puffing on a ciggy, his eyes bulging, fixating on me from under a greasy fringe (a quote from my dad quickly came to mind, which was appropriate for his condition, "the bhoy had eyes like a pair o' dog's baz's!"). He looked bad, much worse than normal, which for him was already quite scary. I momentarily paused musing just how crazed he looked and that there must be serious cut backs in the NHS if they just let him out of the nuthoose walking about like that, scaring children and old ladies!

"Oh thank fuck yer in!" He said as he pushed past me and made his way straight into the living room.

On seeing his worried expression on his face all feelings of frustration evaporated, as I sarcastically said, "Come in why don't cha!?" I patted him on the back. "We were worried aboot ye mannie, fits been going on with ye?"

The Doc recounted his experience in the woods, the strange vision that appeared to him and attacked him. I listened on, slightly concerned about him and a little for myself in his presence.

"River sand? Symbols? Flying vampire cat!" I mused, not sure what to make of this latest bout of paranoia and remembering Don's words, "He's had a psychotic episode." I regarded him steadily and became concerned about the sharpened pencils within arms reach in the corner of the room.

"No, vampire cat demon!" he stressed.

His bulging, goon-like right eye staring out from his lank fringe was actually beginning to unnerve me to the point of being scared. His thick lensed glasses magnifying the creepy effect tenfold, making the eye seem to have a life and maddening agenda of its own.

"Oh right, right," I nodded urgently, making sure not to directly contradict him in any way! "Cat demon, mmmm sounds totally fuckin' scary, man."

I had that awful feeling of realisation, shared by many I suppose, when suddenly it dawns on you that 'yer mates a fucking nutter,' and what's more you've been inviting them into your house all this time and even encouraging them to do their nutter stuff, right under your nose. Maybe also, they were going to turn on you next and you didn't see it coming. I didn't fancy being in the front page of the Press and Journal as the victim, right beside a picture of the grinning mental Doc, I mean, what a fuckin' embarrassment! People I went to school with would read that!

The Doc looked almost tearful as he remembered the sequence of events and I could see that this had been all too real for him, I was a little perturbed myself and I felt compelled to make him feel better.

"It was that place man, really trippy out there, eh?" I said. "And Alchemist-Al's wines, fuck me, how fuckin' trippy must that stuff be? Totally fucks with your brain, man!"

The Doc nodded but looked at me, I thought, momentarily more compos mentis than he had ever done before.

"Yeah, I know, I know, but I tell you, Sean, what I saw, what happened to me, I don't know how I know, but I know it was deliberate. It was like a…a magical trap! And I think Hippie Davie had something to do with it!"

On that point, he seemed most adamant. It still all sounded a little paranoid to me; clearly The Doc was reacting to the friction that was between them, but I instinctively remained sympathetic and engaging with him. We spoke a little about the night's proceedings and the conversation with the law the next morning. I didn't mention that Don and I had been standing a mere two feet away from him as he was led away; besides he might start thinking we were in on the conspiracy. We had a laugh at Doc's protestations about suing the law for being Shamanist and eventually even The Doc relented and admitted he had been a little out of it! This made me feel a bit more relaxed and happy that he was not going completely off his head.

"You're ah' I can trust right now, ah' I can trust Sean."

I tried to console him. "What about Trish!?"

He conceded with a nod, "And Trish aye Trish."

"And Pamela!?" I added.

"Oh god, I'm keeping a bit of a low profile from Pamela right now. I think she may have cottoned on about Trish and me!"

I smirked, "Oh the 'rehearsin' ye mean?" I mouthed emphatically, "What makes you think that? Has she said onything tae ye?"

He paused for a second, obviously debating whether to tell me all the grizzly facts, or not. Though, as usual he decided to just go ahead anyway. He motioned using his hands in a cicular motion to wind the story onto the point;

"Well, you know aboot how Trish likes to...dig her nails right in and stuff?"

I nodded and smiled, recalling The Doc's discomfort sitting down on some occasions. "Yer erse in tatters and stuff like that?" I replied, acknowledging The Doc's many gripes in the past; always containing 'a little bit too much information.' I was somewhat relieved though, as this was relatively tame compared to the stuff he had tried to reveal to me in the past. Such as the time several months back, trapped in the car with him in Stonehaven Park, when he was frightened because his shenanigans with Trish had resulted in and I quote, "giving him a cock like a minky fucking peperami." He, then duly tried to show me it for a diagnosis. I had to plead with him to put it away, shouting, as usual, that studying Biology didn't make me medically qualified. Unfortunately, whenever he was terrified about a particular body part, I was the first person he'd come to. I was relieved on this occasion that he wasn't trying to whip his trousers down, as would be usual, and bearing his bum at me!

"Aye, aye, exactly, exactly," The Doc continued. "Well the hospital were taking a look at it and were quite concerned...they kept questioning me aboot ma erse!...Fuckinhell, doctors kept comin' in and looking at it, then showin' it aff tae ither doctors...and I think the police might have taken photies of it when I was asleep, but I'm no certain, I might have drimt that!"

I tried to remain calm and sympathetic, but the thought of medics lining up to stare bewildered at The Doc's stripey torn arse made me chuckle. I regained some composure then joked, "Shit Doc, did they get the erse doctor from Foresterhill?"

The Doc merely nodded. "Fuckin right they did...and she was a woman!"

I looked intrigued. "The erse doctor is a woman eh? Blimey! Well I suppose not many men fancy bein' erse doctors!"

The Doc nodded approvingly.

"No...no, well aye, of course, they're mair likely to go in for boobs and that!?"

"Gynaecologists!" I mused.

The Doc nodded again; "Aye, aye 'ats right; fit do you cry an erse doctor 'en?" he mused.

"Anustician or anal-analyst I think." But as I said that my face began to contort with amusement.

"Fuck off!" The Doc replied, not falling for it.

"Okay, okay I'm sorry no, I don't know the proper name for the erse doctor, sorry!"

The Doc looked a little triumphant that he'd caught me out, but he continued on unabashed about erse doctors and their wiley ways.

"They wouldn't let up; I think the police were worried about what kind of things were going on in their local neck of the woods. So I jist telt them the truth, that my girlfriend liked to play rough and that!"

"They buy that?" I asked curiously.

"Well nay right awa…but once I telt them mair and mair aboot my sex life, they seemed to start to give in and believe me. Trouble is, they went and fuckin' mentioned it to Pamela did they!? Stewpi't fuckin' interferin' fuckin' bastards!"

My face lit up, it was marvellous; I could imagine Pamela sitting in the waiting room with the psychiatrist and The Doc's mother, "How is his brain doc?" "Well there's nothing we can do about his brain! We're sorry to say. However, his tattered arse is what we're more concerned with at the moment. Eerrm here, why don't you wear these extra thick marigolds…as a safe sex device for his bum cheeks during your rough arse play?"

I baulked. "You mean they had a go at Pam aboot yer tattered erse? And she didn't know anything about it?"

"Well, I'm sure they did, coz when she came to see me after she had been talking to the doctors she had this mad look in her eyes. She said the doctors had mentioned a few 'curious injuries' and she had a few questions of her own for me…an' a knew fae her face that she didna' jist mean the state o' ma ba's!"

"Oh fuck's sake, Doc, what are you going to say to her?"

The Doc smirked with glee and his left cheek knotted into cramp of quite undeserved triumph.

"I, eh, fell doon the stairs in the police cells!" he said winking at me and making the inverted commas with his fingers then sitting back taking a smug drag on his ciggy.

I laughed a little and then looked at him as he smiled back, quickly realising he was serious. "You mean you're going to insinuate that two country village boabies abducted you, did weird things to your erse and bollox and then locked you up for the night?"

"Pretty much...yeah...well aye yeah, a'course!" nodded The Doc before further reflecting on his solution. "...Yeah!"

"Think she'll believe that?" I implored him, trying to guide him, as a friend should, to galvinise some further thought.

The Doc shrugged. "Well, you know what those village boabies can be like? Dinna' call 'em 'the fuckin' filth' for nutthin' dee they?"

I shook my head slightly confused, but remembering the 'gay' business with Gemma and practically everything else, my neck muscles shook themselves into an affirmative nod and my mouth began to agree.

"Yeah, yeah, oh they're bastards for bum abuse a'right!" and played an air banjo, "Tada dum, dum, dummmm!" I meant that in more ways than one.

The Doc grinned back, "Ta dum, showuz yer bum!?"

We both laughed a little and relaxed. The Doc settled down and watched a bit of telly, while I actually got some work done. It seemed the option of working or talking about The Doc's sex romps was acting like a sort of catalyst for me to hit the books. I reasoned that if he moved in and drove away all my other friends and any possible females from ever coming back to the flat, that I'd be a first-class student by Christmas. With Pamela hunting him all over Aberdeen, I also reasoned that The Doc may want to hole up here for quite some time. I offered him my sofa.

I was just debating the length of time he would be here and whether I should convert my big cupboard into a medicine man-priest hole when there was a hammer on the front door. The Doc instinctively dived for his cigarettes and then shot through to the bathroom like a tattered bespectacled rabbit. I mused at how a person could develop an instinctive reflex to save his cigarettes before his life, I may start thinking about quitting if I found myself in that situation!

However, it was only Hippie Davie; he had a knowing look in his eye. "He's here yeah!?"

I thought it strange for Hippie Davie to have so much of The Doc's welfare in mind. As he crept past me into the living room, he resembled a boy who had broken a window with a football and had warily returned to the scene of a crime, to inspect the broken pieces. I took hold of Hippie Davie's shoulder,

"Look...he's very upset and fragile. You have to be very nice to him ok? He's a mate remember?"

Hippie Davie nodded quickly and nonchalantly then looked serious.

"Yeah, yeah, of course man, no worries. I'm Mr. Fuckin' Sympathy in person, brother." He patted me on the shoulder in assurance, before nodding and walking on into the lobby.

He strolled into the living room, doing the obligatory flick over of my open text books and notes with a mixture of disdain and curiosity on his face – difficult emotions to convey all at once, made possible by the varying amplitude of lines on his hippie-wise face. I mused that he was contemplating why people would invest time to study such matters. I sometimes thought the same myself. Hippie Davie cast an eye upward towards the roof over the door and shouted through to The Doc,

"C'mon twathead, come out it's only me."

The Doc appeared, like Mr. Ben, as if by magic behind me, using me as a shield, I could sense his genuine fear of Hippie Davie, surprising really. I didn't realise how seriously he thought all this vampire cat business was. Hippie Davie's eyes locked onto him with a look of sympathy and for a fleeting instant, I thought, a little glee. I hoped he would be careful and not wind him up too much as now wasn't the time.

Hippie Davie flumped down, still looking over at The Doc. "You ok, man? Let's hear it then, wha' happened?"

The Doc recounted how he had seen a demonic figure and how Al's concoctions were a little stronger than he had anticipated. Curiously however, he missed out the runic symbols on the ground and the symbol on his robe. I could tell he was on the defensive and spun a yarn about taking an extra bit of acid he had concealed and so was much more vulnerable than he would normally be. I remained quiet and watched Hippie Davie's expression, as The Doc recounted some of the more frightening episodes, while I, catching Hippie Davie's eye at the point where he was propped up in the back of a Morris minor with a car full of grannies in a tatty robe, holding onto his exposed bollocks, tried not to laugh too much. When The Doc mentioned the medical staff hovering over his bum cheeks however, Hippie Davie creased up laughing as he stared over at me.

"And they had a go at Pamela about it coz The Doc said his girlfriend had done it and, of course, Pamela hadn't the faintest idea of what they're talking about!" I said, barely able to conceal my own amusement at the volatility of the situation. "She's gan tae kill 'im!!"

Hippie Davie's face erupted in dimples, "Oh that's beautiful, just fucking beautiful man!" he said as he planted a fatty on his lips, in Hannible Heyes style and in a very decent impersonation exclaimed, "I luv it when a plan comes together!"

I chipped in, "Hey, you leave 'Howlin' mad fuckin' Merdock' alone! The poor bastard's been through the wars here!" The Doc just looked sulky in response to our teasing:

"Fuck off! Fuck off, ya pair o' bastards! Fuck off! I had to fight demons and protect you fae the police!"

His words however were being drowned out by our mirth. I stuck my flat open hand on my head to emulate a Mohican hairstyle and said, "A pit-eh tha fool!"

The Doc looked a little distressed, so I nudged him playfully. Hippie Davie, though, was choking with laughter and continued unabated, standing up,

"I pity the fool when Pamela gets a hold of him...he'll be howling all right...when she rips what's left o' his fuckin' 'bolloxs right aff!"

The Doc looked wild eyed. "C'mon you guys...Nae the ba's again, c'mon?"

Hippie Davie continued, "Howling mad Mikey, that's a new fuckin' name for him." Tears were now streaming down his face from the hilarity.

I shook my head, as images of The Doc howling and scrambling through the woods, chasing sheep now seemed ludicrously funny. The Doc, though was not finding it at all funny;

"It's **nae** funny!" he exclaimed, stamping his foot down and wincing regretfully. "Pamela's gonna be really mad if she finds oot you guys drugged me...ye, ye...fuckin' pair of cunts!!"

Hippie Davie retorted, "It's all your own fault, ye daft bastard, nae wonders yer erse is in tatters, when you go sheep shagging, yer meant to do it them, nae the other way around!"

I exploded with laughter, beating the ground with the palm of my hand as I slid off the couch, but I still don't think The Doc saw the funny side.

"I have a theory!" proclaimed Hippie Davie when he finally got his breath back. "The initiation was meant to make you face your dark side; we all have one, no disgrace in that. To face it and control it, that's the key. Congratulations Doc, seems you have encountered your personal demons and have come out the other side just about in one piece, albeit a bit unhinged, but then you always were, so no harm, no foul eh?"

The Doc laughed back nervously, but I could tell he was still very tense.

I sat forward, "So that's it? A scary ass vision and humiliation at the hands of the bum doctor...who's a woman by the way! And he's on the road to enlightenment?"

The Doc nodded in agreement, "Aye?"

We both looked at Hippie Davie, who eyed The Doc with a look of a teacher eyeing a disobedient pupil. "Well, it means you're at a crossroads now, however. The demon has been let loose and it still may still try to control you!"

I shrugged. "So?"

"So, you'll have to be very careful from now on Doc. Any dark thoughts, evil motivations could mean you may be sent mad, or lose your personality altogether! You'll be feeding that Demon!"

I shuddered, regarding The Doc's evil gremlinesque little frown. I considered that here be food for a whole host of hellish legions made flesh.

The Doc frowned, focusing on the more important aspect, obviously; "So does that mean that ama Jedi yet?"

Hippy Davie gave a wry smile as he stared out of the window at passers-by. "Mmm, let me see, what do your Jedi senses say right now, Doc, me old Padawan?"

The Doc eyed him with a blank expression, obviously not much of the force managing to fight its way through that creased frown and big lenses. I heard the outside door creak open in the hallway as Hippie Davie and I held each other's gaze. The realisation filtered through, even to my non-Jedi awareness and I almost mouthed a warning to The Doc to go, but Hippie Davie's gaze mesmerised me and I understood he was making me still and rooted to the spot. The Doc looked from Hippie Davie to me then back again.

"Demons, Karma...Pfah! I can handle it, stuff will blow over, things always work out for me in the end, the force of nature is in me and I can control it more than ever now. I'm capable of learning my lessons like a man! If I could handle being hung upside doon in a tee-pee wi' eagles cla's on ma nipples...I kin fuckin' well handle this shit!"

As he spoke, Hippie Davie and I listened to the footsteps along the hall and heard the door handle click. The Doc was still prattling on about his Eastern Cree stories, as our heads then spun towards the door. As the sound of the door swinging open drowned out the words "occidental Scottish-Canadian guy" a cold yet angry wind chilled our faces and very bones, as the figure of Pamela strode into the living room. Her eyes settled on me like a hawk, and then onto Hippie Davie, before fixing on The Doc who glared back towards them, a rabbit caught in their sights, his cigarette dangling from his bottom lip as his mouth gaped open.

A look of triumph spread over Pamela's face and I thought she was just going to spit fire and burn him to a crisp there and then. Her triumphant look quickly gave way to fury and she darted towards The Doc, "Yooooouuuuu! You have some explaining to do."

The Doc darted towards the door at a rate of knots, but Pamela merely stepped back blocking the way. He ducked and dived like a champion boxer, avoiding slaps raining in his direction before spinning around and heading along the hallway. Pamela followed and frantically grabbed various objects, hurling them at him. A coffee cup exploded near some bookshelves making him cover his head, almost falling over towards the bathroom. He fumbled with the bathroom door handle but a copy of Oliver Postgate's "microorganisms" splatted him on the face like a demented dove. He fell back a little and scrambled towards and through the only door left – to my kitchen and tried to close the door behind him. Pamela however, seemingly possessed of superwoman strength flung it open and The Doc went flailing backwards towards my bedroom door at the other side of the small dining area, followed in the background by the bemused bouncing dreadlocked and craning silhouettes of Hippie Davie and myself.

The Doc picked himself up and fixated on my front door. He knew his only chance was to get to it. So like an American football player he stuck his arm in front of him and made a break for it, staring ahead at the space he was aiming for. But Pamela had already anticipated his surge of strength and showing that there was not even a smidge of debate about who really was the superior between the two, she lifted my frying pan from the draining board by the sink, (a handy weapon with a handle) and swung it with due force right at nose height. I think she may have intended to use it as a form of barrier between The Doc and the front door, but her timing was perfect as the little escaping rabbit ran full pan straight into it. It made a nasty *pang* sound as it made contact with his flat simian face and a stunned Doc fell backwards, with quite a beautiful arc, as his head jarred straight upward and his glasses climbed along a slow motion orbit into the distance behind him.

"Fuck me, right in the coupon!" was all I could think to say and grimaced for my dazed-looking friend.

The Doc staggered backwards towards my bedroom door as I could barely make out the phrase "fell doon the stairs..." and "Police bummers..." as Pamela practically lifted him back up to his feet with one hand gripping his tatty old T-shirt. It was a very unchristian way to treat a Christian Death T-shirt. Hippie Davie and I recoiled with shock at the speed and severity of Pamela's response and instinctively Hippie Davie and I held our hands on our mouths, partly in shock and partly in shame as we both had to suppress our laughter. I looked at Hippie Davie, who glanced back at me understanding that this was exceptional entertainment. His acknowledgment of this made me feel it was ok not to intervene and just observe a bit longer, perhaps if blood was spilt I would try to placate Pamela and save my poor old buddy (and my wallpaper). The Doc's protestations were met with a steely expression. Pamela grabbed The Doc by the knackers and he doubled over in helpless agony. Hippie Davie and I added background sound effects, like a wrestling match commentary, "OOooooohhhh," was all that needed be said. Pamela spat her words at the writhing Doc,

"I've seen that Hippie bint of yours; seems she was unclear that you already had a girlfriend...so I put her right on that score!" The Doc's eyes looked like they were about to pop as Pamela applied the pressure to reinforce the last point to his still swollen testicles. This scene was so bad that I felt really sorry for him there and then, as I'm sure Hippie Davie did, too. Any man would, in fact. All The Doc could do was moan as his face turned berry red, his mouth pursed open and outward in exasperated pain. Tears welled up in his eyes, as were in my own just watching.

"Really thought you could get away with two timing me then did ye?" Pamela said. "Think you can make an arse of me like that?"

The Doc tried to keep it going, "Didn't do anything sexual really...she jumped on me...just a kiss I told her straight, I can never have a relationship with her."

Pamela obviously came to the end of her fuse, "You lying little bastard!" With that she practically lifted him off his feet and threw him onto my bedroom door, as if she wanted to push the disgust away from herself, as The Doc was propelled through into my bedroom.

The image of his shocked grimacing face will forever stay etched in my mind as just how justice should be imagined. A slight shocking pause filled the atmosphere which was then interrupted by further wrestling commentary, courtesy of Hippie Davie's sports radio show, "Oooh and that's a smack-down!"

I watched in horror, about to intervene, when Pamela spun around and shouted, "Shut the fuck up! You guys are all alike; I'll deal with you in a minute!"

I instinctively shut the fuck up.

The moaning Doc slumped on the bed like a spent rag. He seemed to be missing the gene which provided such useful survival instincts, however, as he pressed on further trying to sustain the lie.

"I never did anything with her, you got it all wrong Pam, you're making a mistake." His pathetic voice whined out in protest from under a shape that was only identifiably human due to thin legs and docs poking out from it.

"Oh yeah," screamed Pamela, "that's not what the fucking doctors were implying to me! How dare you embarrass me like that! So let's see how much nuthin' really happened' looks like, shall we?" With that Pamela pinned down The Doc and ripped his jeans and pants down.

Hippie Davie and I grimaced in horror as the sight of his white, bony bare pathetic little arse slid into view. Although it was really horrendous, I saw why the doctors had felt inclined to speak to Pamela about it at the first opportunity – there were long black, blue and angry red streaks which raked the length of both cheeks. Long red scars beamed out at us telling of the absurd pain he had endured, just so he could boast to us about his kinky antics. There was kinky and then there was just plain stupid. Pamela gawped at the sight; we all did for a second, while The Doc whined, now just defeated and whimpering that he'd learned his lessons in life. We all felt sorry for him lying there, Hippie Davie and I both felt that he probably had learned his lessons all right.

Pamela obviously felt that there were more lessons to be learned though, as she knelt on his back and with the words, "Oh I'll make sure you'll learn all right, learn to think twice before treating woman like shite," she started smacking his offending backside with motherly force.

Hippie Davie and I exchanged looks of both mirth and embarrassed awkwardness at the same time. The Doc's yelps, between each *thwack,* could be heard down the street, it seemed. I was acutely concerned that I was next and was confused as to whether it would be something I wouldn't object to anyway? I saw the same expression on Hippie Davie's face, as he was thinking the same thing. Maybe we should be in for the same thing; perhaps it was the goddess herself who was administering this punishment to The Doc! Did we all deserve it? Probably not actually!

I wandered down to the harbour a little later after everyone had gone and all discussions, grovelling, denials and apologies had been exhausted. The cool north east air was peppered with gulls and greyness, charged with the hum of people heading home for the evening. As I walked I had some vague notion that perhaps in a magical sense, I was striding towards some kind of twilight of magick, between the worlds of science and reason, my studies following the footsteps of Darwin's logic combined with the mysteries of magick and the experience in the woods. Some might have said that the dawn had already risen on the mysteries of 'magick.' After all, David Hume and the bright lights of the enlightenment, who I owed their scientific clarity, had nailed it as a closed case about a hundred years before. Seemed like in society, just as in my head, logic did win out to be the best option, the only sure thing. However, I also understood that compared to the obvious magnificence of the universe, science as a tool was still in its infancy.

As I approached the building, the glass reception door swung open in invitation like some vampire's gothic castle, with Don's grinning features inviting me in. I wandered in and put the kettle on in the spookily quiet back storeroom as Don set about rolling a couple of small joints to keep us going for the next hour or so. Invariably, we spoke about the preceding events, as our friend's mental state was of grave concern to us.

"Then the silly bollox is having to fend doctors off peering at his stripey torn erse, it was in such a state you see!?" I beamed as Don's face lit up with glee at the revelation.

The laughter could be heard even by the seals in the quay behind us, as they skimmed the sea going about their business under cover of the dark skies and water. I relayed the full story to Don, who sat enjoying the intake of noxious fumes and idle gossip.

I continued relishing the chance to impart this amazing bit of gossip; "...Yeah and get this right? Then Pam turns up and fucking well lays right into the poor little bastard. Christ on a bike you should have seen it man! She was whacking him with any kind of weapon she could lay her hands on man!"

"Oh aye, like fit kinda things?" Don said.

"Jist aboot onything I could pick up fast enough to hand to her!" I said and we exploded with laughter again. "Oh Jeesus dude, what a fucking batterin' he got, I had to pull her off him man, she started sculpin' his bum and everything man!"

Don choked a little, an expression of sheer disbelief on his face. "Sculped his bum!?"

"'At's right...sculped him right on the bum, pinned him onto the bed and started whacking into it, in tune to the words she was screaming out, like this." I did the actions of a mean Pamela punishing a prostate and helpless medicine man with repeated slaps of my hand in concert with the words.

"I'll-teach-you-to-do-kinky-bum-play-with-somebody-else-behind-my-back-ya-dirty-little-bastard!"

Don shook his head, I winced a little myself and continued, "Oh God I started to feel sorry for him there like, that's when he started crying like a baby, man!" Don chipped in tongue in cheek, "Like a baby Doc, Baby Doc Du Twaty-yeh?"

I laughed. "Yeah different Witch doctor! Aye that, too; baby witch doctor getting some un-priestly punishment from the Goddess!" Don nodded his head in agreement;

"Well yeah I think he's definitely learned his lesson now." I thought about Don's words and the events of the day.

"Has he learned a lesson though Don?" I asked.

"Oh yes," said Don confidently. "The goddess has ensured justice has been done that's just something he had to learn!"

I pondered that for a second. I wasn't as confident as Don that stuff will always work out! "That's the trouble with Wicca and Paganism, though, isn't it Don!? There's no system in place to guide people, no definite structure, no 'training' as such. Therefore people like The Doc flock to it in their thousands, talking shite without any evidence for what they are saying, believing whatever the hell they see fit, how do you know it's not genuine mental instability rather than an sincere search for soul? To put it in a few words, how can you separate serious chaps from the cloaks that flap? Separate the esoteric from the crap, the incompetent from the weak and the student from the freak?"

Don looked on with a we-are-not-amused expression, keeping his gaze level with mine. "You should be a fuckin" rapper!" he said sarcastically.

"Wiccan rap!?" I replied and thought, 'there's a thought.' I stood up and started prancing around the reception area, as Don giggled I started ad-libbing rhymes in a public enemy stylee:

"Am a witch with an itch, don't need to get rich, got a goddess that got ma back,

Smoke dope not crack and I'm great in the sack!

Can I get a witness?

Got a ritual to fit you'all, ma posse is ma coven and ma hommie's horned and cloven.

If you're sick – I gotta fix, as I yell outa spell.

Don't believe in heaven or hell.

Can I get a witness?"

I thought Don was going to do his usual apathetic you-are-pathetic look, but I got a start when he leapt up from behind his desk and started spitting out rhymes:

"Hey Yo Muthafucka I am Don and ma homme is Sean,

I don't mean to boast but am hung like King Kong!

Don't need to be told where how or why or what to think so in case you are God botherer get outa my face...!

As the Goddess is my witness; peace out!"

I nearly wet myself with laughter; it just wasn't a "Don" thing to do! I applauded. "Fuck-in-ell mate, you were wobbly for a second, but fuckin' well done, bro!"

We laughed loads and added various lines to the rap, which took on epic proportions throughout the night. Still, the events and the conversation with Don left me with a feeling that I was unsatisfied with Wicca and the notion of consequences. Sure, there was the three-fold rule, but did anyone really understand that, or was it just believed out of blind faith? If so, this was no better than the organised religions – it taught us nothing and rules are made to be broken by any right-thinking human! Rules that are made to be blindly followed are doomed. That was common sense and what I always thought was instinctively naïve of the god in the biblical story of Eve and Adam. It's simple human psychology. State that something should be avoided or not touched and human/primate psychology ensures we do just the exact opposite! So their logic dictates that God made us so he could fuck with us? What a scary thought! Like a computer game, he could set any monster on us if he got bored perhaps he already has.

I mentioned that to Don. He thought for a moment then said, "That's because the organised religions specified stuff for people to follow without allowing people to think about it, coz they needed to be told. Now there's a shift towards a realisation that what we do has consequences! You can't watch Blue Peter anymore, right, without the notion of recycling and ecological balance being thrust down your throat!"

I could see his line of thought. "Yeah like Karma man?"

Don nodded. "Exactly, it's up to us to figure these things out for ourselves, or else it means nothing! We must learn to govern our own behaviours; to understand why we do things! Therefore having proper insight into exactly what the consequences of our actions truly are, in a comprehensive holistic way, rather than being told what we do and blindly follow laws without comprehension of why."

As a bit of a punk, I had to agree, I took a drag of a joint and chipped into the argument;

"Yeah that's what gets me about the organised religions, man, it's so fucking patronising. I really hate it, despise it even. I'm an adult; don't tell me what to fucking do and don't protect me! I'll figure things out myself!

"They want to keep you under control, like a child! Following rules means that you don't have to think for yourself!"

I was getting more animated. "Yeah, I fucking hate that I can't buy a bottle of wine on a Sunday, or there's a level of pornography deemed fit or unfit for me! Fucking bollox man, I should be the fucking judge of that!"

Don, who could sense that I may be about to go on a rant and disturb the nice pleasant atmosphere he had engendered in this building over the years, brought the subject back to The Doc.

"S'right, Doc made his choices and now he's learned the hard way. Maybe if people are protected from making mistakes they'll never actually learn and we're here to learn surely?"

I thought about The Doc and people fucking up in general.

"Yeah it's like Karma right enough, which makes sense, coz we live our whole lives on a journey, learning and maturing. As individuals, we collect experience and not just in a passive way like a videotape; it changes us, we adapt and are modified by it for good or for bad. Just as we evolve through our lives, as a species we evolve, learn co-operate and adapt! It's the natural way, the way the brain is wired, that's why, rationally, a prescriptive set of rules, laid down in scripture will never, can never be an appropriate way for a society or an individual to progress! Such a society would simply be doomed to keep making the same mistakes over and over!"

Don cocked an eyebrow at me. "Like ours?"

"Absolutely, does the phrase 'history repeats itself' sound familiar?" I smiled in response.

"Karma is a funny thing isn't it, Don?" I mused. "Seems like The Doc got what he deserved in a weird kind of way; makes you think about this threefold rule thing, I mean Gardner, right, seems to have made it up? I mean, who knows that for sure? I reckon it's just another law, like the biblical stone tablets sort of deal. Karma seems to kick in, I think the three fold rule is jist bollox! I reckon magick, like life, is all about learning and paying the consequences if your motives are not good.

Don watched the smoke from his joint float in the air in front of him. "Mmmm, gravity keeps us all from floating away doesn't it? Keeps everything ticking away in space and stuff! You think gravity affects our moods and things as well? Sorta would explain astrology wouldn't it?"

I nodded. "Yeah, but some astrophysicists have calculated that the effects of gravity on us from distant stars is so miniscule, it's not worth thinking about. I mean the gravitational pull of Benachie Hill up the road has more pull on us right now than Saturn or Mars does! So does that mean that your character depends on what side o' Benachie you were born or conceived on?"

Don mused a little further, not really listening to me.

"Maybe it's not the stars then, maybe it's the earth itself. That would make more sense wouldn't it? I mean, maybe it's where the

Earth happens to be in its orbit that affects us and the sky is just whatever is there at that time of year, so people go by the stars and mistakenly think it's the stars influence, but they just happen to be the backdrop of where the position of the planet is, in relation to the Sun's gravity or something!?"

I stared at Don with some awe, "Fuck! Fuck that's quite profound man! I see what you mean, like same idea as people mistook the world as flat, coz that's what they can see?"

"Precisely!" added Don as if he was channelling the "mythical spirit" of the great Sherlock Holmes. I thought it was rather beautiful, as he had brought the concept of astrology, which I scoffed at and even felt secretly and deeply ashamed about, right into the realms of scientific plausibility in an instant. I could have kissed him (but I kept that information secret).

"Have you been hit on the head with a very large apple lately Don?" I said still in awe.

Don smiled and shrugged, a little nonplussed and just smiled. "Must be Hippie Davie's weed! Actually what was I saying again?"

I let the word fall around my head, "gravity causes astrology!" Did this man know the gravity of his words?

I knew very little about astrology and apart from the fact that I found it all very complicated and far too mathematical in appearance for my biologist brain, I had concluded that it was probably an outmoded system. In fact, my scientific training and mind-set made me positively bristle with resentment and near spiteful aggression towards anyone who took astrology for granted or, even worse, made some kind of living from doing it. They may as well admit to me that they thought the earth was flat or that they thought H.I.V could be treated with leeches and a few well-placed crystals. I mean, technology had moved on a little since renaissance times. There were more than the seven planets the original system was based on and Isaac Newton had nailed the laws of the motion of the universe. This had seriously now been updated by Einstein's general relativity, widely understood to be twenty-first century thinking in the twentieth. It was an awesome leap of scientific discovery, human genius and imagination. I was proud to be part of this scientific rationalism and illumination.

I spoke my concerns to Don again.

"I sometimes worry about magick and the arts and stuff, as there does seem to be a lot of symbols and philosophies such as astrology that underpins a lot of it, that just does not stand up to scientific scrutiny at all. I mean, casting a magick circle and doing the quarters and using this notion of earth air fire and water, it's no longer valid to describe the real world. We have the periodic table and bosons and particle physics and relativity to describe the real world. We have evolution and...and laser beams and atomic bombs! The material world has been described down to the smallest dot to almost the edges of the fucking galaxy. We know our postcode in space now and there's nothing else but dust and dirt and gas and fucking loads of empty space. So why, if we have moved on that much do we start talking about Mars and Venus this and earth and air elements that? Know what I mean?"

Don smiled. "Well, maybe it's because hundreds of universities and scientists work on all the physical stuff so that we can have technology and chemical fertilisers and a' that stuff that we need. But maybe only, oh I dunno, about half a dozen people in the whole world bother to research the mind and soul to any great extent. I mean that's what occult means, dunnit? Hidden, reserved for the few!? So if you think about it the occult sphere of knowledge is not in step with the technological sphere of knowledge as not many people have had the opportunity to contribute to it."

"Well apart from centuries of Tibetan monks and tantric practitioners, alchemists and masters, I will concede that it's not in the realm of Western science at least. So what does that mean? That we have to conclude that much of magick is obsolete? Those whole sections of it such as astrology should be deleted and the bits that are left absorbed into psychology?"

As I was disintegrating magick and relegating it to the trash can Don had been giving the matter a little more thought!

"Well actually; I think astrology and all that stuff still matters in regard to personality and how we're wired, I mean I don't believe it's going to affect you in a direct way, *via* gravity, but it may be that the influences do exist on the subconscious and collective unconscious, the sort of marmalade that binds everything behind the scene. This might not be an actual physical medium but surely there's enough evidence to show that there is a probably collective 'mental' medium, for want of a better word? I'm happy to call that astral; because working with that in mind shows that it works!? Doesn't it Sean, isn't that what you'd call a 'working model" in the realms of science?"

Don seemed to be honing in on the same notion that Davie had had earlier! 'Maybe we're all stoned and talking shite, I thought for a second.' But to me it came down to superposition of a small part of the mind again, not bound by space and time. Though again I was impressed by Don's analytical powers and sat open-mouthed looking at him intently! He never failed to amaze with me the things he came out with and I often wondered if he was some kind of sage that was just toying with us all.

"Well you know, I just don't know, Don, I just don't know if I can accept this whole idea of star signs and houses and rising signs; I mean, it's the stuff of tabloid papers as far as I am concerned; I just hate it!"

Don smiled at me in an almost "ah bless" kind of way.

"Aye well, don't forget the stars are behind everything we do in the tarot, even in the aspects of the gods and goddesses we call on and in fact even behind some sexual kung fu techniques."

Don was becoming more engrossed with Taoist and tantric sexual techniques and how they might correspond to magick and the fertility aspects of Wicca. I couldn't help but smirk and could barely contain my broadening smile as he sagely imparted his knowledge. I just couldn't take him seriously as the way he emphasised it made him look comical and almost a parody of Peter Cushing in some hammer house of horror film from the 1970s, which I rather enjoyed actually. I have many a fond memory of my grandmother letting me stay up late to watch them at her house during summer holidays, with juice and ice cream. However, that may also explain quite a lot, given my subsequent preoccupation with the occult and witches.

I couldn't resist mocking him in a fake Peter Cushing style emphasis, "Don't forggggggggeett; the staahs are behind everyyyyything we dooooo!"

The more Don got the 'umph' with my piss taking, the more I wanted to annoy him. "OOOh I say, sexual secrets of the Chinese and astrology, don't you mean ass-trology, my dear Van Helsink?"

At this, he shot up and reached into his combat zipper and lobbed his cock out. "I'll show you sexual secrets of the ass, come here ya bastard!?"

I shrieked with shock as he sprang around the corner with his offensive looking fat member bobbling about in his hands like a small baldy ferret eager to break it bonds and launch at me. As he raced around the counter towards me, I had the notion that a fat animated zombie sausage was leading the chase and Don was merely being dragged behind it, barely able to control it like some hellish version of Rod Hull and Emu. My instinct was to jump and run.

"Ahhhh get that awa fae me ya derty basterd!" I ran outside the door into the street in an effort to finally shake him off; but he just followed me outside. He didn't care that it was a floodlit street with passers-by and traffic not fifty yards away. He just stood at the top of the stairs making thrusting movements with his hips and laughing whilst enjoying the moment. This had the effect of making his willy bounce up and down, as if it was waving me away from the top of the stairs. Any passers-by might have thought that this security company must have had some weird training in reception and customer relations skills. I started laughing at the sight of Don in his uniform exposing himself in front of the building. I wasn't prepared to go back in, though; I knew when it was time to go. You had to hand it to Don; he certainly had a great method of letting his guests know they were outstaying their welcome!

I waved goodbye. 'Well, seems like the Karma Police have righted everything,' I thought to myself as I walked back up towards Market Street, 'I'm sure we're in for some peaceful equilibrium now, I can feel it in my bones; sense it in the force even!'

I liked the town centre when it was a bit quieter, there wasn't the hurried head-down behaviour of shoppers creating rivers of bodies pushing and collecting at street corners. In the late evening, instead, small groups of friends ambled together, relaxed and laughing; lone blokes strode deliberately with hands in pockets, taking stock of their surroundings. It was a better time to think. People were that bit more curious of each other and there was a slightly heightened sense about the smattering of pedestrians as the crowds had gone, exposing people that bit more. I liked how the buildings became speckled in a sodium glare as a sense of the soft murmur from pubs could be heard. The lull of fiddle music pushed out through flapping doorways as dram soaked tattooed smokers piled onto the pavement rudely barring my way; caring about nothing else, nor anyone else in the world at that moment, save for the little cardboard boxes cradled in hand on their way to the kerb-side.

Halfway up Market Street I sped across the road, having to be vigilant of accelerating U-turning taxis. Looking down the road to my right was the sight of one of the main harbour quays. There was the familiar and imposing scene of large sweeping hulls and rusting iron just a few yards away and towering over most of the buildings. Improbably huge chains lit by a sun-like halogen glare juxtaposed with boats just serenely afloat like giants of the sea; a huge sense of heavy industry stamped the identity of Aberdeen proudly, imminently and historically side by side with the older granite town centre, peacefully asleep still dreaming of a nineteenth century fishing town. Don's building was beset in the background, melting into the quiet of the evening.

Several safe hours later at Don's wee reception, all was quiet around the building, save for the tinny reverberations of a T.V. set droning on the corner of the reception desk. Don sparked up a spliff and stood at the door, the cool air wafted over his face and through his short crew-cut style hair. He blinked as the coolness momentarily stung his eyes and squinted away from the glare from his Zippo lighter and pleasing aroma of gasoline vapour. The quietness settled down and began to blanket the surroundings with stillness. Something wasn't right; he wasn't sure what it was but he could feel it, giving him an uneasy feeling as his eyes darted around, glancing along the side of the building and then rechecking, scanning the street ahead and flitting over the car park away across the quay. Usually he enjoyed the peace of the harbour at night and liked the early morning seagull-night-time rhythm, seeing what no-one else saw! Save for an occasional cat or hedgehog or the spying gulls. Life at that time of the morning was co-joined, linked by that sense of anonymity and the knowledge that they existed in a quiet left-over land of time, not wanted and ignored by the daytime world. Usually Don liked it and belonged to it but tonight, for no apparent reason, he felt uneasy and anxious, so he snuffed out his spliff and hurried back inside. Almost annoyed with himself, he decided to make coffee, a small trip into the back room, to shake the silly trepidation he felt. This wasn't like him at all.

On hearing the glass door rattle and knock, he wandered back into the reception, keys in hand, expecting to see the beat driver at the door, perhaps having forgotten something! He peered through the glass, looking closer to block out the glare from the lights outside. Then he saw it looming in front of him as a reflection in the glass for a split second. A massive twisted figure, a snarling, demonic, manic face reminding him of some old Peter Lorre film, but with a much more sinister look, peered at him and then vanished. He leapt back from the door in startled shock. He cursed himself for not bothering to reinforce his magical defences here. He had been meaning to do so at some point; an unfamiliar buzzer sound went off behind his desk. Curious and somewhat freaked out, he leaned over and saw a red light. *'Red lights are never good,'* he thought. The fading sticker beneath it read *back carpark* in old biro.

Don grabbed his stick and radio and made his way to the stairwell. He sat in silence waiting, listening and staring down to the basement door that led to the underground car park. He waited again; nothing happened, no-one came. After tentatively creeping down the stairs he saw the bottom door to the stairwell, slightly ajar. He pulled it closed; probably someone had not closed it correctly and now the wind had pulled it open. That must be it! He regained his composure and strode back up to reception. He did not like this at all, that face in the glass, this coincidence. It wasn't funny. He was beginning to think that that was all the excitement over for one night, so he was doubly shocked when he got back upstairs.

The smell of burning plastic stung his nostrils as small whiffs of black smoke billowed from the back of his T.V. set that had gone blank. The video that was sitting on top had buckled in the heat. The ashtray that had supported his spliff was now devoid of said spliff. It was immediately apparent what had happened. It had toppled off and slid down the back of the T.V. set, slowly burning a hole in the circuitry and creating enough heat to melt and deform the video cassette casing as well. Don threw the video off and then in panic and almost a reflex poured a cup of Coca-Cola down the back of it to cool the insides. A shower of sparks flew upwards out of the back with a bright blue flash and smoke that sent Don flying backwards across the desk.

A moment later, the last crackle hissed its way out of the T.V, restoring the reception into shocked stillness. Don's head arose from behind the desk as he slowly patting himself all over to check he was actually still alive. He looked at his dead T.V. set in horror, as one might look on the corpse of a good friend, then to the buckled videocassette and then back to the blank but very dead T.V. He thought, *'Fuck me!'* He looked at the glass reception door, as if to see the face winking at him or something, "Why, why dammit, why didn't you just kill me instead?" he exclaimed in a Charlton Heston kind of way, as he shook the useless deformed cassette in his hand. Suddenly the building seemed alive with noises as the doors of the reception upstairs hammered in the distance and windows seemed to blow open, the familiar sound of the weird poltergeist-like effect that tends to happen when psychic seismic activity is occurring. Don not so much caring about the racket still focused on the buckled cassette in his hand.

"Ffffaaackin" 'ell! Whatever the fuck that was, it sure knows how to bloody well hurt me!" he exclaimed out loud. "What the fuck else can ye do to me now?"

No sooner had the words left his mouth than a loud klaxon filled the room with sound, at the same time water sprayed straight into Don's face from a water sprinkler on the roof above him. As he spat water from his mouth, he had his answer and he could only think to say one thing; "Ahh…Rat's cocks!" he exclaimed.

## Chapter 10:
## Karma Police, Arrest This Man

Some days passed filled with the usual last minute trips to the library to photocopy large and specific tracts of journals and textbooks for cramming purposes. I sometimes amazed myself of just how much information I could digest when the pressure was on; I sometimes felt like one of those memory guys and supposed I might get some circus work if there happened to be a lack of "bat stalking" jobs available in Aberdeenshire after my degree. I had appreciated, however, that my front door had been unusually quiet in terms of interrupting raps at odd hours of the day and night. So I had no excuse but to study, in between T.V. watching and text book cover drumming sessions. Though I did think the flat had a strange feeling at times, sort of like when you wander through a wood and come to a quiet patch where the birds have vacated, perhaps arising from a latent predator lurking about.

In fact, I had that exact uneasy feeling, and on a couple of occasions I fancied I caught sight of a figure looming in the hall, but when I blinked it had gone. Maybe it was the pressure of studying, driving me crazy, I don't know. My car had broken down and despite having several return trips to the garage, it kept breaking down. At one point the mechanic forgot to tighten some key bolts and my dad said that if I had been going at speed, I would have careered off the road and probably would have had a fatal accident. I had been very lucky, but yeah it all added to the mounting stress. However, I just couldn't catch a break at all. The stress was making me come out in hives, bills kept mounting up, my printer broke down, so I had to cycle miles to uni' to print stuff, the list goes on.

The sight of the sun chinking through the clouds made me feel as if I had to do something as I found myself standing still, staring out of the window. I felt like an indoor pet cat, the kind that sits on window sills sometimes with their paws stuck to the glass, looking longingly out into the street, like a little furry prisoner, condemned for some past mice killing spree. I stood staring as if in a trance as the uneasy feeling crept up around me again. Before long, I slung on my jacket and reached for my bike in the hall.

My bike almost seemed to know the way on its own, before I skidded to a halt next to Don and Hippie Davie, who were looking quite relaxed, sitting outside on the café front. A third chair was left pushed out, showing that they had clearly been expecting me. I had a flashback to the canteen on the second floor of the regent building where three chairs were often found by security guards pulled out around a table by ghostly coffee mates. I imagined for a second that that may probably be the three of us, as ghosts, travelling back in time to meet up in our past, to watch ourselves for amusement. However, those ancient washing ghost ladies of the Green would probably chase us away from here.

I sat down as Amber brought me over a cappuccino, "Jeez, welcome to the only psychic coffee shop in Aberdeen!" I said in jest and some surprise.

Amber smiled. "Don't have to be psychic to know you'll be here before long, if these other reprobates are here!" she said cheekily.

I was a little taken aback and indignant, "Really?"

"Nahhh..!" said Hippie Davie, "Don saw ye waitin' at the traffic lights as he came oot the paper shoapie ye dozy prat, now sit doon."

Somewhat relieved that society had not become psychic without me, I joined them. Hippie Davie smirked, "Waiting at the traffic lights, such a conformist for a punk int" ye?"

I had to respond, his hippiedom with a dash of cappuccino seemed somewhat unfair to me all of sudden. "Oh so, riding your bike up on the pavement and pushing past little old ladies is anarchy and living a free life? Thaaaat's all it takes is it? I know, let's get rid of traffic lights all together; people can be free to do what they want, cos you know, people are so naturally cool and groovy that traffic and therefore society will function much better that way!"

I was aware of the slight exchange of eyeballs, as Hippie Davie slumped back a little put out; he grinned, as if to express triumph at winding me up a little, but I knew my remarks had landed. My comments had rocked the boat of their little superior-to-the-masses mind-set and I felt a little unwelcome all of a sudden! Don made an "Oooooo" sound. "Well you must have got out of the 'right wing' of the bed this morning!"

Everyone laughed at his admittedly quite annoyingly clever play on words. I relaxed a little, "You know, I think that's the trouble with anarchy and idea of freedom! It's people! That's why the counter-culture of the Sixties didn't work, people! Hell *is* other people. I mean look at The Doc; if he had half a chance, he would take over the world and make us all slaves, wouldn't ee? It's people like him that become politicians! Yep beware anyone who wants to become a politician!"

Hippie Davie smiled, "What was that thing you said to me the other day? Whoever you vote for, government wins! True that!"

Don nodded. "Yup, we would be much better off with no government at all! Let people do what they want and just sort of govern each other!"

"Oh Christ!" I sat back and looked aghast. "There'd be anarchy all right! Of the worst kind, bloodshed, in less than a week if you allowed that, man!" A line from one of my favourite poems came to me, "*The worst would be filled with passionate intensity, while the best would lose all conviction!*"

Hippie Davie screwed his face a little and smiled out of the corner of his mouth. "What's up, you got an essay deadline looming? Are you just gonna like, sit here and quote lines from all the pessimistic prose you know about? Heheh."

"That's right, ya bastards!" I exclaimed raising my voice in mock anger, "I do have a deadline and an essay to hand in and I'm going to make everyone feel as pissed off as I am!"

Just then a cloud plunged the green into grey and a breeze whipped along the cobbles almost as if the elements themselves were saying, "Fuck off ya lazy bastards, haven't you guys got jobs to do or something?"

Don sighed, "See you! I was happy sitting here, in the sun and now you come along with yer pissed off at the world vibe and...do some sort of fuckin' rain dance and put a downer on everything!"

Hippie Davie smiled and sat back blowing smoke into the passing current, making it billow behind him like a mad dreadlocked Victorian steam engine. The kind that would never actually be on time and probably despise passengers - a lot like modern trains! He added his half penny to the conversation,

"Bogartin' our fuckin' vibe dude!"

I wasn't sure if he was just taking the piss out of Don or whether he was serious, as he did tend to actually speak like that. However, I was feeling a little rebuked by Don's accusation!

"Rain dance? Fucking rain dance?" I started laughing, it was so absurd. "And when did you see me leap up outa my seat and start doing a fuckin' rain dance?"

Don just started sniggering but wasn't going to concede just like that! "Well...you probably did one on the way here, unconsciously you see, coz yer soooo fucking moody! See, us witches have to be careful when we're moody....might inadvertently wish for thunder or something!"

Hippie Davie raised his eyebrows in mock seriousness and nodded. "Yeah dude, probably had time at all them traffic lights!"

With a hand wave, I dismissed his allusion to my seemingly unhappy liking of conformity.

"Pffff, look if you get knocked doon on yer bike by a big lorry turning left, then don't come running to me...if you can still run that is!" I sat back contemplating the possibility. "Wouldn't it be fucking brilliant if we could do that eh? If you or Don pissed me off and I just jumped up and started dancing around the table calling for thunder or rain, just to annoy you!"

They both laughed at this image. Don chortled and sat with his hands out to the side, fingers in yoga pose. "Hell yeah, brilliant way to get rid of annoyin" people, just sorta go Ummmmmmm...shazam thunder bolt right in the..."

Hippie Davie was already ahead. "Or even better, imagine we could make the sun come oot, right in the middle of a rain shower, ye know, just enough to shine on our table or something and nobody else's!?"

Don laughed heartily. "Yeah, abody looking as we sit doon outside and just link hands, look up and have a large sunbeam come down on us, amazing!"

Hippie Davie grinned and opened his hands on the table, imploringly, "Yeah, we should be able to do that man! I mean, what's the point of being fucking witches if you can't bend the rules ever so slightly now and again!"

I wasn't sure if he was joking or not, as I smiled wryly, taking a drag on a cherry tobacco rollie, enjoying the entertainment of my friend's silly chat. Don nodded avidly.

"Yeah, yeah, we can heal; we get to do spells for good luck in love and things occasionally, so...why can't we catch a break with the bloody clouds and stuff?"

I laughed but felt the need to point out the obvious. "Well we live in Aberdeen, man! We'd have nae energy left for anything else! Heheheh."

They both nodded in agreement. Hippie Davie then sat forward a little, then made a little plea, "Right then rain man, you got us into this I want my sun back. I think you should get up and do a sun boogie and get it back for us!"

"Sun boogie...Jeez it's been so long, you know!? Not sure I can remember all the steps to the sun boogie! Is it like a jungle boogie?"

Don looked up. "Rain, rain go away, don't come back for another day."

I smiled, remembering my childhood. "Christ, I remember doing that in the playground, utterly convinced it would work!"

As small rain drops splattered on the table and began to speckle the cobbles around us, Don mused out loud,

"I remember it did seem to work most of the time actually!"

I added, "I remember that, too!"

Hippie Davie shrugged in resignation. "Well, we're fucked then ain't we? Can't you see what's happening? All that rain you guys postponed in the playgrounds has had to catch up on us eventually, ain't it? You two must be due a good few months a' rain now!"

Don nodded in a can't-argue-with-that-logic manner and I pursed my lips in resigned agreement. I thought for a second.

"If only we'd been a bit savvier," I said, "and reworded that particular oral contract with 'come back tomorrow!'"

Hippie Davie nodded a slow agreement. "Yep, if tomorrow never comes, you'd have been blessed with eternal dryness if only you'd thought of that; pity there were no lawyers in primary four wasn't it?"

To my amusement, Don actually slapped the table loudly in annoyance "Bastard! Now why didn't I think of that?"

Hippie Davie giggled, "You weren't a witch then my friend!"

I conceded, "Probably just as well; the whole North East of Scotland would be suffering massive, inexplicable drought by now anyway!"

Don smiled. "Ahh but the rain could come on as soon as I went indoors, that's ok!"

"Selfish little witch," I said.

Don winked and went all coy. "Weellllll, something like that has been said many times before!"

Hippie Davie packed away his tobacco and lent forward, looking like he was preparing to go inside, but then held his hands out to each side. We moved to follow suite then realised he had something else planned.

"Well let's do it guys, let's just get a reprieve for a few more minutes, at least until the brother Don here has to go home and get some shut eye!"

I was a little apprehensive. "You mean like a sun boogie?"

Hippie Davie cast an eye on the public scene, all the people wandering around enroute to the station and so forth.

"Aye, well maybe not as full on as an actual sun boogie, but a little power raising and chat with the gods like!?"

Don grabbed Hippie Davie's hand. "Come on then!"

I, less happy with holding my mates hands in a café table in public, hesitated. "Well come on ya bastard, it's a" your fault onyway!" Don moaned.

It was interesting that what had started as a joke at my expense, about my mood changing the weather, had somehow consolidated into a genuine grievance in my friends' minds. There was obviously no point arguing. Reluctantly I held both their hands and engaging emu-logic I closed my eyes, hoping it would render me invisible to the public. Hippie Davie began some chant, about the gods of rain and weather and chance and the sun god cutting us a fucking break. It didn't rhyme, though and we found it difficult to build up a lot of enthusiasm about it. Instinctively, Don contributed the more straightforward and time-tested magical verse to the proceedings,

"Rain, rain go away, don't come back till another day! Rain, rain go away...!" We all just followed suit, smiling a little. I thought about that caveat I had mentioned and prised it in.

"Rain, rain go away don't come back till tomorrow we say!" I opened my eyes and winked at Don, who immediately began singing it louder, a knowing smile on his face, winking back at me! It was beautiful how triumphant his expression was at that point. How much he had invested in the belief of the situation! Together we chanted, getting louder and more confident with every verse. I could actually feel the energy flicker around us, just like any other circle at Newmachar.

"Rain, rain go away! Don't come back till tomorrow we say!" People walking past looked at the table of loonies in the wind and rain with some worry on their faces. People in the café looked out of the window and laughed, with an "Awwwe-bless-them-poor-deluded-fuckin'-hippies-look-what-happens-when-you-desert-a proper-education" kind of look.

But it worked! The rain stopped as the wind gave a little angry gust of derision in our direction. We felt a natural end to the ritual and the energy seeping away. Just on cue, a chink of sunlight 'floodlit' the table we were on. We looked at each other – Don had an expression of triumph on his face, Hippie Davie just had the usual told you so, not surprised sort of look, while I looked at the other two with suspicion! The people inside the café looked confused and one old guy shouted, "Well done lads," which made the others laugh out loud!

Don laughed, "See if witches are in a good mood, the world's a better place.

A few seconds later, thunder echoed in the distance. Hippie Davie contemplated it for a second and then said,

"Shit, we've forgotten about The Doc!" We all laughed and then eyed each other for a second. Yip, it seems like we had!

Strangely, a shiver rose up my spine as I contemplated The Doc and thought for a second it may be the breeze getting to me. A momentary lull stalled the conversation as each one of us contemplated The Doc for a moment or so. I almost missed his gremlinesque little face eyeing me with envy. Since the day of reckoning in my flat he'd had nothing more to do with us. I did feel a little guilty; perhaps we'd gone over the score teasing him!? It occurred to me that he obviously hated me, Hippie Davie and probably Don, too, whilst he' been sitting here chatting as mates. I never suspected that his mind was plotting and despising us in such a manner all along, though a little bit more talk with Pamela after the fact confimed this to indeed be the case, poor Doc.

Greyness spread around the green like a New Model Army song as we sat, sipped and sifted through our tobacco products. There was a definite oppressiveness hanging in the air and I put it down to high pressure. To try to lighten the mood I started the conversation going about astrology.

"So, did Don tell you his ground-breaking theory of everything Hippie D? (as his name had been shortened further in proportion to how long I'd known him! Equally he could shorten my name to 'S', except it just sounded like a person from the west end of the city being derogatory!).

"You succeed where Einstein left off then, Don old boy?" Hippie Davie enquired as he turned to the unassuming Don, as he nosedived into a black coffee (as a confirmed goth now, he always took black coffee, you had to figure!). "

Wha..? Oh I may have, yes, when I was a little too stoned like, you know...what was it I said again?"

I looked at him, a little in the huff; my philosophical hero of the previous night was becoming a little more like Nigel Bruce's depiction of a bumbling Dr. Watson in the cold light of day. I stressed my words a little stronger to emphasise my annoyance at his forgetfulness.

"The fuckin" astronomy is a result of the earth's position in its orbit and the Sun's gravity rather than the distant stars theory!?"

Don regarded the space in front of him as if the words were written right there in the air, but were boring him like some random newspaper print. "Oh aye, aye, s'why the Earth's not flat...or something!"

I regarded him with a little disbelief; he wasn't the same person as the night before. I shook my head and smiled a little.

"Sometimes I wonder if your nae schizophrenic, ya bastard!" I said with an air of almost mock sympathy.

Don just shrugged "Welllll, depends who is inhabiting my body at the time!" he said in a manner that made me think he wasn't actually joking.

Hippie Davie, though, predictably had run with the idea while we were debating Don's state of consciousness.

"MMMmm why didn't I think of that!" he mused.

"That's exactly what I thought;" laughing out loud and imploring him with my hands. "I'm thinking that as well," I concurred and the laughter rippled around the small plastic table. I shrugged, "It's a much better theory of astrology than distant stars shining their cosmic influence down from hundreds of light years way back in time and space."

Hippie Davie nodded. "Places the influence..."

"If any," I chided.

Hippie Davie looked suitably annoyed at my interruption, which pleased me. "..Innnnfluence with the Sun and the Earth; God and Goddess if you like, I like it!"

"I fuckin' know!" I said in agreement, "Makes a lot more sense, because we must be buffeted by the combined gravitational influence of the Sun, a big fuck off massive thing in space and the Earth, a big fuck off ball of rock that we're glued onto to!" There must be gravitational fluctuations that influence us all the time and they must be cyclical just as the seasons are coz we're hurtling around a wobbly solar orbit. The stars are just the wallpaper we see as it traverses that orbit!"

Don drew on a spliff handed to him by Davie, "Yeah and so for astrology to work, you can just look at the earth herself and the seasons where we're born into; it's like the state she's in when she's pregnant with you that counts...and therefore your mother...or something!"

Hippie Davie raised an eyebrow. "Fuckin 'A" Don old son, that makes perfect sense brother!"

Don's words though were squashed through the scientific filter (just behind my right ear).

"Jeezuz, in fact you can allow for the seasons because the southern hemisphere has the opposite seasons. So if astrology has an effect at all, then we know it must be a whole earth thing rather than a particular season affecting mother and embryo during pregnancy! I looked around in order for confirmation to cement that part of the theory."

Hippie Davie mused out loud, a stream of consciousness emerging forth as he spoke, "Gravity, it's the ultimate force driving cohesion and hence co-operation in the universe! Fuck that may even explain ley lines does it not? As points of gravitational fluctuation on the surface?"

I picked up the pass. "Yeah, gravity is the glue that may even influence the mind and hence even the subtle mind-body will, or force, as you Jedis put it!"

Hippie Davie retrieved the pass, the old one-two as we used to say as kids playing football in the park, a deadly combination that seldom failed to score goals. "Yeah well the ground we sit on is floating on a big bowl of hot liquid init, sorta like a giant floatarium. It's no surprise then, that gravity shifts us around, shifts the subtleness of the mind; has our moods and personalities pinned down from the word go, *ergo* astro-fuckin-strology!"

I headed the ball in the net, "Ha and ley lines are places where geological formations in the rocks give out strange geo-magnetic fields aren't they? According to that author Serena Rooney McDowell, hence it makes your pineal gland go on the blink or something? That could also explain away yer force if you're not careful!"

Hippie Davie shifted in his seat as if to avoid the implications of those words on his internal beliefs. The old 'cognitive dissonance shuffle,' a deft mental movement that seldom failed to score against a reasonable goal.

"Yeah, yeah mister scientist. I think I'm right in saying that some dude surveyed lots of professions and found that people's vocations generally fell into their expected star sign categories. So if that's true, you have a theory right there!"

I nodded the ball towards Don. "Not me. Professor Yaffle there unearthed that little gem last night!"

We laughed and held our coffee mugs up to toast Don's theory, variously saying, "To professor Yaffle! Here's to his gothic genius!"

"Here, here," I said clicking my mug with the others.

Don chuckled to himself. "Who needs a university education; all you need is plenty of dope and a few sleepless nights!"

I felt slightly put out by that statement until Hippie Davie cut in, "What do you mean, that is exactly what a university education is, init Sean?"

I shrugged. "You forgot the frequent masturbation!"

Don, of course, corrected me. "I never forget about the frequent masturbation!"

As I sipped, Hippie Davie's mention of gravity acting like a cohesive force in the universe filtered through to my mind. "Gravity is God!?"

Don looked annoyed. "Oh fit's he spiking aboot now?"

Hippie Davie and I smiled almost guiltily as Don continued imploring us with his arms like an Italian mob boss.

"Can I nae jist sit and hae' a fuckin' cup o' coffee sometimes without somebody gan on aboot science...or Einstein or...mysteries of the bloody universe?"

I felt a bit guilty, maybe he's right, maybe that's all I ever speak about and maybe I'm boring! I was about to counter a little whilst Hippie Davie just chuckled, making me feel as if he was silently agreeing with Don-adding to my paranoia he continued on with his tirade.

"Fuck me, honestly! It's like being stuck in a lift with Arthur C. Clarke and what's his fucking name, other guy, American one?"

"Carl Sagan," I said dryly.

Don pointed his finger at me. "Aye!"

But before he could continue his mid-morning whine at us, I changed tack. "Well actually I wouldn't mind being stuck in a lift with them guys...if I'm going to get stuck in a lift with two guys at all that is!"

Don just tutted.

Hippie Davie, who'd been anticipating Don's grumpy demeanour passed over a fatty. "Brother, chill out, life's getting you uptight and it's spilling into our little debates, this'll never do."

I remembered who started it all off. "It's all your fault anyway, Professor Yaffle! You weren't complaining when you were churning out theories the other night!"

Don lit Hippie Davie's rollie. "Aye, well am nocturnal, I can't deal with this shit in the mornings sometimes!"

I laughed. "It's ten past twelve in the afternoon!"

Hippie Davie, however, leaned forward a little bit more serious.

"Listen brother, there's nothing wrong with chatting about stuff! I mean, thinking and talking is free man, think about it! Everything else you do is either taxed or numbs your mind – school, T.V, all kinds of media, working in some job that forces you to be slave to something else! Sitting here thinking is free, hell if more people just took time out and sat and thought about things, then the world would probably be a much better place!"

Don with his anxiety now lighter by a few draws, smiled over at me apologetically. "Am sorry, am sorry; I know how you're into your 'science,' but it just gets to me. I mean, I don't need things explained like you! I know magick is real, I know the other side exists and I'm satisfied enough with that!"

I felt the need to explain a little. "Well, the way I see it, it is like this right!? I don't actually understand why everybody does not pose these types of questions all of the time!? I mean we all should be debating the question of existence on mass! Think about it, we live in a world where we are told there's a 'God,' a human-like figure that rules the universe watching over us!? Just think about that for a second. That's an awesome assumption and if you ask anyone up there on Union Street chances are they will blindly say 'yep that's right, I believe that!' I mean, imagine if that wasn't an accepted fact that we are just conditioned to believe, if no-one even considered that before and then it came on the news, out of the fucking blue! 'NASA satellites have reported that space is not just full of dust, but a large powerful inter-dimensional alien is sitting out there monitoring your every waking move from another dimension!' Imagine that!? There would be widespread panic; people would take to the hills. It would be like *War of the Worlds* all over again, but ten times worse!"

Hippie Davie laughed. "Bro I never thought of it like that!"

Even Don chuckled at this notion. "It'd be like hamsters in a cage suddenly realising there's somebody standing outside staring in!"

"Or like goldfish in a bowl!" I shrugged.

"God's pets!" exclaimed Hippie Davie. "Imagine that!"

I continued, "It really is a weird, paranormal thing to have to consider, yet most people just accept this without blinking an eye! But I say, if we all truly believe this, without question, then we should be spending billions trying to communicate with that...intelligence and locate it in space!" I implored them further to excuse my point of view.

"That's the way I think! I think about the validity of magick and faery and apparent apparitions because, if there's any truth in them, any at all – and because of my experiences I am forced to concede that there very probably may be – then I have no choice but to think and wonder about it. And that's why I don't understand why it's not more of a mainstream concern!"

Don nodded quietly. "Ok, I never thought about it like that. I suppose everything's been discovered in science, ain't it? All the big stuff, so I suppose explaining paranormal events and things like that would be a major breakthrough?"

Hippie Davie leaned forward, "Mmmm, s'right stuff that defies explanation is probably an indication that the science is just insufficient to explain it! No one really believed in ball lightning until a physicist saw one glide past him in a plane! Or meteors were dismissed for years until one practically landed at the feet of some famous astronomer."

I nodded "That's right! So if any of what we say is real, has any kind of effect that could potentially be measured in the real world – a poltergeist slamming a door, something appearing in front of people on more than one occasion in the same place, or as I seem to have definitely done on more than once, had accurate dreams and visions of events that have yet to happen – then it means science lacks the data to explain it. So that data must be found, as it's so fundamental to how we think about life, the universe and everything; it is imperitive that we investigate this." Hippie Davie smiled,

"What was it someone said? Any culture coming into contact with superior technology would consider that technology to just be 'magick.' 'Arthur C Clarke!" I said triumphantly pointing a finger at Hippie Davie.

At that Don slammed his coffee cup down on the table with a thud.

"Oh forrrr fuck's sake!"

We sat soaking in the freedom of not working, enjoying each other's company, caffeine and tobacco. When the mind is free from work and study, it is unfettered and able to expand into other matters, often the company of my friends who did not question any aspect of magick both annoyed and inspired me.

As Don began to open his mouth another train of thought leapt to my mind, which I felt the need to unburden myself with and so I cut him off before he could utter another breath.

"And take telepathy! The very word makes every rational sane person gawp with distain! But, think about this, it surely must also (quite antagonistically) be an accepted mainstream fact!"

I waited for a second, inviting the opposition from them. Hippie Davie frowned, he knew I must have some obvious bit of evidence but wasn't sure where it might be hidden.

Don shrugged. "We do it all the time!"

"Yes, but I mean in real society, not the 'real people' like us lot."

"Church?" said Hippie Davie hesitantly.

"Precisely!" I exclaimed. "Think about it; every priest, holy man, nun, priestess, man woman or child who ever closed their eyes and prayed is basically accepting that they are telepathic and that, bizarrely, some alien intelligence will receive their thoughts!"

I let the concept wash for a second, they both nodded that was true! "So why isn't telepathy investigated more then?" I continued in defiant logic. "Why is it 'ok' to pray and think you can send your 'thoughts' to some subtle outside agency, but it is ridiculous to believe that a person can send their thoughts to someone else. It doesn't make sense, when you think it through, does it?"

Hippie Davie said, "Yeah I suppose, telepathy via prayer is an accepted fact; it's on the American Dollar Bill man, 'In God We Trust' I guess that's accepting that God is real and he is telepathic with humans – weird shit, huh?"

Don sneered in dispair and his voice raised an octave or two higher,

"It's no fair, all the craziness of other religions is just accepted, the holy sacrament, angels roaming the earth, God talking to prophets. We actually have nothing crazy like that. In fact Wicca is just basically based on observation, the earth, the moon, how we feel about it, how we connect to it and the principles of humanity and nature."

Hippie Davie cut in. "Yes we believe in magick, tarot and the mysteries, but only because they fucking work!"

I actually agreed with both of them. "However much I am sceptical about tarot, magick and the Western mystery system, it all seems to work and prove itself to me over and over again and yet I confess I continue to be sceptical."

Hippie Davie sighed a little. "You're still sceptical after all the out of body experiences and the magick you've had first-hand experience with?"

I shrugged. "In my 'scientific' religion, Davie, it is scepticism and posing continual questions that are the way to enlightenment!" I pondered exactly what I was saying for a moment.

"It's not enough to believe in something myself, or be satisfied with something I can see with my own eyes, or experience with my own mind. I mean, that boils down to faith! Blind faith, my friend, is for the stupid and the ignorant. My religion, of reason, of science, is based on facts and that is the only way! To be able to reproduce phenomena for all, to supply the technique so it can be useful, allow us insight into its processes, or else it is a waste of time, in my view. That's what I think Crowley meant by 'Magick is for all.' I think he was being quite prophetic, stating that magick is a human process by which we will harness the part of the mind that furnishes us with religious experiences and phenomena! If it is real, then fair enough, so we should be able to bottle it and use it!"

Hippie Davie pursed his lips. "It's will isn't it? Will power is the key, doesn't matter what religious background you furnish it with Reiki, Jesus, Wicca, Islam or Tibetan Buddhism. It is will; that's the essence of magick and yes it works! It's like a sophisticated type of positive thinking, or group cohesion, but 'will' works, through whatever process."

I jumped on his exposition, thinking again of my conversation with Arianne and Wolf. "Exactly that, exactly that, you said '*whatever process!*' See, in my view it really is not enough to state that; we must investigate and find out how 'will' alone can shape events, change the course of a person's life history, can produce chance occurrences, heal the sick at a distance, or even change the infra-red properties of a glass of water or alter the aura on a Kirlian photograph or change a whole atmosphere of a place or room, *etc, etc.* And I say, Don and Einstein and Newton were skirting around the issue."

Don's eyes widened in some kind of horror, like he was being accused of being part of an establishment gang he didn't want to belong to, like they'd broken a window and he didn't want the blame as he was only there in the background!

"You mentioned gravity is the glue that keeps 'reality' together, Don!? Well, I think willpower, focused imagination, is just like gravity. It's not very strong, like gravity it is a so-called non-baryonic force, not as strong as the atomic strong force or fundamental particles, but is effective over long distances and bends reality, like gravity bends or buckles space-time. I reckon 'Will' can interfere with the very fabric of space-time, especially the 'time" part, unlike gravity which is concerned with the 'space' part of space-time! With concentrated will, we bend time events in our favour; we are like little planets hurtling through life. Some people are like Pluto, unlucky and not making much impact, some others, such as magicians, the strong-willed people, are like suns and create positive will, even attracting others towards us. Annnnd that's why magick works; or religions if they are big enough. It's like more people equals more 'mass,' 'cept we can call it 'temporal mass,' which ties in with the 'hundred monkey effects' and Sheldrake's 'morphic resonance,' as it affects time and fate and our luck and chance!"

Don applauded. "Temporal fucking mass. Here, here. Another lecture from scientist Sean the sensible."

I shrugged and Hippie Davie exploded into laughter. "Sensible Sean! I fuckin love it...all right Sensible, let's have another drink!?"

"Fackin 'ell," I sighed, I had a feeling if I didn't dowse this immediately, it would fan quickly and stick. "Nah, nah, I would prefer surreal Sean or Sean the, the snake hipped sex god or something!?"

Hippie Davie immediately turned to grin at Don whilst aiming his thumb at me in a derisory fashion. "Fuck affff! You're Sensible all right, Sensible Seanie! Fucking brilliant, like 'Steve interesting Davis,' off the snooker! Hahahahaha." He held his hand up and high fived Don, who laughed in what seemed to me now a cruel kind of way, his little cigarette reverberating up and down, clenched in his little mocking mouth; the bastard! It was clear that the more I protested, the more they would call me by that moniker! I hated my friends sometimes!

As Don shuffled around in his bag for baccy I felt a little ashamed, maybe boring my friends a little, but then I saw Hippie Davie smile at me and wink. "I think you're on to something there, Sensible, maybe some of your ideas are making magick a bit more concrete. I'm starting to appreciate your rational view, heheheh."

The more we sat and laughed the less the sense of foreboding loomed at the back of my mind, though it was definitely still there. I mused out loud that it was good to get out as the atmosphere of my flat was a little oppressive at the moment.

Hippie Davie sat forward, suddenly looking quite attentive, "What do you mean exactly by 'oppressive?'"

I could sense the conversation seemed quite relevant to both my buddies, as Don listened in quite intently also.

"Oh...I dunno; sort of strange, not like my usual flat at all, just a feeling that makes me not want to spend too much time there, y'know?"

Don spoke up while Hippie Davie continued looking straight at me, as if he had a search light which was combing my very aura. "Oh we know!" he said while tailing off a little quietly and glancing over at Hippie Davie as he now became the new centre of the conversation.

I looked at Hippie Davie curiously for the explanation. "Mmmm, there's no mistake, I thought it was just me until Don told me about his work the other night and now you," he said. "It's no coincidence, we're all being had mate, it's as clear as coffee...isn't!"

As he spoke a tingling went up my spine, I had come to recognise this type of response in my body in relation to subtle or spiritual insights like this. I knew what I was feeling was some kind of 'signal,' as I had grown to accept and trust this. The feeling swept over me and instinctively I knew that Don and most likely Hippie Davie were experiencing the same. We all paused looking at each other knowingly as my rational side kicked in. "Had!? What exactly do you mean by 'being had'?" Though I didn't really need Hippie Davie's confirmation, I just knew.

Hippie Davie nodded. "Someone or something has set its will against us, all three of us most likely and I think it's fairly obvious who!?"

"The Fuckin Doc!" exclaimed Don. As soon as he said it a huge wave of feeling swept around us like a "psychic wind."

Hippie Davie's eye's rolled a little in his head. "Wow! You guys feel that? There's no doubt, man! For whatever reason, mad old Howling Mer-Doc has been up to no good, rattlin' his evil medicine man old voodoo bone in our direction!"

I winced. "Jeesus Hippie Davie, what a fuckin' foul thought, puulease!?" I retorted a little perturbed at the image of The Doc with his minky little peperami, involuntarily invaded my mind.

Don closed his eyes, seeming to pick up on some vibe that we seem to have invoked by starting the conversation. "He didn't do it on his own; he was helped by a couple of people; I can see their eyes burning under hoods!"

It was like we knew everything subconsciously and we jointly collaborated to bring the knowledge to the surface! I knew it didn't make sense, but we could all see what Don was saying and accepted it as if we were reading it from a newspaper. A further chill swept across us which seemed to pique at the vision of the cloaked figures.

Hippie Davie rummaged in his pocket. "I know, we'll make sure. I have a little something in here!"

I wouldn't have been surprised if he went stock still and began to project a three dimensional hologram of The Doc doing black magic in the middle of the table, *a la* R2-D2 in Star Wars. But instead he produced some sticks with runic symbols inscribed onto them, which I somehow recognised as being the work of Wolf, but didn't know how I 'knew' that. Hippie Davie tossed them onto the table and studied them for a second. "Yup, yup they concur, a couple of people, being misled by one (Doc) are trying to subdue us." Hippie Davie's lips moved to say more but literally bit his lip. Don and I, however, were still in tune with what was going on.

Then Don spoke, "They feel they are protecting The Doc; I can see them building up energy for him, for some kind of healing, but he, The Doc used it in rage. He's unleashed some kind of demonic part of himself and he's sending it after us."

I nodded; it was clear to me too and as strangely as it sounds, it was as if Wolf's runes spoke to me, recognising me as a friend. I turned to Hippie Davie. He was already glowering back, eyes wide as saucers and an expression of knowing on his face.

"You fucked with him," I said, "you split the dark side from him and did something. I don't know how but you made it real...fuck! Hippie Davie what did you do?"

Hippie Davie regarded me silently, almost, I thought, with a kind of fearfulness tinged with tangible guilt, and there was no hiding it. We all could feel it and knew it. He slouched back in defeat and blew smoke out in an exasperated long stream signalling that his words were to follow in a similar honest grey stream before us.

"Ok, I did, I created a shortcut from one reality to the next, I used the energy of initiation to charge a charm, a kind of powerful old gypsy punishment, which I embellished with a little sprinkling of the goetic stuff I learned and a little of my own imagination. It opened the way for his dark side to come through and give him a nightmare. I thought it would just teach him a lesson, precipitate a bit of karma. Thing is, I totally underestimated just how big that mutherfucker's dark side really was!"

I shook my head. "Ya don't fuckin' say Hippie fuckin Dee!? I mean really, c'mon, it's The Doc!? He's an egomaniac, a little guy, y'know; little guys are always trouble – like Hitler and Napoleon – and that is no fuckin' exaggeration putting them in the same league neither! And you thought you'd release his inner demon??? That's the worst fuckin' judgment call I've heard since...since...since the bloke on the Titanic said Ahhh fuck icebergs! This thing will probably just chunk through the bastards no problem!" Hippie Davie smiled shaking his head a little condescendingly, though also quite amused, "Chunk through the bastards...! Heheh" As he patted some ash into the now brimming ashtry.

"He maybe didnae hear the music 'at's all,'" said Don cutting in dryly.

I turned and shrugged somewhat agitatedly. "Fit fucking music?"

Don smiled out of the corner of his mouth, a little pleased with himself. "The scary cello-sort of music you hear in all horror films...which means, just don't fucking go to that castle, move on, go get a travel inn kinda music or when the doctor boy is about to switch on Frankenstein!"

I was still a little irascible and so picked on him a little, despite his efforts to lighten the situation. "Frankenstein's not the fucking monster; it's the doctor's name. Doctor fucking Frankenstein!! And he didnae switch him on, he waited till a lightning bolt hit him with enough energy to apparently reanimate the corpses he'd sown together. Fuckin 'switch him on!? He didnae fucking buy him fae Fischer fuckin' Price did he?"

Hippie Davie handed me a joint right in front of my face, "Hey Sensible, be sensible, stop being a twathead, smoke that and calm doon, for fuck's sake or you're demon will be jumping oot and ripping a" the cobbles oot the green!" Hippie Davie chuckled. "Oh fuck's sake! Sensible be sensible, brilliant!"

This nickname was going to be used against me, I could tell. I smiled, "Christ ok, sorry Don old son!"

Don just smiled back; he had a way of conveying that he was immune to my rants, kind of like a wise old uncle is to a kid with behavioural problems.

"Yeah, sorry I see what you're saying," I said. "Hippie Davie should have heard the music; there must have been a cello or....or rather an entire fuckin' orchestra playing in the background Hippie Davie, when you were plotting your gypsy head-fuck curse, y'know? Telling you not to go there..!"

Hippie Davie frowned, obviously feeling a little bit got at. "No, that's the thing, I really didn't think it would be that bad bro, just thought he'd get a fright and maybe wise the fuck up!" He leaned forward and caressed his fingers over the runes before scooping them back into a little muslin bag. I almost fathomed they said goodbye to me in my head, but shook out the very notion as nonsense. He implored us with his hands, "See...I reckon he's actually been feeding it consciously himself, unbeknown to us, coz something went way wrong there. It's almost like The Doc was the shadow and that 'thing' he visualised was more real."

At the moment he uttered that, the biggest chill swept around us. We all could see it, see that it was there all along, in the background and now it had a focus for its rage; Hippie Davie and now us!

"Shit!" exclaimed Hippie Davie, "wherever The Doc has been, that thing has been. It's been in your house everywhere, we've got tae do sumthing! I'm kind of ok, but you guys are exposed...in fact it's only coz of the natural protective elementals that surround you from the coven link and so on that it can't actually do something really bad to you, but look at how it got at Don last night, that was some real bad shit, he could have lost his life! Never mind his job and comforts; it is the worst kind of intent. There is real ill will there. It may find a way."

I sat back and thought, 'Yes it's clear, will is a force, if you concentrate enough and to make it work, you clothe it into something that is understood and accepted. The Doc clothed it with a raging demonic creature, as that's how he "sees" it. We see something similar at our end, because the mind can interpret it the same way, even if it's not exactly the same thing we all see, or what The Doc had in mind, it'd probably be quite similar. Hippie Davie nodded, acknowledging what I was saying;

"It's what Tibetan buddists call a Tulpa, a thing created from will, a thought form sent to alter our fate, affect our space-time in as negative a way as The Doc can make it!' I immediately thought of the 1950s movie *Forbidden Planet* and the unseen creature (the Id) which was an expression of the subconscious mind of Dr Morbius; such power unleashed, had ultimately destroyed the highly civilised Krell.

I looked over at Don, who seemed intrigued and a little pensive. Hippie Davie began scribbling symbols on some picture cards he produced like a conjurer from his back pocket, muttering to himself, but I didn't hear him, I was sliding away into my own little place. I felt a mushroom cloud go off in my head. Something strange welled up in me like when I felt the presence of the goddess, a feeling like good poetry being made in my head and coursing through my veins; tears sprang to my eyes as if in response to some force or pressure in my body. I felt like I was expanding outward from my belly and a strange confidence washed over me. Suddenly, I visualised everything, The Doc, his creation snarling at me, his friends, probably from the Dundee shaman tribe, everything in an instant. I felt it there and then I didn't need a circle, a spell book, a charm, a coven, anything at all. It was like I understood the rules of the game and could control it from here.

I didn't require any words or prayer, the 'will' was more like a shape, or a feeling; an emerging form more efficient than words could describe; in fact words were redundant. It was more like a non-verbal preliterate sense of will. I saw a vision of The Doc and his new pals in cloaks. I pushed the feeling of energy I had over the image. It was like a colourful smoke drifting over any words or will which they had. Sometimes their words punched a shape into it like a net about to break, but I just willed it further. It took some effort, but I could feel my willpower, empowered by the goddess, subdue every curse and stupid idea they had against me. I saw The Doc and imagined binding him there with a black ribbon, wrapping it all around him.

Then the demon was there, raging, screaming, threatening. A thought came into my head from some old silly film – 'laugh at the devil and you take his power.' I conjured up the energy of a laugh and examined how this felt in my body. Like a Qi-Gong exercise I sent the will of the laugh, which had a colour all of its own, circulating through my body. I then pulsed and expanded this 'laughter energy' into a gas which permeated every pore of the demon. My will changed its tone and immediately the expression of the 'thing' fell stoney silent and with a strange pitch that seemed to well within me I sent a power forth which made the image burst into bright blue flames. I was aware that somewhere I was making the sound in the distance for real, but I was far removed from that reality. I constructed a circle around me and suddenly bright blue electric flames engulfed my body, sterilising me, cleansing me from all the stuff that had been thrown my way. I could see negative pieces slide off me like molten plastic and disintegrate. I had a feeling that my mind had accepted something about magick and will. I thought, 'my fate' belongs to me!! How dare these fools try to influence me, interfere with my ability to exercise my will, it wasn't fair! And with that, energised by a sense of justice, the flames grew and my mood immediately lifted; I felt euphoric and happy. I let out a sound of joy and slowly opened my eyes to discover that I was standing up, slightly out of breath, with beads of sweat on my brow.

Hippie Davie and Don watched, open mouthed; their chairs scraped right back from me in apparent alarm. I looked down at my hands, which were positioned in front of my chest as if I were about to catch an invisible basketball.

Amber had come out and was staring at me with a mean look on her face. "What are you guys on?"

I stammered, "Sorry, for a minute there, I lost myself, I...lost myself!"

Hippie Davie held up a hand in defence "It's ok, it's ok we're just acting something out, it's cool, it's cool, just sit down and relax brother!"

I sat down, feeling quite drained, a little confused and perturbed.

Hippie Davie was smiling at me, "Fuck, just take this anyway!" It was a picture of Chewbacca the Wookie holding a lightsaber, with some symbols drawn into it.

Don regarded us both, "Gentlemen, we must act! There is no other recourse!"

Hippie Davie sprang up from his chair. "The game is afoot!" I tutted under my breath. "Bastard, I was going to say that!"

Some hours, joints, theorising and magick-making later we sat, we three, in a huddle within a magick circle in my flat. The incense drifted slowly from the altar. Its camphor smell conditioned me to think in 'circle mode,' (where the imagination expands out, after a fashion, to impregnate reality with possibility). Hippie Davie's own particular brand of incense also pervaded the space, kissing us with its presence. A sense of purpose filled the circle, as Hippie Davie, Don and I chanted to build power. The faster we spun, the more we could all feel the combined power multiply and flow. We all shuddered as if in some post orgasmic ecstasy as we instinctively stomped to a halt in synchrony as we all felt the power build to its maximum. We looked at each other through the veil of smoke,

"We're just gonna block them," I said, "that's all...bind them from doing any harm on us!"

"Or anything they conjure towards us!" exclaimed Hippie Davie.

Don had a slight evil glint in his eye. "Or we could send everything back to them and more!"

At that a strange but not too pleasant feeling pervaded the flat; the doors outside in the hall cracked and then too did the floorboards, as if something big had appeared there. In my mind's eye, I saw a massive hooded figure, bigger than the Hulk and exuding terrifying power. I could feel that it was goading us to seek damage; it was something that would have carried our will for revenge, but also feeding on this for its own shape and existence.

Hippie Davie held up a finger to his mouth, looking at Don. "Hold your tongue, young Padawan, the circle is filled with intent, speak in such a way and you'll attract the howling!"

I looked over at Hippie Davie aghast. "The fucking what?"

Hippie Davie shot a glance back, "You see it out there, beyond the circle, towards alllll the elements? Our thoughts and actions dictate how our 'will' will be interpreted here; it works at the speed of thought. We were all thinking what Don said, so saying it out loud carried the force towards that intent, we have to stop it. We have to be sensible, not give in to the dark side!" With that, Hippie Davie picked a small framed picture out from his sack under the altar and held it aloft. "Please, concentrate your minds on this."

I couldn't help but snigger; it was a picture of fucking Yoda, with a wise muppet smile creased along his little green face. Hippie Davie looked at me, his eyes bored into me halting my need to complain and de-rail the spell. I shrugged and concentrated on the face; Don was already staring at it intently.

Hippie Davie spoke, "We focus our minds on common sense and good, we are not here to drain our energies in such frivolous things as revenge, or stupid things like anger. Yoda, our figure of wisdom, Yoooodaaaam, Yooooooodaaaaa, Buddha, Yooodaaaa." His voice grew progressively louder and louder until he was near shouting.

A definite change spiralled around the circle. I found myself mouthing the words "Dad a daaa" louder and louder in harmony. In a flash, I saw what Hippie Davie was doing; saw how every child's dream was passionately linked into this image of good Jedi force overcoming the evil of corruption and dominance. It was powerful, as powerful as or even more so than established religions now as it had a mass appeal to practically every human being with a television around the globe. I saw it and understood at last why a grown man was fixated on child memorabilia. He was a serious magician, a shrewd player of the imaginative forces that govern and bent the group mind that magick fed into. And here's me thinking until now that he was just a spoilt middle class dreadlocked waster that just missed his mum and childhood!

With that, the child-like conviction that Yoda knows best filled the room with a new energy. The "howling," as Hippie Davie had put it, had vanished. Hippie Davie smiled and waved his plastic light saber to the centre of the circle. Instinctively and without saying a word, Don slowly did the same' I was still Wiccan and comparatively old school.I had a gnarled piece of willow wood that had seemed to speak to me from a park one day. I picked it up and joined the other two in the centre of the circle.

Hippie Davie was about to speak but Don interjected, "I've got this, The Batbox Bunch are no more, long live the Three Musketeers, we are all for one and one for all! We three friends, we protect each other and all is protected by each one. We make ourselves impenetrable, for our combined will is too big for the stupid, the weak, the jealous the egotistical, the misled, the fools that transgress against our will to do good and use the Force. So the Force is with us!"

I then interjected, "I call on the Goddess Matt and The Fates. Anger is a short-sighted release of rage; it cannot win against our combined wisdom." Knowing that just saying words was not enough, I concentrated and visualised this happening, felt these goddesses arriving with their beneficial knowledge and power.

Hippie Davie smiled and nodded. "The Force is with us, for the dark side is powerful but lacks vision, lacks sight. As Yang will become Yin, the force they send is spent and we feel it lap on the shore of our spell like the smallest of ripples, absorbed by the great force. Our friendship will keep us protected, all for one."

Then all three of us contributed, "And one for all!"

With that, Hippie Davie set about scattering runes around us and sat quietly looking beyond his closed eyes, staring intently ahead. After a few minutes he opened his eyes and spoke,

"Ha, I see you...I can 'see' their faces, their spell! They did all that stuff but didn't think to hide their crimes. They thought they were justified in 'protecting themselves.' I tell ya, I think The Doc has seriously misled them.

Don spoke up, "Probably been calling us for everything, making out we're a right bunch of psychic bandits or something!"

"Pretty much!" said Hippie Davie "Seems every time we were ribbing him or he did something stupid, he was harbouring a grudge. It's you he seems to hate the most Sean!"

"Gemma!" I said at once. "He hates me because I got off with Gemma."

"Precisely," said Hippie Davie. "Not to mention you called him a cunt in front of Lord Ursio...and vice-versa! But it's same with me and Amber, hated us for it; our relationship made him feel inadequate!"

Don agreed, "Yeah, s'why he hides behind magick and tries to make out he's some fantastic high medicine man, superhuman or something, he just feels inadequate coz he's failed so dismally at life!"

"Text book case that," Hippie Davie continued. "No job, depressed, lives with his Ma, girlfriend that bullies him, no money, no status and no self-esteem."

Don pondered further. "The problem is not so much him, it's what he's projected, what he's made!"

Hippie Davie looked thoughtful for a second. "Yessss, not so much of a problem really, not if you know how to stop things like that; it's not as if The Doc is all that skilled, this rage ultimately driven by his own inadequacies and fears. Only a fool would purposely bring such a thing into existence and try to use it against someone else. I mean ultimately it hates him, like he hates himself, so we just have to give it that awareness and by default he will gain that awareness."

I looked at Hippie Davie a little nervously; I wondered where his morals stood on this.

Don shrugged, "Welllll, I just want it away from me, I don't like feeling it around, it interferes with the ambiance of my work and poor Harry's not happy at all; I mean, it's unacceptable."

I sat back for a moment in meditation, "I dunno, I still worry aboot The poor old Doc, one minute he's a mate, yeah a bit two faced maybe, but still a mate and the next he's consigned to a self-destructing nutter!"

Hippie Davie asserted, "Look, he always was a fuckin' nutter, he's a sinister fuckin' human being that just brings spite and bullshit into people's lives. He'd have no problem trying to fuck you up and he even doesn't care how much lies and deceit and corruption of other people he employs along the way! I tell you, I always knew he was big trouble, that's why I tried to keep my distance from him and now he's contaminated the Newmachar circle and every fucking one else he's touched! I've got to say this Sensible old son, you're way too trusting and you've been a little bit naïve!"

Don nodded. "Yup; av never trusted him, but you kept on saying, he's a maaaate, it'll be a'wright."

I held up my hand, "All right, jeez, well I just thought he was a bit of blow hard, harmless really!"

Hippie Davie, now seeming like a chastising teacher or fed up father, rounded on me. "You can't be flippant or blasé with regard to magick and circles, you're not dealing with people anymore, but ultra-people, not just the mundane, but the ultra-mundane and not only waking consciousness but the depth of the subconscious! Petty jealousies, people with lousy character traits, well they get amplified out of all proportion; I'm telling you, Jeez Mags should have telt you this!"

I cast my eyes over at Don who shuffled a little and then looked down on the floor. "Well am sure Mags probably trusts working with the Goddess, that she'll ultimately sort everything out!?" I realised that I was grasping at straws and sounding a little bit too much like Don.

Don nodded. "Absolutely!"

Hippie Davie sighed. "To tell you the truth, that's my problem with Wicca and circles and Newmachar etc. There's no guidance, no way of weeding out fools, no way of keeping people on a proper path, I mean you leave that to people to do themselves and they will stray!"

I shook my head. "Well, well fucking well, keep people on the path, keep people in their place so they don't stray!? You sound less like an anarchist and more like the fucking church!"

"Yup, Wicca's not about that," Don said, "it's about being free, being anarchistic and being truly human!"

Hippie Davie seemed even more fatherly and grown up all of a sudden. "Exactly! I'm all in favour of that, but people, humans, aren't ready! To paraphrase Sartre, People equal shit! That's why I ain't got faith in anarchy anymore, that's why punk is dead, t'aint dead, it's fucking dreaming, mate! That's why I'm in favour of structure, of tuition of taking steps and adhering to a path, that's why I do believe in *Star Wars* coz it's a readily accessible path and is uncontaminated by corruption, the church or political gain, it's as near as human aspirations for good over evil as we can get. You can't go wrong with it!"

There was what seemed like a long pause as we all looked at each other. My face contorted in contemplation, I had no argument. Don looking bemused as ever, started to smirk, "Well hark at O.B Wonky Knobby there."

We all burst into the laughter of relief.

I nodded, "Too true brother!" I conceded to Hippie Davie in an 'if you can't beat 'em join 'em kind of way. "Actually, I kind of agree with you! I know the problem with religion; I know the problem with human beings!" I continued quite resolutely.

Hippie Davie looked interested while Don seemed to sigh.

"Quite simply put, we're not really homo-sapiens!" I exclaimed triumphantly.

Hippie Davie nodded slowly, seeming to get the idea.

Don just giggled, "You speak for yourself ape man fae Northfield!"

I shrugged, "Av; known more true human beings in Northfield than any other part of Aberdeen!"

Hippie Davie looked interested. "You mean we're half Neanderthal or something?"

I suppressed a smile, relishing the opportunity to continue unchallenged. "No, well maybe, but not even that; Neanderthals were very successful and probably lived in harmony with their environment! No, what I mean is, 'sapiens,' right, means 'sapient,' yeah? Aware! Well I say human beings are not as 'aware' as we'd like to think we are!"

Don nodded in approval. "Yeah I see, like not everybody is aware of magick and how the world actually fucking works, most people just go to their work, watch T.V. and don't actually think much at all, zombies on auto-pilot mostly!"

I agreed; "Well yeah but that's not really my point, I mean quite simply an awareness of how we influence everything around us! I mean, sure we have a conscious awareness of ourselves and that which is around us. We eat, we talk, we communicate our feelings and we can empathise with others, cry when we watch a film, appreciate great art, have free will *etc*. See; yeah art! We make such a big deal of art or paintings, music or poerty, the things that move us and touch our core humanty! coz they force us to think in that moment and grasp our humanity." I became more emotional and more animated with the point I had arrived at; "*But why* does it take a poem or piece of art to move us like that?" I said imploringly. "Why aren't we 'that aware' every second, it's like we're closed off from that awareness in our day to day lives! I mean, look around the world, human beings lack the ultimate ability to empathise in totality! We are NOT AWARE of the consequences of our actions. We don't 'feel' the consequences of our actions, we're closed to it."

The other two looked upwards pensively, as the obvious of what I was saying struck them, they'd never thought of this before. I carried on explaining why I thought this was so.

"There are *degrees* of conscious awareness, I'm sure and the majority of the time we may be in a waking comatose kinda sleep; a kind of 'rolling intelligence,' similar to what earlier ancestral humans may have possessed. Presenting episodes of awareness but unable to be completely aware and cross reference all consequences but definitely ample for 'in the moment' survival; like dogs y'know!? S'why the Neanderthals, for example, never had much in the way of innovation of tool design in thousands of years? They obviously were not aware of their lack of innovation just as we are not aware of our lack of vision and future insight. Yes, we are orders of magnitude better, but not as supreme as the name *homo sapiens* would make you believe. I still think we exhibit significant aspects of the primal animal influences that prevent us from being aware of our complete mental potential. This animal-primate rolling 'in the moment awareness' where we fail to consider future consequences of actions, y'know!? People smoke and eat badly all the time, though we know it's bad. The climate will heat up and affect every aspect of our ecosystem. Take stuff like wars, genocide, slavery, these things are like animal expressions of dominance. However, empathy for human suffering is not part of our priorities, as it is all too easily switched off. So from day to day, I don't think people have enough empathy, or maybe I am just being overly sensitive! But I cannot come to any other conclusion. Science might make us aware of our own human nature, our 'ingroup-outgroup' tribal psychology, impulses, social cohesion and the list goes on. Just as science has given us a fantastic perspective that our own sun is one of many; yet we refuse to act on any of that that information. We cannot seem to cross reference common sense with policy, intimate relations, religious ideology and cohabitation with other groups we share the planet with, with self knowledge. Our history is a slow teasing out of co-operative successful hunter gatherers, to the barbaric human zoo. Psychology informs us that the recent modern mass deaths of the world wars were a result of blind obedience; of switching off thinking. *Yes* there has been a counter-culture of reason and spiritual awakening but it hasn't caught on. Counter culture, in my view, represents the better portion of our 'humanity,' a raising of consciousness, a societal enlightenment towards what the humanistic psychology movement terms actualisation and transcendence. S'why the Beatles had so much in synchrony with Indian mysticism."

"Hippie Davie was clapping and Don was nodding, "Yeah fucking right brother!"

I wasn't sure if they were taking the piss or not, nor cared; my own articulation of this thought seemed quite clear to me and I marched on with the sermon. "Anarchy, feminism, worker's rights, human rights, ban the bomb and other such consciousness raising events, are, however perhaps, too slow in my opinion! So! Therefore we are not '*homo-sapien*' at all. Let's get it right, we should be more accurately relabelled as *Homo demi-sapien*. Half-aware upright, apes! Upright apes on holiday, carrying credit cards, swinging through coffee shops like trees in a fucking forest of chrome, concrete and plastic; that's all we are. And those that believe we're divine, well I say; so why don't we act like it? How could we act like it? Provide people religious morals? I mean nah; you cannot just provide people with rules and expect them to follow them! That can never be successfully enforced by the churches or any other power, just like we were saying the other day Don!

A change of societies, of priorities, of expectations of morals can only improve and come about as a sort of zeitgeist. People, not anarchism nor Marxism or Jism fucking-ism, but just...trust! A religion/way of thinking based on perfect trust is the only way possible. It would be powerful enough if enough people had trust in human nature enlightenment and science! Perfect love in other words; so that, my friends, is MY religion. People! 'Hell might be other people,' to Sartre, but 'people have the potential to be in the company of heaven' to me!"

Don stood up in mock ovation and applauded, as Hippie Davie smiled at me and said, "Well, well, well you ARE a fucking hippie after all!"

I shrugged. "Something like that! Well if being a hippie is all about being true to the ideals of common sense, just like rational science, then I'd be a...I don't know, what's a hippie scientist, Davie?"

Hippie Davie pressed his lips together and shrugged. "James Lovelock!?"

I laughed out loud, while Don looked at both of us with a deadpan expression that spoke volumes.

"Maybe I'm a hippie-analyst or something!" I said whimsically.

Don, of course got a shot away as quick as he could. "More like an anal less -hippie."

"Or a lippy analness or, or wait for it...a hairy analness," Hippie Davie joined in.

Don giggled, but I had a glint of inspiration. "Well you're a hairy-fuckin-mess! So there!"

Don howled like a wolf whilst Hippie Davie just took a bow and ruffled his big mop of dreads at me, apparently proud of being the big hairy mess in the group!

Don then piped up, "Hey, Hippie Davie's also a fucking good 'spaced'-scientist! Does that count?"

Hippie Davie acknowledged this with a resigned frown and I giggled, slightly jealous that Hippie Davie could always gain so much respect, while I always seemed the boring one. I joined in the fun. "He's a psychonaut who explores the laws of the inner universe!"

Hippie Davie looked over, smiling from his eyes. "And you're a cycle nut exploring the laws of the green cross code!"

'Ouch...touché ya bastard,' I thought as I grimaced and held my two fingers up at him, while Don laughed uproariously at my expense.

I felt the need to change the subject back to my argument, which was still at the back of my mind, to put a whipped cream dollop on the top of it.

"Anyway, as I was saying, we are not 'completely aware' and everybody should be 'aware' of that fact, everybody should be taught first year psychology in primary school, the world over. Let's all realise we're the same fucking species and that we're imperfect and get over it! That there's a huge potential in perception awaiting us that artists, poets and philosophers; people like David Bowie have been guiding us to realise. A light years step in self-perception, as awesome to take in as when Giordano Bruno first led us into the path of the heightened awareness of our place in the galaxy in the sixteenth century! And you know what; we're still resisting his initial idea. There are many stars to have awareness of...we should carry on the work of Giordano Bruno!"

Don merely mused, scratching his chin, "Mmmm!" while Hippie Davie muttered, "Very sensibbbbble!"

"Vintage sensible!" said Don nodding in Hippie Davie's direction, to convey his point.

Hippie Davie sighed. "Ah well, back to the imperfect world of twats and demons. Let's get to the real task at hand, getting this fucking influence away from Don and I."

I waited for a second for the gap with the absence of my name to be filled. "What about me then? Gonna leave me to have my fucking eyes scratched oot by the Terror O' Torry!"

Don chuckled. "Terror O' Torry! Heheh you're a twat sometimes!"

Hippie Davie looked at me, holding my gaze for a second. "Are you serious? After what you did? You're in the clear, there's not a trace of anything around you anymore!"

I was surprised and looked innocent. "What do you mean?" I stammered.

Hippie Davie, looking a little impatient, I thought, tutted and shook his dreadlocked head in resignation. "You blasted it all away from you, I'm not sure how, but in terms of your aura man, everything around you that shouldn't be, just blew away like so much cobwebs! I'm not sure what you did, or what you used, but I am sure it worked quite well!"

This time I wasn't so surprised. "Yeah, yeah I'm aware of it! I'm not sure how I did it either, but I really just felt the need to do it. They really annoyed me you know?"

Hippie Davie raised his eyebrows and looked over at Don, who smirked back and blew smoke from the corner of his mouth in mock derision. "Remind us never to piss you off too much then, bro!"

The strange notion that my mates respected me and didn't think of me as a bit of a push over crossed my mind. Wow, when did that happen? How and when did I become such a respected member of a group and when did I become so obviously proficient at magick? I sat back and relaxed a little, watching Hippie Davie and Don with fixed curiosity. Hippie Davie fashioned a piece of The Doc's old robe that he had hacked off earlier into a bunch between his hands. He whispered some incantation over it and then threw it into the centre of the circle, where it landed like a sick dove. Then he lit three candles positioned around it. I felt a little sad and a bit weird as I mused that the last time I had set eyes on that robe was when The Doc had it draped over his head and was entertaining us with the whole "Lord Arse-io" routine. However, I should have known then that it really was no joke, it was serious. Further, deriding him in front of his "pupils" during the Shaman demonstration had been the last straw. It set in motion The Doc's extreme resentment and feelings of humiliation leading us all to this point, talk about Karma!

As soon as Hippie Davie lit the last candle both he and Don stepped back and pointed their self-lit athames, made in Hong Kong, toward the piece of cloth. Even as I tried I couldn't stifle a chuckle, which they studiously ignored. Both Don and Hippie Davie recited in synchrony, "Let The Doc's Tulpa be drawn into this vessel rich in his aura! We command you in the name of the force, the light side and the will of the universe!" I was still chuckling and feeling a little superior all of a sudden. After all, all I had to do was close my eyes and will them into a thousand pieces, so it seemed. Condescendingly, I scoffed, "Bloody hell, what a right carry on you fuckin' Jedis hold!"

Don looked over, looking a little angry now, more with The Doc than me, but my timing was not good. "Fuckin' shut up you, or you'll feel the Force o' this fucking thing right up your erse!"

I balked, "Oooh hark at you, well I never! If Luke Skywalker could hear you now!"

Hippie Davie, however, was resolutely staring towards the piece of cloth. "Give it a rest, you two! Look!"

Don and I both glanced back at the wad of old robe, curiously it did look as if it had grown a little and the shadows did appear to resemble eye sockets. The more we fixed our gaze on it, the surer I was it did look sorta cat-like and crumpled kinda like The Doc's expression could be, if it had whispered, "Without a doubt!" I wouldn't have been the least bit surprised! The candles flickered and instantly it took on even more of a cat-like face appearance. Don whispered, "Fuck me!" at the same point, echoing what was in my own head. He clearly was seeing the same as I was, as we all were. Hippie Davie then lowered his battery operated light saber-athame and spoke sternly to the figure.

"We order you to retreat and leave us in the name of his master Luke and Yoda and the holy Jedi will of the universe. You will go back to whence you came!"

At that point, Don, still angry with me, lost a little self-control, clearly the least vociferous of The Doc's antics over the year or so and usually one to defend him, his treatment by The Doc boiled over. He grimaced and then brought his plastic lightsaber down in onto the cloth,

"Youoooo little basterd." He then started thwacking the cloth with a similar frenzy to the house maid in Tom and Jerry cartoons. "That's for scaring Harry and that's ma video and that's…"

Hippie Davie tried to fend him off. "Whoa, whoa whoaaa, fuckin' hell, cool it bro, remember we have purpose here!?"

The ambience of Hippie Davie's circle however, had gone; I was now chuckling with laughter. "Yooos a naughty demon vampire pussy cat, so yooo is heheheheh." Funnily enough, the image in my head was eerily similar to the sight of The Doc running around my flat trying to get away as Pamela slapped him around with a frying pan in the coupon for cheating on her.

Hippie Davie quickly reaffirmed the initial ambience and sternly chastised Don and I for being foolish; we guiltily fell silent, but I daren't look at him, else I would go off again. Instead, I stared at the cloth that still remained face like, despite its hefty beating, I even though it had grown a little bump on its head. I wondered if whether on the astral a bump had appeared in conjunction with the sound effect up-octave whistle that occured when Tom gets a big volcanic mound of a lump on his head. I so wanted to inform the others of my observation, but Hippie Davie, almost in anticipation, shushed us, even though no-one was speaking! I knew then it wouldn't have been a good time; I bit my lip to repress my mirth and looked on.

Again Hippie Davie spoke to the creature to leave them as did Don. Then he sprayed it with some gummy looking substance and said in chilling tones,

"We bind you and your master The Doc! And now we will get rid of your vile influence on us and the ones we love forever!" With that, he scooped it up and I almost thought the face stared back, with bewildered looking fear. He then marched through to the bathroom and threw it into the toilet and with another quick move, threw his hand with his zippo lighter into the bowl. The element of fire illuminated the room as flames shot upwards out of the bowl, purifying the anger. After a few seconds he pulled the handle and we watched the whirling blackened cloth zip around and around received now by the element of water, dowsing the emotion. I almost thought I heard it scream as the last thing I saw was a shape like an open mouth crying as flames disappeared beneath the foam. Don, Hippie Davie and I, the three musketeers, were free, as the water chugged to calmness and the ringing in our ears subsided.

Don spoke for us all, "Goodbye Doc old son, Goddess help you mate!"

## *Chapter 11*:
## Under the streets beneath the waking world

Life has a tendency to pull you back to the mundane; the clock ticks on, alarms go off, we all jump out of bed to go to work or follow the same routine. It's easier to slip back into a semi-conscious state, in order to get through the day, week or month. There's really no point in being over-awake, overly stimulated for such activities. It's the human condition. We all used to be hunter-gatherers, running in the woods, fighting wild beasts or slaying dragons; but we're mostly hunter–grocery pickers, fighting wild bosses or trying to slay our anxieties. My anxieties were building fast. It had, in the blink of an eye, become my final year. I had wasted my time having way too much fun or just being lazy. Now I had to cram in as much as possible to try to stop myself actually failing! This was looking like it was quite probable, but even the threat of that failed to motivate me completely.

Things with The Doc took a bit of a back seat now for a while and I visited the green less and less. I even skipped the odd Esbat as I needed to pull all my spare time for deadlines. Of course, as soon as I had some credit time-wise, due to cancelling some social thing, I squandered it in front of the telly or listening to music. I hated that! As if I had I gone socialising instead, I would just worry that I wasn't at home doing preparation. I was terrible; I had all the work ethic of a Hollywood version of a Roman emperor on holidays, minus the grapes and array of sex-slaves. Although it was hard for me, I did make some progress.

I thought that would be it, that we were free from The Doc's envy, madness and badness. For a while all was normal, Don nearly lost his job, but the spell we had done seemed to do the trick. The evidence became misplaced and the company suddenly accepted that the old T.V. was more than likely out of commission. They banned T.V's in the reception as a compromise! Don just started sneaking upstairs to the conference room; it was far more comfortable there anyway so I at least found it much more to my liking! However, as summer rolled on, I discovered that I was no longer a student. Real life had finally caught up with me and I found myself working as a postman as a stop gap. It was good for the duration of summer but became more and more tiring as time went on. I graduated with a decent degree, but I just didn't care too much; I had no real ambition or direction. I thought about combining my interest in evolution and psychology but never really seriously tried to do anything about it. For the moment, I was content just being me and sitting with my mates. Perhaps chilling right here down the Green was where I was meant to be. I'd slouch back in quiet contemplation as Hippie Davie quietly rolled himself a mid-afternoon fatty whilst Don would check his pocket timepiece on a chain, thinking; I am expressing my will here just nicely, thank you very much.

The postman job I had, though, was killing me; I was so tired all the time. What had been an enjoyable summer job, which I even used to look forward to doing, was becoming more wearisome as time wore on. The six-day-a-week getting up in practically the middle of the night was taking its toll as my weekends evaporated into desperate attempts to catch up on sleep and then prepare for work again on the Monday morning (which was really Sunday night). The colder and darker the days became, the grimmer they became. Snow wasn't good for plodding through, especially in blizzards, but at least I could pull my bag behind me like some member of Scott's artic expedition who'd taken a wrong turn in Greenland and found himself, Narnia-like, plodding under the floodlit streets of Dyce, with everyone's mail for the whole trip in one bag.

At least I had most of the afternoon free to wander down to the green and sit and enjoy a coffee or two with my mates. However abject tiredness often meant I would be asleep within twenty minutes of my weary behind hitting the sofa. Some people, it seems, are made for the working life and even thrive on it. But my physiology was such that I needed to just sit for long periods of time and I knew in my heart that I would probably never find a boredom limit for day time T.V, sitting enjoying a coffee 'n ciggie or two or even having a nap. The working world is not fit for a peaceful existence. There you have to be content with only fifteen minutes for a coffee break. Fifteen minutes? My body is just getting warmed up after fifteen minutes, it's almost cruel to make me stand up and go back to a job; a coffeless, T.V.-less job. Why would I ever prefer going to work all day anyway? I had a nice comfy furnished house but all I seemed to do in it was sleep!

So working all morning was wearisome to say the least, however, as I was to discover, such interruptions to my normal sleeping routine were going to have a strange and beneficial side effect. It seems that oscillating sleep hormone levels washing through my brain could have similar side effects as quaffing fairly modest doses of Alchemist-Al's wines had. Later at home as I slumped onto my sofa I became aware of a slight bobbing feeling and the sensation of something over my head. I opened my eyes to be met with a bright and disorientating light in my eyes. I squinted but the brightness merely dulled slightly, but I couldn't see or make out anything. 'Why,' I thought, 'is there such a bright light in my living room? Had the aliens finally come for me? Were lots of little beings with long E.T. necks coming to take me away?' Then I felt the sensation of turning around, as if I was drifting slightly, the room focused into view and suddenly, with a degree of shock and surprise I realised exactly where I was. I was, it seems, bobbing along my ceiling, the bright light had been the light bulb which was in my face and my actual body was slumped below peacefully snoozing alone on my sofa. Yet here I was watching everything, thinking rationaly in an 'awake' type of consciousness and very aware of my living room and everything in it.

I could hear the sounds of water in pipes running through the flats around me, amplified with some weird sense of life. The murmurring ghosts of the people who had left their imprints in this place faded in and out of range and I could hear my ex-girlfriend Jen walking and wringing her hands in anxiety in the next room even though I knew she wasn't there in person. 'It's her ghost,' I thought, as I bobbed along the ceiling; 'it's an imprint of her emotions, nothing more.' Though I also knew it was connected to her and even could communicate with me, if I had the notion to. I wasn't afraid, only curious; 'What kind of imprints do we leave on this world?' I thought, 'we are not even aware of it, yet what we do remains! It stays like a stain here.' No sooner had I had this thought, I suddenly felt myself rushing at high speed, towards and then straight through the wall of the room to my left. I could sense the cavity between stones and see old pieces of wood and dusty dry clumps of foam as I rushed past them. Consequently, I found myself barrelling along over hills and streams faster than a jet fighter.

In the next moment, I was walking past a very busy street, filled with people wearing all colours. The people were modern, but some of them were dressed also in very old fashioned looking clothes. I watched with interest as a horse and cart slowly moved unperturbed by large buses and shiny impatient cars. The place itself was at once old and very new. I could sense it was a clear day, in the present but also the scene sometimes seemed vague, old and black with chimney smoke. I felt like I was seeing a number of scenes all superimposed at the same time. However, despite this, this was not in the least bit confusing or chaotic. I knew some people could see me, as they stared at me and walked out of my way, whilst others seemed to look through me and walk straight towards me, forcing me to glide past them like some cloud around a fast-moving vehicle. I was very familiar with this mode of consciousness, as shadow walking had been second nature to me once before.

I was drawn down a cobbled street and I found myself walking with purpose along it; I walked between a bank and some old building, which also momentarily took on the texture of strong golden looking bricks and mortar rising up to take the place of the tattered old shacks there. There was a feeling of newness of resurrection and strong new purpose trying to obliterate the dear loved but forgotten shacks, which seemed to emanate a life and purpose of that life now gone but now eternal also. It was like they had staked their claim to exist forever. They somehow lent a texture, a feeling and a sense of "being" and connection to the environment. As I walked down the street I could see old souls waft along there, piercing eyes stared out of dirty faces wearing rags that would defy belief, even by today's homeless standards. These souls had suffered more it was clear and they emanated this, which commanded a bit of respect and sympathy. They watched me like I was from another planet and I immediately felt guilty. Even my postie job couldn't compare to the hours of toil and lack of freedom their faces seemed to convey and I felt hugely privileged in comparison.

As I walked further down the sloping cobbled brae, the smell of dampness and faeces burned my nostrils and the back of my throat. I now had to watch where I was walking as slimy things and wetness was strewn all across the cobbles at my feet. It was disgusting, how could the council in this place allow the rubbish to accumulate like this? Further down the street meant further darkness and even though it was daytime, I was aware the area was plunged into a kind of perpetual night. A gaping hole emerged as a doorway to utter blackness beckoning me to go in further. I was reluctant but I could see people coming and going, going down into the darkness that was their home. They lived in hell, it was clear to me, but I wondered why they would voluntarily remain there, taking their chances in the dark and filth. Something told me that many who went down into its dark winding stinking interior would never come out of again alive. Dogs skirted about like rats, reminding me of some L. S. Lowry painting come to life. The dogs and people alike seemed unaware of the gloom, as if it was their home and they knew nothing else. I was very wary; people were staring and I felt really out of place. An old man started walking towards me, a sinister glee in his eyes, seeming to understand I didn't know where I was. He mouthed something like "Here kitty, kitty, are you lost?" in a strange but very sinister Highland accent, which sent a real shiver through me. Smiling was all I could do but I knew this was just making it worse, making him advance further. I tried to brush him away with my hand, trying to motion I was fine, that I didn't need help. But I could sense that he could sense my feelings of anxiety as my voice sounded weak. I tried to will myself to sound more self-assured, but only a squeak came out. He strode further almost subduing me as he came for what, I did not know, nor would like to find out.

Then I remembered the second floor of the regent building, how "Harry" had jumped back from me. Ah! A circle of protection – witchcraft! It came flooding back to me. Instinctively, I drew a circle around myself and then remembering a pathworking at Newmachar where the Goddess gifted me a cloak of power and protection, I summoned it. It appeared in my hands. I almost clapped with glee. I had forgotten I was a witch, a magician. I could put my imagination to use. I slung the cloak around me and then asked the Goddess to guide and protect me. Immediately, I could feel myself grow in stature and I even felt myself stabilise, become more solid and heavier. I was filled with confidence.

I turned to the man who had paused and spoke very clearly, "No ta mate, am a' right, cheers!"

He stopped dead and spun around on his heels, seeming to curse as he did so. People stopped staring or didn't seem to notice me at all. I resumed my journey into Hell. Hell was a maze of winding tunnels, disorientating, smelly, damp and rife with people with disease. Suffering pain clung to the walls, asserting itself as part of life here. I had imagined hell as a child and seen in my mind's eyes glowing rocks and fire. But this was much worse I would trade this for fire and brimstone any day. At least fire cleanses.

I was becoming concerned that I may never find myself out again, or that my cloak would forever be tarnished with the smell and sense of decay. I could understand why in the Middle Ages people thought smells could bring disease. I felt here that indeed it could. The smell seemed to permeate to your very core. I knew I was just here to observe, I could feel that but I wondered if I was making a huge mistake wandering down these dark corridors. Despite my cloak and magick, the fear tore at my senses. I was afraid that I would emit my insecurity to all and sundry down here; the "wolves," I was sure, were not too far away from me. Then I heard the voices, modern sounding voices, people who talked with more joy in their voices than the other residences of hell. I drifted towards the source and then found myself motionless in the doorway looking at a crowd of people. They were dressed in robes; black robes with emblems of high magick sigils and other symbols resembling a "Fields of the Nephilim" album cover sewn all over them. I was invisible to them apparently, but I still kept perfectly still and quiet, just in case. One guy, who looked a little like Kurt Cobain with long hair and a pock marked face looked suspiciously in my direction. He drew on a cigarette and looked for all the world like some pirate, or a follower of misrule. Although he did look like my kind of person, my heightened instincts told me immediately that he was a seeker of danger, despite the cost. He had no grounding, no rules it seems. He was, in short, trouble! Something about him reminded me of The Doc. Then no sooner had I thought that then I was aware of The Doc himself. I couldn't see him in the darkness in the crowd but I knew he was there. Then his little face morphed into view. He looked anxious, scared even but also filled with an intensity for revenge. His whole body exuded a dire need to inflict vengeance. No change there; I was almost pleased to see him!

I really didn't want to be standing there, but I was filled with curiosity. What on earth was The Doc doing here? Who were these evil looking Nephilim pirates? It certainly wasn't the Dundee crowd. They were by and large very nice and pleasant people, who'd visited Mag's circle once. And most of all, where the fuck was I? Had The Doc actually ended up in Hell? I supposed there was no other place left for him.

As I stood there I found it was difficult to observe and I quivered and felt sick at times. As the ritual proceeded, there were animal like howls and explosions of emotions and energy that I could see erupt and cover everything, including the participants and the walls. Screams and howls filled the room and the hooded figures danced and flung themselves around the cavernous room. The scene was like a spectacle from *Tam O' Shanter*, the movie if directed by Quentin Tarrantino!

Instinctively I backed away and pressed myself hard against the wall in front of the cave-like opening opposite a cellar like room, which I half sunk through like it was made of treacle. I couldn't understand what was going on, but I knew enough that it really wasn't good. The Doc himself was crying and his body shook with rage as he mouthed inaudible incantations and dedications through clenched teeth, like a wronged schoolboy swearing revenge and dedication to the devil himself. I saw him clutch something in his hand and I realised, with a huge sense of disappointment and sadness, that it was a picture of us, the Batbox bunch in happier times. I felt sorry for him, I wanted to hug him and I wanted to shout out to him to not go any further, that he was making a huge mistake. But he wouldn't have heard me anyway.

The chanting and snake-like hypnotic lull of the group seemed to amplify and focus The Doc's dark intent. The pirate of the group leaped and yelled and squatted on all fours and ran around The Doc like a possessed dog, licking at his calves and occasionally screaming, his head arched back like a howling wolf demon. I could see a mirror and then another mirror with drawings on it that was held up in front of The Doc. I could see that the first mirror was actually a door with a mirror on it. Then there was a frightening clash of breaking glass, like the universe itself was being rent in two. Then darkness and silence fell, soon followed by the sound of panting men beneath hoods for some agonising, evil minutes. It was the type of evil silence, born out of expectation before a strike of death. The will that drives war and slaughter, the mind of the predator focused at its most lethal sharpness. Injustice freed with unstoppable lust. I realised, in that split second, there was no need for a Devil or Hell, only people and their intentions. Unchecked, the worst intentions of people cling to the walls like marmalade and decay, like I had seen during the ritual, which was basically a type of spiritual pollution.

I froze, fear permeating me, I felt as if I was there in person, not as a shadow anymore but vulnerable, present and visible. Suddenly there was an inhuman screech and the sound of wings filled the air. A lean tall demonic figure loomed upward, confused, licking its lips regarding the crowd before it. They knelt, not seeing but perhaps feeling the awesome sick presence of the beast in the room. The Doc looked dazed, like a school kid that had stayed up too late, not understanding what was going on, slightly afraid, lost and drained of energy. The others looked wide-eyed around the room and at each other but not seeming to see the strange terrible looking hawk-like presence of the wizened awful structure in the centre of the room. I'm sure if they had they would go mad or instantly try to reverse all that they had done. I was sickened and afraid, daring not to even move. But then suddenly a hawk like shrill filled my ears and the thing turned towards me piercing holes where eyes should be gaped in my direction. Its face seemed to be formed loosely from old sack like material as it had suffered the worst kind of curse, too evil for even human semblance at all. Then with an *awwwwnnnnnhhhhh* sound, like an animal about to fumble for some awful sentence, its face seemed to loom out of the dark, filling the room as if it was searching for me, trying to latch onto me, probing in the darkness, feeling my presence like a hungry owl sensing a helpless mouse in the dark, desperately scrabbling for it, with only a matter of time before latching the prey in a merciless and final deathgrip. Terrible talons waited, ready to bury into my innocent body, to inflict me with madness, fear and disorder. I wanted to flee; I even thought I should but my shadow body at this time seemed to have a will of its own. A strange feeling occurred to me, like at the back of my mind another part of my brain was making decisions. It was like my soul self parallel to me, was me as well, but out of sync with my ego. As the pitiless pits of eye socket ate into my image and focused some old timeless hatred of will towards me, my voice rang out with courage I swear I would never have guessed was in me.

"Aye - But Hail to thee HEY- KA-TEY! Guardian to me in Hell whose torch-light will not die, I fear not the shadows or the lifeless and accursed! Hail Queen of night! Nothing that moves in this dark place can bear your power and might, ruler of all spirits, Witch-Queen, Torch-Bearer, Phosphorus and Soteira! And with that my arm raised up and I made a sign with my fingers a sharp memory of another 'me' shot and seared across my brain like an emotional dart. Far away in another time my grandmother had shown me as a child how to make the sign to call Isis in times of fear. My fingers arched and stood between me and the demon creating a blinding light for a few seconds which lit the tunnels. In a flash I saw an awesome brilliant white, female shaped figure, curiously like the lunar goddess amulets sold in every new-age shop tapered at the top, hips visible and no real defined legs. She appeared to hold aloft a torch as an intense white light streamed around the cavern, like an exploding flash bulb. It was magnificent! Even all the coven members stared in my direction and I could see The

Doc's confused face for a fraction of a second, look towards mine. The demon reared back, unable to withstand the light of the Goddess, normally having real contempt for women's form and now fearing its intensity. It gave me the time I needed, as I ran backwards towards the exit of hell, finding myself hurtling towards the cobbled street like a jet's shadow on the ground. But it was behind me and it would not stop following me, raging it seemed to yell at me as I burst out of the tunnel. A gravelly rasping voice scratched its way along the walls behind me; "I will fynd yoooo and I will hauuuuunt yoo," which seemed to mean hunt and hurt all at the same time.

I understood that all I had done had been to create a small pause against the inevitable wave or pulse of 'will' that was flowing towards me like a fucking torrent. A burst dam of the damned, 'will' fuelled by hate and something I didn't understand or could be prepared for, aimed to engulf me in destruction and chaos. I opened my eyes suddenly on my couch, feeling very hot and disorientated. I shot forward and knelt, vomiting onto the floor as I did so, surprised at the ferocity of illness that was upon me and confused as to how much was fact or my screwed up imagination. Was I working too hard? But I knew deep down I had in actual fact witnessed something, as if by chance, something that had and was happening.

I collected myself and made a cup of tea. I had to think! How much of that was my imagination? I saw it for real, I was sure of it, that had to be a real place, but where was it? I know it wasn't Aberdeen, as the buildings weren't granite grey! It was more like some Scottish or Irish old town, kinda like Dublin. I had been there for a few days before starting university. Although deep down I was sure I had seen a little of Edinburgh, although I had never been there before in my life! I was feeling quite shaken and came to the conclusion that doing nothing was unacceptable. Even if it had been some weird figment of my imagination it was now, in a sense, very real. I snatched up the phone and tried to get through to Don.

He answered half asleep, "Hello what the fuck do you want at this time of day? Somebody better be deed!"

I felt a little guilty as to him this was probably the equivalent of six in the morning. If it wasn't for the fact that I knew he had an hour or twos kip after four a.m. whilst getting paid for it, I would feel even more guilt! "You'd better get over to the Green, we've got big trouble!"

Some hours later, the other musketeers sat solemn faced whilst I recounted the events from earlier that afternoon. Hippie Davie, for the first time, looked quite aghast at times, especially on mention of the strange coven antics and the smashing mirror routine. Davie and Don exchanged horrified looks as I described the strange lank demonic form and the way it fixated on me.

Don spoke first. "Sooo Doc was holding a picture of all of us?"

"It looked like it, to be honest," I replied solemnly, although secretly I was quite relieved that if I was fucked, my friends were fucked, too. Humans are quite illogical when it comes to how we treat and care for the people that matter to us most.

Don shook his head in frustration, "Fuck! I thought we'd dealt with all this shit!"

"I don't understand!" I replied, I thought we had too...Do you think I might have imagined it, like maybe it's a result of some deep down guilt or something?"

Hippie Davie lent back and looked skyward, seeming to contemplate life as a cloud for a few seconds. "Nah...I don't think you imagined that and I'm fairly sure if you were to put your hand on heart, you'd admit that you know you didn't just imagine it either!?"

I nodded, "Yep!" I knew it, too.

Hippie Davie continued, "Nah, that definitely sounded like astral projection all right, no doubt about it in my mind, the shadow body, the flying through the walls and away at high velocity, the way you were drawn down towards where those guys were, it was like you were being shown that. Jeez Sensible, the more I get to know you, the more I realise that someone up there, as it were, is really looking out for you! It's like you have personal protection from the Gods or something!"

Don then spluttered across the table, waving his arms in my direction agitatedly. "Ooohh that's a'right is it? A' right for, fucking, him!" He pointed rather rudely right at me, "but what about normal people...like me, what about me!?" He was now whacking himself in the chest.

"Normal!?" I exclaimed, now I knew he was scared" He was describing himself as "normal!"

Hippie Davie however was looking quite genuinely concerned, which was starting to unnerve me a little. "There's no stopping a thing like that, we can protect ourselves, even protect each other but, it would be a constant state of defence, it would really start to drain our energies after a while, I'm sure! It's not just The Doc, it's those others now and then this 'other' thing, which isn't actually The Doc, but perhaps a demonic something given a form to do his bidding, if you will." Don put his hand to his temples and hung his head.

"Right, it's a good move, if you think about it, we stop him from being able to do us any harm, so he gets a big bastard to do it for him instead!"

"Exactly right Don," said Hippie Davie, "Though I doubt he'd have thought of that himself, or even have the know how! Nah this is a strange kind of magick, I think we're a little out of our depth here. I'm going to try to phone Wolf in Spain and you guys should talk to Mags about it."

The lights in Mags's living room always seemed to make everything seem very still. There was always a lingering scent of incense and benzoin in the air that made you want to just stay there forever, like when you never want a Sunday morning to ever end kind of feeling. The many objects, knickknacks, fairies and dragons staring down from the bookshelves made you feel like you were intruding into some strange fairy realm. Mags brought us tea and a whole host of chocolate biscuits. It was most pleasant, like visiting a lovely old aunt, where instead of talking about the price of bourbons, we spoke about magick and Wicca and all things interesting and fantastic.

"So what do you think Mags?" I said, "What do you think I saw? Was it real and what can we do about it?"

Mags slurped her tea and thought for a few seconds. One could almost feel the force of concentration being focused by her superior brain.

"This spirit seems quite ugly, grotesque." She mused for a moment. "Yes Davie is right it will take a lot of energy and effort on your part to defend yourselves against such a sheer manifestation of rage and hate. But I don't think it's a part of Michael, not like the last time."

I raised my eyebrow and looked at Don, assuming naturally that he'd opened his trap and blabbed about the batbox bunch and the Three Musketeers and all the extra-curricular magick practice we had been indulging in! However Don was making exactly the same face back at me and our expressions blinked into confusion as we stared each other out for a second and then swivelled around, almost in synchrony back towards Mags. I was curious,

"Did I...? Did Hippie Davie mention that to you at some point...?"

Mags merrily bit into a chocolate biscuit seeming to ignore me for a second. She looked over her spectacles at me with a triumphant smile on her lips,

"I'm your high priestess! Let's just say that as you're in my coven, I have insights into what you get up to in the magical realm from time to time!"

I baulked, "Really?"

I must have sounded quite aghast as she give a little giggle and said, "Don't worry, I'm not spying on you and to be honest I do trust you guys; you are rather sensible."

Something about the way she said that as she glanced smiling at Don made me look at her suspiciously, but then I thought, 'Nah, she can't know absolutely everything...can she?'

Don broke the train of thought, grinning maniacally at me. "Sensible all right, we don't call him 'Sensible Sean' for nothing!"

Mags chuckled, a little too much for my liking. I had come to accept it, though. "Aye, that's me a' right!"

Don sounded a little anxious as he spoke, "What exactly can we do Mags; how do we get rid of it, how do we stop this crap from happening?"

I fathomed then, that the experience at his work place had shaken him up a little bit more than I had realised. It also occurred to me that if The Doc could inflict that type of chaos into Don's life, then what was this latest scary, vile creature capable of doing? His anxiety was beginning to affect me, as we sat there in our high priestess's living room eating toffee pops and slurping tea.

Mags looked pensive for a moment. "Well, it sounds like some older wicked soul has been charged with new intent; the magicks that sustains it and gives its whole existence in this world is the 'will' of directed hate. That mirror you saw was obviously a symbolic doorway from whence it came, or was summoned as the case may be. I get the impression that they weren't one hundred percent sure of what they were doing!"

I realised the truth of it as she spoke. "Oh yeah, yeah that makes sense and I guess it's now trapped in this world, mad as a hatter, hell bent on getting revenge. But what is it, though? Where did it come from?"

"A demon," Mags said flatly!

Don sighed, but I contemplated this for a second. "A fucking demon? I kinda only thought Christians believed in all that Heaven and Hell and demons kind of thing. Do we believe in demons now, I musta missed a meeting!?"

Mags merely smiled a little out of the corner of her mouth, "Oh yes, these things exist alright. Some say quite externally to us, others say we make them. Yesss, well and people make demons on the astral plane that can take on a kind of personality all of their own if it's...bad enough or enough people contribute to it. Enough hostility done to another human being can, in effect, be given a thought-form that we see as a thing having personality, sickness, vengefulness or being abusive to the point of manic. It comes down to intent, intent and energy!"

I stared at her and was just about to say, "I don't like the use of the word energy," but she smiled and stopped me in my tracks with an almost sympathetic look.

"The force you feel in the circle, the power, the chi whatever you want to call it," she said, "feels very real doesn't it?"

I shrugged. "Yes, yes of course, of course yes!"

She pushed her point a little further, choosing as simple a way as she could to help me accept the reality of the vision I had had. "Characters in Shakespeare's play, or the Lord of the Rings are real to you and I aren't they? The power you imagine you feel in a circle and that others feel at a distance also has a reality and influence in the real world doesn't it? Well then just add the two together! *Et viola*, a timeless character or energy that can influence how you feel and how you think."

I thought for a moment of an allegory which was stuck in some recess of my mind; that of Jesus blowing a life force into a bat he had moulded from clay. I mused for a moment that this story was a reference to how the magical mind can will something to be; 'I bet that is a reference to some deeper hidden grimoire embedded within the Bible,' I thought!

"I guess it's like the Jewish golem or the Buddhist's tulpa," I said, "but I can never quite grasp just how 'real' these things actually are!"

Don shifted a little in his chair, glancing briefly at Mags, tutting in a frustrated manner and then looked up at the ceiling a little intently. Mags maintained her look at me, frowning, looking serious and deep in thought. "Yes, yes and it takes quite a lot of concentration to infringe upon the choppy sea of everyday life, but there you go, it's possible!"

I thought about my analogy with gravity and other forces. Will was like gravity affecting the temporal aspects of existence. Just as gravity affects space time, will bends and contorts the temporal fabric of space-time. It's true physicists have shown that there is no such thing as "nothing;" space is constantly in flux, matter being produced and then annihilated at some very basic energy level. Will may not be affecting three dimensional "stuff" directly but it can definitely interact with it and influence how it progresses through time! This demon did seem to fit the analogy, it was like a black hole, an energy-sucking black hole that existed in this world for one reason only, for destruction. It would forever take and take, fed by hate and in order to sustain it and make itself bigger it wanted more and more violence and negativity. The idea came to me, like a rip, a seam coming loose and then looser and looser; rending space and time, in direct opposition to creation and stability *i.e.* chaos, a demon.

We all sat sipping our tea, alone with our thoughts. What to do, what to do?

Don spoke. "Well clearly we can't make it just go away and we can't ignore it, as it's sure as shit not going to ignore us!" He turned his head towards Mags. "How do we kill it? Kill Doc? Please say we have to kill The Doc!"

I chortled. Mags, who had been deep in thought for the last few minutes, said, "Well, you can try to bind it and then trap it, that's the first thing you can do really!" She got up and for a moment, with some excitement, I thought she would bring down an ominous looking large dusty looking book from the top of the shelves; however, she just shifted it aside and then reached towards a dusty tatty looking old shoebox.

"I've got something in here that I picked up from a little pub in Eire on a visit a few years ago to see some stone circles. The thought of a pub comes to mind as you guys were always drinking together in the Prince or at that café you like. As your friendship and magical relationship has been linked by drinking together, you've effectively swore an oath of loyalty." She turned around slowly and looked down at us temporarily over her glasses in a need-to-know-only kind of manner. "And oaths of magical friendships are not things he should be breaking lightly!" She continued bustling about the top shelf. "Aye, we just happened to chance into a lovely little inn in a nearby village that day, there was a very strong feeling in there. I went in and met a nice woman; she was doing card readings for a few shillings and half a Guinness. Well, we got chatting and at the end of the day she brought out this and handed it to me. She said I had permission to use it for my family whenever we had need of it."

Mags placed a small coin-like disc on the table; it was clearly quite old and grubby but still inscribed on it were identifiable markings in a triskele shape with a menacing looking toothed bird in the centre.

Don looked at it in awe. "Is this something to do with the Morrigan?"

Mags smiled knowingly, "No, it's actually a power amulet that links to Badb. She's a powerful crow goddess of land, justice and war. Moreover...righteous war, or defence of your land; defence of your oaths around the claim to the land at your feet. If used correctly she will momentarily confuse and confound your enemy making the situation bend in your favour! Now between the two of us, that day, we could tell that this particular amulet was made with magick skill, to be active and still very much is. That pub was on or near a place of worship to Badb, we both agreed on that." Mags looked up over the rim of her glasses, a look of dear affection spread over her face as her voice softened with the emotion within, "So...in essence this amulet is a gift straight from the Goddess for this purpose! It will serve you well!"

Don raised an eyebrow and looked at me, "Sounds pretty good! Could she maybe send a leprechaun then, Mags?"

I rested my temple on my hand. Leprechauns! Demons! Maybe I have had a bit too much dope in the last couple of years!

Mags merely nodded. "Don't underestimate leprechauns! In my experience, these sprites are immensely powerful; they are like elves, extremely powerful, but don't tend to care about the affairs of humans. You might see them as funny little people with hats and buckles, but I see them as gods; they're the gods of the old religion, the remnants of the forces our forbearers connected with on the land itself! But no, there's no need to invoke anything other than the Goddess; she will be of great value to you in this case." She handed the small coin-like talisman to me.

My thoughts were filled with disappointment, as I reached over towards it, but curiously, as soon as I grabbed it, I felt oddly optimistic and assured.

Mags looked at me with a twinkle in her eye. "It'll be far more effective on your home turf, for you can never find anywhere more powerful and protective than your true home!" Next she bustled off to the kitchen and returned with a small dirty looking stone.

Don looked in awe at it, "Wow, an ancient crystal of some kind, Mags?"

She chuckled. "Yes, well it is quite old; it has certainly been in the cupboard for coming up to three winters now!"

We looked at her quizzically, in reply to our expressions she looked down over her glasses at us. "Rocksalt!" Don and I slowly mouthed the word without any affirmation of understanding. "This will hold the entity in place, binding it to Earth; it can't stalk you on the astral if it's bound to Earth can it? Also, it will give it some mass just long enough for you to deal with it...I recommend dissolving it after that, in the mighty North sea; give it a real taste of Aberdeen!"

We sat and chatted a little longer, but time wore on and we knew it was time to move on. As we stood in the hallway, Mags hung a thread around our necks with a small eye symbol scratched into it with symbols representing our names. She also had one prepared for Hippie Davie, though she hardly knew him.

"This will serve as a cloak of invisibility, so that the evil eye will not find you or have perception of you," she said.

I stopped for a second; she hadn't made these during our visit! "Jeez Mags, did you just happen to have these?" I exclaimed, lifting the token from my chest closer for inspection.

"Oh, no dear," she said matter-of-factly, "I just knew you'd be in need of these sooner or later!" I looked at the small wooden medallions; the thread was quite intricately woven with beads and patterns. It looked like it had been made months ago.

We stood facing each other on the Green; Davie's face was aglow with a proactive aura. "What'd Mags say?"

Don spoke up, "We're calling in international occult forces!"

I looked at Hippie Davie. "Mags reckons we can soften this or deflect it with our combined will; trap it in rocksalt, to bind it to the earth using friendship, our home and the goddess as a strength!" No sooner had I said it then I had the nucleus of an idea emerging in my mind!

Hippie Davie nodded and raised an eyebrow approvingly. "Cool, cool that's actually very similar to what Wolf said, so we're in business!"

I related to Hippie Davie the Badb triskele, Ireland and the breaking of oaths. "What did Wolf say exactly then?" I said curious and now buoyed by the optimism cascading through the conversation.

Hippie Davie glanced down; his eyes gleaming, contrasting against his bronzed skin; awash with Vitamin Hippie D.

"Wolf basically said the same thing really – that Doc's new demon, was probably risen using some old grimoire or something but more likely an evil presence related to some dark episodes in that location. The intent, the spell was acting out of spurned friendship and so is fighting us all individually. But it wouldn't pick a fight with all three of us at once; so we should stand together!"

Instinctively, we stood closer and Hippie Davie put his hands on our shoulders and we followed suit.

"This is it then comrades, brothers, mates," he said. "We're not going to be bullied by anyone; if someone starts on one of us, then they start on us all. Together, we are stronger."

I nodded. "Yeah, nobody fucks with my mate's T.V. 'that's just taking the fucking piss!"

A tear started to roll down Don's cheek, "And they fucked up *Star Wars*, dude; they fucked it up, fucked it right up…"

I could see he was getting overly emotional. "Shhhhhhh, they can't destroy *Star Wars*, dude; it will just become more powerful now, think about it!"

Hippie Davie smiled and patted me on the shoulder, clearly approving of my words of encouragement to Don.

Don lowered his head and quickly nodded in affirmation, snuffling a little as he did so.

Hippie Davie however was now quite offended. "Well that just strikes at the very heart of us; any demon that swipes at *Star Wars* is definitely declaring itself an agent of the dark side; and so gentleman, *C'est la guerre.*"

Don looked at me a little confused and still a little emotional said; "Ch-cheese?"

I shrugged; I thought it had something to do with cheese as well, but didn't want to say it out loud.

Hippie Davie looked at both of us in turn, a slight look of concern and confusion on his face. "No, no….war my friends, this means war!" He exclaimed, his words echoed a little in our heads. As we considered it, a buzz of excitement rallied around between us.

"Yes," said Don, "aboot time an awh.'"

"Fuckin' right!" I exclaimed, "Only so much shite ye can take is there? I'm fae Northfield after awh! And up there we stand by our mates!"

Hippie Davie patted us both on the shoulder. "And we're not going to take any shite from any o' 'em Edinburgh chaos magician cunts are we?"

With that, we agreed a plan of action, we needed to defend our home and we needed a focus of something here in Aberdeen that represented the heart of the city for us. Somewhere that represented a power base, somewhere that was plugged into the history of the place and where we could summon up the deva, or forces associated with friendships and bonds. Somewhere that knew us and was a magical temple for us and other Pagans like us, where anyone with an ounce of spiritual awareness would be drawn to in this city. We all thought for a few seconds but without too much trouble, the name came to mind instantly, we looked at each other and smiled. We said it aloud simultaneously, "The Prince of Wales!"

## Chapter 12:
# The Prince and the Queen of Night

"But how, for chrissakes, are we going to manage to do a surreptitious magical circle, involving expelling demons, in a busy pub?" I said sitting at the back lovingly caressing my pint of Dark Island.

"That's a tough one all right," said Don. "Maybe we could come in early on Sunday and do it!"

"Nah, we need permission, but how? Who's going to ask? What are we going to say? I wish Hippie Davie would hurry up, what the fuck is he up to?" I said, frustrated as we had been sitting there for a full ten minutes now waiting for him to sit down with his pint so we could continue with the plan of action.

Don leaned backwards and peered up towards the bar. "He's chattin' up the barmaid!"

I sighed and shook my head in genuine frustration. "Oh for fuck's sake, can he no' think of anything else!? Fuckin' hippies! I tell ya, never go to war with a hippie; it just doesna work!"

Don shrugged. "Well hippies generally don't go to war do they? They just form Woodstocks an' 'at and run aboot naked, fucking like mad all over the place, high as kites!"

I frowned. "Yeah, yeah, they should get their act together shouldn't they!? Get their priorities right!"

Don looked at me and gave a little ironic laugh. I began to smirk as I put my pint to my lips, "Well...war's a serious business; somebody's got to do it!"

Just then Hippie Davie lolloped over, hair bouncing with triumph as he plonked his pint down in a statement which said, *you're going to love this*, kinda way, *see what I've just achieved.* Hippie Davie sat down and our eyes followed from the brimming, spilling pints to his face, sporting an expression of *easy when you know how*, kind of matter-of-fact concealed smugness.

"You're going to fackin' love this!" he said. "I was chattin' to my mate Fiona there and av' managed to get us in here after hours in the early hours of Sunday morning!"

"No shit!?" I said, a little taken aback that it appeared so easy! I hadn't realised that his 'friend' Fiona was in the building, nor indeed was I aware that he was still 'friendly' with her, if you know what I mean!?

Don, however, raised an eyebrow in suspicion, "What do we have to do?"

Hippie Davie cast his eyes away and mumbled into his pint, "Oh a little spot of tidying, maybe a little bit of mopping that sort of thing!"

I was just contemplating what that might entail when Don pulled his pint out of his mouth and almost choking on froth as he spat out the words, "Baggsy not doing the toilets!"

As quick as a flash, Hippie Davie repeated the same thing and then they both turned towards me. I stared at them both a little stunned as the implications quickly filtered through to me; they had bagsied it. The bastards knew I was powerless to overturn the rule.

"Oh fuck me!" I said. "That's not fair! That's not fair at all."

Don sniggered shaking his head, "Geez on a Saturday night as well!?"

I shook my head pissed off at the injustice of it all.

Hippie Davie shrugged. "We had to get in, didn't we? So that's the way we're going to do it. The way I see it, we clean up dead fast, all help each other out like, then we'll have a few hours to ourselves. We'll set up candles, bring our robes in and stuff, it'll be great, I can just imagine it, a rite in here, evoking the spirits of this place, of Union Street, of Aberdeen itself into the circle, be fucking awesome man. All smelling of incense and weed...and piney fresh, especially if you make a good job of the toilets Sensible!"

I was beginning to enjoy the image until that point and then saw them pass a look between each other! Mates eh? "Ye bastards! Ye bastards!" I said and huffed as I drank a big gulp of Dark Island to console myself.

The time came around soon enough and we found ourselves sitting in the Prince, each with our sports bags under the table, sipping beers. In truth, we had been in since early tea time, as a result of having nothing much better to do and the excitement of the task ahead. We decided to have a few drinks first, so that we could cope with the hard night of work ahead. We had huddled together in my flat to come up with an idea to banish this demon from us, stop the chaos magicians from being able to strike at us and finally send that thing back through the rip in reality, as we had now come to perceive it.

The banishing ritual itself focused on magick being evoked into the bar and infusing this with the Spirit of the Prince of Wales (It's that 'deva' of a place, the sense of a place; the continuity among the comings and goings, the sense of a pub you get when you get drunk and stare at the panels and pictures of the walls, with the kind of affection you had when you stared at the hood of your pram or blankets in your first cot). This was most important as we felt we needed permission from this spirit to do the ritual there and enlist its help. It must have seemed strange to anyone who glimpsed us on that Saturday evening. At around 10 o'clock when the throngs were three or four deep at the bar; we sat, three of us in a triangular formation, at the back of the bar, wedged in a compartment near the fireplace at the back. A team of women and handbags made a useful wall between us and everyone else. Hippie Davie murmured an incantation and we felt ourselves melt into the scenery, becoming invisible. We closed our eyes and imagined ourselves outside the door, on the astral, as it were.

Hippie Davie whispered, "Are we all here?"

Don nodded and I said "Yes."

Hippie Davie smiled, but I was a little confused, "Hey Don, how'd you manage that; how'd you manage to just nod!?"

Don shrugged; we all smiled then laughed a little. Hippie Davie knocked at the door and then we waited a little, "OK, try it now, Sensible!" I tentatively pushed the door and it swung right open; amazingly the sound of chatter in the bar seemed audibly louder, exactly as if we'd walked in from outside.

We each visualised walking through the bar and sitting quietly in our seats, a spare chair sat facing us, into which we invited the guardian spirit of the Prince of Wales and then we waited. Strangely, I felt the need to hang back a little, it didn't seem right that we all just sit straight down. I telegraphed my hesitancy to the group, Don immediately understood.

"I kaen get pints for everybody then!" I smiled and then in my mind I fought my way to the bar, but the regular bartender was not there. Instead I imagined a thin-faced late-to-middle aged-woman with quite lank straight black hair faced me at the bar. She had a fairly mournful expression which did not change; I understood straight away that I was probably picking up on some ghost of barmaids past. She poured the drinks without a speaking but did say what I thought was a genuinely appreciative thank you, when I thanked her and gave her some money from my pocket. She bowed her head a little but remained transfixed, staring at me, with an almost imperceptible smile across her lips. I went back to the table where my two compatriots, motionless and without speaking awaited me. Any onlookers might have seen three very still guys sitting with eyes tight shut lift their drinks in synchrony and slowly place them back on the table in silence. We spoke, asking with all our hearts for the spirit to join us and then we waited.

Minutes passed and all I could feel was the tight grip on Don on my left and Hippie Davie on my right. I felt a silly sitting there but decided to put all my effort into feeling for an impression or image or vision that might occur. I wasn't going to just imagine it; I really wanted the vibe of the environment to form itself in my mind. And it didn't take too long, as a large form appeared in the doorway of the hall between the rooms. It seemed like a large balding figure in a traditional barman's garb. He was quite foreboding – massive, strong with big arms and big hands – but at the same time he wasn't representing the complexity of the place or the magick. I figured he was some kind of guardian as he did not speak but only seemed to stand there watching. Presently, the corner of the room caught my attention. A shape unfurled itself by the fire and a large brown shaggy shape, that I felt was a Great Dane, got up and walked slowly and lazily from the corner of the fireplace and collapsed beside us in a heap of fur. I gasped in fear and excitement as a very strong cold feeling spread over me and culminated in tears forming at the corner of my eyes, one escaping, brimming over to my cheek. Somewhere in another world, I felt the grip of my friends become stronger and tense for a second or two. The Great Dane spirit rolled its head over its front legs and made a contented *huffle* noise. The bar seemed eerily quiet, as if you could hear a pin drop and I was sure that if I opened my eyes we would find ourselves alone in that corner of the room. The thought scared me so I concentrated on the animal that was at my feet between myself and Don. I began to think it was going to be difficult to communicate with a dog when I realised that the dog did indeed have an owner and that owner was behind me. The atmosphere had gone very, very cold indeed, although my face and right leg were now burning from the fire I could feel in the hearth. I turned around and saw the bar was filled with people, all manner of people. I saw an image, a vision in my mind of a little old man with a gnarled face sitting watching us on the other side. Closer to me, I felt the presence of a man sitting, smiling at us wearing a top hat which seemed a little torn, like some story book tramp.

I could sense women with bags and lots of people with instruments, fiddles and whistles looking like they were getting ready to play. There were just far too many people and I understood that they were all the guardians of the Prince of Wales. I looked again at the man with the torn hat; he had a black coat on with a chequered waistcoat underneath. He had a very kind face. He kept his gaze level with mine the entire time. I asked him for permission, but before I got the words out he smiled and nodded. Simultaneously, the Great Dane raised his massive head and then lowered it on my lap. It felt amazing, so warm and loving and the weight seemed to surround me entirely like a hug or a loving embrace from a very familiar friend. I thanked him and then thanked everyone in the bar. They didn't even seem to notice me but at the same time I knew I was there with them and they allowed that. I felt a huge surge of belonging, of eternal bonds and love. I belonged here, here was a focus of my home town and I felt safer in that place than in any other place on earth right at that moment.

As with all rituals, it was plain when the time had come to return, to come back down to earth, as it were. I felt the image of the guardians subside and caught the impression of the last faint wisps of music. I became more aware of my friends and for an instant wasn't sure if the few bars of fiddle music I heard came from the jukebox or came from the people I had just perceived. I realised I was now completely back behind my eyes, which slowly opened, adjusting to the light and sense of reality. Hippie Davie was blinking, clearly just back to earth a few seconds before me, Don was opening his eyes, like a new born baby; big pupils struggling to take in the smiling faces of both Hippie Davie and myself.

We took a few seconds smiling at each other and waiting to come back completely. Curiously I still felt the weight of the Great Dane on my left thigh, to such an extent that it was becoming uncomfortably heavy.

Don gasped, "Hey Sensible, half your face is bright reed!"

Hippie Davie nodded, "That's coz he was sitting too close to the big fire!"

I put my hand to my face, "Fucking right! Whose idea was it to sit here?" The empty fireplace to my right looked very dusty from years of lack of use.

Don was the first to talk about what he'd seen. "Well did ye all see 'im?" and he motioned to the door way to the connecting halls. I turned to look where he was motioning and then back at Don, excited and incredulous.

"You mean you saw a guy there?" I said.

Don nodded. "Yep a big guy, huge hands, baldy and cleaning a glass, towel over his right shoulder!"

I didn't particularly remember seeing the towel or glass but knew they were there all right, as soon as Don mentioned them.

Don continued, "He was definitely like the bouncer in here, could crush you into a fine powder if he wanted too, kinda thing!"

Hippie Davie was nodding animatedly. "Yep, yep I think I saw the same guy, but he is definitely a boxer or a wrestler or both, he's definitely a guy to call on if need be."

"You don't have to," said Don. "He's here all the time and whether we call him or not, nothing is going to be able to get past him in here. Demon or not, he would flatten it to a small disc and just turf it outside! I have his assurance of that!"

"Well done Don, well done!" I said nodding in his direction. I felt he had secured solid protection, whereas I realised I hadn't paid much attention to the big guy, so I was glad Don had taken care of that, good old Don.

Hippie Davie was smiling. "What else?" His eyes were bulging with glee and his eyebrows were making his face contort into a gesture of exclamation.

"You mean the people?" I said and with that the image of the top-hatted man and the feeling of the place washed over me like a strong emotional wave, I couldn't stem the flow of tears welling up as I said it, Hippie Davie just smirked and his eyes bulged even bigger emphatically as he slowly nodded towards me.

Don gripped onto the table and reeled at the intensity of the feeling, saying, "Oh gods!"

The image of the man with the top hat was very strong and intriguingly dominated my thoughts, as if a part of them had bonded with me. I could see it in my mind's eye and it just remained there, it would not leave. I wondered if it ever would!?

"I saw a guy sitting right there!" I said pointing to the table where the women now sat. Again a huge feeling swept over us as I pointed.

"No shit!" said Hippie Davie, "I think I spoke to the same person; he was a magician, a very magick man and believe me, we are quite privileged that he chose to reveal himself to us tonight. His name...started with an H, Hendry or Horacio or something like that!"

As he said it, I knew it was right and then realised the magician aspect was correct as well!" "Tarot!" I said, I think he even had a card in his hat!"

"Yes!" said Hippie Davie, "This man was crafty, a conjurer, maybe even a gypsy but also very knowledgeable in the craft of the wise."

"Nah," I said, "Not a gypsy, a countryman of some kind, perhaps a travelling man who earned a living here and there telling fortunes and doing spells for people but also of a strong mind, an intellectual and skilled sorcerer in his time."

Don nodded. "Ohhh I'm getting that, I'm getting that, yeah."

I laughed. "Yep Don old son, seems you weren't the original 'top-Hat, top hat!"

Don shrugged. "I don't mind; I feel good carrying on this tradition!"

We each looked at one another and smiled; we had done it. We had connected with something and all this time I could still feel the weight on my leg.

"And his dog is like his familiar or something, also wrapped up in both the friendliness and the protection of the place!"

Both of them looked at me quizzically, "Dog?"

Don gave an ahhhh sound with a conciliatory smile, "I thought there was something, maybe under the table, but I wasna sure!"

"Yeah I said, you can say that again!" I relayed my story of the dog, the people and the music and how I felt we were welcomed in and totally protected in this place.

Hippie Davie glanced around as I spoke, "God yeah, I think I may have been aware of this at some level, but I was totally focused on trying to speak with the one person."

With that, we raised our glasses and toasted our new friends and to the Spirit of The Prince of Wales.

"To the old top hat!" I said and felt a chill of appreciation running down my face and spine.

Eventually, the last drunkards left the pub and a strange calm descended almost straight away. The bartenders and barmaids hurriedly packed things away and tidied up, counting coins and pulling the dregs out of the pipes. I felt like an intruder. It was awkward as the staff really didn't seem to like us hanging about, disturbing their routine. Clearly they thought us a bit strange as they eyed us suspiciously while they worked. However, Hippie Davie's obvious influence on their boss was apparent as he joked and smiled with her in the background, the chemistry between them was quite clear. I eyed Don feeling very jealous of Hippie Davie's relationship with this attractive older woman. As I looked at Don it struck me that he was feeling jealous too! I was a little giddy after the ritual and, to a large extent, the beer; not to mention quite knackered by my job. I wasn't relishing the work we still had to do and I was now thinking that it was a really bad idea. Surely I would have very little energy to repel demons after mopping toilets for the next hour or so!?

We each set about our tasks. I had no choice and was resigned to tackle the lavs. I decided to just go head to head with the men's first. Christ it was bad! It's an unpleasant aspect of male behaviour that to urinate somewhere in the general direction of a urinal is kind of acceptable, I mean; statistically some will go where it is meant to. The more beer consumed on the premises translates as more urine on the floor and walls and even, it seemed, around the sinks. Much to my horror, it seemed that urine was not my only problem. There were also other even less savoury items to dispose of. I ran out retching from time to time, saying; "Uuurgh fuckin' Christ, fuckin; Christ sakes," much to the barely concealed amusement of Don and Hippie Davie. "How aboot a swap? Anybody?"

Don was hiding way back in the kitchen area. "I'm not havin' much fun either, it's knee deep in sauce and greasy pots here!"

I, however yearned for the sanitary conditions of a kitchen in comparison to the dank dirty men's toilet. "I don't mind grease, yeah; let's say we swap for a bit?"

A short bubble of silence was then met with a "No, Fuck aff!" I looked over at Hippie Davie behind the bar, but before I could say anything he shook his head.

"I have to clear all the pipes and deal with the barrels and things, I'm the only person allowed to do it and you don't know how to anyway, do ya?" Annoyingly I thought that he must have been making that up, that it was complicated and required a lot of skill, I'd never known him to do a day's work in his life!

I mocked him a little, "Yoo don't know how anyway do yaa;" in a childish voice as I returned back into the pungent atmosphere of the toilet.

I could hear Don reassuring Hippie Davie under his breath as the door swung closed. "He gets like that sometimes when..."

That was like a red rag to a bull to me, I clenched my teeth, seething with injustice and a sudden desire to pick a fight. I hauled at the door with all my strength so as to shoot my head back through and shout, "Gets like what, exactly?" But in my haste to pull the door open dramatically, I *thwacked* the inner door straight into my own head. I howled in frustration and pain. I could hear the others giggling outside. I kicked the mop across the toilet but then, a little hurt, picked it up in resignation, instantly regretful as the handle had touched the piss stained floor.

Some half an hour or so later I was forced to run out again, retching or 'cowkin', as we say in Aberdeen, a much more adequate expression than merely retching. There to my total disbelief were Hippie Davie and Don sitting at the bar having a smoke and each supping a pint of beer! They looked a little sheepish. I was incredulous and virtually speechless for a moment.

Hippie Davie smiled and said, "Oh fuck's sake, here we go!"

I raised my voice, "HERE WE GO!? FUCK'S SAKE!!? HERE WE GO!? Here I go you mean, here I go...mopping up three colours of fuckin'...SHITE through there!" I motioned back into the toilet, the emotion straining in my voice as I looked back into the pit where I had crawled out of, "Ah canna believe...and you sit there having a jolly fuckin' time!? Oh ME! Let me tell you, you won't have to worry about Demons coming to get ye tonight, coz I'm aboot to hae yez both mur-dert myself' afore the night's oot!"

Hippie Davie motioned with his hands for me to calm down and revealed that he was actually in the midst of pouring a third.

"Relax, relax will ye for crying out loud, I was just about to give you a shout. We thought it was time for a wee break, we can have one each; but no more after that or else Fiona will give me fucking shit for it! Don in the meantime was giggling uncontrollably, taking amusement at my bad mood.

I simmered down (instantly at the sight of free beer) and pulled up a seat. As the three of us sat there just chilling out, smoking and sipping beer listening to the radio in the background, I realised I was probably as happy at that moment as I had ever been. "Fuck, I wish I owned a pub!" I said out loud.

The other two immediately concurred nodding in approval "Aye, this is good," "Aye, aye, exactly what I was thinking aye!" they replied in succession.

I sighed and shrugged. "...Sorry aboot being a bit moany earlier on!"

Hippie Davie patted me on the shoulder. "Comes with cleaning toilets, forget about it!"

I felt I had to justify my ill temper. "Mind you, you bastards were enjoying it a bit too much, you can't deny that!?" I turned to look at Don, making him recoil slightly into a look most sheepish. "And you should know better, you're my best mate an all."

Don shrugged. "I was only funnin'!"

Meanwhile Hippie Davie just stared ahead at me in a kind of mock seriousness. I did a double take as I sipped my pint, beginning to smile at his foolishness, reading the exaggerated mock concern etched on his brow and eyes. I protested,

"What? ...Well I've known Don for ages, we're coven brothers; we go way back to previous lives and everything!" I looked over at Don who nodded in affirmation.

Hippie Davie now began to exaggerate his feelings of rejection by quivering his bottom lip; it made him look like a lost teddy bear with all those dreadlocks and beard. I resisted the urge to hug him for a second. He shrugged a little in resignation, which immediately shot a bullet of guilt that lodged in my chest and stayed there.

"Oh it's all right dudes, I can always see your love for Don and each other, it's kinda nice man, no worries!"

I looked over at Don shaking my head. "Nah, nah, well yeah, that's true, but you're kinda in that same group anawh?" My voice quivered as I strained to disguise the emotion; as a mere man I was dreading showing this too obviously.

Don chipped in, completely emotionally unrestrained and having no problem finding the words my macho self could never let me say, "Sure, we love you as well, man!"

I was jealous. Hippie Davie reached over and patted Don on the shoulder, "Likewise brother, likewise!" Before giving each other a large bear hug.

I began to feel very awkward; I was able to say that to Don, but only after a couple of years and even then, he wasn't like other blokes, he had no barriers to feelings. It was easier. He didn't bottle everything up like the rest of us. Now he was sharing a hug with Hippie Davie and their ease sharing feelings in such a way made me more jealous and slightly uncomfortable at the same time.

Hippie Davie started fiddling with his tobacco pouch, "Cool, cool, well I always kinda thought you didn't like me too much at first, dude!"

I sucked my top lip, "No, no not at all, I..." I cleared my throat a little to maintain my normal tone; I was worried it was getting a little higher pitched in order to suppress the underlying emotion that was building as I clenched the muscles in my throat. 'Damn beer, damn hippies,' I thought.

"Not at all, I erm, kind of thought the same as you, really, you didn't like me as much as perhaps, Don or The Doc and stuff!" I was careful not to use words like "felt" or "cared."

Hippie Davie looked a little put out. "Nah man, c'mon did I give you that vibe? Naaah dude, I can honestly say I never did not like you, Sensible!"

I now felt a little embarrassed and felt the need to qualify what I had accused him of now! "Well, yeah, you know, not 'not liked,' you know but I mean, with all the Jedi stuff and sometimes we seem to argue about, well my scientific views, which is a stumbling block for me. I suppose that I gathered you might be a little exasperated with me at times...it's nothing! Forget about it!"

Hippie Davie fidgeted and shifted a little closer,

"Man I can honestly say I'VE NEVER thought bad of you or been exasperated by you! In fact, I totally respect your views and thoughts, dude, that's true! Just ask Wolf, he'll tell you! Am always bigging you up to him man!"

The thought of Hippie Davie bigging me up to Wolf both surprised me and caught me off guard, making me a little emotional. I puffed my cheeks and clenched my lips, just to make sure they wouldn't visibly start to quiver. I shuffled, still thinking how to respond (it took careful consideration at this point) when Hippie Davie held his hand up in a friendly gesture. I shook his hand, it was a good feeling and all a proper bloke requires for emotional contact with another bloke, as stipulated in the rules that all males get drilled into them when they take you into that little room in primary seven and read out the man-rules handbook! (Or as my former girlfriend Jen had referred to it – the bastard's handbook). But of course, Hippie Davie being a Hippie and me being a member of the cooler anarchistic counter culture also, meant that no rules, however sacred were, erm, sacred!

"Oh c'mon Sensible, I luv ya man!" He then got up and flung his arms around my neck. That was too much, I hugged him back.

"I luv ya too, man! Like, totally respect you too and everything." But the last words didn't get out, drowned out as they were by escaping sobs wrenched from a throat near clenched to the point of cramping up with the effort of holding in the emotion.

"Awwwwwwwh isn't this cute!?" Don said slowly and deliberately getting up and covering us both in an effeminate group hug.

Hippie Davie continued, "You guys are family to me, man!"

Don chimed in "We're all brothers of the craft!"

I reaffirmed, now no longer hiding my emotional outpouring; "The musketeers, man, best mates!"

Then it occurred to me it was way after closing time, we had been drinking beer all day and we were in our favourite pub in the middle of the night, essentially to defend each other. The ritual had begun and we hadn't realised it! I looked down at Hippie Davie's open army bag; the Badb triskele glowed up at me.

Then I pushed Hippie Davie away a little.

"Fuck me, it's the beer man, it's the beer talking. I joked a little, "We're getting all maudlin like guys do at closing time! It's the power of the Badb triskele, man, we'd better be careful; we can't handle this man...we're not even Irish or anything! It's getting to us!"

Don and Hippie Davie turned to look at and their laughter broke the tension! Instinctively, Hippie Davie realised what I also had at some level. "Ok let the rite's begun!"

We finished cleaning up quickly and cleansed ourselves and prepared ourselves mentally. We had done a good job of cleaning and making the surroundings that bit more hygienic. We set about creating our circle and positioned the candles and incense accordingly so. When we put the lights off completely and the effect was quite stunning in that old pub in the dark. I cast the circle while Don called the quarters, that is, invoked the elemental forces of Earth, Air, Fire and Water around the circle at key points. Then we walked the circle with the altar candle in silence and we each envisaged the light of the Goddess entering and imbuing the circle. Hippie Davie then sealed it with the force and Don called down the moon as a protection into the circle. After some concentration and memory work, by all of us, we were undoubtedly successful. The very room seemed to now glow with an aura, so much so that I looked around expecting a light to be on somewhere. It was extraordinary!

The next step was to try to visualise and invite in the spirits of the pub itself, who we now considered as our friends and very powerful allies. I placed the Badb triskele on the makeshift altar and in an act of intuition decided to consecrate it with Guinness and invited the spirits of the Irish pub into here. Then I concentrated and sent a prayer to Badb asking for help in battle, as was our Celtic right! It worked, an eerie presence crept over the pub and it became darker and electrified. A loud bang echoed from the back of the pub. I looked over at Don who was looking downward, in an effort to control the intensity statring to overwhelm him. I then looked at Hippie Davie who was grinning manically and in a manner that, if I were to turn around and see him like that were he sitting on a couch with me, for example, I would jump off shrieking, 'Get the hell away from me you freak.' It was like he was plugged into the mains, his dreadlocked hair seemed to be standing up in response, as if he had been struck by lightning and his eyes gleamed with a mesmerising kind of madness.

He looked back at me, "Well fuck, that's worked all right!"

Don and I then sat hidden, wearing Mag's talismans, under heavy cloaks that we had prepared. We doused these with consecrated water and imbued them with sage smoke. Sage has a curious power of its own, a strong spirit ally that can cleanse a place. We used it to blind the demon or any forces from knowing our tactics. We knew this was an extremely strong negative force. It would relish a fight like a predator, instinctively going after moving prey. So we were going to present it with a target. Bravely, Hippie Davie was to stand in the circle, apparently alone. This was to create a space, an astral-mental imaginary space, where will and imagination were to be used to visualise a rite that would create an area between worlds which would suck the entity towards it, like a vacuum. For this, Hippie Davie was going to use a rite which he said was inspired by, among other material, the Star Ruby. He predictably enough had entitled his version 'The Star Wars Ruby!'" This worked as a most effective banishing ritual for those with the skill to utilise it. The original was a Pagan/Hellenistic ritual created by Alistair Crowley; Hippie Davie understood the reality of this rite. Crowley had created it from other rituals devised by early nineteenth century occultists combining powerful words and magical phrases aimed at clearing a space in readiness for further magical operations or meditation. Now Hippie Davie had created his own version in true Shamanic/Jedi style, using his own allies, - the Force!

First he performed a version of the qabalistic cross. Facing the east, in the centre, he drew a deep breath and closing his mouth with his right forefinger pressed against his lower lip. He forcibly shouted out,

"Apo pantos kakodaimonos (Completely away Evil Spirits)." He touched his forehead and shouted out,

"Force Unto thee!" in a small emotionally charged voice, almost under his breath. It really felt like he meant it, as he paused, to allow the words time to be acknowledged. He traced his hand to his groin and shouted,

"Oh Solo" and then his right shoulder and said,

"Strength of the Force!" to his left;

"Blessings of the Force." Then he clasped his hands locking the fingers and cried out;

"Hail to the trilogy." Hippie Davie then advanced to the east as he imagined a pentagram on his forehead and making the sign of Horus roared out:

"Chaos."

And then put his finger to his lips whilst adopting the stance of silence.

He advanced to the north and made another sign, roaring out "Leia."

To the West he cried out; "Leia and Solo."

And to the South he bellowed, "Solo."

Completing the circle widdershins, Hippie Davie walked slowly to the centre and raised his voice with the words (IO. Y. O. D. A.) Whilst adopting five distinct postures such as holding his hands in front of his abdomen and then leaning back throwing his hands in the air, like he was catching a large beachball from behind.

Any magician seeing a spaced Hippie dance about with a light toy saber glowing on the floor would probably smirk sardonically. Don and I could not see, but started to visualise everything. This was a good tactic; as it meant we were more attuned to the level of imagination and not being distracted by the reality of the empty pub where we sat.

The pub was now transformed by words of power and images of the mind, which were getting stronger and stronger (and thus more and more "real") with every passing minute.

Hippie Davie danced in spiral movements, imbuing the movements with energy, every footstep deliberate, like a Red Indian ghost dancer, alive with the moment. When he felt that he was fully tranced out and in the moment, the moment where the energy he was building was almost too much for one person to handle, he leapt to the East. He bent his head back suddenly like an epileptic wolf and shrieked, his body arching and assuming the stance of a clawed hawk.

"I am Mando'a as the Jai'galaar, the shriek Hawk." He danced around and around on the spot and shouting "The Force is a wheel, turning as I shriek; I paralyse and bring dread to my enemies and I collect their very souls unto me."

Under my shroud I saw, again, the idea of will being like a singularity, a small black hole, bending space and the fabric of reality itself in space-time.

Then like a manic wide eyed tranced out fiend he leapt backward to the west and then stood up abruptly; making his body into the sign of a T-shape, shouted out,

"I am a hero of a thousand faces; I am Luke of light and the blessed path! My destiny awaits and it is written I SHALL-NOT -FAIL! My will is reconciled with my destiny; I am at one with the Force!"

Then he walked with his eyes closed to the south and stood to face it. With his eyes still firmly shut, he said,

"I use my eyes not, but trust in the force, with love and with the trust in the force."

Then he bent down and picked up his lightsaber that had been deliberately placed near to where he now stood. The pub reverberated in a smoggy green light from the toy lighting up the incense smoke. He continued;

"As I am bound to the force by love and will, so the force is bound to me; this is my weapon, this is my truth and it runs through my wand, my saber!"

As he said this he raised the weapon to the south and then held it upright in front of his head as a salute. Then he turned around and knelt and saluted to the North.

"I salute you Yoda, as a force spirit-Daemon! To all those who cross and become enlightened ones, as Luke my father daemon shows that all evil will be consumed eventually by the force, there is nothing to fear as all will be so, so mote it be!"

He stood for many seconds motionless and with a huge smile on his face, laughing and smiling at the North of the circle. From where we were, Don and I, "saw" the spirit outlines of Yoda, Obi-wan Kinobe and Darth Vader exactly as we'd seen in cinema many years before, for this image was timeless and thus part of the fabric of our space in time.

Hippie Davie stood up and shouted out,

"About me flames the pentagram and in the column stands the six-rayed star!"

Immediately I saw the pentagram fluoresce around Hippie Davie in the circle and I was certain Don did too. I "saw" Hippie Davie in my mind's eye stride forward and step into the middle raising his light saber over his right shoulder and sling down his back, fighting ready he sneered into the midst,

"Come on Demon who stalks me; I call on thee to face me here!"

We had gambled on Hippie Davie being somewhat a first wave of attack here, but as he stood there, after his flawless *Star Wars Ruby* I didn't think any demon could stand up to him. His will filled the pub and I knew it would never feel the same again; anyone with half the ability to sense atmospheres would feel Hippie Davie's will in here now, I was sure of it. To use the space time analogy, he had created a small star; just as if matter had coalesced in the vacuum of space to create gravity and light, mimicking creation itself.

As Hippie Davie stood there challenging the Demonic force, all was quiet. We didn't have its symbol to call it or trap it, but that was ok. I had actually seen it! So Hippie Davie had made me draw it on a scrap of paper and he had fashioned a sigil from instinct which he felt suited the image I had described. He tossed it onto the ground on top of a symbol he had chalked on the floor.

He further continued to evoke its presence;

"I command you demon of hate, command you to come and fight! I evoke you here by the might of Yoda and the will of the force!" Again he stood still waiting to strike, but something was different this time. This was our cue to begin our part and Don and I began our invocations.

The Pub seemed darker, very much darker and Hippie Davie's nerve began to waver, just a fraction, as a real thick darkness spread all around him, leaving him feeling very vulnerable and alone. He was in a very dangerous place and he knew it. To his dismay, a very large pitch black shadow appeared behind the bar to his left. He turned, expecting the image to disperse with the light of logic and direct sight, but it did not. Instead, a mouth appeared and snarled at him; as clear as day he saw it. He froze, resisting the urge to shout on us out of sheer fear. Instead he bravely gritted his teeth and faced it, a lone Jedi in the dark beneath Aberdeen's Union Street in the quiet, in a pub between the worlds.

He arched his light saber towards it, directing his will as strongly as he could,

"I now control you beast of hate, you will do as I say, arise, step into the circle before me and face me!"

But it did not move into the space, instead the vision morphed into a devious grin as the light from his lightsaber faded to a dim glow and then peter out as he held it towards the direction of the black demonic void. Hippie Davie gasped as he was plunged further into complete darkness; it was like being alone in a sea with a shark somewhere in the dark with you sensing, but not seeing it! He waited for the strike as he summoned what will he could to form a circle around himself. However it was not enough because as soon as fear crept in, he was weakened and it was now stronger. Anyone ever taking part in any kind of exorcism or banishing will know that fear is the weapon of such entities as it erodes the will and belief, corrupting faith.

The windows rattled a bit in the wind outside and the candles flickered. Loud cracks and bangs could be heard all around the pub whilst the back door over at the other end of the kitchen rattled madly and loudly in its hinges. He knew this wasn't a coincidence. The entity was showing its strength, a strategy geared to kill off any confidence Hippie Davie still had. Still, Don and I held our positions. Hippie Davie now crouching moved right into the centre of the circle, eyes darting to and fro towards the sources of various creaks and sudden thumps. The centre of the *Star Wars Ruby* appeared less lit and powerful than it did originally almost fading into a wispy shadow of what it had been. Fear was punching holes in the protection; Hippie Davie's star was becoming a red dwarf! He slowly placed the palm sized piece of Mags' rock salt in the centre of the sigil we had created for it on the floor.

Timbers squealed and floor boards creaked, as if something large was stalking over them. Still Don and I held fast our positions and remained still. We were concentrating on an impenetrable wall around us, in a manner reminiscent of the antagonist in John Wyndham's 'The

Midwich Cuckoos,' where the teacher Gordon Zellaby kept his thoughts away from the "children," by concentrating on an image of a brick wall.

Hippie Davie began to whimper,

"No...no, no...you cannot get to me, please; I'm in my cir-cle of protection."

He punctuated the word "cir-cle" expertly as this had the effect of actually puncturing his circle, as if the lack of confidence made a hole in his defences, a hole in the circle. The principle was the same as kids at school arguing in the playground. As soon as one bottles it and loses their nerve, the other kid senses this and goes straight for the kick in the bollocks! Astoundingly, Don and I could see in our mind's eye a large dark silhouette fly over the bar and traverse the space towards Hippie Davie, like a large stalking shape. Amazingly, Hippie Davie was looking at the same thing; as it entered the space with him. This was a very dangerous place for him now.

For a second Hippie Davie's head seemed compressed and nausea filled his senses, his energy was being attacked and he was going to be quite ill and lethargic if this was allowed to continue for another minute. He looked up and then he finally caught sight of the astral image that inhabited the space with him. The spectre loomed over him, allowing him to see it a bit more fully, setting the final jolt of fear into Hippie Davie's mind, perhaps in an attempt to unhinge it, perhaps lesser men would have been. It was huge, it was terrifying and deformed. A perverse, evil manic grinning face filled with teeth and large empty eye sockets fixed on Hippie Davie in the dark.

Hippie Davie instinctively scrabbled backwards almost crying out in revulsion. Reaching to the altar he held aloft the Badb triskele from Eire in an attempt to stall it for a vital second and create confusion in the midst of battle.

"I call upon all my allies here; HOLD the infernal here." He threw the old Badb triskele talisman towards it and scrambled back out to the side of the circle towards the North. The disc tinkled on the ground with a pleasant chiming sound which seemed to freeze the surroundings in time. A soft sound like a bird in flight settled like a calm in the circle. The atmosphere again changed and I could imagine the big boxer bouncer loom out of the shadows and grip the demon like a vice. Hippie Davie felt the image of the top hatted spirit walk into the circle and lend his magick to it. Hippie Davie lit a small candle which was connected by chalk lines to two others, creating a large triangle where the sigil and rock salt lay exactly in the centre.

Hippie Davie stood up and walked into the west side of the circle faced the centre of the circle and lit the next candle; he could sense the Demon struggling in the centre being sucked into the sacred space and absorbed onto the rock salt, right underneath wherein the column stands the blessed six-rayed star. The demonic influence being rendered ineffective in turn. It was trapped but it was going to need a bit of will to rid us of it altogether. As Hippie Davie continued to walk anti-clockwise to the south-east to light the last candle he looked over to our position and shouted,

"Now!" That was our cue; as I said before, fear erodes confidence and faith and here is where "religious faith" has a very real power, as it consumes the mind and eradicates fear, the unknown and uncertainty. That is why the human mind craves it. But for us, faith was a burning star light that would not be dimmed; as Erneh had once told me, "For a witch, there is absolutely nothing more powerful than the Goddess." For some time Don and I had been concentrating on one thing, murmuring incantations and invocations, turning our imaginations towards another ancient night, for me, Turkish/Greek and Don, Italian! We threw off our cloaks of invisibility and stood up walking towards the circle. Hippie Davie held aloft pieces of rose quartz in one hand and a small incense burner in the other with appropriate herbs for the respective Goddesses burning in them. There was a sudden surge of sensation, smell, sound and intent. In synchrony we spoke almost as one at the top of our voices, strong and confident. I spoke aloud;

"I invoke Hekate! And she rules this night and rules all spirits herein; Come Hekate, she who will bind and banish you never to blight my priests again; back whence you came by the force of my will, you henceforth are banished!"

Simultaneously, Don chanted,

"I invoke Trivia! And she rules this night and rules all spirits herein; Come Trivia, she who will bind and banish you never to blight my priests again; back whence you came by the force of my will, you henceforth are banished!"

We spoke this mantra over and over getting louder in synchrony as we stepped forward. We met in the middle, west of the banishing triangle and clashed out pieces of quartz together forcibly. At the same time Hippie Davie joined us with his quartz and light saber, looking tired but smiling. We then started spinning in a circle, going widdershins whilst chanting the mantra all the time. We became louder and louder and faster and faster. Every time Don and I said, "Force of will" Hippie Davie joined in with the "Will of Force!" simultaneously. It had a magical and mesmerising effect. We then grew further apart until we were at the edges of the circle. We drew an Earth invoking pentagram over the sigil and the rock salt; then we sent the whole pentagram spiralling faster and faster. I mused that it was like an event horizon and it began to shrink, gaining pace as it did so. We saw the flames of the pentagram grow larger and stronger in our minds until it consumed the target within. In our minds we called on the elementals of earth to help hold the demon in the salt.

Eventually the pentagram shrank and disappeared into a singular spot, as our imaginations followed it down to the level of the atoms of the crystal lattice. I was reminded in a flash of the prison for General Zod in Superman 2. We all then sat down and Hippie Davie directed us to visualise being together on the astral, chasing the influence away from us. We saw each other surrounded in purifying flames, Hippie Davie with a strange bluey-green glowing light saber and Don holding a bow with a crown on his head.

"Wow, I think I can see you guys with weapons," I said.

"Mmmm wow Sensible you seem to be holding a large knife which seems to be on fire!" said Don.

Hippie Davie acknowledged this as if it was quite apparent, "Yep, let's go, all for one!" and we all repeated "And one for all!" Then we chased after our quarry.

As I visualised the scene and allowed the image to form in my mind, I had an impression of a small, squirming animal-like figure caught in a trap. I was contemplating just how much this was my own imagination filling in the gap; or whether it was an impression of some reality when the image quickly changed, without any apparent effort on my part. The image now gave way to a strong impression of a spinning neutron star or something that reminded me of that. I realised, somewhere deep down, that I was seeing it 'for real,' not clothed by my mind but more like it really was, a representation of it actually. It wasn't an entity at all as such, but conscious mental energy; a small vortex of will power gone awry, given birth by concentrated effort and then sustained by its own mass. Like a rip in time and fate it was a little gravitational lens to bend our fate, to deflect us from our real destinies and cause untold havoc in our lives; the personification of ill will.

And that's what it was all about, I realised, in that moment with my Goddess consciousness expanding my mind. Life was about living according to your own will, fulfilling your own destiny and being at peace with that. The phrase that Hippie Davie had pointed out with glee that Gerald Gardner had transposed to Wicca from Aleister Crowley came to mind, "Do what thou wilt shall be the whole of the law; love is the law, love under will!" However, life was a constant struggle to attain that against the slings and arrows of other people's agendas or wants and needs. We often have to toe the line rather than be ourselves.

We chased the entity. Occasionally Don would fire a bow at it, causing it real pain, I imagined. I thought that after this intervention the demon would never come to Aberdeen again, we were safe! It was banished, it was gone! We all then picked up a corner of the small piece of cloth which lay under the salt and sigil, bundled it all together and tied it at the top. Don would drop that into the briny water of the quay later, the rock salt forever dissolved among the mighty North Sea. Thus we thought it could never make itself a body here again and be forever dispersed in the north east. (Its body, if it ever tried to inhabit the astral realm with us here, would forever have this quality).

There was only one thing left to do and that was bind The Doc and his crew, so that they wouldn't be able to direct anything like that towards us again. We had some of his hair and some photos of him that we attached to a small sackcloth doll we had acquired for the purpose. We all meditated on it silently for a few minutes and when we were ready we spoke to it.

"I call you, Doc!" I said making contact with it and my wand. "I hope and pray that you will see I always loved you as a friend, as a brother even and I have done little to merit your hatred towards me; with that in mind, I bind you from further attacking me! With regret and love, I wish the Goddess helps you find healing. But I will not allow you to obstruct my will to live my life in accord with my own will and destiny."

Don and Hippie Davie spoke their mind also, each being careful not to create further negativity. All half decent magicians worth their salt know this.

Using magick for defence, of course is legitimate, especially in a case like this. However; I think magick should basically be viewed as a martial art, such as Aikido or Jujitsu. Every person has the right to follow their own will and destiny and it harm none as we Witches say! So if an aggressor is trying to prevent you from following your own will, magick, like Aikido or Jujitsu is best utilised to redirect the energy back like karma or deflect it. I especially think we magicians should take our leave from Morihei Ueshiba (O Sensei) the founder of Aikido. Aikido was developed for world peace; to teach people the error of their ways; O Sensei understood this idea well. Magick should be about spiritual development and self-alchemy; making yourself "gold." If you start acting like a power mad bully or try to influence every aspect of your life then you will never develop as a person.

We ate furiously; to ground ourselves as daylight crept under the door. We thanked our friends, our new allies and also we thanked Badb and each Goddess in turn. We tidied up and with much fatigue shuffled outside and locked up.

Don turned to Hippie Davie, as he locked the door, "Phew, thank fuck for that, you think that's it; for good like?"

Hippie Davie nodded. "Oh fuck yeah, we sent it back alright...though...neither of us should venture into that basement place in Edinburgh, wherever it is!? I have a feeling that it may still have some reach under there, lurking in the darkness!"

I knew it, too. "Mmmm yeah, it'll still have a bit of reach there, where it was made as it were, but not as much, I have the impression that it is a shadow of its former self, but still a nasty presence nonetheless. I pity anyone that spends any time there, but fuck it, not our fault, people will never know how close it came to be being free and people will never know how we stopped that thing from getting out and creating problems. We should be thanked for locking it up in those dark cellars below reality, wherever that was. I guess it will eventually disappear without any attention anyway!" I didn't know where this place I had seen had been, but I felt it was very dark, dank and old, as if a series of almost medieval looking streets, still intact, under the very city itself. I could see it in my mind's eye. The entity would be cautious but always present and much more pissed off. Although, how could this be? There wasn't really a weird old cavernous town underneath Edinburgh was there? Of course, that couldn't be for real! I mused that this place obviously existed in the astral and so must be long gone, therefore the presence must have been removed from the physical, thankfully!

Still, we felt a sense of relief after that night, free from a presence we'd grown used to. It was difficult to describe, but it was only now when this nagging presence was gone, that we realised the weigh that had been there, like an albatross around our necks. We had rid ourselves of the terrible demonic form raised against us but how could we be sure this was going to end our woes in this department.

Some hundred and fifty miles away, on a cobbled street a guy with chaos magick symbols inscribed on his leather jacket was punched square in the face for looking a bit too long in the direction of a group of lads out on a binge pub crawl in the west end. He received a beating which meant he would flee Edinburgh for some time and go home. It would end up being a good move for him, he would befriend old friends from school and feel less of an outsider and not need to prove himself by the excitement of black magick. He also would discover the healing arts after as his own bones slowly mended.

A few days later, one of his mates, a neurotic person, would start dreaming of the demon walking around in the darkness. He saw it cock its massive shaggy head backwards and scream up through the streets at him to set it free, accusing him of locking it there. He would wake up covered in sweat, as the beast's screams morphed into the sound of air brakes of large buses squealing outside in the street as he awoke. He eventually developed so much paranoia that he ran into St Giles Cathedral on Parliament Square, Edinburgh and flung himself on the floor sobbing. There was no exorcism; he was taken to a sanatorium, where he spent the next year drugged and lost to the world. He realised he had done something which could not be repaired, that he was responsible for something that would continue to haunt him for a long time to come.

And The Doc, who had been dossing with a guy who had to go home after being beaten up, had no choice but to return home himself. Walking alone back towards his mother's house in Torry, he walked tall, the mighty shaman that no one should mess with. In his mind, people moved before him in swathes as he walked through the crowds. As he walked along the streets of Torry, two boys of about thirteen years old walking in the opposite direction saw him coming. They nudged each other, amused at the sight of a greasy-haired bespectacled lank goth-like man with balding hair and big clumpy boots walking towards them. The Doc stared ahead, to command the respect he deserved and walked towards them sneering. The kids passed by laughed and began to taunt him.

The Doc sneered, "I'm not the kind of person you should mess with, boys!"

This was like a red rag to a bull to these tough kids. "Oh aye!? You? Fa the fuck are you? Ah yoor Fuck-all!" and then they ran around him chucking stones at his head and kicking him and jumping away swiftly from The Doc's slower reflexes. The Doc had no choice but to take to his heels and run inside. They chased him, in scenes reminiscent of the small dinosaurs in Jurrasic Park attacking the thief. Like that bad case of Karma as well they enjoying mocking him whenever they saw him thereafter. The Doc hated everyone from his bedroom in his mum's house; it was all he could do. After all "Hatred is the coward's revenge for being intimidated," is it not?

## Chapter 13:

# We are all Stars

They say that the greatest technological innovations take place in time of war. We felt as if our motivation to defend ourselves and stop our T.V.'s from exploding had resulted in us becoming more proficient at performing rituals, visualisation and magick in general. We decided to work on aspects of magick and continue to meet and perform various magical operations as a practice. We met as often as we could to train in magical exercises aimed at improving our powers of visualisation, magical imagination and strengthening our astral bodies.

Obviously Hippie Davie knew a lot of more "practical" applications of magick than Don and I, that much had become clear to us. What we could do effectively was cast a circle, draw the quarters and work with the elements, the rest was kind of left to intuition or little bits of this and that we'd observed in the Sabbats and Esbats. We didn't know much theoretical magick as it were, as I suppose Mags and Erneh ran the circle as a very family-orientated tradition. They didn't presume to teach us or make us do anything to prove ourselves. This was quite frustrating after a fashion, as between them they had an encyclopaedic knowledge of various systems of magick. Erneh, for example, was also a mason and had been involved with Golden Dawn systems of magick, but he never spoke of these things. Don and I never asked him, as we were just too intimidated by him. Often his language and references left us both as baffled as before and we were both too proud to say, "Excuse me, I don't actually know what you mean by that and if he said, "Sorry old chap, what bit exactly?" I would have to look him in the eye and say "Any of it!"

So it may have come as a bit of a surprise to Hippie Davie in one of the musketeer circles when he asked Don and I if we could just go and do the lesser banishing ritual of the pentagram just to make sure the area was sufficiently cleansed. Don shuffled on the spot and I Looked over at Hippie Davie, "Well we can both do the preparation if that's what you mean?"

Hippie Davie was busy looking over some notes he'd made and absentmindedly motioned over, "Sure, sure dudes, whatever, if you wanna do it between yous that's fine by me" and continued studying the ritual he had devised.

Don and I then looked at each and shrugged.

I motioned with my hand towards the South, "You do east and south, I'll do north and west?"

Don shrugged again. "Fair enough!" and then turned his back towards the east, as I cleared my throat a bit behind him and waited. A few seconds later, he turned around again and started whispering to me, "Wait, I da' want to go first, you can go first an' I'll follow on!"

I sighed; "Oh for fuck's sake Don, it's jist me and Hippie Davie, there's nae Mags or Erneh judging you here!?" I whispered back. "C'Moan!"

Don shook his head, "No, no, it would make mair sense for me to do the West and North, coz I'm feeling all kind of emotional and watery like the west and I'm comfortable with the North and being all earthy today and onywy you should do the Air, cos you're like, all thoughtful and stuff!"

I shrugged; I didn't see why I should go first. "What the fuck? I'm as earthy as you! And anyway, I'm nae feil; you're jist sayin' 'at cos you don't want to go first...fuck's sakes!"

Don shook his head. "Look, see; you're all fiery and full of pent-up anger; you definitely should be doing the fiery south!"

I gasped in frustration, raising my voice in whisper mode which was whispering but, ironically, was actually louder than normal speech; "Well I wisnae fuckin' fiery till you started, wiz A?"

Hippie Davie just sat chuckling from his bean bag seat in the far corner; arms folded, now enjoying the show. "You really are like an old married couple int' ya?"

I decided it would be quicker just to stop arguing with Don and as we tried to swap places we kept bumping into each other, like Laurel and Hardy, if Laurel and Hardy had made a film where they practised Solomaic style magick (their catalogue not quite as complete for them not doing so). The frustrating thing about Don sometimes was that the more you got pissed off at him the more he just fired innuendos back at you.

"Fuck me," I opined as we shuffled places.

"Mmmm ok, I thought you'd never ask."

"Just...go West Don."

"Go Weeessssessst baby you and me, that's our destinnneeee!"

I turned round and tutted; "You can be sooo, so annoying sometimes!"

Don grinned, "Oh punish me then, if you want to!"

I looked over at Hippie Davie and raised my hands in resignation. He smirked back and we all started laughing. I looked down at my feet shaking my head in laughter. "Fuck, you can't even have a proper argument wi' you, can ye?"

With that, we composed ourselves and completed the quarters, turning towards Hippie Davie expectantly.

Hippie Davie just looked back clearly expecting a bit more. "Well yeah, good idea with the Wiccan circle, but I still reckon we should do the lesser banishing ritual of the pentagram just to be on the safe side, you know, besides, you can never practice that enough, know what I mean?"

I nodded in agreement and looked over at Don, "Ok fair enough, Don? Do you wanna maybe have a crack at that this time?"

Don looked thoughtful for a moment and shuddered, as if he was shaking off some chill,

"Well, am still kinda a watery an' a'thing! I'll maybe pass, I'll jist watch you the now!"

I nodded. "Yeah I thought so!" I turned towards Hippie Davie. "Yeah, frankly we don't have a fucking clue what you're talking aboot, Hippie Dee!"

Hippie Davie looked to and forth from Don and I, a little surprised. "Really? Sorry I just assumed, you know about the qabalistic cross and stuff like that, do you use your own version?"

Don and I just looked blankly back at him. I spoke up.

"That's another thing, I know about pathworkings and the tree of life and stuff, but what the fuck is all that qabalistic magick and stuff that you keep mentioning? Where does it come from? I mean where does this whole thing come from anyway?"

Thereby began the formal disclosure of the teachings of Hippie Davie, or as we came to know this, the five-fold path to Hippienlightnment, steps I to V.

"It was easy in principle," he said,

"Illumination can be gained in steps, tis the way of evolution after all, revolution recapitulates evolution."

# The Hippienlightnment Handbook, steps I to V.

## Step I

"Let's begin with some Qigong," Hippie Davie said. "I'm a big believer in the technology of the East. This is a way to feel your power, to feel the force! They call Qi/Chi in China or in Japan Ki. So we start at the beginning. This is the Tai Chi Qigong, let's learn these and learn how to move and balance the Qi."

We learned and tried to memorise eighteen separate single movements designed to stimulate and move the Qi. We also learned the basic standing meditation postures. This was simply standing still and shutting up, as Hippie Davie put it, with hands resting near the 'one-point.'

The remarkable thing about this was that only after a week or so of daily practice I could feel the Qi pushing against the palms of my hands when I breathed in. It was difficult at first to still the mind and even have the stamina to stand more than a few minutes. But after a very short spell, I felt like I could stand there calmly all day long if I needed to and could feel this well of Qi or power pulsating at my one-point or lower Dantian (a meridian point three fingers below the navel and two finger width deep).

During trance-like meditations, I felt my concentration becoming focused and my will sharpening as a weapon of my mind. I felt like a 'tree" strong and just focused on a point (that's the only way I can describe it). Better still doing the qigong forms after this short meditation period allowed me to feel how the Qi followed the will! All witches, Shamans, natural magicians, priests and priestesses of any description or martial artists should do this first!

## Step II

The next set of lessons involved hermetics, Hippie Davie explained. "Now I shall explain the qabalah, from the point of view of the hermetic tradition. This is not the Jewish Kabbalah, rather these aspects, although related to that stem from a series of meditations and connections to the tree of life, which is not accepted in mainstream religious Jewish Kabbalah or Christian Cabbalah. This is the magical or hermetic applications as developed by various magicians since medieval renaissance times, such as Eliphas Levi to the more modern practitioners that developed it further such as the Golden Dawn and Franz Bardon."

Hippie Davie then placed a piece of paper in front of the altar candle. "Imagine a tissue paper in front of a candle. The candle is the light of the most divine aspects we call God, or ultimate reality, call it what you will. The tissue is there because to see this ultimate reality directly would drive us blind and insane. It's too big for our unenlightened minds to comprehend. This tissue is like a veil between you and the god version of you. There are ten separations between you on the physical, we call Malkuth and the divine planes we call Kether. The planes are like dimensions or stages; these are emanations from light to solid, from energy to condensed matter."

I wasn't comfortable with this notion of creation; it was a little biblical for me! Don was also looking a little disappointed as he intoned; "I dae think I can have anything to do with this really, I canna believe in a God and stuff like that."

Hippie Davie shrugged. "You don't have to; it's about your own psyche really. The creation story is there to inform you that you are not a separate individual all alone in a dark universe. It says you're part of a continuum, that's all, the thing has fractal geometry; 'As above so below.' This is the hermetic mantra, derived from Hermes Trismegistus and you should know by now that that is fundamental to all magick, any magick, any system of influence that we work with. This doesn't mean you should accept that's how creation really happened, but it does provide a framework that links your inner psyche to everything around you; inner forces such as powerful beings like angels and stuff like astrology and tarot all stem from it too. Basically, everything you know as an occultist links up here and more. Importantly, it provides a map to enlightenment, or as qabalists call it illumination if you align your aims, mind and soul with it."

Hippie Davie didn't like just talking; he was a real advocate of doing! He demonstrated, "Now I shall show you the basic and most important method of grounding and preparation for magick work. It should be done at the beginning and conclusion of all work. It is the qabalistic cross."

Hippie Davie showed us how to perform this and think about the Qi as we did so. It proved to be a good method to improve visualisation and did leave you feeling kind of polished and grounded. It also started us thinking about creating a little tree under our skin as it were. After a while, I could see a white cross glowing brightly behind my eyes. You may think it was odd perhaps, that witches were invoking crosses inside themselves. But as Hippie Davie pointed out, we were magicians and magicians understood that all religions should be routes to enlightenment. If not, then they're not very good for you or your mind.

Hippie Davie's teaching was incredibly stimulating and Don and I could really feel their effects. We were very grateful as we developed.

Hippie Davie spouted forth philosophy like some time honoured sage,

"All things are as equal to the magician, whose perspective is like a hawk looking down on the landscape ready to pounce on some gem of truth like prey, no matter what the source," he said. "You must be like a hawk in battle, keeping your eye on your goal. Don't be pushed or pulled or persuaded or hung up by someone else's truth; for as one magus has said, truth is not quantifiable or conveyable. You cannot convey real truth, real enlightenment. You can only develop that yourself in the same sense as a Zen master will guide the student via koans (questions aimed at allowing the student to arrive at truth himself). Or to put it another way, as the great philosopher Bill Hicks would say, "Hey come join us on the evolutionary bell curve!"

Hippie Davie was smiling and I laughed out loud with a knowing smile on my face, meanwhile Don was looking at us suspiciously, clearly thinking "Bill" was an unlikely sounding name for a philosopher.

Then Hippie Davie continued, getting to the point that he knew Don especially had on his mind,

"So you ask why consider Jesus? Well, accept he was a magus, one who has helped bring illumination into the world, as Buddha before him and Muhammed and other bearers of light. They have achieved God consciousness on this planet."

I asked, "Do you think Jesus was the son of God?"

Hippie Davie shrugged. "I don't know! I only know he was a great qabalistic master and the deity associated with him is a powerful way to spiritual healing in meditation. Therefore to me he is a master and a great ally."

We read books about Hermes and Hermetic magic. We learned about the qabalah and עץ החיים (Etz haChayim), the Tree Of Life and what Hippie Davie meant by 'Christ Consciousness.' I likened this to my earlier theory of *homo demi-sapien*. Here was a method of actually working towards and achieving more '*sapience*', or illumination as Hippie Davie had called it. What's more it was clearly mapped on the qabalistic tree of life; where and how this could be achieved through meditation and magick!

### Step III

Hippie Davie considered, after much discussion and reading of qabalah that we were ready to experiment further with energy and Qi. What I liked was that he linked this, essentialy middle-eastern technique, to other energy work such as Wiccan power and Qi.

"The middle pillar exercise is about creating a lot of energy and flooding your aura and mind with it. There's so much energy of Qi produced that it repairs the aura as you sweep it around yourself and down through your own middle pillar. This qabalistic exercise maps the Etz haChayim into your own energy body system, or Chinese system of meridians. The points of the qabalistic sephiroth also closely match the Indian system of chakra points. There seems to be a weird coincidence of these three separate alchemical systems, which I think either points to a common origin or even a co-evolution of the awareness of the mind-body energy system we call Qi."

I began to appreciate Hippie Davie's wisdom of developing a familiarity with Qigong and especially standing meditation first. None of the books on magick or Wicca had ever told me that, but it made perfect sense and I didn't actually know why western magick books and practitioners weren't informing us to find it out and use it as soon as possible. With the middle pillar exercise I could feel the energy actually transform around my one-point into a 'solid feeling" pillar of energy. The regular meditation, especially, stilled the mind and made me feel as if I was more in touch with my real self. My advice would be, try it for yourself; you can develop that technology in mere weeks.

"There are other very useful qabalistic visualisations and exercises and we shall become proficient in each one," Hippie Davie said. "There is the lightening flash, the path of the flaming sword and visualising to build the little tree under our skin, employing all the god names and then angel names to vibrate and develop and stimulate all the energy points that correspond to the sephira there."

There was a hell of a lot to learn, but I found that after putting in effort to learn the sephiroth of the Etz haChayim, everything else just slotted into place. Of course, actually doing it rather than just reading about it created firmer memories and I found after a few weeks I had learned all the associations, colours, names and positions of all the sephiroth of the Tree of Life and where it interjected on my own aura. We had to be careful and not overdo it, as on some evenings I was so spaced it was like I had taken large doses of hash, but it was just the effects of constantly altering my mental state and expanding my consciousness. Fortunately on the first few occasions when I was completely out of it and feeling sick and scared that I couldn't handle the effects, Hippie Davie appeared at my flat and helped talk me out of it. The answer was simple; standing meditation (I hadn't been doing it enough times). All I had to do to become smarter and a bit more human was stand still and shut up.

## Step IV

We kept journals and learned how to access the borderlands. This was the twilight between wakefulness and sleep. It was actually quite easy. Every night we programmed ourselves by self-suggestion to remember our dreams. Every morning we lay still and focused on gathering our dreams before they faded. We used hand held recorders and documented each dream. Patterns emerged and symbols became clear. After a few weeks, whatever 'sensor' kept watch in our subconscious and borderland allowed us to creep into the borderland in a more awake state. Don, especially completely mastered lucid dreaming extremely well, though I couldn't quite acquire the skill consistently. I always felt too tired!

## Step V

We each became proficient in utilising sigil magic in Step V, making talismans and blending oils and incense. We resolved to practice clairvoyance everyday by raising the power to our third eye by intoning the qabalistic god name YHVH and focusing it at that point just above and between the eyes. Then we'd shuffle the tarot pack and try to decipher which card we held. With practice we became better and better. We also used the blue-ray candle method; meditating on the flame of an indigo candle for five to ten minutes every day. This involved imagining the flame sending indigo light into our third eye. This had a knock on effect of helping me sense spirits during evocations and elemental work. We even began to utilise the "jing" the sexual energy that we realised we had been squandering all these years, into a force that could be combined with the energy of the middle pillar and circulated this back through our bodies. This was thanks to Don's input, as he'd been experimenting like this for years. We learned how to make our magical bodies stronger and more resilient. This, we found not only forged our energies anew for magical work, but had a direct effect on our normal "basal conscious" state. I understood what Hippie Davie meant by saying everyone is a star at one with the force in a perfect Jedi galaxy. The whole world mentality was deficient. In our seemingly enlightened state the notion of fearing a god and deferring to authority was corrupt, or at least had served its function and was now out of synch with the incredible power of each individual which constitutes a society. If everybody was/is a star, then authority had no right to determine what we did in life. Hippie Davie told us that this is what the philosopher Freidrich Nietzsche had said, that no one system could possibly be correct and that each person had the right to live their own path to work towards being a potential 'superman'. This was an idea that echoed the notion of Christ consciousness. I liked it, as a comic book reader, the idea that we could make ourselves more human and super-human really appealed.

Davie also educated us further saying that Nietzsche had also stated that there were no facts, only interpretations of truth and that *"convictions are more dangerous enemies of truth than lies."* I liked this perspective. I couldn't believe I had never heard of it, but I was quite happy that logic had already concluded what I internally believed, that all humanity needed was therapy. Humanity needed self-awareness about egos and persepective. I didn't believe in original sin, just original ignorance. Understanding that everyone was also a star was just that change in perspective; exactly just as Giordano Bruno helped change our perspective of reality, God and humanity in the 16th century.

We really were becoming brighter stars among the long black night. Modern living really didn't permit a person to shine, we were very much at odds with society which we had to rebel against, to assert our right to burn brightly; we were experiencing the real living star wars.

We have the right to find our own true path in life. If not, we serve a false Death Star, a parody of real life, floating junk out in space, reeking of repression and false idols, serving the empire. Any idol which does not come from within is a false idol.

The constant working of our magical will was having this strange side effect of making us burn more brightly from the inside. We were becoming spiritually uplifted and shining brighter and brighter on the astral planes. We were stars in our own right, singularities that were drawing the power of fate and the universe towards us. We were becoming confident and at peace with ourselves. If you are a star burning bright in space, you are as the goddess intended, as it were. The divine plan was quite simply that you be a vibrant living part of the universe. You're actually not here to be bossed around and live a mundane miserable life, well not only that anyway, but to be called forth under the inertia of your own power.

It's simple – it's about nurturing your own personal piece of "the force" and merging it with the universal force, be your own "will to the Force!" Rise up, wake up and perform the rites of Hippienlightenment and claim your life back! To quote Sean Connery in the Untouchables, "Here endeth the lesshon!" Such are the words!

For many weeks and months we had been practising and working together. My real interest was in out of body travel. My experiences with Wolf and on other occasions left me hungry for more. The experience I had gained in the borderland state made me feel like I was travelling out of my body at times. Frustratingly, I just could not do this at will when wide awake. I just had to wait for the odd time when it occurred naturally, if I was very tired or half asleep on the couch. Neither Don talking me through it nor hallucinogenic drugs such as *Salvia Divinorum* had any effect. The latter just made me pleasantly stoned for about fifteen minutes!

I needed help! So we devised a ritual where we each tried to connect with spiritual helpers or guides on the other side. Hippie Davie came up with praying to higher intelligences with the aid of the qabalah and some guidance in the name of improvement of the individual. Don and I gave the script a once over and then made additions or alterations to lend it a bit of a Pagan twist. The ritual took place and we meditated on our aims. We performed the Qabalistic Cross and the Star-Wars Ruby all blended in within a traditional Wiccan circle. As usual, the atmosphere was electric and the very light in the room visibly changed and became brighter during our operations. Don went first and approached the universe as it were and asked for spiritual guidance whilst lighting the relevant candles as well as burning the appropriate herbs and substances. Hippie Davie followed and took some time and pretty much ended up half comatose on the floor, after ingesting the relevant herbs and substances. He seemed in a totally different place, almost completely unaware of Don and I, his face alive with smiles, looked animated as he occasionally made gestures that made you think he was deep in conversation, without making a sound; then collapsing on the floor, arms outstretched in an almost euphoric, messianic posture.

Finally, it was my turn and I decided to give it my all. I really wanted to progress and discover more of the mysteries, my rational mind still drove me to need some incontrovertible event or experience that would dispel all doubts about everything being no more than a figment of my imagination, with no other 'real" power. I followed the instructions but at the point where I had to address the spiritual powers of the sephiroth of Binah I decided to imagine what was going on in terms of space-time and 'will' being comparable with gravity again. It was like putting on a pair of magical infrared goggles in the night time. I imagined the veil of Pakoreth as like a wormhole to a part of the universe that was brighter, clean and just easy with no problems such as on the rocky little oasis in space we call Earth!

I concentrated on making a singularity in the space-time fabric of will and tried to imagine my will bending space and time, creating a tunnel from one universe to another. I found it very difficult and so I decided to invoke the God to help me. Since my dreams of him converging with me, he was never far away and it felt easier for me to start with this visualisation. I thought it would give me confidence if I could feel his will add to mine. I imagined a large antlered powerful figure emerge from the undergrowth and foliage and stand behind me, towering in the room, the smell of the forest pleasantly filled my nostrils and I heard the sound of hooves echoing in my brain. I stepped back into the aura of the God and allowed it to fill my own. I stumbled a little and stamped my right foot, feeling the expansion of consciousness which was really a type of expanded trance state. I felt like, 'ladies and gentlemen, we are now floating in space.'

Concentrating very hard, I made my request as Hippie Davie had written but deciding to place more emphasis I said,

"To provide myself with change and development and help to astral travel for the better of myself and the better of society, perhaps so mote it be!" I then visualised a crown upon my head and said with every ounce of honest passion and will I could muster, "With this natal crown, the crown of my being, the crown of my soul I pledge my goal of being at one with my divinity." The finally, thinking of the spirit of nature that has been present in my mind all my life, "Please lady Brigid, shining one, holder of the torch of illumination, light my way, take me with you on the path I will."

I waited. Nothing really happened as can be quite usual in such exercises of visualisation for gods, goddesses, spirits or relatives crossed over, whatever it might be. I decided to maintain a little discipline and waited longer, slipping into a meditative state. Some long minutes passed and I began to hear Don and Hippie Davie shuffle slightly. I could feel the ritual coming to an end and food started to spring to mind. I was content that I had put all the effort I could into the ritual and I was satisfied. Perhaps I may start to have a bit more success, at the very least I felt confident that I probably would. With my eyes shut I began to rouse myself, slowly coming back to Earth and visualising returning and flying back toward the the altar in the room and made myself more aware of my surroundings.

I turned my head to the left and cocked one eye open. Don was crouching down looking at a bottle of Cairn O' Mohr dry oak leaf wine. He looked very groggy and I thought for a second that he was going to be sick. He sat down and poured himself a drink. I turned to look at Hippie Davie who was still on the ground but now up on his elbows smiling like an extra from *One Flew over the Cuckoo's Nest*.

A few seconds later, Don tripped on his robe and went flying across the centre of the circle, spilling wine all over the food and us to boot.

"Oh great, right in the fuckin' tattie crisps bowl ya bastard!" I observed, as I had just loaded it earlier.

Hippie Davie began giggling uncontrollably.

"Well they're 'tatties' now, tatties o'er the side boys, ye've had yer chips! Heheheheh!" With that we felt the circle had come to an end, as if some timer had gone off and plunged the atmosphere back into it just being a silly afternoon, as opposed to being portal to another universe of angelic beings that would help us escape from our mundane lives.

Magick is often like that; there can be extreme amounts of concentration and visualisation with all the correct correspondence and incense and so on and generally not much occurs in the end. Some people expect hallucinations, fireworks, apparitions and the very fabric of space and time to rend and reveal fantastic hidden facets of reality, as if in the film *The Truman Show* when the set is ripped revealing the people in the background. But it isn't like that; usually you're standing in funny costumes staring at a living room wall or picture of someone's child's school photo on a fireplace mantelpiece in a smoke-filled room. Yes there are changes in "energy response levels" and definite changes in atmosphere; though it's the psychological changes which are more abrupt. Magick is a technology of the mind and subconscious rather than the conjuring tricks we expect it to be because we have seen it in the cinema as children, Sinbad, the Lord of the rings etc. Yes I had had experiences as a result of doing this. But mostly, the circle is cast, much concentration and visualisations are performed and then we go about our day, feeling psychically empowered, euphoric or cleansed after eating tattie crisps!

Many more occasions passed where we got together to flex our magical minds. We meditated; we fasted to gain some enlightenment, to be all we could be! I orientated myself to the moon every night and renewed my pledge to be at one with my own personal divinity and also achieve better control of out-of-body travel. This was a religious fixation of willpower and mindfulness. Focusing the will in this manner was a religious method for the anarchist and rationalist in me. The technology of magick, quite simply was a religion for the atheist. And it works! It's a long forgotten and hidden psychology from the masses.

I could really feel a change in my own persona. Now everyday challenges and events were a backdrop for my personal journey. I felt more relaxed about life, as surely a man who keeps a personal faith that he is quietly working towards achieving knowledge of his own actual purpose in life could do no wrong! How could I? In a sense it was my Goddess-given right to try to find myself in this way, to reiterate the words of CRASS and the Levellers: *"There's only one way of life and that's your own."* And here was the mental technology to free me from the chains of social dumbness and open my eyes to the wonders of humanity and the universe. For were these "not only queerer than we suppose, but queerer than we *can* suppose?"

The long hours of postying were just incompatible with actual life. I was always tired, exhausted even and the thought of a nine to five in an office working the usual five days a week really appealed. Despite call centres being the 1990s equivalent of Victorian workhouses I quickly jumped ship and started a job in one such place. I couldn't believe it when they told me I was being timed every time I went to the toilet, but remarkably it turned out to be true. Sadder still, was the fact that four years of studying at university had got me here. Graduates were given precedence with such temporary jobs, although the pay was minimum wage. I don't know what the worst part was - doing the ostensibly monotonous job and pretending to be earnest and concerned about it all or taking the daily crap from the supervisors there. These were of a typical creed, ambitious power dressing people in their late twenties and thirties, who whilst slavishly serving, worked their way up from the reception desk or office pool. They had one thing that united them all, a seemingly ingrained resentment for graduates (and a complete lack of common social decency). They hated me because I wasn't concerned about my average call time. I was consistently at the bottom of the league, mainly because if lonely old people phoned in to chat, I would indeed chat to them. The policy was to 'handle' them and get them off the line as quickly as possible. Consequently, people who actually cared about their average call time too much – *i.e.* everyone that worked there – just cut them off after a few seconds. It was as easy as pressing a button and then the next call in the line would be talking into your headphones. It did my head in no end. I would often feel forced to punch out the toilet code on the PC so that I could get up and go for a walk. This meant my average toilet break times were not exactly premier league either.

One of the most mystifying things to me was the speed at which the other graduates in the team conformed to the culture. They would wax lyrical about customers and call times at tea breaks and become obsessed by the fucking league table which loomed on a large board in front of the desks. Small rewards – chocolate eggs, the small coloured ones made of cheap stuff, not even Cadbury's – were given out for the quickest overall team members every week. Christ, you could buy a whole bag of them on the way home. I didn't get it. Pavlov came to mind. These had been otherwise very intelligent university students a mere few months previously and now they were vying for chocolate eggs and giving a shit about how fast they could piss and get back to their desks to be rude to old ladies.

I refused in principle to "push" for promotion, as it were, for anyone! It was actually a tad depressing, as far as I was concerned; I had this job only really because I quite liked eating, living in a house, buying beer and essentials. I seemed to lack the critical gene that made people conform, maybe I was a waster? I certainly felt like it at times! It was obvious that's what the supervisory staff thought of me, too. They wanted to sack me and tried to justify this by stating that I shouldn't be wearing a nose ring and that if I did not remove it, I could no longer work for the company. (Yeah I know, I was on the phone, figure that one out, I couldn't!). I complied and removed it at my desk before starting my shift, but retaliated by dying my hair bright blue. As I walked in, my supervisor shook her head and tutted. I found it despicable that people could control how you both appeared and behaved simply because they employed you; they owned your soul as well. My soul yelled "fuck off" in return; my soul sang Rage Against the Machine songs. However, wasn't anyone else thinking 'that there is something wrong with this picture?' I didn't think I was particularly an upstart or a delinquent; I just wanted to live with an element of "realness" or imagination.

I began to think, "Jeez where would I be without magick to turn to? Where would I be, what would I be? All I wanted was to be all I could be, to experience fully what I was put on this earth to do. Surely there was a purpose to all this; surely sitting in an office building surrounded by fucking automatons that cared so fucking much about their bathroom tiles or what car they drove was not the last word in civilisation was it, could it be? All I wanted to do, all I wanted to be was "real." I craved a bit of realness from people around me. But people don't deal in real! I laughed out loud at this thought; I was starting to sound like Hippie Davie, who despite being Scottish often spoke with an almost Californian-like mystical hippie drawl. People accept real as getting a job, contributing to society and working to acquire qualifications and map out professional development. That's normal, certainly, but it isn't real! It's what makes us live or be a person but it doesn't make us human. I was reminded of a quote I caught somewhere that was attributed to the mystic called Osho on meditation: *"Meditation is nothing but a device to make you aware of your real self – which is not created by you, which need not be created by you, which you already are. You are born with it. You are it! It needs to be discovered. No society allows it to happen, because the real self is dangerous: dangerous for the established church, dangerous for the state, dangerous for the crowd, dangerous for the tradition, because once a man knows his real self, he becomes an individual."*

I decided that's why punks and counterculture people prefer each other's company; they are that bit more real, more sensitive, artistic, imaginative, more searching than the average non-punk/counterculture person. I couldn't identify exactly what more "real" was. I guess it was just more open and unafraid to experience more in the name of life, scientific and spiritual inquiry (*i.e.* the mystic).

Several weeks had passed after the oath that I had taken in the circle with Don and Hippie Davie. I had all but forgotten about it. That morning, as I was about to plug in my headset, a voice crackled into my ear, quite loud and crisp, "Use your heart." I was very startled by this as I hadn't keyed in as yet and hadn't expected to hear anything at all. In fact I was savouring the few minutes I had before I had to start talking. I looked around thinking someone was taking the piss. I began to rationalise that it must have been a spike in the system, a random error or something like my headset acting like a radio antennae. But I knew it hadn't been random, I could feel it. I began to feel acutely concerned that I might be losing my mind. I tried to forget about it and got on with the monotony of yet another day giving people as much time to pay their bills as I possibly could, without even listening to their woes.

That same evening I found myself awake suddenly in the middle of the night. I tried to move but realised that I couldn't. I couldn't even muster the will to move my pinkie. I was experiencing sleep paralysis, though I was now quite awake. Seizing the opportunity, I decided to stop fighting it and lie there thinking about my etheric body. I closed my eyes and meditated, imagining myself in standing meditation feeling my aura. At a given point, I intuitively opened my eyes and now saw into the room, just as I would be if I had been standing meditating. But I wasn't actually there, I was lying paralysed in bed, but my mind gazed into the room. I was totally awake and totally in control. I didn't know what to do. It seemed I could do anything, go anywhere I wanted. However, it occurred to me to try to connect to what I felt was guiding me, what Hippie Davie and Wolf had alluded to in the past, that 'someone' who was looking out for me, a powerful ally in spirit. I steadied myself and concentrated on that thought. I braced myself and called out into the void for that which watched over me, to my most powerful, holy and sacred ally.

When you are travelling on a familiar road like, for example, on a regular commute, you are aware of the direction you travel in; that is normal. Have you ever glanced across the motorway and realised that your experience of a certain bend or landmark is now totally different from the experience of that same place when you travelled through it in the opposite direction earlier that day? The time of day may be different; all the familiar bends in the road are there but you're now just facing and travelling in the opposite direction, complete with 'the experience' of going *somewhere else*! But that's all it is. Your experience is now focused on the journey, going somewhere else. You never actually quite, consciously, equate this stretch of motorway as being the same piece of road that you travelled through earlier because your attention is drawn to the relevant aspects of the road, the other side of the same objects you knew from the opposite drive. Although you are on almost exactly the same point on the map, in Cartesian space, all your expectations, feelings and experience about the journey are different because you are locked in one pattern, in one direction, going somewhere definite and your perception is a mere countdown of the experience of your one way journey - like life! The one pointed mode of experience, the logic of that and the countdown to the end! The cars on the other side of the road are experiencing that parallel universe perception that you had inhabited earlier that very morning.

This is as close as I can get to relaying what it felt like at that moment. I'd been narrow minded, selfishly only able to comprehend my own point of view. This mindset was pathetic, like an insect crawling on a window, totally unaware of the world around me that we share. As soon as I experienced any perception of anything, this was compartmentalised, collapsed to a point, like an insect's view of the world or like the notion of collapsing the wave function into a simple selfish point, that my ego then grasped and held onto. But now, all of a sudden my awareness expanded well beyond that limitation. I felt suddenly beyond that, more like a wave connected to everywhere at once, to every viewpoint, which was not only of this dimension. The old, 'point consciousness' was clearly painfully inadequate, I kept thinking that was just like an insect's 'point-perception.' Processing only one point at a time, one isolated action at a time (like cinema film creating the illusion of seemless life). A Point consciousness, blind and lacking the notion of our human universe completely...yet an insect may crawl upon this human landscape nonetheless, while we watch or even fail to notice it!

Who watches us watchers of insects? The room became very 'real' and an intense light now contracted into a feminine shape, alarmingly close to me. I couldn't make her out, but suddenly she became both male and female and for want of a better word 'Christ-like.' The feeling of love and appreciation this being had for my life and soul actually radiated from it like a powerful heat. This intelligence before me emanated empathic feelings for my limitation of experiencing myself as a single point (the illusion of my own ego, for example) and beamed sympathetically at me. All feelings of self-loathing and self-doubt instantly vaporised before it, never to return. I was immediately and quickly transformed before this radiant heat. The radiant being didn't speak but a series of booming emanations seemed to periodically reverberate around the room and I soon realised that they corresponded to movements of its mouth. The entity was speaking, but I was ill equipped to comprehend the meaning at that moment.

I knew the realisation I had about my inability to perceive more than one direction more than one action, more than one aspect of reality at a time was a huge limitation. We humans are actually nowhere near describing the universe. I was both relieved and in awe of this knowledge at the same time. I didn't know what I was facing, I thought of the Goddess and the woman from my infantile dreams. As I tried to grapple and hold on to this thought, it dissolved and I knew I was her, she was in me and she was just another direction in the road I was travelling in parallel. My brain was starting to turn into a mess, I was also The Doc at times, I was also Hippie Davie. This was a type of information that I just couldn't quite process with my limited and linear logical mind. It was both disappointing but strangely obvious now that my precious scientific tool was now no longer of much use to me anymore.

The entity was sometimes a figure in the room but also seemed to fill the whole room and I felt like a small seed stuck to it. That's the best way I can describe it, a small kernel on a large piece of bread. I felt that the being spoke of love, not earthly human love but a love that represented some kind of universal perfection. I knew I wasn't quite prepared for this, but that it was happening anyway. Somewhere my body lay scared and confused. I knew the ally who was my guiding force somehow knew that I wasn't ready. I looked towards it one last time and an eye fixed on me. It was extreme and frightening like the eye or Sauron from Lord of The Rings, but at the same time loving and sympathetic and seemed to me to look like the eye of Isis or Horus. It gave me the distinct impression that it was time for other people to wake up and learn about this aspect of themselves. Part of my life's work was to attempt to tell some people of this, that there is an actual reality worth striving for, there is love in the universe and there is hope. Further this realisation was attainable as something within us all. A sustained act of will would bring this awareness and power, or force, for want of a better word, into people's lives.

As I began to cycle home in the early afternoon, after my shift the next days, I couldn't stop thinking about both the vision and the voice I had heard crackle in my ear prior to that. I felt completely different, calm, much more at peace and self-assured. I knew there was a connection to my mood and my experience with the powerful guiding ally. I had been completely altered, for the better. I felt like a new confident individual, who I really should be as opposed to the neurotic underachiever, the 'bent out of shape by society's plier's' person I had tended to be before the experience.

As I came to the traffic lights half-way down Bridge Street, I looked around at the traffic, the drivers, the gulls, the grass blowing in the wind across the road, the people and I was struck with a feeling of familiarity. It was a notion of how I saw the world as a child, how I assumed everything was connected in a strange ego-centric way. As if I had been familiar with the patterns and ebbs and flow of recurring themes in people's personalities and the very wind that stirred the atoms of the tarmac around like grey paint on a dusty sketch. I felt, what could only be described as, a heightened sense of self-awareness; but not an altogether unfamiliar sense, more a remembering and re-engaging with that state of mind. I realised in that moment that my mind up until that brief second or two, had become more and more on autopilot. As we watch T.V, sit at the office or go shopping for our next meal we are practically going to sleep. Although there's definitely nothing wrong with that; nothing wrong with relaxation after a hard day's work; it does have the effect of switching us off. Wake up.

Several vivid minutes later I was careering towards the Green and my two mates who sat in the distance chatting, sipping coffee and smoking joints. Hippie Davie was wearing a wide brimmed hat and Don's top hat dominated the small round table on the cobbles. It was a scene that looked like Fields of the Nephilim had given their roadies the day off.

As I dismounted, I felt more than ever that some inner calm had descended upon me, like in my heart I knew I was doing the right thing with my life. As I drew near I thought it was kind of funny that I was about to espouse theories of heightened states of awareness to a stoned out hippie that spent all his daylight hours either napping or getting nicely stoned and a gothic night watchman who spent all his night-time hours doing the same between prolonged bouts of *Star Trek* and *Babylon 5*. Their whole ethos, their way of life seemed to be reducing alpha waves as much as possible, *i.e.* becoming "less alert" than they can be!

So I wanted to relay the experience to the other musketeers as I sat down and excitedly tried to explain how I felt more awake and more "me" than usual this morning. Hippie Davie looked thoughtful and nodded, his eyes scanning over some distant memory of a familiar experience.

Don wrinkled his nose as if I had brought a stinky fart to the table with me. "Sooo, fit yer saying is, is that most of the time, you cycle aboot traffic half-a-sleep?" He cocked his eye up at me and smiled disarmingly. "Am going to have tae keep an eye oot crossing the road in future I can tell ye!"

I waved him off then relayed how I felt that I had some kind of change in perception and awareness. Certainly I felt an odd feeling of spiritual calm emanating from deep within me. The more I began to realise where this feeling was coming from, the more I relayed this to the other two.

"It's funny as I sat there at the lights waiting to go, I began to realise a few things about the world and consequently myself, about how I feel about what people think actually doesn't matter. I mean, I felt this feeling of suppression about my life and how others saw me just melt away, slide off me, kind of thing. I've always had at the back of my mind, this thing like I didn't really belong in places, in jobs at university; like I'm a kind of impostor or something. Yeah that's what it was, an impostor syndrome. Well I've sorta woken up to realise; how can that be true? If you're all about finding your 'own true will to force,' as you always say Hippie Davie, how can you be an impostor? You are exactly where and what you should be, if you are trying in your heart to aim for that. That's what the Tree Of Life is all about isn't it? And maybe some people don't like me and bitch about me at work and stuff. It's normal isn't it? I mean, it doesn't matter, it's normal, everybody does it. Gawd I would get upset about shit like that before, but now I realise it's all a load of crap, it doesn't matter; no-one actually cares.

Hippie Davie sat back and smiled. "You know what, you're right about that; I think that's a good analogy, perhaps you've woken a little bit more from dreaming!" And he started humming a tune I didn't recognise and he stated singing in a punk-like sneer, "*In the city of the dead...it wasn't anything you said, except I know we both lie dead.*" He stared towards me as if expecting some recognition, though I must admit I had never heard it before. What did that matter? I can't know everything he knows or else we'd be the same person and we weren't, simple as that! Don mused for a moment,

"Society...is a nightmare! And magick is the enema that allows you to wake up from life!"

Hippie Davie and I looked at him nodding. "Fuck Don," Davie said, "that may be exactly right, exactly right, I think you hit the nail right on the head there mate. But...you did mean anathema right?"

Don smirked; "I know what I meant!" and winked. We chuckled and sipped coffee, waking up in the Green in the afternoon sun for the umpteenth time.

I articulated my thoughts about "everyday" intelligence and consciousness being a little bit switched off.

Hippie Davie's brow frowned and I could almost see my ideas penetrating his brain and lighting a small fire therein.

He rested his hands on his cheek in contemplation; "Wow, you know, the more we talk about this, the more it makes perfect sense. I mean what you said Don, about magick being the anathema of a dreaming society, makes sense. We don't use our minds like we used to. I mean where's the DaVinci's, where's the prophets? Where's the Buddha's? Where are they these days? There's an awful lot more of us on the planet now, than at any point in history, so there should be more saviours and geniuses? So where are they? Probably sitting watchin' Jeremy Kyle and eating nachos, that's where!"

Don rolled his cigarette thoughtfully. "It's like we're blinded by convenience, like we're existing in a gilded cage perhaps!?"

Hippie Davie then bounced back, folding his arms on the table with a slight thump. He was having one of his animated moments, which always gave me a bit of a start. It was as if his brain suddenly came to life jolting him from his usual laid back semi-comatose self. It seemed to me as if he was suddenly being possessed at times, so great was the change of energy and enthusiasm.

He continued on; "I think it's probably true that older civilizations had a good awareness of the world, had a connection with it, like you described Sensible. But with civilization came slavery, came mundane life, came a gradual disconnection to nature and perhaps our own individual nature with that. Maybe sleeping or unconscious is too strong a term, but more like a gradual dimming down of this type of connection, awareness or awareness of the whole as it were. That would explain why mystical systems like the qabalah or the Egyptian rites could be developed then, when enough mystics had a good connection to their own nature and their connection to everything else."

He prodded the table, affirming the thread and firing out the next.

"You could argue that there is definitely a lack of awareness or insight into that kind of mental possessing now and we've become more left brained. All the psychodynamic energy is being used by the left brain so we have computers and planes, but at a cost. I mean everybody knows the North American Indians had a respect for nature that we just don't. Ask anyone, not just hippies like me but anyone, anyone up there on Union Street right now and they'll tell you; we've lost our connection to nature. Everybody can say it, but nobody really understands how we lost it, or what it is to get it back."

I wasn't entirely sure that the American Indians or any tribal people for that matter didn't actually change the environment they inhabited. I remember watching a documentary where archaeologists could tell from lake-bed layers and ice-core samples that primitive people had burned many acres of forests in pre-historic times; so much for "close to nature" (bollocks). Although his argument that industrialisation forced a change in consciousness did seem fairly reasonable to me, I felt that was, perhaps, inevitable. I remembered something Professor Speakman had said in passing in the lift on one visit to the department to check in with the bat project, "The current trend towards obesity, which is beginning to gather pace in Europe and the U.S. before that, could be attributed to a lack of predators on the human race and a metabolic evolution towards something akin to island micro-evolution."

So I threw the idea into the ring, "You know what guys; the dodo right, was a pigeon of sorts, but it became fat and flightless on the islands of Mauritius where it had evolved. It had no predators. When people arrived they found it stupid, helpless and fucking half comatose it was asking for its own demise. I say the human race has become like the fucking dodo. We've become fat, dependent on home entertainment, our minds have become lazy; and if we're not careful we'll die out just the same; blissfully unaware that we could have ever taken flight in the first place."

Hippie Davie who had been thinking himself into a cloud of blue smoke emerged and shook his dreadlocked hair in agreement.

"You know, Sensible old son, I think you're on to something! If more people were to use magick on a personal level, guided by a few clever wise men and women, we would have seen a society based more on...on freedom...on marching towards a destiny where fairness wins out even, where people become more like some version of Nietzsche's supermen. I mean, if loads of people became aware of these 'other dimensions of human consciousness,' such as only very few do now, then there would be a lot less bickering and more thinking about the big picture! I think more people would gain awareness that we're all the same, that race is an illusion and something like the soul is the real reality. That it does boil down to the global village of humanity. I think what you say actually feels right you know? It feels true, but very few people seem to even be aware of this, but what can we do?"

I shrugged. "I guess we're doing it, we're thinking for ourselves, we're trying to explore our will, magick, destiny, alchemy and tread a path that basically hurts no-one and keeps everybody sweet. I guess the answer is not to preach, that seems to be what the forces of control do, they preach, it's like psychological warfare! What we can do is to just lead by example I suppose. I mean look at you Hippie Davie! You're doing it; using the bardic tradition of using a known saga –*Star Wars* – to align yourself with your own will and destiny and teach us the same!"

Hippie Davie smiled and pointed towards us and in a mock Darth Vader voice said, "Yoor destiny lies with me!" Making us laugh again.

Don piped up. "Maybe we should be looking for a new prophet!? Like an anarchistic one who doesn't want power or followers but actually wants people to think for themselves!?"

Hippie Davie nodded. "Yeah, like Elijah or Thoth or Hermes Thrice Great. Some say they were not even human but possessed of prater-human intelligence, imparting their wisdom onto the old priesthoods and philosophies of the ages."

As was customary, I threw a spanner in the works, "But if they tried that now, society would declare war on them in the name of God!"

Hippie Davie looked pensive for a moment, drawing on his spliff like Freud drawing on his pipe deep in thought. Only a century and a beard and some hair beads separated them.

"Well, maybe we don't need a modern day prophet, well actually the last prophet that I've taken any notice of was quite clear that, you don't need to follow anyone or anything per-se, but your only duty is to develop your own divinity."

I nodded in affirmation with my own inner sense of libertarianism; this was obviously rather like CRASS again to me. "Like a spiritual anarchy you mean?"

Hippie Davie shrugged. "Yeah, exactly, there's only one way of life and that's your own true will. The term 'will' referring to your own inner self (souls) true path in life, as opposed to the rusty tram lines you might be stuck on because of the need to work, love and consume."

Don and I nodded. We could get the idea, but Hippie Davie was a little sketchy on the how. "You're talking about Aleister Crowley of course, Hippy Davie?" I said.

Hippy Davie gave a cheeky smirk. "Yeah brothers y'know, the guy that pretty much invented most of modern Wicca!?" He smiled a broad dimpled grin as he watched us with his head bent back a little, like a math's teacher surveying his pupils.

Don wrinkled his nose. "Fuck off! Aradia invented Wicca; no-one can claim invention of the craft!"

I nodded an affirmation towards Don. "Yeah, c'mon Hippie Davie, you're always having a dig at Wicca. You're not telling me two blokes in a country club somewhere dreamt it up over a couple of Brandies and a cigar!? Even if they did contribute towards it, there are plenty of people that would say they've had witchcraft in their families long before they came on the scene surely!"

Hippie Davie nodded, "Witchcraft, yeah, but Wicca, specifically is a re-energized folk tradition mixed with modern twentieth century magick, from the Golden Dawn really and Aleister Crowley, the prophet of modern magick...I'll admit that Doreen Valiente had a larger part to play in it right enough."

"Well fair enough," I said, "I must admit I haven't delved too deeply into Crowley, he's a bit obscure sometimes, I'll stick with Vivienne Crowley just now thank you very much!"

Don tutted, "Aye, well when the Goddess directs me to read a Crowley book I will."

Hippie Davie sighed a little. "Look no disrespect brother, but surely the Goddess helps those who helps themfuckinselves!?"

Don looked quite irritated at Hippie Davie's swipe; he hated being preached at.

"Look here ye...ye big dreadlocked twat. Firstly, am sure it was Jesus that said something like that, so you can stop your friggin' preaching! Yer getting as bad as the boy." He motioned towards me, indicating that I was often a pain in the arse when suggesting that he should read certain books or correct him on some scientific theory he'd gleaned from a badly concocted story in the Daily Mail. "Secondly, who actually needs to read books wi' you two cunts goin' on and on a' the effin time." He turned around to Hippie Davie and put his hand over to receive his spliff, then purposely held it up to his lips and triumphantly smiled as he mocked us.

Hippie Davie conceded and smiled. "Aye, fair enough, but actually, there are proof and a point to it all, you see! Mr. Crowley did get it all to work; he showed that if you have enough patience and you practice the right systems, like we're doing to increase our willpower and access our mental abilities as much as possible, then you do in fact start living in accordance with your will. You do wake up a bit. It's what the humanistic psychologists call self-actualisation!" I had heard of that from the psychology lectures, but hadn't realised they meant illumination. I stated that to Hippie Davie. He shrugged.

"Yeah, well it's just that Crowley was way ahead of them and understood this technology we call magick. Finding your true will is like finding yourself in a personal way and with your whole soul. I mean who wouldn't want to do that!?"

We sat back and watched the shadows grow longer as a darkening sky swallowed up the hustle and bustle below, creating a bowl of blackening cobbles. Grey granite facades were blotted out of their detail up and down the Green and beyond in distant Market Street. On cue, the city lights blossomed, flickering across window sills and walls, in their inexorable fight to hold back the darkness; resulting in lonely pools of glare. I was over-dozed with coffee and now it was beginning to get unpleasant and headachey. I could tell that Don was definitely getting annoyed with us, as his last outburst had revealed. I was also starting to get annoyed with his grumpiness, which I usually found funny and comforting; but at other times like this I wanted to kick his stick away and knock his top hat off and stand on it! Hippie Davie could sometimes be hard work as well. From the moment, I had met him I always felt a little drained in his presence. It's true, I really like him and he inspired me a lot but as I watched him I noticed how he would sometimes fail to conceal that he felt a little self-satisfied and superior with his profound, grownup knowledge of philosophy or magick.

However, now I regarded him as an equal, as a friend, just as fallible, or lazy at times, as I was. I liked this observation, as it hit me that I really had changed greatly in a short space of time. I felt more "real" and much more capable of handling life and all its foibles, it was as if the constant middle pillar and meditations had strengthened me and perhaps my soul really was ticking over more in accordance with my life and life direction, who knows?

Hippie Davie had gone to the counter and had a little chat to the now giggling Amber. I had a little chuckle with Don about how it felt like everybody seemed to 'get some' except me. As Hippie Davie was returning, Don in all earnest was casually posing the question, "Well, do you want a blow job then or don't yeah?"

He said this quite sarcastically and loud enough to know it would annoy me as I shrank a little in my seat as onlookers swivelled their heads in my direction, he really was cruising for a kick up the pocket watch and chain. I shook my head as Hippie Davie grinning also began shaking his dreadlocks in a mock slow motion fashion,

"Fuck-in-ell, well, I take it back; you two are not like a married couple after all, far too many blowjobs getting bandied about for that!"

We laughed as Don agreed, "Well aye, that's the good thing aboot Wicca, the maximum period you can be hitched is a year and a day, then you get the chance to re-do it or renegotiate the marriage bonds."

Hippie Davie sat down putting his finger over his mouth. "Ssshh, don't tell the general public that, for God's sake. If that gets oot they'll be lining up at Newmachar for miles! Heheh!" It was a funny thought, but probably not so far from the truth. We probably didn't want our cosy little club to be infiltrated by the suits and the profane. We didn't want the conversations at the circle to become dominated by latest robe fashions or where to buy accessories for all the Wiccan holidays.

Hippie Davie burst open a packet of Maltesers and we instantly cheered up again as he handed them round. We sat back throwing them up in the air and catching them in our mouths like trained seals...albeit probably diabetic ones.

Hippie Davie, munching like a happy terrier looked around the café surroundings, as if he'd just noticed that he was in one, like the chocolate had temporarily made him quite sober for the first time in ten years. He raised his finger in the air indicating that his mind was churning around some concept that he had to share, so Don and I decided to capitalise on the opportunity of not having to speak by cramming another couple of sweets in our mouths. Finally Hippie Davie spoke,

"I've been thinking, about our talking about no prophets anymore and people living a slave-like existence and not having the access to the stuff we have; maybe we should do a ritual of some kind to wake people up, maybe it's our duty in a way?"

Don and I looked at each other. I immediately thought it was a waste of time and expected Don to concur, but he looked in agreement with the idea.

"Yeah, let's do something, if it helps people accept us and our way of life, then it's no bad thing!"

Don was always the one who hated the fact that he had to explain each time he said he was a witch or followed the craft of the wise, as he put it. People didn't give you that hassle if you said you were a Taoist or Buddhist! Despite the fact that he went out of his way to look very different, which possibly made him appear to be an attention grabber, he actually got annoyed with people staring or reacting to him as an outsider. Don just wanted to stamp his own style as "normal," so he could just get on with his day.

We put our heads together and came up with a plan of how to go about this new venture. This is when the three musketeers were at their best. We were in our element discussing how to put a magical ritual together and how to up the ante a little bit from what we had done before. Certainly from working together so much and using lots of our spare time meditating and diligently practising, we were very strong as a group and knew we could handle just about anything. Finally, we decided that we needed something that would supply a little bit of information for the rational mind to chew on and provide something to use as a talisman that could be charged and would link the personal object to a collective social prayer for change, towards a more enlightened society.

Don had an idea first. "Maybe spray paint some symbol with different slogans here and there and charge each one in a circle!?"

We mulled that one over. I thought it wasn't bad but slightly disconnected, as it might cause confusion or be drowned out by all the other graffiti or bill boards. I thought about some of my CRASS LPs, where information was sometimes disseminated on the cover or in a booklet.

"What about a small booklet or photocopy that can be done and handed out and maybe we can do a sigil on each one and charge the symbol?" I said.

Hippie Davie nodded. "But wait, a sigil doesn't have to be a symbol, it can be a work of art or something we put our efforts and intent into. I like the idea of information, but a photocopy sounds too sterile or boring, why not a picture or piece of art?"

As Hippie Davie put that image in my head, suddenly I had the perfect idea, "A comic strip, a fucking comic strip where we gradually give out information and inform people about self-illumination and free will!"

Hippie Davie was excited and followed on my line of thought. "And we can have a hero who finds his own true will and then begins to change the world for the better by showing other people how to do it!"

Don now was smiling, liking the idea. "Aye, or he goes about Scotland or Britain, kinda like Kwai Caine in *Kung Fu*, ye know, getting involved in situations and sharing his wisdom or doing magick to help people!"

Hippie Davie then finished off the idea, "It has to be a Jedi, a guy that wakes up and realises George Lucas had a secret code imbedded in the film that was designed to wake people up and use their own power, own force against the might of the empire! It's perfect, the original films are a call for humans to get back in touch with nature and their own personal hero and we're just carrying on the work!"

We talked it over; Davie was a fantastic artist and had drawn some comics himself with exquisite detail and Don and I understood the medium well enough to make decent story boards for it. It was simple; each comic once created would then be consecrated and charged as a powerful sigil. We were sure Austin Osman Spare would have approved of this use of his method. The sigil would work on the astral level of the collective consciousness and will the readers into realising that they can be the hero, as the hero doesn't have any other special power except faith in his own self diligence, self-propelled will and a realisation that the mind is much more capable of things than we're lead to believe is possible!

We worked on it for days. Don took to phoning me out of the blue all the time with ideas, which would turn into hours of discussion and vice-versa. All I wanted to do was work on it and the other musketeers were no different. Hippie Davie drew, painted and sketched and I began to love the characters, based on us. I was voted to be the main character, as it seemed fitting that a nerdy scientist should become a superhero. It was a tried and tested formula after all. My moniker went through much iteration but we eventually settled on "Rational Russel." I felt it was a bit of a piss-take or what they actually felt my name was, but was content for the purposes of the comic to let it go. Hippie Davie was re-named 'Alistair Starman.' He wanted to just keep his own name, but Don chided him, saying that Hippie Davie would be a stupid and annoying name for a hippie in a storybook, as 'Davie' sounded way too conventional. Don was to be the inspiration for a third character who was there to keep me grounded and add clever sarcasm and wit to the comic strip, modelled a long way on one of my favourite comic book characters John Constantine of *Hellblazer*. We finally hit upon a name for the comic and *The Hippie, the Dippy and the Lippy* was born. The whole comic was to be one big sigil, which would come out periodically and hopefully would just wake people the fuck up to their own potential even just a little bit and usher in an eon of mutual respect, awareness and that through the lessons of the social sciences, we all should know by now that we're all the fucking same and that all religions are, essentially after the same thing as well. It's quite simple really, isn't it, when you talk it through!?

I had a niggling doubt about whether this was actually lawful, though in a Wiccan or magical sense, weren't we coercing people just a little bit? Don and I decided to ask Mags and so, not waiting until the next full moon came, we thought it would be good to go there and see her in a wee visit. It would be good to take Hippie Davie along as Mags had a high opinion of him and so I knew it would just be a nice interesting chat. I enjoyed driving places with my mates; it was a change from hanging about the town like a trio of tramps for a change.

Mags looked over her spectacles at us; she had been deep in Terry Pratchett's latest novel and we all felt a little guilty. However, she seemed in a very good mood, buoyed by the book's contents no doubt. She went to make tea while the three of us, unlikely looking people to be visiting an elderly lady in the quiet cul-de-sac in the very middle class estate in Newmachar, sat patiently. Mags came through smiling, "Well tell me, how you got on with the nasty business of that thing in Edinburgh?"

The thought "as if you don't know!" fluttered across my thoughts as if it were tickertape being lead behind a bi-plane.

Hippie Davie sat back comfortably; arms spread out on the sofa, threw a spliff up in the air and caught it in his mouth. He looked at Don and I who had paused and tensed for a second, "You...you don't mind if I?"

Mags shrugged. "No I really don't mind, s'up to you!"

Don and I both relaxed and turned our attentions to our cups of tea. Don daintily lifted his tea up to his face, with his little finger jutting out. I smirked and nudged Hippie Davie's knee, he looked at me and still smirking I nodded towards Don. He was dressed in his usual regalia, his large top hat sat on the table top next to the tea pot and his large jangly three million hole Doc Martins stretched out seeming to take up the entire living room carpet. He had on a dusty looking velvety waistcoat and black sort of cassock complete with a black cravat. His face was painted black and white as usual and this "spectre" sipping tea politely just seemed all the more comical! Hippie Davie began to smirk as well and the two of us began chuckling louder and louder until it was very obvious we were laughing at him as he studiously sipped his Victorian cuppa.

He looked over the rim of the cup at us, a little taken aback that we were laughing at his expense. "What the fuck's wrong with you two?"

"Nothing, nothing!" I replied and picked up my cup emphasising my stuck out pinkie. "Paasss the sugaah, will you dear chap?" I motioned to Hippie Davie.

Hippie Davie swept up the sugar bowl and offered it to me with a pronounced low nod of the head. "Certainly my good man; would one care for one lump or two?"

Don wrinkled his forehead, not sure if we were taking the piss out of him or just mucking around. Hippie Davie then picked up his cup also sticking out his pinkie and we both just sat there like that, grinning at Don. Hippie Davie then wiggled his little finger to accentuate the gesture, which led Don to take stock of his own pinkie jutting out, he clearly hadn't even thought about it. "Awh fuck off...fuck off! There's nothing wrong with a bit of etiquette! A gentleman always has a bit of etiquette!"

Mags tutted. "That's not very nice language for a gentleman Don, now surely!"

Don grovelled an apology and presumably went a little red in the face...you just couldn't see it under the make up. Hippie Davie and I chuckled under our breath, as triumphant as a pair of ten year olds that had got a class mate into trouble with the teacher.

We explained our thoughts and experiences to Mags. She smiled; well old Gerald (Gardner) would approve actually! I remember him saying that Wicca needed to grow as much as possible, though he was certain that would annoy certain secretive powers that would become aware and activated if people gained enough awareness in the magical realms. I remember he sneered and said that our brand of magick, under the banner of Wicca, was a re-awakening of the old ways that could not be stopped. I never quite understood what he meant by that; I always assumed he was talking about the church and the authorities, but I also had the sense that he was referring to these so-called corrupt secret chiefs or secret powers that worked to slow down human evolution or spiritual development. He was convinced that humanity was far less advanced than we should be. He contended that older civilisations had been eradicated and their knowledge covered up. He said he knew, for instance, that the Knight Templar had started a crusade to reintroduce illumination back into Western philosophy and thought, but they had virtually been wiped out overnight by the powers of darkness as a consequence."

Mags paused and thought for a moment, before nodding and conceding her point, "Gerald really strongly believed that Wicca was the latest expression of what the Templars had tried to instigate (their psychic sensor, if you will) and it was a current that eventually wouldn't be stopped. We had to win, he said, humanity depended on it!"

Then she wrinkled her nose, "Pah, old Gerald was a bit over imaginative at times, he liked conspiracies!"

Hippie Davie made a loud "Mmmm" sound in acknowledgement," Well yeah, I can see how enlightened beings may go over to the dark side and serve the empire!"

Mags nodded and chuckled.

I agreed, but impatiently implored Mags with my hands to explain more. "But, but, ok, what do you mean by psychic sensor exactly?"

Mags raised one eyebrow and gave an almost imperceptible sigh as she searched for an analogy. Although she was very patient and clearly enjoyed our company, this was the problem having a conversation with a certified genius; it sometimes made you feel a little bit slow.

"Well, think about it like this, you have probably experienced your own sensor when you've had out of body experiences or when you've been asleep and had an astral journey."

Don piped up, "Hud oan, is that no the same thing?"

Mags swept his question aside. "No."

Don looked at me and then back towards Mags looking now very confused,

"No dear, an out of body experience is when your mind creates a facsimile of your actual body from the power in your cells and then perceives the world through this medium. The perception is better because you are 'perceiving' not just physical matter but everyone's imaginary representation of matter, the manifest 'thingness' of everything (just as this cup is physical glass and silica atoms, it also has a definite 'cupness' in the world we know) just as everything has a 'physical existence' of everything. So an out of body projection can perceive that and everything and everybody is as it seems now, only more so and sometimes time effects are skewed because the facsimile body is free from the effects of mass and gravity which affects time, so with the right know-how, the facsimile can traverse time too…but that takes a lot of practice."

The penny dropped for me, "Ahh, is that what I call my shadow body then?"

Don glanced over a little jealously and probably still pissed off that I had an OBE in the woods and woke him up and, in his mind anyway, stopped any chance of him having one.

Mags smiled back. "Mmm ah yes, I think many people just see a dark outline and refer to it as that yes! So anyway, that's quite different from astral projection! Mmm yes, that's, right a lot of people get them confused." She paused for a second whilst she absentmindedly indulged some whirling thoughts around her head and sipped her tea. Meanwhile, back on less lofty mental plains Don and I waited like two pets dogs at tea time, eyes fixed on their master patiently waiting for

Mags to continue. "Astral travel is more of a dreamscape travel, it's in much more dream-like landscapes and magical landscapes like the qabalistic sephiroth or tarot can lead you into. You know, all the lands, gods, monsters of the mind and myths that have been created and reinforced by numerous wills of magician, sorcerer or romantics alike over the millennia? These lands there are much more malleable and plastic landscapes but obviously they are real. Some are semi-independent creatures and lands, whilst others are much more real than this cup and room around it here, as they exist in heavenly dimensions that don't change or falter like ours do in time!"

Don and I nodded. It made sense, though no-one and certainly no book I had read up until that point had spelt it out quite so frankly.

We barely had time to digest this when Mags pulled the conversation back to the topic, which was handy because I had temporarily forgotten about it myself.

"So you will know that when you are in your shadow body certain things are not possible. You can't do certain things or seem to have the power to perform certain things! This is your own personal psychic sensor. It's a moral higher function that is similar to your higher self preventing you from doing what your ego or id would have you do on a whim. It is basically your own limitations. Well similarly a group mind evolves or creates these social psychic sensors! It's part of the fabric of our beliefs, ideals and social glue really that binds tribes together. You should perhaps aim to inflate your psychic sensor to connect to that Templar/Gnostic current and then tap into the collective unconscious of Aberdeen."

What Mags said made perfect sense, of course. I liked it because it encroached on Psychology principles I had learned at university about group dynamics and social identity. It also chimed with Jung's concepts of collective unconscious, which was something I could just about adhere to, despite my initial distaste for the lack of a physical evidential "link" it seemed to suggest. Though here was a magical explanation which tied into Social Psychology 101.

# 0: The Force

## Chapter 14:
## The Empire Strikes Back

"Christ, this is amazing, we've actually done something, we've actually achieved something and created a product!" I mused, totally enthralled by the five-page mini comic book that we had created. Hippie Davie's artwork was beautiful. He was a talented artist and Art College had really missed a trick by allowing him to drop out all those years before. Hippie Davie scoffed, "I don't like the way you just said product like that Sensible! You're starting to sound like a greedy little capitalist!"

I nodded; "You know what, you're right, let's not contaminate this talisman! It's not a mere product, it's a work of art, work of absolute beauty," I said as I leafed through admiring Hippie Davie's work, "and doesn't deserve to be bundled as a thing to be sold and consumed, it's art and art deserves to have a life of its own. It should exist to inspire and brighten up other people's lives."

I found it a bit sad that the system, as CRASS would refer to the commercial and political machine, absorbed everything and rendered it as trinkets to be hoarded and possessed. In a perfect world art should be free! And this is exactly what we intended to do with this comic; disseminate it to people who were worthy and who would respond to its message. Clearly the average "comic reader," we decided, was more than halfway to being receptive to the ideas that could be communicated by the hidden mysteries. They just needed a little shove. Although Don did threaten to break the spell, saying,

"Aye, bit, maybe if we charged a little bit, we could each get a few pints and a big bit of hash out of it?"

We had decided to arrange the will of the magic operating through the sigil as a powerful beacon to stimulate chakras associated with spiritual advancement. We included a caveat that it be in accordance with people's own will, rather than creating something that would make people slavishly turn to Paganism or the occult against their will. We just concluded that there were many intellectual people out there that would be receptive to their teachings, except that the current system we were ruled by did not provide the means for people to uncover these routes. We were just trying to redress the balance.

The comic was a story of a scientist who was very sceptical of the occult but who had met a hippie in a bar (Prince of Wales) one evening and had decided to attack him on his views on Paganism and magick. We decided to clarify exactly what the difference was between magicians and materialist scientists in that it boils down to imagination.

The scientist, 'Rational Russel,' believed that human imagination, although a useful tool in the history of science, was only a product of the brain and therefore "unreal." It evaporated on return from daydreaming and had no influence at all on physical reality. In fact this very notion was laughable and this had been revealed as so by the heroes of science such as James 'The Amazing' Randi.

The magician may also concede that magick and its effects are a result of the imagination. They just ask the question, "How big is imagination?" and they quite simply believe that imagination can drastically affect a person's personal reality (just like the psychiatrists/psychologists believe) and we also know to be true. But imagination clearly also affects actual physical reality to some extent as well, as reality and imagination are completely inter-twined (you can't have one without the other). That is, energy, information and time all mix!

The story starts as a savage attack on the superstitious beliefs of the hippie but by the end of page five the scientist is confronted by a strange sensation when the hippie uses the force to make him feel his inner energy and also predicts in a dream an exact situation that he finds himself in. The story was mapped out that the scientist would start off incredibly sceptical and condescending but keeps seeing the hippie use magick and it works for him every time, such as healing or knowing the future.

He decides to investigate using the method of gathering data and hypothesis testing and finds a pattern. Consequently he follows the five step path to enlightenment as mapped out by ourselves and Hippie Davie and becomes an adept, a much more chilled, wiser and happier individual, who has freed himself from a life of a crap nine to five laboratory job and who then travels Asia learning more about being a real human being. He comes back a changed man and revolutionises science creating a new science of magick!

There was nowhere to contact, no link to the Pagan Federation, but the astral link was powerful. We expected people to begin searching themselves and connect to that fate we had made possible. We wanted to create a shortcut through time, a wormhole to a better reality.

Don used his privileges at his work to key into the colour photocopiers and print off a couple of hundred copies. At night, the company copy room became a factory of multi-coloured pamphlets spilling out of the guts of a machine more used to churning out minutes of meetings or memos to all department heads or the occasional arse cheeks at Christmas. I liked the juxtaposition, as I sipped coffee and watched the free comics pile up, eating into some giant ecosystem-destroying oil company budget. I glanced over to Don, who I could tell looked a little concerned at the use of the all the colour cartridges and paper. It would surely be noticed and if it was traced to him, he would just as surely get the sack!

Hippie Davie must have read my thoughts, as he said, "Well fuck 'em, do you know how much profit these oil companies are making? They've got the world over a barrel like drug dealers have over the junkies. What gives them the right to make astronomical profits over the stuff we need for day to day life?" I guess he was spot on really.

We decided to put it all in a box and wandered into Plan 9 comic shop with it. We didn't think they'd be interested, but 'the boy with the bright red hair', as we tended to refer to the guy that worked there, seemed quite excited by it, like it was a right on idea. He was very impressed by the artwork and effort that had obviously gone into producing it. We all sat in silence as he consumed the comic panel by slow panel. We practically held our breath and gave each other relieved and excited looks every time he sniggered or when his face obviously sank into concerned concentration.

Eventually he finished and looked at us with an affirming nod, "Yeah, yeah it's no bad, kinda funny in places...I think I know what you're going for and it's a nice idea as well...But I'm worried it's a bit 'lecturey' in places."

The other two each swivelled their heads towards me in silent accusation, as if we were psychically communicating or moaning at each other, unbeknownst to the boy with the very red hair. I felt myself go a little bit pink, but then I thought I'd better clarify,

"Wait a minute do you mean sciencey lecturey or magickey lecturey?"

The boy with the extremely red hair flicked back through the pages and then looked up, "Yeah a bit of both, but yeah, the hippie does go on a bit as well!"

Don and I then swivelled our heads towards Hippie Davie and gave him a told you so kind of look now making him go a little pink under his hippie bronzed cheeks. We then all took turns explaining the plan and the eventual unfolding plot to emerge in subsequent issues and he nodded and appeared to "dig it," as we spoke. Eventually we came to an agreement and he accepted the box, a bit confused that we weren't charging anything at all for them. Don then decided to assure him this was only for the first one hundred issues, after that it might cost fifty pence a time.

Outside, we chastised him for falling into greedy ways. Don halted us with the palms of his hands,

"Now jist wait a minute, you're the hippie and the indie-punk guy, you might not care about profits or covering all the overheads we have, but it's like you said Hippie Davie, Lucas used the system to defeat the system. Well, all we're doing is the same int it? I don't think there's anything wrong with making money to buy more paper, or...or keep us in 'stimulants' for the creative process!"

Hippie Davie and I had to agree, it was probably sensible to recoup some money for inks and paper and for the general time spent on it. As we ambled along Union Terrace towards Union Street, Don was tapping his finger tips, like some fleshy little glockenspiel, muttering to himself;

"Yep at fifty pence each, coupla-hundred copied next time and a run o' ten comics, that's nearly a grand, a good three hundred sobs each!"

I wrinkled my nose a little; "Listen to Alan Sugar back there." Then I thought about Don's statement of "best part of a grand." Well I suppose a little bit of beer money wouldn't go a miss.

All we could do was then sit back and let our creation roll out to the public and see what happens. Would people wake up a little? Would the environmental movement catch fire throughout society and gain much quicker pace within our generation? Would people start communicating more or co-operating more? Would we start protesting a little harder about the stuff that affects us?

Three days later, I wandered around to the comic shop. We said we'd leave it for a week, but I was curious as to whether anyone had taken any. To my surprise, there were only a couple left. As soon as I walked in, the boy with the incredibly red hair gave me a big smile and a bit of a hero welcome.

"Well I doubted that people would go for this, but a lot of people are saying it's really great having a comic about Aberdeen and magick going on like that; a lot of folk have been asking when the next copy is coming out. Then he looked keen, obviously now being a bit of a fan now himself. "So when is the next copy coming out?"

I shrugged. "We're still putting it together; it all depends on the rest of the team as well.

The boy with the impressively red hair smiled back, "Well you'd better get yourself to yer café or whatever coz the other two are away to work on it this afternoon!"

I shook my head sighing a little. "You mean they've been in?"

"Yes," replied with boy with the shocking red hair smiling widely. "I've seen them both in this afternoon and both said they were away to work on it. They said to tell you to go down to the Green!"

I looked a little sheepish; was I that predictable?

As I left the shop, the boy with the indescribably red hair shouted over the counter, "Oh and can you have a word with Don, tell him I really do think three pounds an issue will put a lot of people off, especially as most people are now expecting it to be free, you know!?"

I nodded and made a note of that.

I made my way through Union Terrace Gardens, enjoying the Victorian splendour of granite and trees and relative silence just metres away from the main shopping fare. I skipped up again onto Union Street, hurried over the bridge and then dived over the road to nip through the grim Aberdeen Market, a strange mall-like maze that was built in the 1970s and now remained frozen in that era. A little collection of cheap stalls and odd little shoe shops selling cheap tat that surely nobody actually wants. Even the little coffee area with its tea stained laminated lino tables and brimming tin ashtrays that were too small for all the ash and shoddy plastic chairs looked frozen in the previous decades. A radio playing ABBA somewhere solidified my observation. This was a mall erected before malls became proper modern malls of the late eighties and nineties with chrome and over-sized portions of food and shops selling expensive gadgets and gifts. The Aberdeen Market was like Aberdeen's cheap little version of a mall, before Americans showed us how to do it properly. I snaked my way through the mall and snuck out the back way straight into the Green. Turning the corner, I immediately spotted the thatched head of Hippie Davie and then the top hat of Don resting on the table. They were hard at work, scribbling and discussing the comic. I felt a pang of sadness as I watched them, transformed from the usual sleepy, take it easy pair into a high pressure advertising executive meeting or something like that. I'd created a monster.

"Fits up guys?" I nodded as I approached, slightly peeved at their pace of productivity in my absence.

"Oh we've got this great idea that we can link Jedi-ism to the same ideals as modern day Knights Templars!" Don affirmed enthusiastically. "And Hippie Davie here knows a lot about it!"

Hippie Davie saw my eyebrow rise as I turned my head towards him; he knew it was his cue to explain a further.

"Yeah bro, I've been reading up on the Templars and their association with secret societies and so on and it seems to me that they were definitely all about illumination and spiritual progress. I reckon they brought back documents from the Arabian Peninsula showing how to move your inner spirit up from the physical level to merge with the level of a personal God. Effectively a sort of mixture of Gnostic Christianity, Sufism and powerful magical alchemy."

I listened intently; I had no idea of who the Templars were except that Mags had mentioned them. I acknowledged this; as usual inspired by Hippie Davie and his way of thinking, which always seemed to me to have a real core of intuitive truth about it.

Hippie Davie fired on, "They were religious knights which stood for chivalry, becoming a better man both externally and internally. They were the first super humans brother, the first Jedis! And you know what else? They were eradicated almost overnight by the Catholic Church like Mags said Gardner said, by order of the Pope in the twelfth century. It seems to me that the church back then, the ruling system, was ultimately responsible for suppressing human nature whilst aiming to dominate external nature. They burned woman, they tried to kill off all traces of witchcraft and label any path to personal development as devil worship. It was a war against humanity that rages still. I mean, that's what we're all about isn't it? Trying to redress the balance, trying to broadcast a wakeup call through the matrix of our collective unconscious with the message to regain your humanity, regain your force and regain your divinity! I tell ya the more I think about it, the more I think old Gerald was onto something brother!"

Hippie Davie by this time was standing up in mock soap box preacher style, speaking out to the large invisible crowd on the Green, but in reality it was Don, a couple of pigeons and myself. Hippie Davie deserved a better audience than this; it made me feel that the sigil-comic idea was right. Someone had to redress the balance. Hippie Davie's talk about the Knights Templars made me think about The Doc, how he tried to bullshit that police officer and I actually felt a little nostalgic at times for his bullshit comments. He had been, after all, a source of amusement, a never ending wellspring of misdemeanours and stupidity that did tend to make you feel superior.

Strangely Don seemed to be thinking the same thing, "Hey guys, did you hear aboot The Doc?"

We both shrugged; we hadn't heard from him, nor even wanted to for several months.

Don looked a little smug, enjoying being the bearer of the little titbit of gossip that he had. "He's back in the fucking nuthoose, apparently!"

I could see Hippie Davie wincing and I knew he felt a little pang of guilt, just as I did, though I didn't know why. Though, perhaps we had mocked him too much at times. Perhaps we should have concentrated on helping him and grounding him. Perhaps we indulged his grandiose notion of himself, or did not challenge him enough, as Gemma had.

Don though, apparently did not harbour the same sense of regret. "Yep, got a mate that bides nae far from his Ma and kaens a cousin o' his as well. He's been keeping an eye on him for me." Don seemed to know an awful lot of people all over Aberdeen, his friend of Dorothy network. I guess they were kind of like the men from UNCLE that dressed like your auntie. "Aye he's eh, shaved aff a" his hair and had a breakdown and just went down and signed himself in! Poor bastard, but he's better aff in there, he's nae built for reality is he?" This coming from the man who had come to the Café 52 on the Green with a face painted like 'The Crow' and was wearing an English gentleman waistcoat and top hat upper half combined with a Scottish kilt bottom half and who, after a quick change, would be on his way to work where one of his best mates was a ghost he'd named, for some unfathomable reason, Harry!

We worked on and then eventually made our way down to the harbour to continue, all night if need be, at Don's work. We had to wait until the beat driver had fucked off, so Hippie Davie and I just wandered around the quayside taking in the sights of the giant vessels silently bobbing atop the tamed waters of the harbour. Everything was just plain nice at the harbour, as all the heavy machinery, winches and tons of sea-faring hulls all lay, as if sleeping, static and restful under the strange unnatural glare of harbour lights. A halogen-lit reality interposed against darkened grey skies and granite streets and alleyways. The murky oil-tainted water looked ill and sediment choked as it occasionally washed and splahed up and down the sides of rust-stained giants. Huge, unnaturally massive chains (that made you feel you were in some fairy story like Jack and the beanstalk) dipped, and then quickly disappeared, beneath the foreboding black depths. I liked just wandering around looking at stuff with Hippie Davie, getting high on his supply and taking in the surreal sights of this weirdly lit and oddly quiet place devoid of people at this time, like spaced out tourists. It crossed my mind that it would be relatively easy to steal a boat if we knew how to drive one, if drive one was the correct phrase.

Occasionally, a massive vessel would drift surreraly quietly outward to sea, illuminated like some alien spacecraft. Seemingly coming from nowhere and then slowly departing into the night amidst the drone of industry, both machine and human, only to be swallowed by the silence of blackness and colourless lapping waters.

Eventually, Don's beat driver had gone and Hippie Davie and I ambled up to the marbled hallway where Don was chatting on the phone making some calls to the central office to check in. He talked for ages. People always liked chatting to him because he was just so innocuous and friendly, so the woman down in London just seemed to go on and on, talking nonsense and innuendo with him, annoying us slightly. We raised eyebrows at each other and did that big eye thing that telegraphed impatience, though we had no right. This was his workplace after all.

We ended up in the conference room and spread our storyboards and ideas around the table. We even had the cheek to use the flip chart pad in the corner to debate formats, story lines and ideas. We were getting paid in coffee and good company and that seemed quite good enough to me and I suspect, Hippie Davie. However Don had quickly assumed the role of chairperson as he could have chucked us out at any time. It was like he owned the place.

We decided to have a formal meeting and Don sat at the head of the table, put his fingers together in front of his face in a triangle, in an' I'm-a-court-lawyer kind of way' and instructed us to sit down. Nodding towards me, in mock serious voice,

"Now Mr. Sensible, can you present the latest ideas from the dialogue in little bubbles department?"

I smiled and then stood up and cleared my throat. "Well, eh, the little bubble department is being held up at the moment by the scribbley, department as apparently, they don't have enough room on the panels for all my writing annnd their big swishy drawings!"

I sat down and then Hippie Davie stood up all business like to reply.

"Well, first of all I didn't get the memo that the art department had been re-titled as described!" We all laughed as I grinned broadly to the other two, taking ownership of my latest bit of ad-lib. Hippy Davie continued with the presentation.

"Even if I was stoned, I doubt I would have agreed to that one, we're indulging in serious fine-art here...not the wall scratchings of a fucking mental patient. As for swishy drawings!? Surely the board here recognises that it can't be a proper comic book without swishy drawings, the bigger and shishier the more serious a comic it is! Sshhhesh...everybody knows that!" Don and I nodded and made the appropriate shrugs and noises in approval. "And further, Jeeeziz – have you seen how much he writes?? And that's after editing...I mean, I think we can get the point in a lot less pages, else I'll be spending all my time just drawing a cunt sitting in a coffee shop with his mouth open, panel after panel!" I felt a tad put out and embarrassed, but laughed along. I had to admit his point was funny and I had a sneaking realisation myself that he was of course, right.

Don in a comical take on some big business executive leaned forward on the table. "Fine, right listen you bubble-heed department!? Cut it doon and you, just draw bigger panels – more pages will just mean more profits! There problem solved. Right just fucking get on wi' it then, we have got deadlines people, deadlines! Let's go, go, go!"

I stood again, "Ah, excuse me sir, but there's s'posed to be a bit where you say any other business!"

Don retorted "Mind yer ain business is the only ither business! Silence in court, I mean...meeting!"

Hippie Davie chuckled. "Aye, Mr. Sensible is right, you canna end a meeting without an 'any other business,' it's a law!"

Don grunted, impatiently swivelling around in his chair looking up at the ceiling like a brain damage victim. "Och, a'right, fit else is there then?"

I stood up. "If you please sir, there's the small matter of..." I directed my voice straight at him accusingly. "...You beein' a fuckin' greedy bastard and trying to make lots of money out of this venture!"

Don swivelled around angrily and stared at me, pointing aggressively, "Now look you, your job is to do the inking and thinking, if it wisnae for me, we'd be out of pocket! We have overheads, all this printing and production costs money you know!?"

I slapped the table with the palm of my hand and leaned over towards him, metaphorically getting into his personal space.

"With all due respect, Mr. Top Hat department, it costs you fuck all; given that we steal it all from the oil company you're meant to be guarding from people like us!"

Don pompously re-arranged himself in his seat and then fervently jabbed his index finger repeatedly towards his own face,

"Well that's right! As the main investor here, it's my head on the line, it's me that can lose my job, it's a'right for you two; you don't have careers to protect do you?" There was a short pause while he allowed the message to sink in before clarifying his position. "Am the one taking all the operational, strategic and financial risks here..!" He looked very serious as he reeled off the next point, straying into new waters, developing more of an American twang as he went. "This mutt's gotta hunt me some turkey, you get me? As a business model it's a fucking nightmare!"

I almost shouted out that watching porn and sci-fi all night was hardly a "career" but instinctively stopped; I didn't want to be "that guy." I had no right to be judgmental. Besides, he was so lost in the part that I decided to be diplomatic. Well, I didn't want the business talks to break down at this stage in the game, didn't want the wheels coming off just yet; not while I was still driving this bus. You have to be savvy when dealing with a nervous investor like Don. I knew it was down to me to keep him on board with this one. We needed him, it was as simple as that, we needed each other! I held my breath and reminded myself, 'play the corporate game for the time being and we could still all come out of the other end of this and prosper!' The tension mounted in the board room.

Hippie Davie, though, interrupted before I could retort. "Ok, that's fair enough, Don, we totally appreciate what you're sayin' and get that it's well risky. Let's cap the price at one pound fifty an issue and use the funds to buy any pens *etc.* that we need y'know - buy the occasional inspirational substances now and again to fuel further creativity!"

Don motioned in the air with his hand in a gesture of *'obviously, thank you,'* and replied leaning back in his chair eyeing me triumphantly. "Ok I think that's reasonable, the top hat department can run with that."

Bastard! He's done it again! Hippie Davie had moved in and sealed the deal right under my nose! I had trusted him as an ethical investor, a good guy; but there he was revealing himself as just another corporate shark. He would hang me out to dry in an instant in his bid for promotion. Oh yeah, he tries to pretend that he's not interested in games, climbing the corporate ladder, but that's bullshit! Bullshit I tell ya! He's stitched me up good and proper, made me look like a right bag a' fuckin' doughnuts! I learned something that day, that there are no friends in business, you have to have teeth and you have to be prepared to use them. You have to be able to switch morals at a moment's notice. Well they think I'm some schnook that can be played, used as a pawn!? Well, their biggest mistake is underestimating me! Christ, I'm the ideas man...I'm core competency for this venture! I should be vying for tactical leadership! I'll be back in this board room and I'll be making the rules. I'll talk to the guy with the impeccably red hair and set things up my way. These two mooks will be in Jump Street in no time.

I turned around to see Don grinning and looking down at his lap and I had a good inkling of what was going to happen. He stood up and started waving his penis up and down in the air, "Motion waved!"

I tried to correct him, "Well that is a nasty wavey motion...wait a minute, don't you mean motion carried?"

Hippie Davie was laughing. "Member waved, motion carried."

Don then slapped his penis onto the table with a painful sounding thump. "Done, meeting adjourned!"

We laughed a lot afterwards; it was clear that Don wasn't exactly going to turn into quite the model capitalist that I had feared he might.

However that glint in his eye never quite went away, he would be forever possessed! Money was the worst alchemy, money changes everything. Still...I suppose a few more quid in my bank account wouldn't go a miss either!? I mean, my car was on its last legs...be nice to have a comfy reliable new car, with a good stereo. In my defence, a car shouldn't be just about getting you from A to B, nothing wrong with a bit of comfort, gadgets maybe, gadgets would be cool!

I wondered about the day time meetings that took place here; Christ, the dayshift really had no idea about the nocturnal after-life operations did they? I stood up feeling a little perturbed that I had felt such a surge of animosity towards Don and had almost attacked his competence to lead such a high powered meeting.

"Gawd you know Don, I felt a bit caught up in the moment there, jeez – you think just having a meeting in a place like this brings out some inner career climbing, corpo-innate instinct or something?"

Don flashed a warm smile back at me, now himself, also over the heat of the board room battle.

"Aye, it must be a strange kind of demonic possession that goes on at business meetings and stuff; it's like the priesthood of the damned or something." We apologised to each other as we felt our humanity drain back. I mused into the air for a second or two, thinking about that, then mouthed, "Corporate theft of the soul, replaced by a soulless nine to five demon."

We actually created quite a few copies right up to number five. We were now about a month ahead of ourselves. All we had to do now was another bit of talismanic magic to charge and consecrate the next few bundles as actual physical sigils. We were so proud of our sigil *Star Wars* social catalyst. To us, it was up there with Sergeant Pepper or Christ the album by CRASS. We set to work creating an atmosphere in the board room. We had brought in candles and other effects. I had Hippie Davie collect some of Alchemist-Al's wine so that we could combine the sigil magick with a possible astral visualisation; Al's wines would help with that. We all felt that the maximum amount of effort was required.

I was certain that out of body mind projection and shadow self-journeying was the key. I mean, this is what our shamanic ancestors did to explore the inner universe and as a result all of magick and occult knowledge was built and created from that wellspring of ancient knowledge and tradition. If I could just repeat the experience and hold it all together, then I could see more of what was going on, astrally speaking, instead of just feeling and believing it all.

Although I had come to terms with the fact that there was much more to magick than people realised and I obviously knew my own abilities, I still craved even more proof. Over the last few years my world had, slowly but surely, been twisted upside down; my sense of reality had taken quite a pounding and my rational brain had been presented with a reality that collided with the nice comfortable materialistic world view that I had been very comfortable with. An image came to mind of a comic I once read, an experimental story pitting Sherlock Holmes against Bram Stocker's Dracula. The panel where Holmes witnessed the vampire shape-shift and fly out of an open window was clearly in my mind. The great detective had had to come to terms with the reality of the supernatural and his own cognitive dissonance, with the dictum "once you have eliminated the impossible, whatever remains, however improbable, must be true!" I still clung to that. However, what was far more probable to me now was that I knew that human reality was far more extensive in this universe than the current mechanical version led us to believe. Our oberservations of time, mind and matter had to be updated as well as our perceptions of ourselves. We, humanity, just needed to radically alter our perspective and mentally soar through the heavens, just as the Christian philosopher Giordano Bruno had first demonstrated, so that we notch up our level of awareness and consider ourselves all as deserving to own our true will, just as any other divine creature in the body of our beautiful sparkling lady Nuit.

We cast a circle and grounded ourselves. We sat around the floor sipping on the strong looking brew in our hands. I held my cup in my hand staring into the candle's flickering flames. We all glanced at each other as we became aware of the growing silence enveloping the room. I remembered a line from a beautiful poem from school and spoke it quietly,

"*As the silence surged softly backwards, when the plunging hooves were gone!*"

Hippie Davie smiled in recognition, "Wordsworth?" "No, no whatshisname! Walter De La Mare! I remember it from Northfield Academy."

The silence then did surge softly backwards and brought with it quiet contemplation. The darkness crept over us and cut us off from reality, now illuminating everything with candle light. My head began to swim and I put my hand up to my face. This ale did seem much stronger than I remembered, or perhaps it was the first stages of food poisoning, who knows? I knew it was a bad sign that I was beginning to experience so much doubt at this point, just at the point of losing my grip on my sense of reality. My precious rational mind, which had been asserting itself, as light faded in both the room and my sanity, would have no chance to resurrect any confidence or straight thinking in me now. I could feel the panic rising in my mind. My rational mind, no longer able to orient itself was flooding my body with fight or flight chemicals. My head spun a bit more and my brain reacted to my further dizziness by emptying my stomach, I heard Don say "Oh shit," as I bent over and started vomiting. A few seconds later, Hippie Davie was at my side, his reassuring touch spread through my torso, making me feel a little bit better straight away. I recognised the same type of feeling that Wolf had been able to impart on the night of the fox and somewhere my subconscious mind flagged that Al's Ale's obviously made us hypersensitive to the energy and intentions radiated by another person. I knew Hippie Davie was giving me some kind of healing with his touch, whether deliberately or not. I looked into his eyes and saw real love and kindness there. I came around and became anchored by Hippie Davie's energy.

"Relax, relax, we're cool man, it's cool," he said. "Feel better?" I did. I nodded,

"Yeah, yeah, geez I'd forgotten how potent this stuff was, I was knocking it back like lemonade!"

I had at least regained some semblance of rational thought, but my perception had changed. The flames of the candles no longer seemed like the incandescent particles of ignited carbon and chemical energy being released as hot plasma that I knew them to be. Rather, a manic dance ensued where strange beautiful sprites continually and spontaneously reinvented themselves, bursting forth from the glowing wicks circled all around the room. It was like a Disney cartoon, as they popped into existence in synchrony. But I was sure in that instant there was something very much more alive about them, a second for us, perhaps an hour or even a lifetime for them. They sang, danced and celebrated their existence, much too hot and quick to linger with ours, glancing through the veil at us, perhaps with some understanding, perhaps without caring. I thought, 'all our world began with theirs and will be destined to end when their world grows cold and lifeless, the end of entropy.' This was harmony, everything in a slow balance between extremes. However, like the see-saw tipping, all that could ever be is temporary in this world.

I was mesmerised, "I never knew fire elementals were this beautiful!" I mouthed out loud. I turned to Don and Hippie Davie.

"You know, the universe, us, everything comes from fire and when you think about it, fire itself is so blindly destructive but out there in the vast coldness of space, it nourishes everything on this planet and drives all life, weather, climate everything!"

Hippie Davie looked impressed at the thought and Don nodded concurrently. Hippie Davie responded, loving the philosophical thread, as I instinctively knew he would,

"Life is maybe a slow motion flame going from one being to another. Hey dude, life takes that raw flame and metabolises it into the force!"

I pressed on, "But it's all destined to return to a ball of energy, all destined to cool, as entropy runs its course or maybe even implode only to explode back into another universe. I mean that's the best possible scenario that it keeps bouncing back into an eternity of big bangs! Otherwise, whatever way you look at it, everything we know is just going to flicker to ashes, disappear and what's the point? That's what I've always thought was the biggest joke; that everything we care about is finite! Ashes to fucking ashes!? So if God exists, surely he would know that? So what's the point?" But in my heart I now knew this thought was nonsense and limited, like the insect-like point of awareness, seeing only in one linear direction that I sensed in the presence of my ally, the being that linked with my mind, my essence, my soul in some kind of hyper-space. Entropy is not the end of the story, there was much more to be revealed to us yet. That realisation had been hugely exciting, stirring me but at the same time stilling me; leaving me content with this newer revelation, this new hope.

Don looked solemn. "We're here aren't we? That's amazing; maybe that's all the point you need?"

Hippie Davie pressed his lips together into a big smile and lay back, basking in the flickering light. He raised his bottle up to take a swig and stopped momentarily to reflect on the conversation.

"Well, probably this is the point, I mean we're here, tooled up so to speak, trying to dream ourselves into another type of reality!" He put on a fake American accent, "Another dimension, a dimension not of sight or sound but of the mynnd! What was it you said, Sensible old son? If part of mind can have knowledge of events that haven't chronologically occurred yet, then mind can exist out of chronological time. Hence, my good man," now nodding towards me in Sherlock Holmes tones, which I appreciated greatly and felt somewhat humbled by, "Hence my good man we must therefore exist, effectively, forever!" He lay back fully now gazing up at the stars. "I loooove that! Makes perfect sense!"

In that instance, I became further aware that we'd come quite a long way since our first meeting near the central ref' when I used to feel quite inferior to him and now I felt very comfortable in his company. I respected him and loved him as a friend and clearly he felt the same way towards me.

"I suppose I've never said this out loud," I said, "but this, all this stuff, it really is fucking real isn't it? We're skating close to realms of imagination and a method to use our brains like no-one has really done before!?"

Don tutted. "You mean nobody in a few hundred years has done before!"

Hippie Davie held his finger up from his prostate position, as if that was all the energy he could muster to move;

"Yep, s'right, we're just doing stuff that was widespread and stamped out of existence by the powers that be, the churches and rulers of the world's people. We're just remembering, rediscovering what is ours!"

Don stood, raised his bottle in the air. "And claiming our right to evolve and discover our roots as sorcerers of Aberdeenshire, the people of the ancient stone circles, the people of the stones! Sorcerers of the Silver City!"

We all cheered. I stood up also and raised my bottle into the air, as an illuminated sleeve waved over the matted Hippie shape on the ground, punching a fist in the air, a movie scene all of his own making; *The Breakfast Club* meets *Fear and Loathing in Las Vegas*. I pressed on with the flow.

"The three musketeers, on a mission from...on a mission from the Goddess!"

Hippie Davie chuckled, mocking the Blues Brothers, "We're on a mission from God-dess."

I smiled and kept going, "And we will fight, fight for our right to paartaay!" This was met with some hoorays and yays from the background. "And now we're gonna carry the news, to all the young dudes!"

We sat for a few more minutes chatting and laughing. It definitely broke the tension we all felt underneath. Then I became aware that I was feeling quite sleepy. After a pause I watched a tiny fleeting piece of glowing ember from a candle wick float upwards in a snaking motion into the air. It somehow reminded me of the fleeting nature of time and that we had a job to do.

I called for a blessing and for the Goddess to watch over us and Hippie Davie called for the force to be with us! Don, however, began to weep slightly,

"And I pray to the Goddess that you are kept safe, for I will not be with you!" Don was at work after all, he needed to keep a foot in this world. Don was very apologetic and assured us that he would sit up tending the circle watching over us as we descended into sleep, into the spirit world.

This actually made me feel quite reassured. The thought of my limp body lying still in this creepy building while my shadow body went journeying far and wide was a bit worrying if you thought about it too much. So we swigged the last of what we had, smoked the last few puffs of Hippie Davie's power mixture and lay down. My head was already swimming madly as I lay down and this time I was under no illusions that I was about to fall into a deep trance like sleep. The practice had made me much more aware of the symptoms and the feeling of drifting and bobbing around like a small dingy on the choppy sea of my own conscious awareness. I tried very hard to retain my self-awareness, telling myself over and over that I was going to remember, that I was going to see and feel. I kept looking at my hands in my idle day dreaming, trying to see them as black shadows, trying to break free. The blends of substances though, were my best friends. The ale loosened my bonds and the smoke helped me drift free. A few times I felt as if I was looking from above where I was lying, in a bobbing like fashion, though in my excitement I would snap back to ground level. I stayed with it and just kept telling myself it would be a matter of time, treading that tight-wire in the borderlands between falling into the chasm of deeper sleep and remaining aware.

Eventually though, it happened; I was floating freely and my eyes gently opened to gaze at the scene. I actually expected to just be looking disappointedly towards the boardroom door, but amazingly I seemed to be sitting at the table some ten feet away from the sleeping bodies, just watching. I had a memory of feeling a bit dizzy and I now realised that I had been doing the spiral out of body transition just before settling down there. I began to feel the panic sensation but this time controlled it much better and began to breathe easier. Curiously, I watched Don get up and stare down at my body. I didn't linger at that scene though, as intuitively I knew it would not be good to fixate on my own body, lest I be sucked back in towards it.

Even though I had done this a few times now, I was still extremely amazed and excited that I was now experiencing viewing myself almost dispassionately from across the room. I then looked over towards Hippie Davie, half expecting to see him there grinning at me but all I saw was his body lying there and the strange pulsating aura around him. I knew it to be him trying to release. Before I knew what I wanted to do, my shadow self-barrelled down towards him at break-neck speed. It was a curious thing that the shadow body did seem to react to thoughts before it became consciously articulated to me. It was disconcerting, in fact, because sometimes you weren't sure what you were going to do next or how "you" (shadow self you) were going to respond. I mused that my shadow self seemed much braver than my rational self, or maybe that bit more reckless which worried me as well. While I was experiencing all these musings I became aware of a tug on my right arm. Instinctively I lunged backward to see the image of Hippie Davie, or some kind of outline that I just knew was a reference to Hippie Davie in my mind. I was grasping his arm. Curiously, the image disappeared and it was as if he dissolved back into a formless cloud. Again and again, I tried until at the third attempt I pulled him out. I seemed to have the knack down a little bit better. It required very delicate, very constant pressure. Now I was holding onto a very doped, sleeping image of Hippie Davie. His head rolled around and he could barely focus on me. Instinctively and I don't know why, I kissed him! It was a very weird thing for me to decide to do but that's what my shadow self did. As I did so I reminisced how in fairy tales the princess would kiss the frog or the fairy queen would kiss the hero in order to either send them to sleep or cause them to be magically transformed into something else. 'Christ,' I thought, 'people knew all this stuff already!'

Hippie Davie's eyes blinked and looked into my face. I didn't know what to do, so I hugged him in excitement. I could feel his excitement as well and we both spun around the room like a couple of excited animal cubs, falling over ourselves laughing and just feeling amazed to be there.

We came to a halt and I heard Hippie Davie shout to me, "Look at Don!"

The sensation was very strange and hard to describe. It wasn't like Hippie Davie was actually standing before me, it was like glimpses of him and when he spoke, somewhere in the back of my mind, I knew it was an actual sound murmuring from the mouth of the half comatose figure that was actually lying beside me.

We both glided towards Don who was peering down at Hippie Davie. He had a curious look on his face and seemed to be doing his best to remain quiet. I had half a thought that he was about to jump on him and make love to him, which amused me a little and then almost as quickly scared me, as I thought that I certainly would be next. (Also and ambivalently, I felt a little hurt that he wouldn't do me first!).

Don had no idea that we both now stood in front of him, it was so freaky! I tried to shout at him but I realised that speaking was becoming very hard indeed. I watched as an outline of Hippie Davie seem to flicker and appear behind him. I was thinking that perhaps this is how very clairvoyant people saw ghosts and stuff and it was taking me all my effort and concentration to just see glimpses, even though I was looking out from a virtual shadow body that my mind seems to have constructed a few feet away from my actual body. I knew that all the concentration, magical exercises and shadow body exercises I did whilst doing qigong had helped to achieve this state. Now that I was in this state, this was normal for me. I did have the gift to do it as a child and it was just a question of remembering now, how to move around. I realised without physically seeing that Hippie Davie was trying to slap Don on the arse but there wasn't a peep from Don, except we watched him casually and absentmindedly scratch his arse while he took another puff of his cigarette.

I was aware that Hippie Davie was focusing on wafting some of the smoke of Don's cigarette around. Although it did curl a little, this was probably more to do with the draft from an open window. Don spoke out loud however;

"If that's you two fucking about, you can just fuck off! Stop playing aboot here and go aff and get done what you're supposed to get done...and...Gods go with you!"

That's what I absolutely loved about Don. Practically anyone else in the world would have attributed that to vortexes of air, but not Don, he was very clear that it was his friends playing out-of-body tricks on him and on this occasion, of course, he was absolutely fucking spot on.

I caught a vision of Hippie Davie, who was amazing to perceive on the astral. I saw glimpses of a blinding psychedelic vision, clean and bright, his whole being seemed to revolve around his smile. I mused; there was no doubt *'what a good soul this man has got, he's amazing.'* I had never quite seen him in that light, though I suppose I always knew he was that person underneath and perhaps that's why I became friends with him so easily. I had the impression of Hippie Davie speaking to me, 'Ok brother, we have got work to do!' but I never actually heard it as such, this was in my mind. No sooner had I heard/imagined my arms had already interlocked with his and we were now speeding off together in a blinding flash, very much, I thought, like the start of Dr. Who.

I held onto Hippie Davie and the experience was odd, as I could feel his arm both physically and also as an emotional energy close to me. We moved around each other and then tried to enact the ritual we had devised. It was odd trying to concentrate on performing magick in this state, as the energy was very hard to control. Expanding it made me feel huge and light and contracting it made me feel quite solid. I felt that if I could sustain the solidity, then Don might actually see my outline in the room. I knew instantly that the disembodied energy of "Harry" that I'd seen all those months before was indeed a person trying to make himself solid on the physical plane. The poor bastard obviously was a barely conscious part of a mind without a body that occasionally jumped ahead of his death time and tried to keep going in that location, as if he might continue his actual life somehow.

We were aware that we were in the boardroom but something was different, something wasn't right. Hippie Davie's voice to my left said something but I couldn't make it out. Communication was becoming harder, I couldn't think straight; I felt drowsy, incoherent. I struggled to regain control. I tried to look at my hands which worked and helped me stabilise my thoughts and awareness of myself, of where I was. This spurred me on to using my will to remain here and stabilise myself further.

The bundle of comics seemed to emanate a faint silver light, so I had a feeling that the intent and the sigil we were working on was having the desired effect. The idea was to broadcast a *"magical current,"* as Hippie Davie had put it, out into the astral version of the city. We needed to identify our psychic sensor and physically "fly" to it and merge it with the gnostic current. We then needed to identify the deva of the city itself. However we couldn't seem to visualise the city or connect with it as we'd assumed that we would be able to in our etheric bodies. We couldn't see it. Instead the room grew darker and the walls seemed more foreboding. I concentrated and began the words of the consecration of the sigil. We held hands trying to raise energy and use the cone of energy we had been working on earlier.

But our voices and energy just seemed to bounce off the walls and echo all around us. After a few seconds of chanting Hippie Davie and I slowed down and we looked around the room perplexed as the idea of our voices echoed continually, seeming to bounce off every surface and grow ever more sinister. The sound faded eventually but we knew that all our efforts and intent were having no real effect, that it was just being reflected back to us in this room. We instinctively knew at the same time what the other was thinking; we had to get out of this room. There were definite 'spidey senses' going off like alarm bells in my mind and in my aura.

The room seemed different, the area where Don had been standing next to our sleeping forms was now replaced by a hard, featureless pitch black wall I felt Hippie Davie next to me and thought *'Where the fuck are we?'* We linked arms, expanded ourselves and spun around slowly ready to aim for a window or a doorway, but everything now looked hard and black like volcanic glass, from floor to ceiling. Now we found ourselves just spinning slowly in a small black cell. We tried to drift through it but frustratingly found it solid. I began to panic; I had never been in this situation before. I never felt like I could not get back to my body or snap back awake. Now I was out of ideas, what should I do? I was glad Hippie Davie was here, but he seemed as impotent and as trapped as I was, like a spider trapped in a glass. I could feel his panic add to mine. I started to get emotional, thinking of Don sitting by our twitching bodies, confused and scared when we would not wake up, probably watching us moan and thrash around in panic. But then maybe he'd get Mags, yeah Mags, she'd know what to do, or Wolf! He's an expert at this. I started to call out for Don and Hippie Davie seemed to join me, "Don, Don get Mags get Wolf, help, we're trapped, can you hear us, Don?"

It was no use, time seemed to pass, minutes, maybe hours and we just remained in the room, now pitch black. We could feel along the wall, looking for a way out. It was a terrible feeling, like perhaps we'd be here for an eternity, just searching in the dark; never finding a way out. I could hear Hippie Davie say something about the force and the Gods. He was praying, I joined him but again, the words just seemed to bounce around us. I was scared, I began to feel claustrophobic and I was sure that back in the real world somewhere my body was having a panic attack and Don could not get me to come round. It occurred to me that we were in a kind of Hell where even the Goddess could not hear us.

I thought for a second. There was only one thing I could do, try to create a magical space in here that might allow the divine in and break this horrible nightmare spell. I stood up and faced what I thought might be the East. Using the concentration I knew I could muster, I began the lesser banishing ritual of the pentagram. I reached up and touched my forehead, 'here goes,' I thought, 'let's sees if this works when I need it.' I thought of a Goddess that was close to my heart, Athena, protector and warrior Goddess. I reached up to her with all my heart and visualised above me a brilliant white crystalline light, saying;

"ATEH ATHEEEEEENNNNNAAAAA" and brought it down to my heart, then down to my feet to connect this divine help within myself. "MALKUTHHH," at the same time, I visualised the small tree of life surrounding me as I then made myself the small tree, echoing the whole of reality and the universe, the big tree. To connect the idea that is central to all good and proper magick; as above, so below. I wondered for a second whether it would work in my shadow self, as Malkuth, the earth was surely somewhere else right now. But it was ok, it was energy and mind that mattered, not the location, which was very reassuring to discover. The words echoed around me and boomed in the darkness, going nowhere but at least they filled me with a bit of hope.

I drew the energy back up as a brilliant white glow to my centre again and spread it to the right saying;

"Ve GEBURRRAHH!" And as I did so I thought about the power! I could see a white cross form vividly within me. I imagined the little tree within me pulsate with power and purpose, emanating from a bright red sphere on my right shoulder. My spirits were lifting now as I began to feel invulnerable and capable of drawing help to our plight here. I drew the white light across to my left side and intoned;

"Ve GEDDUUULAHH." I thought about the glory of the divine sense, the glory of the creation force of all human beings filling me, her glory surrounding me;

"Hail ATHENA," I said, as I felt my entire shadow body just becoming a cross of energy, which was a weird experience indeed. I drew the energy in front of the centre of my power and cried,

"LE OLAM AMEN." I immediately felt reinvigorated and powerful. My mind calmed and I felt a greater sense of control and confidence for what I needed to do.

My will was on full beam for the task at hand. I felt that even before I had drawn the first banishing earth pentagram that I was going to succeed. I could sense Hippie Davie joining in, following my lead. The momentum of will and steadfast belief carried me forward. A slight trepidation surrounded me as it seemed to take forever to let the God name of the East quarter sink to my feet and actually fill my aura. In this state I could really feel it was an elastic band being pulled, filling with potential energy. When it is spoken and just "felt," one uses instinct and a sense of timing, but in this state it was like my shadow body was changing colour and changing shape to become an image of what I thought was something like the actual god itself. This was very strange and actually very frightening to experience, but made me feel powerful, thinking it may also feel frightening for whatever was creating this hell, imprisoning us. I pointed my symbolic athame at the first banishing earth pentagram to charge it as is common. I saw it in front of me thick and white, as if I'd spray painted it onto the very space in front of me. Then as the God name was ready to be released I let it flow from me:

"YYYODDDHEY-VAAA-HEYYYYY." I did what I usually do, felt the name vibrate to the very end of the universe. The effect was awesome. The entire environment shook as if a bomb had gone off, a voice booming loud as a jumbo jet vibrating the air and everything around. My own shadow body was vibrating and oscillating in an odd way and for an instant I felt incredibly huge. However I knew I wasn't finished, I wanted to or in fact needed to complete the entire cycle. I turned around and proceeded with the south repeating the procedure. Again it seemed to take ages to charge my own body with the god name of the south quarter. And then I let it go as before, this time I was excited because I knew it was going to be good, now spurred on by the first attempt, I poured fourth;

"AADO-NAIII," roaring forward and in that instant my shadow body ignited and was aflame. It wasn't the kind of purifying flame I often imagined myself surrounded by to cleanse myself. This was something else; it carried with it an uplifting emotional high. The flame roared with it as the word still deafening roared with the flame across blackness around me and to the very depth of the universe itself. In fact I was embarrassed as I fathomed that if I was shouting this from my real body where I was then people might be hearing it on Union Street. I spun around and started the banishing earth pentagram of the west quarter. Again it seemed an age to charge it with the god name, I bellowed out,

"EHAAIYYAHHHH!" This was again louder than a jumbo jet taking off right next to us as emotion swept up through me. Finally, although all was peaceful and quiet I spun around to the North, repeated the final incantation and drew the last banishing earth pentagram. Lastly, I roared forth;

"AAAGALLLLLLAAAAA." By that time, I wasn't sure if this last word would have much effect, but I was wrong. The word itself seemed to squeeze me to a thin almost atom width and then gently released me. I felt like I had been taken apart and put back together again. I felt like I had been wrung out like a wet rag and what was left was light and good. My feelings of anxiety had drained away. After each word had sprung forth I tried to centre myself by recoiling back to the centre and I put my index finger to my mouth in the style of the god Harpocrates, symbolising silence, stopping me broadcasting at the key moment.

Again like with every practise I had done recently with the LBRP, I felt like I was alone and standing on a column in the centre of the universe. So I held myself in Osiris risen position and called forth into the ether,

"Before me GABRIEL." Again I tried to vibrate the name as much as I could by letting it fill me, vibrate and release as before but quicker this time and trying to sustain a poetic rhythm with it, too. Usually I tried very hard to imagine the archangel in front of me and usually I've just about reached the limit of my concentration. It had taken me many months of almost constant practise to get any good at visualising an actual person with garbs and associated paraphernalia. A pentagram I could just about sustain. This however was admittedly still a bit beyond me.

But I didn't even need to try to imagine anything, for no sooner had I vibrated the name when a white object began to take shape in front of me. At first, I thought it was a hazy white blurry outline and I felt very pleased with myself to have achieved that. However somewhere else my body took a sharp breath in sheer surprise. Little did Don know at that moment this was because I was looking through virtual eyes towards, first, the image of a flaming sword which flickered for only a split second, before being replaced with an array of vivid flashing colours that seemed to be driven by a strange intelligence of their own in front of me! I recoiled backward in fear of the strange alien lights and nearly smashed into the back of the prison room. There was something eminently terrifying and beautiful about them.

I stammered and then just resumed my position and continued on, knowing that now that I had started, I had to complete the ritual.

"Behind me RAPHAEL, to my right MICHAEL and my left URIEL!" My vision was filled with the most beautiful array of bouncing, spinning coloured orbs reminiscent of some modern UFO sighting. Finally I intoned:

"About me flames the pentagram and in the column stands the six rayed star."

I always thought these were just words, something to say at the end of the ritual to give a bit of closure perhaps; how wrong was I!? I realised I could hear something like a helicopter overhead, chopping the air into bits. The area right in front of me suddenly seemed to stretch and just as suddenly pop back into place. A massive deep red flaming pentagram spread out beneath my feet and burned its way across the space beneath where I hung. As it spread out over the black obsidian like-surface, some of the black glass-like wall was scorched white as if frozen in bleached peroxide suspense. I sensed Hippie Davie behind me, a still and pleasant light hung in the air. The air seemed to beautifully and slowly vibrate with the coloured orbs, pulsating and moving together as if communicating in a method way outside of my normal range of aesthetics. I thought to myself, 'how fucking incredible was that? I mean, who maaade this stuff? How did they know what they were doing?' The LBRP was clearly an amazing, fantastic technology which was filled with the secrets of the universe!

The beautiful fiery red pentacle descended and then raged all around us. In that instant, I called on the Goddess to help me, as a boy calls on his mother in the dark. She was my last hope. But the prison we were in wasn't going to yield without some more tactics to attack us. It began to shrink in on us and the claustrophobia started to make me feel more solid and heavy. The room shrank and my head began to feel squashed, squashed so much that it made a horrible taste in my mouth and an almost sickly tickling sensation down the middle of my face. I could hardly breathe as I kept asking for the Goddess to help me However; the LBRP had taken some of the substance from the initial obsidian hard texture so that I could push against it. A female voice rang in the darkness; *'open you eyes.'*

Momentarily, I opened an eye and I was suddenly aware that I was writhing on the floor gasping for breath. I crawled onto my hands and knees now aware of Don in floods of tears on the phone. My head was soaked from Don throwing water on my face repeatedly and my body was soaked in sweat. Hippie Davie too was coming round gasping, his sweat drenched dreadlocks trailing on the floor in front of him as he made a gasping/groaning sound followed by an "Oh my Gods."

Don was weeping but sounded a little relieved; he sunk down on the floor sighing,

"Oh thank the Gods, thank the Gods, I thought you'd maybe been possessed or killed by something or poisoned by that fuckin' wine! You're back, you're back oh thank the Gods!"

We all looked at each other in silence for a second as Hippie Davie and I collected ourselves. We felt like we had just crawled out of another reality and it felt good to be back here in person, although I was worried that I may snap back to that horrible place again.

I stared into Hippie Davie's eyes, "That actually happened didn't it?"

Hippie Davie returned my gaze, his eyes wide and terrified looking; he nodded quickly,

"Yeah, what the fuck? What the fuck happened? Did that actually just happen?"

I put my hand up to stop him even talking about it for a second; I was still in shock, still quite scared by it. I turned towards Don but before I could ask him anything he just closed his eyes and said in a resigned voice, "A phoned an ambulance" I looked at Hippie Davie and the mess around the board room, "Fuck!"

We tidied as much as possible and my heart jumped as we heard the siren sound get louder outside. That was our cue all right. Hippie Davie and I walked downstairs to intercept them and apologised. They were ok with that, as they said that they'd rather find us upright than comatose on the floor. The worst part though was the police car that had arrived a few seconds after, as Don might have mentioned in his fearful state that we'd drank wine with a possible hallucinogen mixed in it! The paramedics shone annoying lights in our eyes and checked reflexes, blood pressure and heart rate. Their conclusion was that we were quite intoxicated and under the influence of some as yet unconfirmed stimulant. I thanked the young woman by my side as she packed away the tubing of the blood pressure cuff,

"Least we're alright then eh? So sorry again, about this!" I said, though she replied sympathetically;

"Yeah, I'm just happy that you're doing ok at this moment Mr Anderson...though it's these people who you'll have to convince now!" The young and quite sweet paramedic motioned her head towards the older and much less sweet looking police officer imposing her black uniform of dread onto the scene.

It was a little embarrassing as the police were quite patronising and stern with us. They questioned Don extensively on our presence there and his role in the drug taking. We tried to tell them we had flaked out in the toilets and Don had had no part in the wine taking, but they were very sceptical to say the least. It was spiralling out of control. They could see through our lies. They walked Hippie Davie and I into the waiting cars for further questioning and as we were getting our heads pushed into the back seat of the police car a dog team van screeched up and two dogs with their handlers further poked their fucking noses into our business. They insisted on checking the building and found their way to the boardroom with its cloud of incense and dope smoke hanging over it. They had found a bottle, which we'd emptied but still had enough dregs in it for analyses and they also found all our little private stashes of pot hidden in the back room. We were probably going to get police sentences in court but even worse was that Don was probably going to lose his job. I felt sick and completely impotent. Just what the hell had gone so drastically wrong?

The next day I sat depressed and defeated in a small room just waiting, waiting for more bullshit and condescending officers of the law to come and interrogate me and make me feel like an idiot. I surely was anyway, I had ruined my mate's career of getting paid for watching telly all night and now we were all going to receive a criminal record. I felt humiliated and as if all my energy had been robbed from me. I couldn't stand to think what my parents would think and it made me feel that four years of a degree were probably down the drain as no-one would employ me now. I was ruined! I sat at the table, taking little solace from a rollie cigarette and a cold polystyrene cup of coffee. I had been told to just sit there. So sit there I did.

Eventually, a female officer of some kind walked in; she looked like an overly professional looking woman. She reminded me of Dame Judy Dench in that she gave an air of pleasantness but concealed a plausible ability to shoot you callously on the spot. She eyed me coolly as she sat down and then clasped her hands on the table in front of her. She motioned to the police guard, who exited the room and closed the door behind him. She handed me another cup of coffee in a proper cup and placed some cigarettes on the table in front of me. I was grateful for the coffee, a distraction from the boredom and blankness of the room. Something about her made me think she wasn't like a normal police officer. She projected an aura of slick authority with a penetrating stare. She was hard to read, looking quite stern but at times a little sympathetic with some understanding in her eyes. She made me feel at ease, at least.

"Well then, Mr. Anderson, my name is Dr Wallace! I'm glad we can finally have a little chat with you, it seems that you've been drawing a little bit of...attention to yourself of late wouldn't you say?"

I held my head in my hand in resignation, "It's all a fucking mess, we weren't doing anything that bad, but the way you guys are talking it's like we were running acid house parties in the oil company offices," I snatched my hand from my forehead making a plea with my open hand and outstretched fingers. "

I mean for Christ sake, it had nothing to do with Don, Hip...erm Davie and I just had a swig or two too many of that friggin' concoction he got off a mate! We didn't know it could do that to us! I've been trying to tell you that since last night!"

Dr Wallace just smiled tight-lipped at me and glanced down at some notes while I spoke, as if she was preparing the case for prosecution.

"First of all let me clarify, I am not a member of C.I.D; though I am somewhat affiliated with the law. I'm a trained psychiatrist and I've been following your case for a little while now. I'm here to help you Mr. Anderson, help you to see the error of your ways." She said, condescendingly, but also with an authoritarian kind of kinkiness that made me listen further. I didn't quite understand what she meant by 'a little while now!' surely we've only just been brought in!? She maintained eye contact with me, staring into my eyes and for a second I felt she had an almost hypnotic gaze, like all I wanted to do was just give in and agree to anything she had to suggest. She carried on in a measured studied tone,

"To help you back on to your true straight and narrow!" Her voice made me want to believe ever so much that she really could help me out in this tight spot, I listened intently, waiting for a life-line. I would agree to practically anything if it helped Don and Hippie Davie, but especially Don. Though I became a little concerned at the word psychiatrist and I wondered who she did work for?

"So not police? Are you from a hospital or Health service then?"

She gave a slight laugh, "In a manner of speaking, yes I am a psychiatric specialist, but don't be alarmed at that, I'm not here to judge you, at least not at present, Mr. Anderson." She said smiling warmly with a hint of irony. "No I work for the government; I head a small civil service branch that is concerned with the mental health, habits and welfare of the local populace."

As I put my hand to my face, looking concerned and trying to evaluate just what the hell that meant, she pressed on. "I won't go into the details, suffice to say that we're actually also affiliated with home security and therefore are not widely known and that we tend to operate quietly in the background. We" She paused a little searching for the right words. "...step in occasionally when we can see that the health service, for example, may need a bit more qualified assistance, such as in situations like yours, Sean."

I shifted in my seat, under her knowing glare and picked up the sensation for a second that her friendliness masked some feeling that she thought I could be dangerous. I became cautious and suddenly felt I was in some kind of verbal jousting match. Maybe she thought I was in some politically-driven anarchistic group that posed some terrorist threat. I had to allay her fears, make her see that I was quite a rational person and far from a threat. I had to sell it as just a fuck up whilst experimenting with mushroom wine and nothing more. Again she tried to reassure me,

"I'm just here to help you Mr Anderson...this meeting is nothing for you to worry about. You can just relax for the moment, what you say to me will all be in the strictest confidence." I watched her wave a pen over a small notepad. I was acutely aware that this meeting could potentially be very much more for me to worry about. I caught on quickly that she may have the power to consign me to a mental hospital or something. I had to keep my cool and not telegraph that I 'knew' what she was up to. My game now was to convince her that I was a fairly innocuous and perfectly regular citizen.

I smiled and cleared my throat, nervously carring on, trying to appear calm and very rational. "Situations like mine? What do I have to do with home security; I'm not a threat to anybody! I was just having a laugh with my mates."

All of a sudden her tone of voice changed although her expression did not. "A laugh!? Like the laughs you had that put poor Mr. Hutcheons into mental rehabilitation? Tell me, Mr. Anderson, do you think it's normal to terrify people out of their wits? Yes, quite literally out of their wits? Or a normal thing for a twenty-something year old man to experiment with the occult and play with toys and start seeing devils in the local pub after hours?" I was shocked, really really shocked. I started to mouth an apology, but she parried on.

"I've looked at your file and your achievements, Mr. Anderson and it seems like you're a bright and sensible young man, with a good future ahead of you." She regarded me coolly for a moment.

"I will come straight to the point, Mr. Anderson. In my opinion you have gone off the rails a little bit in the last year or so, messing about with magick and drugs, to the detriment of your life and as a science graduate, I would have thought you would know better." She smiled, a little triumphantly, allowing the words to penetrate. I nodded in agreement, desperately trying to convey that I was receptive to all suggestions. She carried on, pressing home her advantage,

"You need a little bit of guidance. You seem to do nothing else except sit around looking at reality through a drug haze, listening to these friends of yours. You're not living like an adult at all, don't you see that? You must have realised this fact for yourself from time to time Mr. Anderson, you're an intelligent person. You need to start acting a bit more like one and basically grow up a little bit. That's all really!"

I felt in a strange daze and I couldn't seem to resist the urge to start repeating some of the words she said.

She immediately lowered her tone and became sympathetic. "No, you're no threat to society Mr Anderson, you're one of us, one of the good guys and you like our society don't you? You're meant to be a sensible lad really!" She paused to allow her words to sink in, I felt good that she at least understood me! I agreed.

"Yeah, I love society me, I want a career. I just want to live a normal life!" She nodded approvingly and then her eyes burrowed deep into my soul.

"Yes I'm only here to make sure you're not thinking of peddling any um, any more politically motivated and sophisticated...guides really! You see where I'm coming from?" She eyed me coolly and gave a slight curt smile. "It's not the kind of thing that we like in our department, such needless rocking the boat! It's just going to upset people, lead people down a dark path Mr Anderson. Not so far from where you are now. People can't handle these 'occult' ideas." Something in the way she phrased that made me feel a pang of real fear and I wished stronger people like John Lennon were still alive. However, I blotted out that thought. I hate conspiracy theories, they're the ravings of the paranoid and now starting to link this doctor's sentiments to the death of John Lennon was nonsense. A CRASS lyric welled up in my mind, 'Just because you're paranoid doesn't mean they're not after you.' Ah shut up CRASS, you're the ones who got me into this mess!

Besides, I wasn't exactly in Lennon's league anyway, or even universe. She made me feel really stupid. Of course in the cold light of day it was hard to explain our actions at the Prince of Wales in a rational way. I did also feel quite guilty about The Doc, suddenly these nagging doubts that I had about this all being a bit of a fantasy came to the fore. Maybe I had been getting carried away. I tried to explain my rational point of view about magick. By now I was past trying to figure out how she knew so much about me, assuming that both Don and Hippy Davie had blabbed our whole story.

"We were just practising, trying to improve our mental skills and develop a better version of ourselves; you know? Just trying to find our true path in life, our true will as it were!"

Dr. Wallace only held her gaze with me for a second smiling, somewhat frustrated; I could sense that she was annoyed by my explanation.

"Oh we understand that, Mr. Anderson, but the problem you have is that you're using these *self-hypnotising* techniques to undo your mind, because you just don't know what you're getting into. It's dangerous!" The word *self-hypnotising* reverberated in my head. I felt a little drowsy, incapable of concentrating and glanced at my coffee cup, becoming suspicious that it may have been doped with a sedative. I glanced up in slow motion, as she walked around the table confidently, and a tad overly seductively, for my liking. Her demeanour suddenly different from the Judy Dench persona I had been accustomed to fencing with; now more dangerous, much more threatening to my situation. Though there was nothing I could do about it, I felt helpless and unresponsive.

"It's all just in your mind, Mr. Anderson. But then you're trying to lead other people to start indulging in that nonsense too..!? Let me demonstrate to you what might happen if you attempt to do what you were doing. Attempting to influence other people, influence reality like that; well that's not *your* job. We've seen the, err comics!"

I was startled at her language and change of character, I was finding it all too confusing and the words *self-hypnotising* seemed to crawl around my brain as if on some carousel, scourging the inside of my skull.

She eyed me like a hawk focusing on prey. "You can do what you want in the woods or behind closed doors, but you shouldn't try to play with the big leagues Mr Anderson. Who do you really think you are? Well you're not entirely well Mr Anderson. You are starting to exhibit a 'messiah complex,' brought on by the dissociation and delusions you have inflicted on yourself. You see, all you have succeeded in doing is to programme yourself into believing all this medieval mumbo jumbo, by self-suggestion and the group suggestions of your friends investing in it also. Don't be too hard on yourself; it can happen to even intelligent people, you just wanted to believe! It's a flaw in your personality Mr Anderson; we see that you score very highly in *absorption,* which is a personality trait associated with fantasy and a ready belief in paranormal explanations for events that actually have a more...mundane explanation. Now, you're an educated person Mr Anderson, you can understand that can't you? The problem is those friends of yours, filling your head with nonsense and psychedelic hoodoo nonsense." I tried to mouth my understanding apologetically but my mouth and body were just going through the motions. Her voice was speaking directly to my brain. I felt as strange and powerless as an alien abductee. She rounded the table entering my personal space, placing her hand on my shoulder as she spoke.

"But see, my poor dear, no-one actually wants your brand of personal salvation! This occult nonsense you're trying to push. It's harmful; it can upset a lot of young kids, cause violence and unchecked aggression. You know it yourself Mr Anderson; human beings are petty, selfish really and not quite...self-aware! Do you want a lot of Michael Hutcheons' wandering around causing havoc? Hordes of spurned lovers trying to hex spouses or young men trying to hypnotise innocent young women!? Well I'll tell you something; we certainly don't and we don't want to have to clean up the mess that you might have started, had we not intervened!" I felt a huge pang of remorse. Although I kind of knew this, I hadn't really given this problem much thought. I felt impulsive and stupid.

Dr Wallace continued on in soft tones, helping me realise the obvious; "Even your own mind Mr Anderson, is not ready for that. Your mental stability will always run into trouble and because the great change you expect will not happen, the cognitive dissonance produced by your psychotic state will be very, very harmful to you Mr Anderson!" She eyed me almost lovingly for a long few seconds. "I'm here to help you Sean, you'll definitely thank me for stepping in like this. All this stuff has to stop, that's all!" She smiled like a friendly nurse as she squeezed my arm, "We'll get you back on track, don't worry. There is a way home, a life-line if you're willing to take the first steps?"

I was now sobbing as the full ramifications of her speech hit home. However she wasn't quite finished with me yet, as she looked down at me with a trace of cynism;

"Let me demonstrate to you what will happen to you if you ever try to go through with anything like this again." I struggled to take in what she was saying, but it all made sense and I had to process it, I had to come out of this using as much logic as possible. My mind was melting through the grate, it was damage limitation now, salvaging as much of my core personality as possible was my only concern.

I suppose a large part of what she was saying was correct and made rational sense. I felt very woozy and elastic, as if my breathing was causing my body to expand like a balloon. Dr Wallace whispered into my ear;

"You think coming out of your body is real; this is not reality, it's all in your mind, Mr. Anderson, I can prove it. As a trained psychiatrist I can simply make a suggestion to you and make you think you're experiencing an out of body reality. But I will show you exactly what will happen if you persist in playing with magick." There was something threatening and sinister about her voice during the last few words. She continued now, confident that she could be much more frank with me,

"And this is exactly what will happen to you if you try any nonsense again. We can't have you running about stimulating the British egregore unchecked!" I was too out of it to understand what she was saying, except that she was scaring me and I felt helpless. With a few small commands that I barely heard, but sounding faintly Greek or Latin, I felt catapulted out of my body and into another room room. Though, unfortunately, it wasn't the interrogation room; I was right back in that horrible black hardened rock prison.

I felt sick, as the panic rose in my throat, the sense of imprisonment grew ever more real and there was nothing I could do. I was a million miles away from the other musketeers, they couldn't help me now. Then I remembered the LBRP and tried to move to do it. But I couldn't even move I was stuck fast, I couldn't speak or will anything to happen at all. I felt trapped within the volcanic glass like structure. This was far more severe than the last time and I thought of Han Solo trapped in the carbonite, as that's exactly how I felt. I began to think that perhaps I was doing this all to myself. I wanted to cry but couldn't even do that, I couldn't even scream for help. It was crazy; of course I had made it up. I mean *Star Wars*! For fuck's sake? Of course, I had taken too many mind-altering substances; like the UFO crackpots I wanted to believe. I had listened and had been too impressed by Hippie Davie and now I was in frozen carbonite like in *The Empire Strikes back*; my subconscious had been given too much free reign. I'd broken my Brain, just like Sandy Rourke had fucked his and it was horrific.

I was held fast, there was an overwhelming sensation of suffocation and complete restraint. I kept thinking that I was dying a horrible death, but wasn't sure when death would come. I thought of the medieval Christian view of Hell, a thousand deaths every day or trapped in a solid tree stump, unable to move. I'd mocked that before, thinking it was impossible or unlikely, but now it was only too real.

I latterly became aware of movement when terrible things slithered around the inside of the walls on cue, like disgusting slugs that made me want to scream and vomit. But I couldn't, I was helpless. I could feel them on my face and body. Pain now seared into me where they fed on my very spirit. I was going to be diminished to practically nothing, although that could take years, who knows!? It was torture; it was indeed Hell, a suffocating inescapable Hell. I knew then that Hell did exist. I was there and maybe I was here because of The Doc or because I dabbled in magick. This is exactly what Dr. Wallace seemed to suggest and I believed her. I just needed to repent and be free. I tried to shout as the last of my will ebbed away. It's all in my head, I'll be good, god knows I'm good, god knows I'm good! I repeated the line same as in the David Bowie song now pleading in my head.

Time passed and then eventually a small female voice made its way to my consciousness, "Stay true, It's just another ordeal, your ego doesn't really exist I am always with you." But I wanted to cry with rage. I was in Hell, which had been as a direct result of listening to the Goddess, listening to this inner voice in the first place, she can't help me now. I suppressed it; I no longer had the energy for her to fill me with her presence. Somewhere not too far away another voice, that of Dr. Wallace, was reassuring me that that is what psychotic people do, they listen to voices and become detached from reality. I was a scientist after all; I had to stay grounded to reality. Only science should be my religion; that would keep me away from situations like this. Science would keep me away from the gates of Hell. Science could be the voice of reason separating me from the unknown abyss of humanity's dark centre.

# Epilogue:
# When will we three meet again?

I woke up in a strange room. I starting crying and sat up looking around making sure it wasn't a dream or hallucination. It felt like I had been trapped for weeks and I gasped air in panicked gulps. A nurse ran though and helped me calm down. A sedative was injected into my arm. I was in the Royal Cornhill Hospital. I had been in a comatose state for two days. I was frail and emotional and my head hurt. Something had been done to my scalp, but no-one seemed to be able to explain what. There were bruises on my forehead above my eyes, which I was assured, had been as a result of a bump as I fell, though I felt like I had had a light saber slowly inserted through my third eye. Of course, this just made me realise all the more that I had spent too much time in fantasy land with the others. I asked to speak to Dr. Wallace, but no one seemed to know who she was, only that I had been referred here after a chemically-induced imbalance of my brain caused me to lapse in and out of consciousness under police supervision. They said that I seemed to have trouble maintaining a proper sense of reality. The toxins had been removed and now I was convalescing. Charges had been dropped and my parents were frantic. I felt very sad and guilty on seeing my mum's face, the worry had drained her and even though they were relieved and happy to see me I could sense my dad's anger, disappointment and even lack of understanding at just how I could prove to be such a chronic waste of space. It was going to take me ages to build up my self-esteem again.

Yes, sometimes weirdness does crop up in my life, but now I do the sensible thing and ignore it and rationalise it away. I now have a steady routine laboratory job as a biologist for a water treatment company. I have also moved down to Edinburgh to make a clean start. I love the city here and feel grounded. I love the Sherlock Holmes statue and the Conan Doyle pub. I love the fact that this city, as well as being the most beautiful I've ever seen, was the seat of the Scottish Enlightenment. I walk past the statue of "Saint" David Hume, atheistic philosopher on the Royal Mile and I smile with pride. I know which side I'm on now. I'm on the side of common sense and rationality. Science is the only way to truth! I can happily focus on a career and get job satisfaction that I'm using skills from my degree and feeling very mundane and normal. My experiences have made me detest people that talk about the paranormal and I, more than most people, can now understand just how easy it is for self-deception and self-delusion to set in, I mean wishful thinking is powerful thing is it not?

As for the other three? I never checked on The Doc. He disappeared off the radar and wasn't the sort of person I should be friends with in the first place. In retrospect, he never really liked me anyway. Don? Well I still talk to him from to time but he has become a recluse, never going out much. As for Hippie Davie, I had never seen such a change in a person. He moved back in with his parents in the west end, back to an upper-middle class lifestyle. I felt quite confused with my relationship with Hippie Davie really. My session with Dr. Wallace had made me realise that he enjoyed playing mind tricks on Don, The Doc and I for kicks and even took the piss a little bit at times, such as having us running around in robes, high on acid. He was a bit of a fake, making us think he was a messiah or something. Once I realised this I felt disappointment and anger. Even the thought of talking to him made me feel almost irrational feelings of resentment. Though this was always laden with a sense of confusion as somewhere deep down I knew I had trusted him and felt that that trust had been valid. I couldn't quite consolidate why I held these two almost diametrically opposed views and feelings!?

I felt compelled to call round a couple of times but he was always quite quiet and reserved in his father's house. His father was a surgeon and quite an austere person to boot. Hippie Davie had cut his hair and was looking for a job. I felt I wanted closure and understanding, surely we had been good friends and something in me made me feel like he did respect and like me, regardless of how I felt. However, his father didn't approve of me visiting and made that abundantly clear. Hippie Davie also seemed more guarded and off with me. It was like we were both too embarrassed to talk about any recent events, so contact just gradually dwindled and then just seemed to end as I moved to Edinburgh. The last I heard, through Don who had a friend of a friend, was that he had gone to learn I.C.T. and was now working for a bank, earning quite good money. I don't speak to anyone else now; Mags passed away, I went to her funeral and that was the last I saw of Mara and Gemma and well, everybody else!

Though I feel relieved, feel like I'm probably on track to whatever lies ahead. I can pay the mortgage. I enjoy the cinema and like spending time with my girlfriend. I live for curry at the weekend and *Buffy the Vampire Slayer*. I often think about Hippie Davie and the ideas we had. When I do think about meditating and finding my true will, it sends a shiver down my spine. I feel the need to blank it out. I mean, living a good life is surely your true will? I choose to live here, that was my choice, my free will and I think I'm happy. I think I must be happy? I truly am.

If only I could come to terms with this weird feeling, though, that all my days feel somewhat the same. Whether it's a shit day, a dull day or a terrific day, I have this sense of existence ticking over. Like when I'm in my car. Whether it's trundling along Gorgie Road going to work or the Straiton Road towards IKEA, or when the engine is revving overtime on the M90 towards Aberdeen on a long weekend daytrip; it's still all just driving. I'm always just sitting still on my bum, in the car, going in 'that' direction beyond the windscreen, only thinking about the next point in existence. I have that feeling that I'm a computer program in a cold dead clockwork universe of colliding energy through space and time. I mean, of course I'm being stupid because I'm the driver of my own car; no guardian Angel is going to drive it for me are they? There is no stepping out of the car mid-journey, no halting the program because I'm on track. I have what I want, well what I need. I mean, I'm glad, especially now, as my parents and family would say, I've grown up, I've found myself. Like the 'Talking Head's' song says, "Same as it ever was, same as it ever was." But...I'll leave it to the singers to sing their fucking songs; I'll just drive the car and sing along on my way to another 'day in a life.'